RESISTANCE IN VICHY FRANCE

RESISTANCE IN VICHY FRANCE

A Study of Ideas and Motivation in the Southern Zone 1940-1942

BY

H. R. KEDWARD

OXFORD UNIVERSITY PRESS

Oxford University Press, Walton Street, Oxford OX2 6DP

OXFORD LONDON GLASGOW NEW YORK
TORONTO MELBOURNE WELLINGTON CAPE TOWN
IBADAN NAIROBI DAR ES SALAAM LUSAKA ADDIS ABABA
KUALA LUMPUR SINGAPORE JAKARTA HONG KONG TOKYO
DELHI BOMBAY CALCUTTA MADRAS KARACHI

British Library Cataloging in Publication Data

Kedward, Harry Roderick
Resistance in Vichy France.
1. World War, 1939–1945—Underground movements—France
I. Title
940.53′44′8 D802.F8 77-30165
ISBN 0-19-822529-6

Printed in Great Britain by
Billing & Sons Limited, Guildford, London and Worcester

PREFACE

THERE are several good general histories of Resistance in France and a mass of partial or special accounts. Most of the general surveys are written chronologically, some are broken down into the different movements, and a few look at separate sections of the community or at separate geographical areas. There are also many accounts of the Vichy regime, and a growing amount of historical research is now being concentrated on particular aspects of Vichy which were, for many years after the Liberation, a subject of taboo.[1]

This study is indebted to all of these previous and current histories but it does not attempt to synthesize them, to replace them, or even to repeat them to any great extent, and anyone wanting an adequate picture of the period would be advised to place this book alongside many others. It does not give a history of Vichy nor a chronological survey of Resistance. What it does is to examine the various ways in which people became Resisters. It deals with the unoccupied, or southern, zone only and therefore stops when that zone was invaded and the whole of France finally occupied in November 1942. This concentration on one zone was partly dictated by the enormity of doing a similar study for the whole of France, but more positively by the belief, held firmly by Resisters themselves, that the southern zone was very different from the occupied zone owing to the absence of Germans and the greater authority and power of Pétain and the Vichy Government.

This is, therefore, a limited study of French Resistance which restricts itself to the zone least affected by the Occupation, and I am only too aware of its weaknesses for that reason as well as many others. No reader can feel entirely happy making general-

[1] Histories of the period which are recommended for general reading and which are easily available are marked by an asterisk in section 7 of the Bibliography. For a complete account of current research and publications there is no substitute for the *Revue d'histoire de la Deuxième Guerre Mondiale* which appears three times a year and is published by P.U.F. It comes from the Comité d'Histoire de la Deuxième Guerre Mondiale, whose publications and sponsorship of research into all aspects of the war make it an unrivalled international centre of scholarship.

izations about the whole of French Resistance on the basis of what is given here, even though most of the ways in which people arrived at Resistance in the southern zone can also be found in the north.

The material presented comes rarely from the established histories, whose facts and interpretations I have generally left to make their own impact. What I have used extensively are memoirs, the Resistance Press, and oral testimony from Resisters themselves. For five years, from 1969 to 1974, I used the summer vacations from university teaching to visit different regions in the south, particularly Lyon, Marseille, Montpellier, and the *départements* of Haute-Savoie, Dordogne, and Corrèze, meeting and interviewing Resisters. A selection from this oral evidence appears at the end of the book. Ideally I should have visited every region in the southern zone, but as my research progressed I became certain that I was not going to write an area-by-area history, and that my main interest was in types of motivation and ideas of Resistance rather than the particularities of local history.

There are few, if any, 'official' documents to underpin a study of this kind. In fact, there are very few documents for any kind of history of French Resistance, though there are more for de Gaulle's France Libre and the British S.O.E. (Special Operations Executive) than for the movements which grew up within France itself.[2] Once the official archives for the Occupation period are released, it will be possible to see if reports from prefects, police, and other government agencies can throw any new light on the formation and operation of the Resistance, but until then the national and local archives have very little to offer the researcher.[3]

This dearth of official documentation is neither a surprise nor a deterrent. It is not a surprise because it was clearly in the nature of Resistance activity to avoid all paper records which might fall into the wrong hands, and it was argued by some Resisters that even newspapers and tracts were an unnecessary

[2] The most interesting documents for the relationship of France Libre to metropolitan France are the series F1a 3710-3796 in the Archives Nationales.

[3] The series F1cIII 1135–1198 in the Archives Nationales contains a selection of administrative reports from prefects to the Minister of the Interior, but on their own they constitute an unsatisfactory source and have not been used in this study.

risk. No historian could therefore expect to find minutes of clandestine meetings, or reports on membership and organization, let alone any information on the motives and backgrounds of the Resisters themselves. Nor is it a deterrent, since the great wealth and diversity of memoirs and the richness of the clandestine Press are more than ample compensation. These are in no way an inferior substitute, but rather, like documents themselves which have their own inadequacies and bias, they are sufficient to fuel the hypotheses and arguments of historians indefinitely. It is from the Press that we get most of the clues about motivation, for the newspapers reveal unerringly what made people sufficiently angry and defiant to move into opposition. They are also full of ideas, not just about the war, the Occupation, Vichy, and Resistance, but also about the past and the future of France. Implicitly or explicitly they document the political and social sources of Resistance.

Memoirs, whether written or spoken, go even further. They come from a bewildering variety of sources but unfailingly point to one central historical feature of Resistance. At a time when there was a complete breakdown of customary forms of political behaviour, a vast national movement was created by people starting from the most basic of political structures, from small groups of like-minded men and women determined to do something and influence others. These basic units can be found emerging throughout the southern zone at different moments between 1940 and 1942 and in response to different provocations. It is the object of this study to present and examine their emergence and to trace their aims and motivations through their propaganda, their organization, and their activity.

The explanations for Resistance which I offer may well seem too neatly categorized: they are, of course, structured well after the events by someone who has no personal experience of the period. On the other hand, I have tried to eliminate as much hindsight as possible and to give the reader some idea of the confusion and isolation which were undoubtedly felt at the time. For this reason a great deal of information about the period, which is now known but which was not generally available at the time, has not been given here, whereas many of the views of the period on which Resisters made their decisions have been retained. For the same reason I have not anticipated later actions by individuals, groups, and movements when first introducing them. It would falsify the unknown quantities in Resistance, the uncertainties involved in making decisions, and the unpredictable developments if I were to accompany the action of an individual or group in 1940 with the advice that he or she was later to become an established leader, or the group a successful movement. Such advice is the method normally chosen to tell readers what to look out for and to mark the broad line of successes and failures in history. In 1940 a vital aspect of opposition activity was that it had no such lines to follow, and I feel it important for understanding the real difficulties of the period for some of this uncertainty to be recreated, at least in the material dealing with 1940 and 1941.

My debt to people who have helped me is enormous. In particular I wish to thank the following for their great generosity in helping me in many different ways: M. Henri Michel, M. Claude Lévy, and Mme Dominique Veillon at the Comité d'Histoire de la Deuxième Guerre Mondiale in Paris, as well as the librarian there, M. Rauzier; M. Victor Joannes at the Institut Maurice Thorez in Paris; Docteur Suzanne Lambolez-Weinstein in Paris; M. Alban Vistel, M. André Plaisantin, M. André Latreille, M. et Mme Louis Dupic, M. Roger Pestourie, M. René Carrier, and M. Maurice Moissonnier in Lyon; M. André Besson in the Jura; M. Jean Vittoz in the Haute-Savoie; M. Albert Solié, M. Henri Cordesse, M. Georges Bouladou, and M. et Mme Philemon Pouget in Montpellier; Mlle Madeleine Baudoin in Marseille; M. Louis de la Bardonnie and M. René Larivière in the Dordogne. Some of these people also gave me an interview on their Resistance past, and to the others who kindly allowed me to interview them, and whose names appear in the bibliography, I am equally grateful. At home I have benefited greatly from the suggestions and encouragement of Dr. Theodore Zeldin and Professor Richard Cobb in Oxford, Professor Douglas Johnson in London, Beynon John and many other colleagues at Sussex, and many students, both graduate and undergraduate, who have channelled information to me from France. Finally I am indebted to the Leverhulme Trust, the University of Sussex, and the French Government for much-valued financial assistance and to Miss Meriel Price for her remarkably careful typing of the manuscript. As for my wife and close friends who have given me so much support and help, I cannot begin to thank them enough.

Sussex 1976 RODERICK KEDWARD

CONTENTS

I. Confusion

When the French Government declared war on Hitler's Germany in September 1939 the French people had, for over two years, been experiencing a dwindling sense of control over national and international politics. The conflicts of 1934–6 which resulted in the victory of the Popular Front had involved issues which seemed clear and fundamental, and in the polarization people had found an identity. But once the first government of Léon Blum had fallen and power had passed to an inchoate set of politicians in the centre, the clarity began to disappear and a suspicion rapidly grew that the country was drifting. Positions firmly adopted in the period of conflict began to weaken; policies which had appeared positive became negative. Anti-Fascism failed to produce government support for the Spanish Republic; the Matignon agreements for new industrial relations were undermined by the obstruction of employers; the increase in wages was whittled away by rising prices; the common front of Socialists and Communists disintegrated; belligerent spokesmen of the nationalist Right began to compromise with the advocates of peace, and the symptom of it all was the policy of appeasement, culminating at Munich, which seemed to owe less to the initiatives of France than to the determined diplomacy of Britain. Within three years of the 1936 elections, when public opinion had been actively involved, the attitude which had periodically marked the history of the Third Republic had re-established itself: a hardened belief that politics was a game played by others. It was this which made people at the time talk of decline and degeneration. They felt alienated from decisions at the top, and it was not a clearly divided France but a confused and disoriented France which responded lamely to the war exhortations of Daladier.

This confusion grew steadily during the months of inactivity on the German front, known as the *drôle de guerre* ('phoney war'), and it spread wildly in the weeks of invasion and defeat in May and June 1940. From the start its effect was to encourage positions and solutions of reassuring simplicity on which people came to depend and round which they united as a way of avoiding the complexity. At the very outbreak of war this effect can be seen in the way people united against the Communist Party after the pact of non-aggression between Nazi Germany and Soviet Russia had utterly confused the international situation. Announced on 23 August 1939, the pact seemed to betray everything that the Parti Communiste Français (P.C.F.) had stood for. Since 1936 the P.C.F. had unceasingly called for intervention against Franco's rebellion in Spain, had been the only party to vote against the Munich agreements in September 1938, and had put anti-Nazism at the front of its foreign affairs programme. It had also voted for increased arms expenditure within France, setting national defence within the meaning of the term anti-Fascism.

The consistency of the communist position in this period had given the party a kind of purity in foreign affairs, against which the policy of non-intervention in Spain and subsequent appeasement of Hitler at Munich looked suspect and compromising. There was undoubtedly a good deal of guilt in the country about both Spain and the concessions to Hitler, particularly among the Socialists, and with it an unacknowledged feeling that the Communists might have been right. The Nazi–Soviet pact provoked an outcry which showed this feeling to have been deeply seated. Almost without exception, non-communist France condemned the pact with outspoken hostility. Few people were prepared to see it in the perspective of the appeasement policy which their own politicians had been pursuing, nor were they willing to acknowledge that the Soviet decision was linked to similar dilemmas in foreign policy. Instead the pact furnished the opportunity for most of France to externalize its own guilt and unease in bitter denunciations and punitive measures. For supporting the pact the P.C.F. was made to suffer for its three years of purity. Within a month the party was forcibly dissolved, its Press heavily censored and finally suppressed altogether, and its militants subjected to arrest and trial on the most slender of legal pretexts,[1] a persecution which, like all scapegoat persecutions,

[1] Louis Dupic, communist Assistant Mayor of Vénissieux near Lyon, was arrested early in October along with forty others, but the police had no charge to make. He commented that it was just like the old monarchist 'lettres de cachet'.

masked the real problem by acting as a diversion from it. The war against Hitler was not in any way helped by an internal war against the Communists, but it appeared to be functional in that most people found some sort of unity behind it. Russia was accused of an insidious withdrawal from the war situation and the French Communists stood no chance of being understood when they explained it as a Russian bid for peace. When they went further and argued that France should emulate Russia by negotiating peace and avoiding war[2] they were never believed to be serious, even though France at the time showed no sign of actively prosecuting the war and had conducted just such negotiations a year earlier at Munich. This anger against Russia, vented on the French Communists, helped to hide from the French people their own lack of enthusiasm for the war and allowed the government to appear less indecisive than it would otherwise have seemed.

The P.C.F. did not situate the pact in its full perspective either. They never used the language of appeasement to describe it but explained it as Russia's only course of action to protect the citizens of the first socialist country from the machinations of the imperialist powers who hoped for a conflict between Nazism and Communism. Stalin was seen to have triumphed over these powers by the signing of the pact, a victory which the party said could be measured by the extremes of anger expressed in Britain and France once the pact became known. Indeed, had there been no Nazi–Soviet pact and had Hitler followed his invasion of Poland by an attack on Russia, there is surely a strong possibility that Britain and France would have done nothing to help the Soviet Union. But while presenting this explanation of Soviet policy, which was a more complex and plausible explanation than the 'insidious withdrawal' version produced by the rest of France, the P.C.F. did not admit the confusion which the pact caused within the party, nor the difficulties of aligning policies of the 1930s with the new situation produced by the pact. Instead, after a confused week in which the communist deputies voted for the credits

[2] The letter from Florimond Bonte and A. Ramette to Édouard Herriot, President of the Chamber of Deputies, dated 1 October 1939 included the words '. . . il y a la puissance de l'Union Soviétique qui peut permettre la réalisation d'une politique de sécurité collective susceptible d'assurer la Paix et la sauvegarde de l'indépendence de la France'. (Reprinted in *L'Humanité*, n.d.)

necessary for France to wage war and appeared to be continuing their support for national defence, the party indulged in its own simplification, condemning the conflict as an imperialist war caused as much by Britain and France as by Germany, and promoted by the Fascist and capitalist elements within France against the interests of the people.

The two reactions to the pact, anti-communist and communist, fed on each other and produced on both sides the hard evidence of fact which made theory into experience. Communist militants experienced the *drôle de guerre* as a period of arrest and imprisonment and pointed out that the French prisons and concentration camps contained thousands of French but no German prisoners of war. Victimized in this way they argued that the war was not theirs and that their true enemies were the rulers of France, a category which extended well beyond the personnel of the government. *L'Humanité*, which re-emerged clandestinely in October 1939, produced, over several months, a list of internal Fascists which included, by direct charge or by association, Daladier, Blum, Bonnet, Flandin, Doriot, Gamelin, Weygand, and eventually Pétain, as well as the Comité France–Allemagne, specifically mentioned on 17 May as 'the Fifth Column of capitalism and Fascism' in France.[3] Since one of the hallmarks of Fascism in Italy and Germany had been the suppression of communist parties and communist trade unions, and since all the named people either authorized or endorsed the suppression of the Communist Party in France, this wide use of the term did not seem extravagant to the average member who had remained loyal to the party after the pact. On the other side, anti-Communists saw their suspicion of the party justified by the tracts and speeches which flowed from the P.C.F. calling on its members, whether at the front or at home, to repudiate the war,[4] by the much-publicized desertion of Maurice Thorez, the party's General Secretary, from the French army, and by the party's support for the Russians in their invasion of Finland. There is

[3] *L'Humanité*, no. 47 (17 May 1940).

[4] A four-page tract, 'L'Humanité du soldat', dated 1 May 1940 included the words: 'La vérité c'est que la guerre actuelle est une guerre impérialiste. Les financiers franco-anglais et les gros industriels allemands se disputent des matières premières. Leur querelle n'est pas notre querelle. . . . C'est la guerre contre le peuple, contre les soldats.'

nothing inaccurate or false about either of these experiences, communist or anti-communist, and the historian must give them both rather than try to reduce one or the other to the level of insubstantial propaganda.[5] Both are integral elements in the state of French opinion and experience at the moment when Hitler turned his armies against France and precipitated a collapse and confusion from which new simplifications emerged.

Had the separation of Communists and others during the *drôle de guerre* been less pronounced, the widespread indifference to a war which few people in France had wanted would have been more overtly recognized. In the Hérault, Paul Crouzet, mayor of a small village, noted in his diary the sense of injustice felt by the peasants at the front when they knew that in the towns many workers had been retained in the factories. By February 1940 the soldiers on leave were, he said, totally without enthusiasm, and their return to the station at the end of their leave produced demonstrations by the women of the village against the war.[6] Yet this went hand in hand with opposition to Russia and the Communist Party, and such combinations of attitude could be found throughout France during the winter of 1939–40. It was a period which did nothing to arrest the disorientation of the pre-war years but added a further degree of frustration and bewilderment, mixed with a certain relief that the war had not brought the horrors so widely predicted, and an element of military complacency articulated in the government's slogan, 'Nous vaincrons parce que nous sommes les plus forts.'

Once the invasion occurred and it became clear that France was not the stronger of the two main combatants, the government's propaganda was inverted by a panic-stricken population. If victory would go to the strongest then it was Germany who was heading for victory. J.-Pierre Bloch, Deputy for the *département* of the Aisne, believes that this conclusion was quickly reached by most journalists who were reporting, or in

[5] The case for a greater historical relativism in the treatment of the communist reaction to the Nazi–Soviet pact is developed in H. R. Kedward, 'Behind the polemics. French Communists and Resistance 1939–41', in S. F. Hawes and R. T. White (eds.), *Resistance in Europe 1939–45* (Allen Lane, London, 1975).

[6] Paul Crouzet, '*Et c'est le même ciel bleu . . .*' *Journal d'un maire de village 1939–40* (Didier, 1950), pp. 112–13.

many cases not being allowed to report, on the German advance.[7] As the rout of the French army quickened, the conviction took root that it was not just a battle that France was losing but the entire war,[8] and there followed the natural reluctance of soldiers in retreat, or soldiers of the reserve defending positions behind the front, to risk their lives in what increasingly seemed a futile display. There were exceptions to this feeling of futility but they were made rarer than they might have been by the mass exodus (*exode*) of population which is inseparable from the history of the defeat.

The *exode* was partly planned as an evacuation of civilians in the *départements* bordering on the front, but was to a far greater degree the spontaneous flight of millions from the north, the Paris region, and even the centre towards the south as the German armies advanced. The first signs and the first verbal evidence of the rapidity of the German progress came with Belgian refugees who included young men who would have been conscripted to the front had there been time, and the sight of these did not induce confidence in the French lines through which they had to pass. As the invasion gained momentum, retreating French soldiers and refugees often found themselves falling back on towns already occupied by the Germans, and news of this fact provoked an even earlier departure from towns west and south of Paris, where the rumours ran that the Germans moved twice as fast as normal soldiers, and that in the hot days of early summer they were advancing *les torses nus* through the ripening cornfields. It was a small step from here to believing that the Germans were in some way superhuman, that they were conquerors by sheer force of physique, and such primitive reactions accentuated the sense of defeat and promoted the search for those responsible for exposing France to such a catastrophe.

By mid-June the *exode* had reached phenomenal proportions.

[7] J.-Pierre Bloch, *Mes jours heureux* (Bateau Ivre, 1946), pp. 24 ff. Among the first German victories in May which the Press was not allowed to reveal was the fall of Namur and Brussels (Roger Stéphane, *Chaque homme est lié au monde. Carnets 1939–44*, Sagittaire, 1946, p. 36).

[8] De Gaulle's insistence in his broadcasts from 18 June onwards that France had lost a battle but not the war was in direct response to this conviction. He was not, of course, at the front when the French army finally collapsed, having been given a post in Reynaud's new government. He left the front for Paris on 6 June. (Charles de Gaulle, *Mémoires de guerre*, Plon, 1954, i. 43.)

Estimates of the total number of people who left their homes with as many possessions as they could load on to bicycles, carts, cars, lorries, trains and buses still vary between 6 and 10 million,[9] to which a further 2 million Belgians must be added. The Belgians had left first and were instructed to make for the south-west of France, and they were closely followed by French people of all classes and ages who swelled the populations of small provincial towns to as much as six or ten times their normal size. Cahors in the Lot grew from 13,000 to an estimated 60–70,000,[10] Brive in the Corrèze from 30,000 to 100,000, and Pau in the Basses-Pyrénées, a major centre of exile from the north in 1914–18, from 38,000 to 150,000. Other towns of similar or smaller size experienced the same kind of influx.[11] On the whole people made for a town with a *préfecture* where it was believed the services would be better and accommodation in hotels more plentiful.

Almost four years before, under the Popular Front legislation introducing paid holidays, workers from the big towns had, for the first time, made their way to the coast or to relations in the country for a fortnight's holiday. Myths of a good country life with ample food and plenty of living space had been crystallized by the experience of these *congés payés*, and were uppermost in people's minds as they took to the roads. One by one the myths were exploded. There was no surfeit of food, even in regions of mixed farming such as the Dordogne and the Corrèze, and the shops in small villages were rapidly emptied, while in monocultures such as the wine-growing areas in the Languedoc there was an immediate scarcity. As for accommodation, the barns and outhouses of peasant farms suddenly seemed less than ideal when investigated as potential residences for an unknown period of time. The towns therefore carried the weight of the *exode* and in Toulouse

[9] Jean Vidalenc in *L'Exode de mai–juin 1940* (P.U.F., 1957), p. 360, gives 6 million. Nicole Ollier in *L'Exode sur les routes de l'an 40* (Laffont, 1970), p. 260, gives between 8½ and 10 million.

[10] Vidalenc, op. cit., p. 338.

[11] Figures for all the reception areas are given in Ollier, op. cit., pp. 239–40. They are taken from an official count in early August of those who had registered as refugees at the *mairies* or local railway stations. Highest numbers were registered in Creuse (304,000), Dordogne (220,000), Corrèze (210,000), Haute-Vienne (169,000), Hérault (132,000), Tarn-et-Garonne (109,000), and Puy-de-Dôme (100,000).

people slept on the pavement.[12] The desperation was all-consuming and the irrationalities it produced were traditional. Anti-Semitism increased alarmingly, in the Press and on the roads, since those who could buy their way out of the situation were invariably believed to be Jews.

The *exode* was a contagion, but not one produced purely by fantasy. The German bombing of towns and shelling of roads allowed well-based stories of high civilian losses to circulate, justifying the images of German bestiality largely inherited from World War I. There was an unanswerable logic in the wish to get away from it all, and the government itself had endorsed this logic by its flight from Paris to Bordeaux. René Cerf-Ferrière was one of those caught against his will by the cumulative power of the *exode.* Mobilized to defend a small village in the Loiret, he found himself at the head of a few men armed with shotguns and with the classically heroic task of defending a bridge across a narrow river against an approaching division of tanks while refugees poured through the region on their way south. Against the orders of a superior officer, he decided it was better to join the *exode* and survive to fight elsewhere. Some of the men treated him as a deserter. 'They had every right to,' he commented.[13] It was in ways such as these that the *exode* gathered its strength. The dilemma of staying or leaving reduced itself to a basic question of survival, and the 'common sense' which prompted Cerf-Ferrière to leave with his family for Brive in the Corrèze was working on a larger scale to convince the government and its new leader Marshal Pétain to end the nightmare and ask for an armistice. Yet when Cerf-Ferrière heard the news his reaction was one of incredulity: 'Lui, Pétain, solliciter Hitler? Incroyable.'[14] Among the many ambiguities of attitude found in 1940 this was not a common one. Most of those who experienced the uncertainties and fear of the *exode* and took the decision to leave their homes reacted with relief to the end of hostilities. The Armistice itself was initiated by Pétain but an end to the war was willed by the majority of France.

During the invasion the communist view of the war, developed

[12] Vidalenc, p. 344.

[13] René Cerf-Ferrière, *Chemin clandestin 1940–43* (Julliard, 1968), pp. 20 ff.

[14] Ibid., p. 25.

by the party in the last months of 1939, was preserved intact. But whereas during the *drôle de guerre* it had been confirmed by the experience of persecution, by June and July 1940 it was less in touch with events, for once Communists, in common with other soldiers and civilians, became victims of the German army, the claim to be detached from the war could not be made, except at a theoretical level. It was no longer the 'war of others'. This dilemma was not openly confronted at the centre of the party, though it weighed heavily in certain regions. *L'Humanité*, produced clandestinely in Paris, was the only regular communist paper until the autumn of 1940, and it kept the party's antipathy to the internal rulers of France at the front of its policy, avoiding a clear statement on its attitude to Germany. It is this choice of policy which provides substantive evidence of communist priorities at the time, but it is not at all easy to conclude that the P.C.F. gave no consideration to the facts of invasion and defeat. From no. 4 dated 7 November 1939 through to no. 56 on 19 June 1940 *L'Humanité* developed its vehement case against the internal enemies of France and accused them not only of starting the war against the interests of the people, but of embarking on the 'Hitlerization of France' and opening the way to defeat and disaster. The precipitate collapse of France in May and June, after so many assurances from the government that the French defences were impregnable, encouraged conspiracy theories of the defeat and the P.C.F. was well provided with one: 'By betraying the Spanish Republic, Blum–Daladier–Bonnet prepared the invasion and defeat of France' and 'The traitors of Munich have opened France to invasion.'[15] By these accusations the party showed that it could not accept the defeat any more than it accepted the war, since the same 'Hitlériens' and 'agents de Hitler' within France were seen as responsible for both. The explicit association of internal enemies with Hitler and the references back to communist pre-war policies in favour of the

[15] *L'Humanité*, no. 56 (19 June 1940). It should be noted that issues of the clandestine Press, whether representing the Communists or any other group or movement, were often published without an exact date or number. References in the footnotes of this study only give a date and number when they occur on the original publication, although sometimes a date occurs in square brackets, indicating the conjecture of the archivists in the Bibliothèque Nationale where most of the clandestine Press is collected.

Spanish Republic and against Munich perpetuated much of the party's anti-Fascist image.

Beyond this there was little in the way of practical guidance for the communist militant faced with the German invasion, though the party leaders called for the arming of the citizens of Paris to defend the city[16] and, as an antithesis to national defence, appeared to revert to the Leninist doctrine that imperialist war should be transformed into class war. On 10 April and 9 May *L'Humanité* appealed to German as well as French Communists to rise against their own governments and on 17 and 19 June proclaimed in dual headlines 'Prolétaires de tous les pays, unissez-vous. Proletarier aller Länder vereinigt euch.'[17] This restatement of a traditional theme was evocative for the old rank and file of the party who had joined the P.C.F. in the 1920s, but it was never developed into a serious call for revolution. In fact the *Cahiers du bolchevisme* of January 1940 were adamant that the situation of 1939–40 was not the same as that of 1914–18 and that the policy of transformation of imperialist war into civil war could not be repeated. The only policy relevant after the Nazi–Soviet pact, it stated, was for the P.C.F. to make its own calls for immediate peace, and to this end the party criticized itself for not having voted against the war credits at the beginning of September. This autocriticism was set out in a long theoretical article and gives some indication of the difficulties the party experienced in understanding the pact.[18] As Charles Tillon noted, long before he left the party, the pact never provided a clear guide for action within France.[19]

At the regional and local level, where the *Cahiers* were not available and copies of *L'Humanité* at this point in the war extremely rare, the experience of persecution and the necessity

[16] Reproduced in *Le Parti communiste Français dans la Résistance* (Éditions Sociales, 1967), p. 49.

[17] *L'Humanité*, no. 55 (17 June 1940); no. 56 (19 June 1940).

[18] *Cahiers du bolchevisme*, 17ᵉ année, 2ᵉ semestre 1939–janvier 1940, pp. 7–13. The auto-criticism concludes with the words: 'Toutefois il y a encore beaucoup à faire pour que la clarté soit complète dans tout le Parti. En procédant à une auto-critique sérieuse léniniste des erreurs et des fautes, le Parti et sa direction rendront encore plus compréhensibles aux travailleurs les raisons qui ont déterminé le changement de la politique du Parti Communiste' (p. 11).

[19] Charles Tillon, *Les F.T.P.* (Julliard, 1962), pp. 82–3.

to go underground in order to preserve the party's structure were of more importance in conditioning attitudes than the niceties of theory which filtered down from the centre. In most regions there were Communists who split away from the party in the first months after the pact and it is accepted that there were confused, if not acrimonious, discussions within the party in many areas,[20] but by the time of the invasion the problem of keeping the party together had been eased by the persecution which had given Communists an urgent sense of solidarity and a clear-cut issue on which to concentrate. It was this issue which provided the *militants de base* with an accentuated feeling of class war, whatever was decided at the centre, and it was the conviction that the rulers of France and the invading Nazis were inseparable in their Fascist intentions which gave these militants a basis on which to build their reactions to the defeat, to the Occupation, and to the government of Pétain. At the same time the difficulties in communication from the centre to the localities allowed considerable local variations in ideas and activity, variations which were of vital importance in preserving the vitality of French Communism in the period of maximum dislocation.

In one respect the reaction of Communists and non-Communists to the defeat was identical: in the need to find someone responsible for the disaster. No one admitted responsibility; everyone blamed someone else. Ordinary soldiers blamed their officers, the General Staff blamed the politicians, the politicians of the Right blamed those of the Left and vice versa, the government of Pétain blamed the ministers of the Popular Front, they in turn blamed the army, most people blamed the Communists, the Communists blamed the internal Fascists, and the Fascists blamed the Jews. There was enough fragmentation here to refloat French politics for a generation. Nothing of the kind happened. Instead Marshal Pétain proposed a simple alternative. He offered himself as a gift to France to attenuate its misfortune, called on the people of France to support him, and stated that there was no need for anything to divide the country in its hour of suffering.[21]

Pétain, as saviour, did not drop from the skies. There had

[20] Raoul Calas, '1938–41. Une Période sombre, *Notre musée*, no. 32 (Feb. 1969), 1.

[21] Broadcasts of 17, 20, and 23 June 1940.

been a nationalist campaign in the 1930s to have him appointed as an autocratic ruler of France, and Pierre Laval was only one of many who at some point voiced his belief that 'the salvation of France lay in a Pétain government and that the Marshal was determined to assume this responsibility'.[22] Among veterans of World War I who identified him with the victory of Verdun and who remembered him as the most popular of the military leaders in the field, he was widely regarded as a providential figure, and Pétain encouraged this view without committing himself to any political position. At the outbreak of war he was in the margin of politics as Ambassador to Franco's Spain, and it was Reynaud who brought him to the centre by inviting him to join his government once the first military defeats were known, a calculated move to inspire the country with confidence. Once the enormity of the defeat was suspected, Pétain became the obvious candidate to secure the co-operation of both army and populace, and his 84 years seemed no disqualification.

From this earthly basis of power, Pétain's fatherly appeal to unity, his concern for the refugees, his moral fervour, and his Messianic offering made an impact at the end of June which can only be called religious. Out of the chaos and confusion a man who seemed to be above the level of political intrigue and propaganda told the French they had a simple choice, to stay confused, divided, and helpless or to follow him. He would 'atone' for the misfortunes of the nation. The majority of France, and on 10 July the vast majority of French politicians, chose Pétain and responded to his moral paternalism and simple solution with an equally simple idealism based on the belief that problems could be removed if party politics were rejected. The Armistice and Pétain were seized on as the only way of ending the incredible confusion caused by the rapidity of the defeat and the chaos of the *exode* but they were invested with a positive quality as solutions that would lead to peace and a return to normal life as if the whole nightmare had never happened.

In fact the simplicity of Pétain's appeal was not as politically

[22] Cf. G. Hervé, *C'est Pétain qu'il nous faut* (La Victoire, 1935). The Laval remark of 1937 is quoted in Geoffrey Warner, *Pierre Laval and the Eclipse of France* (Eyre & Spottiswoode, London, 1968), p. 135.

naïve as it was made to seem later. In his early broadcasts Pétain gave his approval to most of the obvious activities left to the French once the war appeared lost: the reception of refugees and their eventual resettlement or repatriation, the care for the homeless, the return to work and production, parcels for prisoners of war, the protection of the army's morale and concern for the individual soldier, in short everything which involved welfare work and the moral rehabilitation of the country. This met with an obvious but profound response and in particular played on the second phase of the *exode*. While the refugees were on the roads, panic, despair, uncertainty, hardship, and a sense of injustice were some of the ingredients which characterized the *exode*. Once they began arriving in the regions of the centre and south designated to receive them, the refugees were no longer alone in their problems. Municipal councils who had to find beds, food, and clothing for numbers which far exceeded prediction and for a period which might be weeks or months depending on developments in the war found their resources stretched to such a point that the normal process of administration was inadequate.[23] People were recruited at once for voluntary work, an emphasis was put on philanthropy, and the problems placed in the forefront of local affairs, dominating newspaper headlines and council business. It became a matter of local pride not to be defeated in this particular issue, for a local victory won was more than a little compensation for the larger defeat. The *exode* was thus important not just for what it did to the refugees but for what it did to the reception areas. The activity of providing for the refugees may have had political elements within it, but it was essentially something *a*political which affected left-wing and right-wing authorities alike, and it was this kind of activity that Pétain claimed as the moral support he wanted and a sign of the national unity to which he had given himself. Whether they liked it or not, local authorities involved in dealing with the *exode* were associated with the paternalist appeal of Pétain and this made a return to hard-line political infighting, once the refugees had departed, extremely difficult. Such considerable investment in non-

[23] Evidence from Jean Deffaugt.

political achievement could not be easily withdrawn, and the immediate beneficiary was Pétain.[24]

The decision to approach the Germans for an armistice which Pétain announced to the nation on 17 June must be separated from the terms of the Armistice itself concluded on 22 June, but both produced a mixture of shock and relief in the country at large. In what became the unoccupied zone, surprise that Pétain had capitulated was expressed mainly on the frontier with Italy where the war had not been lost. French troops on the line from Lac Léman to the Mediterranean had easily withstood the Italian offensive and among the various units positioned there the experience of 1940 was totally different from that of the defeated army of the north and north-east. But there was relief there also, for by the time the cease-fire came into operation, the Germans had taken Lyon and were approaching Grenoble and the Franco-Italian border. Elsewhere in the South and centre relief was the dominant emotion and when the terms of the Armistice were known and it was found that the Germans were actually to withdraw from Lyon, Saint-Étienne, Mâcon, and parts of the Indre, people in those places saw reason to celebrate, even though the Germans took with them the prisoners of war who had surrendered in the evacuated areas.[25] In Saint-Étienne, wrote Pétrus Faure, which the Germans left on 6 July, a large crowd gathered in front of the Hôtel de Ville, erected a tricolour, and sang the Marseillaise,[26] and in Lyon also the departure of the Germans produced an illusion of recovery, though it must be said that at the local level to be spared occupation was a real, not an illusory, benefit.

[24] An example of the vast local campaign mounted to organize the reception of the refugees is provided by Danielle Josse in a study of Brive in the Corrèze. At the height of the *exode*, the population of Brive had trebled and the town saw still more refugees passing through, since it was at an important crossroads of north–south and east–west. The local administration was radical-socialist and was entirely preoccupied with the problems of the influx from June to September. (Danielle Josse, 'Brive-la-Gaillarde 1940–42', unpub. Mémoire de Maîtrise, Académie de Poitiers, 1971, pp. 34–54.)

[25] Lucie Aubrac, *La Résistance, naissance et organisation* (Robert Lang, 1945), p. 24.

[26] Pétrus Faure, *Un Témoin raconte . . .* (Imprimerie Dumas, Saint-Étienne, 1962), p. 50.

With relief went passivity and a good deal of indifference. In the Dordogne, wrote H. G. Bergeret, 'the majority of the people . . . were delighted the whole war was over. . . . They were convinced that the prisoners would be allowed home and that a peace would soon be signed. It was the beginning of summer. Life was easy. They believed it would always be like that.'[27] In Périgueux, according to Choiseul-Praslin, there was a general atmosphere of resignation and relief,[28] and in Brive Cerf-Ferrière reported a widespread indifference and *je m'en foutisme.*[29] In Crouzet's village in the Hérault the pre-occupations of the villagers were entirely local and personal,[30] and the curé of Petit Bornand in Haute-Savoie recorded the passive way in which everyone returned to work.[31] Aimé Autrand is emphatic that opinion in the Vaucluse was one of submission 'to a destiny against which it was impossible to rebel'.[32] This general picture is well known but it needs re-emphasizing because no one in any area in the southern zone has suggested that attitudes were different. There were degrees of relief, of passive acceptance and submission, and there were, as we will see, individuals and groups whose rebelliousness or anger at the Armistice conflicted sharply with prevailing opinion; but Jean Cassou's observation that 'everyone returned home' can be accepted as more than a literal truth.[33] 'Chacun est rentré chez soi' sums up the psychology of the defeat; it is a metaphor of the French state of mind in the latter part of 1940.

As a literal truth it can clearly be faulted. There were over one and a half million prisoners of war who could not return home, though many of them expected to do so in the near future; there were refugees, from Alsace-Lorraine in particular, who chose to remain in their place of refuge or who were

[27] H. G. Bergeret (real name Maurice Loupias), *Messages personnels* (Éditions Bière, Bordeaux, 1945), p. 5.

[28] Choiseul-Praslin, *Cinq années de Résistance* (Éditions F-X, Strasbourg–Paris, 1949), p. 20.

[29] Cerf-Ferrière, op. cit., p. 26.

[30] Crouzet, op. cit., pp. 162 ff.

[31] Jean Truffy, *Les Mémoires du curé du maquis* (Imprimerie Abry, Annecy, 1950), p. 11.

[32] Aimé Autrand, *Le Département de Vaucluse de la défaite à la libération. Mai 1940–25 août 1944* (Aubanel, Avignon, 1965), p. 63.

[33] Jean Cassou, *La Mémoire courte* (Éditions de Minuit, 1953), p. 29.

forced to do so, and there were people who had no intention either of submitting to the defeat or of returning passively to their everyday lives. But as a generalization it is substantiated by a mass of detail. Most French people in the southern zone abandoned the wider issues and problems of the period to Marshal Pétain and turned inwards on themselves. This submission was later called blindness; 'l'aveuglement le plus complet' was Paul Viret's phrase,[34] and many post-war authors have toyed with the term 'le temps des autruches' to describe 1940.[35] But among the major factors which allowed Pétain to gain such an ascendancy and which rationalized the regressive dependency of those who followed him were the arguments of realism and clear-sightedness which seemed to point in the same direction. Survivalism had its own irrefutable logic and those who said 'no' to the Armistice and rejected Pétain seemed a greater danger to society and appeared to be acting more blindly and absurdly than those who accepted him. Above all it seemed sensible to wait and see, and the comment of General André Beaufre, justifying a policy of *attentisme*, is widely typical of attitudes in 1940:

> However you looked at the problem, the match had been played and lost. Without admitting we were permanently defeated, it was necessary to retire and wait until better days. To stand obstinately against the defeat made no sense. The important thing was to know in what way to retire.[36]

The attitude towards Britain was something of a test case in these arguments of realism. Among the factors variously blamed for the French defeat, the conduct of Britain in denying France more intensive air support and evacuating Dunkirk was as frequently mentioned as any. To continue believing in Britain's goodwill, still more in her capacity to avoid the same fate as France, was already by the end of June seen as foolish, but after Britain had attacked the French fleet at Mers-el-Kébir on 3 July killing over 1,200 sailors it was seen as a

[34] Paul Viret, *L'Affaire François de Menthon* (Gardet et Garin, Annecy, n.d.), p. 8.
[35] Cf. Georges Groussard, *Service secret 1940–45* (La Table Ronde, 1964), p. 311.
[36] André Beaufre, *Le Drame de 1940* (Plon, 1965), p. 259.

dangerous illusion with more than a hint of treachery.[37] Anglophobia in France in July 1940 was as bitter and as outraged as anti-Communism in September 1939. It certainly played a substantial role in persuading the deputies and senators who met at Vichy on 10 July that France was entirely on its own and that the only realistic policy was to consolidate the nation behind Pétain. In the division to decide whether Pétain should assume full power or not, the eighty who voted against full powers for the Marshal were seen by most of the 569 who voted in favour as opting out of the political realities. The Germans were not far away at Moulins and the British had attacked the French fleet. It was the pressure of 'realism' not the machinations of Laval or anyone else which brought an end to the parliament of the Popular Front elected in 1936 and pledged to carry forward the fight against Fascism. It was then Pétain, Laval, and the other Vichy ministers who, without the consultation promised on 10 July, ended the Third Republic and instituted an authoritarian state. There was little initial protest. A dislocated, fragmented nation saw no point in regrouping and restructuring its separate units. Apart from the Communists, who continued to be opposed to the rulers of France and called Pétain's government on 7 July 'le gouvernement des pourris', party politics were disclaimed.

The dislocation was embodied most obviously in the division of France into two major zones, occupied and unoccupied.[38] Within the occupied area, the three *départements* of Bas-Rhin, Haut-Rhin, and Moselle, which comprised Alsace-Lorraine, were annexed by Germany, and the industrial areas of the Nord and Pas-de-Calais made into a Prohibited Zone, administered directly by the German High Command in Brussels. The rest of the occupied zone was effectively under the control of

[37] The attack on Mers-el-Kébir was part of 'Operation Catapult', the British action designed to achieve 'the simultaneous seizure, control or effective disablement or destruction of all the accessible French Fleet'. It was mounted by Churchill in the period of maximum suspicion of French intentions after the Armistice, when it was thought, on little or no evidence, that the French navy might be made available to the Germans. See A. J. Marder, *From the Dardanelles to Oran. Studies of the Royal Navy in War and Peace, 1915–40* (O.U.P., 1974). The attack is set in the whole context of British foreign policy towards France in Raymond Thomas, 'The Vichy Dilemma in British Foreign Policy' (unpub. Univ. of Sussex D.Phil. thesis 1976).

[38] See Maps 1 and 2, pp. 297–9.

the Commander-in-Chief of the German Army of Occupation in Paris, though theoretically the zone was subject to the civil authority of the Vichy Government.[39] The instrument which kept Vichy's powers in the north at arm's length was the demarcation line between the two major zones. The line was extensively manned by the German authorities, whose unilateral decisions about what and who should be allowed to cross permanently frustrated Vichy's attempts to reconstruct a united France, and kept the south isolated from the richer and more populous sections of the country. At the start it was an almost impenetrable frontier, with only 300 letters allowed across each day, presented unsealed at Moulins, and a wait of twenty-four hours or more for any person returning home after the *exode*. All other crossings were forbidden.[40]

The area occupied by the Germans contained 67 per cent of the population, 66 per cent of cultivated land, over 75 per cent of mining and industry, 97 per cent of the fishing industry, 62 per cent of cereals, and over 70 per cent of potatoes, milk, butter, and meat. The southern zone was superior only in its production of wine and fruit, though it had a few pockets of industrial strength of interest to the Germans, particularly the mining of bauxite for aluminium.[41] Almost all the industry of the south was dependent on the petrol and coal in German hands and worked only at a fraction of its full capacity during the second half of 1940, owing to the rigour with which the demarcation line was controlled. There was thus an initial unemployment problem in the south despite the fact that so many men of working age were in German prisoner-of-war camps, and the problem was exacerbated by the 300,000 or more refugees still in the southern zone in October 1940, most

[39] For the different administrations of the zones, see E. Jäckel, *La France dans l'Europe de Hitler* (Fayard, 1968), p. 45 and *passim*. There was also a reserved zone to the west of Alsace-Lorraine which the Germans initially separated from the rest of the occupied zone, under the threat of annexation should the French not obey the terms of the Armistice. The line marking this zone was no longer effectively policed by the end of 1941.

[40] In September 1940 postcards were authorized but only of a pre-printed kind on which the sender could tick the relevant information such as 'en bonne santé', 'fatigué', 'blessé', 'tué', etc.

[41] Michel Cépède, *Agriculture et alimentation en France durant la 2e Guerre Mondiale* (Éditions Génin, 1961), pp. 69–70. A. S. Milward, *The New Order and the French Economy* (Clarendon Press, Oxford, 1970), pp. 235 ff.

of them unable or unwilling to return to the annexed provinces of Alsace-Lorraine or to the Prohibited Zone of the Nord and Pas-de-Calais.[42]

It became rapidly apparent that food, as well as resources, would be a severe problem in the southern zone, and the Vichy Government instituted organization committees to superintend the provision and distribution of all raw materials and foodstuffs and some manufactured products. From the end of July 1940 rationing was steadily introduced to cover all commodities in short supply, though the system of distribution operated unevenly owing to the separate policies of departmental prefects, who tried to hold back the foodstuffs which were more abundant in their own area. The British blockade was widely blamed by the Vichy Press for the sudden shortages in the shops, though it was only a partial blockade and decreasingly effective, particularly in the Mediterranean. The real cause, the German Occupation costs and demands, was never openly analysed so that the public was basically ignorant of the economic exploitation of France, which only began with the 400 million francs paid every day by the French to their occupiers, with the rate of exchange imposed at 20 francs to the mark instead of its pre-war level of between 12.30 f. and 12.95 f.[43]

The unoccupied zone was known also as the 'zone libre' though in general parlance it was usually referred to as the 'zone sud', begging no questions of freedom or independence. In the spa of Vichy the government was safe from the urban pressures which would have been felt had it opted for residence in Limoges, Clermont-Ferrand, or Lyon, though the bulk of the national Press retreated from Paris to these urban centres and yet contrived to be fully Pétainist and subservient for the two and a half years during which Vichy France was effectively in existence. The town of Vichy, with its hotels, parks and gardens, and bedroom-slippered image was less an environmental cause of the government's policies than a symbol of them, and Pétain was adulated in all the major towns which he visited on his extensive and successful tours of the southern

[42] Jacques Delperrié de Bayac, *Le Royaume du Maréchal* (Laffont, 1975), p. 84.

[43] For a detailed account of the growing exploitation and the divided German policy behind it, see Milward, op. cit.

zone.[44] There was, nevertheless, a basic anomaly in the fact that an autocratic, right-wing government should be established in the area of France which, generally, had voted for parties of the Centre or Left during the Third Republic,[45] and this potential challenge to Vichy was countered at an early date by the dissolution of the municipal councils in all towns with a left-wing majority, and the suspension of all the elected departmental assemblies, the *conseils généraux*. By the decree law of 16 November Vichy allowed the system of democratic election to continue for only the smallest communes with a population of under 2,000, while for all others the mayor and members of the local assembly were subject to appointment either by the local prefect or by the Minister of the Interior. It was a wry comment both on the sparsely populated nature of most of the southern zone, and on Vichy's propaganda intentions, that the Minister of the Interior, Peyrouton, could summarize the law on the radio by saying that over 85 per cent of the communes would still be able to elect their own local councils.[46]

[44] One such tour is lovingly described by René Benjamin in *Le Maréchal et son peuple* (Plon, 1941), and it can only be said that the language of adoration in the book makes it more, not less, authentic as a document of the time.

[45] The departmental strength of the Radical, Socialist, and Communist parties in the last elections of the Third Republic in 1936 is presented in G. Dupeux, *Le Front populaire et les élections de 1936* (Cartes et graphiques) (Colin, 1959). His maps show that in the area which became the southern zone the following *départements* had been particularly strong in their support for the Popular Front: Allier, Aude, Corrèze, Dordogne, Drôme, Gard, Haute-Garonne, Gers, Hérault, Isère, Puy-de-Dôme, Pyrénées-Orientales, Bouches-du-Rhône, Savoie, Tarn-et-Garonne, Vaucluse, Haute-Vienne.

[46] Broadcast of 12 December 1940. The rural strength of the southern zone was seen at the time as one of the most significant components in the political structure and ideology of Vichy France. 'La Marseillaise' was rewritten to reflect this fact, though it was not widely used:

> Aimez enfants votre Patrie
> Le jour d'espoir est arrivé
> Du travail et de l'harmonie
> L'étendard vaillant est levé (bis)
> Fiers artisans de nos campagnes
> La paix enrôle ses soldats
> La terre a besoin de vos bras
> Pour nourrir nos fils, nos compagnes
> Courage paysans. Tracez droit vos sillons
> Semons, fauchons,
> Qu'un air plus pur ravive nos poumons.

(Jean Duhamel, *Journal d'un Français moyen*, Imprimerie de la Vallée d'Eure, Pacy-sur-Eure, 1953, p. 216.)

The absence of collective opposition to this massive reorganization of local government was as symptomatic of the stunned and confused opinion in defeated France as the parliamentary vote of 10 July: no local authority resisted the abrogation of its powers. France in the second half of 1940 was fragmented into a mass of individual experiences and regional differences by the effects of the defeat and the *exode*, it was geographically and economically divided by the terms of the Armistice, it perpetuated a major conflict between the Communists and the rest of society, and it was deeply divided on the question of who was responsible for the catastrophe. On the other hand, it was largely united in accepting that the war had been lost, that an armistice leading to peace was a realistic policy, that party divisions should be buried, and that Pétain was the only man to whom the survival of France and the protection of French honour could be entrusted. Psychologically speaking, this simple subservience can be seen as derived from the feelings of confusion, and there was an obvious chronological development from the one to the other, but the two also coexisted in most areas and the elements of unity which France showed in the following two years continued to be dependent on the anxiety which still lay underneath. The hold of Pétainism remained strong while few people exposed the problems it appeared to have resolved, and its early strength is evident in its monopoly of patriotic and realist arguments.

This monopoly seemed undisputed in 1940, but between 1940 and 1942 it was increasingly challenged, and the following chapters focus on some of the individuals and groups who mounted the challenge and produced the phenomenon of Resistance. In so far as Pétainism and *attentisme* were a simple means of avoiding the complexities of the situation, the history of Resistance is the study of individuals and groups who either perpetuated or reintroduced complexity; for the idea of continuing or restarting the war against the Germans and of developing an alternative to the government of Pétain seemed anything but clear and simple to the majority of people in Vichy France.

II. Continuity I

ONCE it has been said that France in 1940 was stunned by the defeat into a state of confusion and insecurity, it becomes important to qualify this point. It is true that for most French people the traumatic events of May and June led to a questioning of the past, and to doubts about attitudes and actions which had previously been accepted or taken for granted: the decision on 10 July by the politicians of the Third Republic, who had thrived on party division and conflict, to disown their traditional source of political vigour, provides an obvious example. More generally, the cult of Pétain was carefully nurtured by the belief that a break with the recent past must be made if France was to profit from the crisis and regenerate itself. To do so the country was said to need a period of calm and security and people were expected not to act or express opinions which would disturb this calm or endanger the period of respite assured by the Armistice and the policy of *attentisme* which followed. In an essay in *La France libre* in 1945 Jean-Paul Sartre described the strange vacuum in Paris created by the Occupation and the sense of a life from which the dimensions of past and future had been removed: 'We were constantly aware that a link with the past had been broken.'[1] His picture is forceful simply because this awareness is developed into an all-pervading mentality, so that Parisians are seen as caught in an anguish of day-to-day life, devoid of past concerns and ultimate meaning. But although this was more true of the occupied zone than of the southern zone until November 1942, it is finally misleading for it assumes, without stating it, that *all* continuity was broken, and this is usually how the word 'trauma' applied to a historical event is understood. Certainly a traumatic experience can change people's behaviour, but it can also intensify pre-existing behaviour so that among certain people a strong continuity of action and opinion is observable. Both are true of France in 1940, when the hold of *attentisme* and Pétainism would have been complete

[1] J.-P. Sartre, 'Paris sous l'occupation', *Situations III* (Gallimard, 1949), p. 24.

had it not been for certain elements of continuity and change which questioned the general submissiveness and kept the situation from becoming closed. The elements of continuity, examined first, show clearly that among certain people the experience of the defeat and the arrival of Pétain to power did not bring changed attitudes or a decision to suspend previous behaviour during the crisis, but rather accentuated patterns of behaviour which had been formed in the 1930s or earlier. The expression of these in 1940, even by only a small minority, reminded the French that choices derived from past convictions could still be made.[2]

In Paris, and to a lesser extent in Vichy, those who wanted an active, positive collaboration with Germany, the creation of a Fascist-style nation, a single political party, and a significant role for France in a New European Order, provided just such a challenge to the more static, comfortable image of the Vichy regime. By 1941 the explicitly collaborationist newspapers had little but scorn for Pétainism, and in their policies for a dynamic alternative they restated most of the Fascist positions developed in the 1930s. It was this continuity which led Jean Luchaire and Robert Brasillach at their trials in 1945 to say that it was not they who had changed but others, and that what they said during the Occupation was exactly what they had said with impunity in the 1930s. Charles Maurras made similar references to the past in defending his denunciation of Resisters to the police: he spent his life opposing those who threatened his ideal of a strong France and in this respect Resisters seemed to him no less subversive than the Dreyfusards of forty-five years before.[3] The naïvety of apologetics such as these points to the dogmatic obstinacy of all three defendants in their refusal to see that changed circumstances altered the significance of their beliefs, but the same

[2] Sartre put the ideas from his essay of 1945 into his fictional trilogy, particularly its third part, *La Mort dans l'âme*, in which the 'freedom' of the characters from the past and future is one of the main issues. By contrast, two other novels on the period of Occupation, Jean-Louis Curtis's *Les Forêts de la nuit* and Roger Vailland's *Drôle de jeu*, emphasize the continuity of personality among their characters from the 1930s into the war. Curtis has claimed that Sartre's approach is no more than an abstract one, and that his characters are no more 'free' than those of Balzac. See J.-L. Curtis, *Haute école* (Julliard, 1950), pp. 165–205, and *Questions à la littérature* (Stock, 1973), pp. 100–15.

[3] Geo London, *Le Procès de Charles Maurras* (Bonnefon, Lyon, 1945), pp. 50–7.

kind of obstinacy in the defence of previous values can be found in the continuity elements which pulled in the opposite direction, away from collaboration.

It is impossible to present these elements in the southern zone in any accurate chronological sequence, for the very fact of their continuity from the pre-war period means that they were all there in 1940, some interdependent, some running parallel to each other without knowing it, and some related only by suspicion or even hostility. Historians of 1940 need the split-screen technique of cinema or the innovations of novelists who allow their pages to be read in any order, but in the absence of these they can at least say that there is no logical or inevitable place in which to start.

In Toulouse the old and partially paralysed archbishop, Mgr. Saliège, had been president before the war of the Association catholique d'aide aux étrangers set up to help refugees from the Spanish Republic, whose cause he had supported, in contrast to most of the Catholic hierarchy in Italy, Spain, and France.[4] Descended from a rural family in the Auvergne, he was said by those who knew him to possess all the obstinacy of the peasant, and he and the Rector of the Institut Catholique at Toulouse, Mgr. de Solages, did not hide their attitudes to the defeat and Armistice. Political refugees came to them from Austria and Germany, and after the Armistice and the division of France into separate zones Toulouse became one of the distribution points for those escaping from the German-occupied territories of the north and Alsace-Lorraine and looking for somewhere to hide or ways of getting out of the country.

Saliège did not need to create new means of communication to convey his opinions to the people of Toulouse. The weekly *Semaine catholique de Toulouse* carried a mixture of news and reflections to practising Catholics of the area and on 7 July 1940 they could read the archbishop's warning against 'suspect propaganda and erroneous judgements', on 8 September his brief reflection that 'Nothing is final on earth . . . while hope

[4] Jean Guitton, *Le Cardinal Saliège* (Grasset, 1957), p. 164. Cf. Cardinal Baudrillart, Rector of the Institut Catholique in Paris, who derived his horror of Communism from the Spanish Civil War and became an enthusiastic supporter of the anti-Bolshevik crusade launched by Parisian collaborators in July 1941.

continues. Coffee, alcohol and other things may be lacking but such restrictions do not prevent a nation's recovery, nor a Goliath from finding a David', and on 15 September the clearly expressed wish that 'occupied France should know that those in the free zone continue to think as Frenchmen, and that they dedicate their prayers and their actions to the liberation of the country'.[5] A full reading of his personal messages confirms the impression of these extracts. They develop a concept of Christian patriotism based on a rejection of *attentisme*, though without any overt charge against Pétain, a concession to public sensitivity which did not compromise his work with refugees and political victims. Both he and de Solages were involved with Christian Democracy before the war and this continued to be the political framework within which they operated, later revealed by de Solages to a shocked representative of Vichy at the Vatican when he said 'I would prefer a victorious France governed by Léon Blum and the Freemasons to a defeated France governed by Marshal Pétain.'[6] If this was not said openly in the summer of 1940 it was nevertheless to other Catholics of democratic or socialist tendencies that the political refugees were sent from Toulouse on the next stage of their escape from Nazi persecutions.

In August 1940 Edmond Michelet in Brive received from Mgr. de Solages fourteen such refugees, including Dietrich von Hildebrand, Professor of Philosophy at Munich. Two months earlier on 17 June, the day of Pétain's announcement that he was seeking an armistice, Michelet had typed and handed out in the streets a tract with six quotations from Charles Péguy, who had been killed in 1914 at the Battle of the Marne. One of these quotations stated categorically, 'In wartime he who does not surrender is my man, whoever he is, wherever he comes from, and whatever his party. He does not surrender. That's all I demand. And he who surrenders is my enemy, whoever he is, wherever he comes from, and whatever his party.'[7] Brive at the time had a socialist and radical-socialist

[5] *Un Évêque français sous l'occupation. Extraits des messages de S. Ex. Mgr. Saliège* (Éditions Ouvrières, 1945), pp. 42, 45, 46.

[6] Jacques Duquesne, *Les Catholiques français sous l'occupation* (Grasset, 1966), p. 163. This excellent book gives one of the best insights into how people divided under the Occupation.

[7] Josse, 'Brive-la-Gaillarde 1940–42', p. 108.

municipal council, preoccupied with the problems of the *exode*, and no official recognition was paid to Michelet's initiative. According to evidence from the curé Alvitre, the anticlericalism of the council led them to view Michelet's opinions, coming from a well-known Catholic, with suspicion.[8] The tracts reached few people, but this was of less significance than the continuity of ideology they expressed. The last of the six quotations was Péguy's invocation of the two values he himself incarnated, Christianity and liberty, the two most important words for Michelet since he had left the ranks of right-wing Catholicism within the royalist and nationalist movement of Action Française and had moved into the circle of Christian Democrats during the 1930s.[9] Instrumental in his political conversion was the curé Alvitre, known as one of the 'red priests' for his membership of Marc Sangnier's Sillon movement, denounced before World War I by the Vatican for its secular methods and socialist opinions.[10] It was Alvitre, whose parish was in a working-class suburb of Brive, who plied Michelet with copies of the Christian Democratic paper, *Le Petit Démocrate*,[11] and who became his close friend when Michelet began to share the opinions of the Christian Democrats with a conviction as militant as his previous opinions as a member of the Camelots du Roi, the youth organization of Action Française.[12]

By the late 1930s, having supported the Spanish Republic

[8] Evidence from curé Alvitre.

[9] Edmond Michelet, *La Querelle de la fidelité* (Fayard, 1971), pp. 18–30.

[10] Formed by Marc Sangnier in 1898, the Sillon was a militant social Catholic movement which exposed social deprivation in a series of meetings, tracts, and exhibitions until it was condemned for 'politicization' and 'social modernism' by Pope Pius X in 1910. During its existence the Sillon was centralized round the leader 'Marc', and young members fought for him and the movement against young militants of Action Française in the Camelots du Roi.

[11] *Le Petit Démocrate* was the paper of the Christian Democratic Party (Parti Démocrate Populaire) founded in November 1924. Georges Bidault was one of its editors before working on the larger paper *L'Aube*, which was started in 1932.

[12] Evidence from curé Alvitre. At Périgueux there was another 'red curé', abbé Jean Sigala, Professor of Philosophy at the Collège St Joseph, who returned to his teaching after a brief period as a prisoner of war and made no secret of his hostility to the Armistice and his wish to continue the fight by any means. Repeatedly reprimanded by the Vichy authorities, he provided leadership for the opposition in Périgueux similar to that provided by Michelet and the curé Alvitre in Brive. (Georges Rocal and Léon Bouillon, *Jean Sigala (1884–1954)* Éditions Coquemard, Angoulême, 1954).

and opposed the agreements of Munich, Michelet was known principally as the animator of the Équipes sociales at Brive, a Catholic organization with centres in several large towns, embodying to a considerable extent the aims and ideals of the universités populaires at the turn of the century, and open principally to young workers and artisans who wanted serious part-time education. Michelet said that a number of the students were railway-workers, and other evidence states that several were trade-unionists and members of the Communist Party,[13] and it was to this audience in Brive that intellectuals of the P.D.P. (Parti Démocrate Populaire), the Christian Democratic Party, or those sympathetic to it, were invited to lecture on topical subjects like racism, totalitarianism, Nazism, religion, and inevitably, on the ideas and writings of Péguy, the most controversial figure in twentieth-century Catholicism, venerated by Catholics as far apart as nationalist Right and socialist Left.

The tracts that followed those of 17 June reflected in full the ideals of the Équipes sociales whose members took a hand in their production and formed a distribution network. In this way their pre-war ideas were perpetuated into the situation following the Armistice without any change of value or any sense of doing something totally new or dangerous. The attitudes of Michelet and his group were no secret in Brive and there was nothing particularly clandestine in their early activity, until the German and Austrian refugees started arriving and even that was not a complete departure since Michelet, like de Solages and Saliège in Toulouse, had helped numerous Spanish refugees in the previous few years. Brive thus continued as a focal point in Christian Democracy and it was here that the dominican Père Maydieu stopped in June 1940 on his way to Bordeaux after escaping from a prisoner-of-war encampment at Orléans. Dressed in civilian clothes, he made the journey by bicycle and on the road from Brive crossed the caravan of ministerial cars carrying the newly formed government of Pétain to Saint-Étienne and eventually Vichy. 'As I wanted to show my hostility,' he said, 'I raised a clenched fist, made the sign of the Popular Front, and shouted "Salud" like the Spanish Republicans. Who would have guessed that this ostensible "red" was a Dominican Father and an officer of the French

[13] Michelet, op. cit., p. 46. Evidence from curé Alvitre and René Jugie.

army?'[14] Père Maydieu had been editor of *La Vie intellectuelle* during the 1930s which with the journals *Sept*, *Temps présent* which succeeded it, and *Esprit* represented an intellectual peak in liberal Catholicism comparable to the period of Lacordaire and Lamennais in the nineteenth century. Interconnected were the political newspapers *L'Aube* and *Le Petit Démocrate* and the two parties, the P.D.P. and the Jeune République, in which the old militants of the Sillon were mostly located,[15] and Père Maydieu was a figure as respected as any in this world of vigorous religious and political ideas, while in his capacity as chaplain to the Amis de Sept and the Amis de Temps présent he was a vital part of the substructure of the Christian Democratic movement. The Amis were groups of like-minded Catholics which grew up round the two journals, and they illustrate that recurrent feature in the French Press by which regular subscribers were used as promoters and distributors and thus formed an allegiance to a paper similar to membership of a political party. Such a paper was more than a publication, it was the centre of a widespread organization, and Père Maydieu visited Michelet's house partly to renew contact with the Amis who had met there regularly in the 1930s. In Lyon, Marseille, Montpellier, and Clermont-Ferrand other Catholic Democrats made the same initial move, maintaining the structures which had buttressed their ideas before the war and which served to keep people with similar attitudes together in the confusion of 1940.

Temps présent had been run in Paris by Stanislas Fumet. After the Armistice Fumet settled in Lyon and tried to continue the journal, finally obtaining authorization from Vichy to reissue it as *Temps nouveau* in December 1940. The Amis regrouped and as a focus for discussion and a matrix of activity the new publication simply took the place of the old one, continuing its aim of showing the incompatibility of Nazism and Christianity but with a more indirect and ironic style to

[14] 'Le Père Maydieu', supplément à *La Vie intellectuelle* (Aug.–Sept. 1956) (Éditions du Cerf), pp. 69–70.

[15] The Jeune République was founded by Marc Sangnier in 1912 after the papal condemnation of the Sillon. It was an explicitly political movement and Sangnier was a deputy to the Chambre des Députés from 1919–24. The P.D.P. was more moderate in tone and membership, but there was a considerable overlap in ideas.

meet the demands of the censor. Fumet's house and the offices of the journal became the meeting place for the Christian Democrats, Protestant as well as Catholic, who lived or decided to stay in Lyon, and the opinions of this grouping would seem to have been genuinely collective, for there is ample evidence of the contacts between them and the mutual trust which existed and little memory of serious dissension.[16] They set out principally to remind those who accepted the position of Vichy towards the Germans that Nazism was an ideology and not just a political regime and in this the continuity of purpose from the 1930s was unbroken. The two Jesuits, pères Fessard and Chaillet, who after Chaillet's return from a mission in Budapest in January 1941 were actively involved in the preparation of extensive propaganda to warn the Lyonnais of the dangers of Nazism, had both written books on Hitlerism before the war, animated by the same intention. Fessard, an editor of the Jesuit journal *Études*, was a specialist in Hegelian philosophy and his publications in the 1930s included *Épreuve de force* written in 1939 and suppressed by the Germans in occupied France, while Chaillet had written *L'Autriche souffrante* in 1938 after the Anschluss.[17] They were both closely identified with the Amis de Temps nouveau but their intellectual sanction went beyond the ideas of Christian Democracy in France to the encyclicals of Pope Pius XI against Nazism and the idolization of the state, in particular *Mit brennender Sorge*. In Marseille this influence was openly expressed by a publication called *La Voix du Vatican* whose first number appeared in July 1940 produced by the Dominicans of Saint-Baume, giving regular transcripts of broadcasts by the Vatican radio. The language was non-specific, but to those attuned to the nuances of papal utterances and determined to find a positive statement, these broadcasts were a re-emphasis of the arguments in the pre-war encyclicals, and were read as such in the circle of Christian Democrats in Lyon.

In September 1940 this circle was joined by François de

[16] The influence of Stanislas Fumet in 1940 in stimulating criticism of the *status quo* is particularly stressed by André Plaisantin (see Ch. XI). His unpublished notes on the origins of Combat in Lyon were kindly made available to the author.

[17] F. and R. Bédarida, 'Une Résistance spirituelle: Aux origines du Témoignage Chrétien 1941–2', *Revue d'histoire de la Deuxième Guerre Mondiale*, no. 61 (Jan. 1966), 13. An excellent and indispensable article.

Menthon after his escape from a prisoner-of-war hospital. An ex-president of the Catholic Youth Movement, Association catholique de la jeunesse française (A.C.J.F.), which had furnished the P.D.P. with several of its leading members and many of its regional administrators, de Menthon was a Professeur de Droit at the faculty of Nancy, a landowner with a family château near Annecy, and after being wounded in the last fighting in the Vosges before the Armistice, had returned as a respected war veteran. Not without difficulty he succeeded in obtaining a post at the faculty in Lyon and quickly made contact with other academics, Pierre-Henri Teitgen, a colleague from Nancy who had also escaped as a prisoner of war in the late summer and had found a post at the University of Montpellier, Alfred Coste-Floret at Clermont-Ferrand, René Courtin at Montpellier, René Capitant and Paul Coste-Floret in Algiers, and Marcel Prélot who had been evacuated to Clermont-Ferrand with the University of Strasbourg. Teitgen and the Coste-Floret brothers had been members of the Jeunesses démocrates populaires which had started under de Menthon and Georges Bidault in 1932, and these old Catholic Democratic links, strengthened by academic sympathies, held during 1940 to form the nucleus of an intellectual movement in the law faculties across the southern zone. Jean Baumel, who was himself giving courses in Roman Law at Montpellier, remembers that the opposition of Teitgen and Courtin to the Armistice was sufficiently open in their lectures to provoke violence and attack from a student minority, constituted as a Pétainist body within the University.[18]

To these colleagues and friends de Menthon proposed a publication to fight the lethargy in public opinion and to continue the intellectual activism in Christian Democracy which had marked its pre-war history. For those who had been formed, politically speaking, in opposition to the conservative echelons of the Church, there was nothing passive or merely self-justifying in publication. They had conceived their statements of principle in the 1930s in the expectation of conflict, and the same combative mentality informed the first number of a paper which de Menthon drafted in his home at Annecy

[18] Evidence from Jean Baumel.

during October and early November. In it he presented his view that the war could still be won and that the French must refuse all help to Germany and unite round the patriotic image of Marshal Pétain. He condemned the lies emanating from the official news under the aegis of Tixier-Vignancour, currently head of the Vichy radio, whom he described as 'that *minus habens*', language which showed the limited public to which the paper was directed.[19] The title de Menthon decided to use was *Liberté*, a word as central to him as it was to Michelet in Brive and those round *Temps nouveau* in Lyon, and the separate articles in the typed three pages, which are dated 25 November 1940, certainly establish the liberty of France as the aim of the author, a liberty understood as it had been by the Christian Democrats in the 1930s based on intellectual freedom and the force of truth. At the head were two quotations from Foch and Pétain which stand as a key to this mode of thought: 'People are only defeated when they accept defeat' (Foch) and the proclamation by Pétain at the start of his personal regime, 'I hate lies: no one will lie any more to this country.'[20] The struggle is principally seen in terms of opinion and ideas, though the example given of resistance against the Germans in the occupied zone, which the paper calls 'admirable', is the march of several hundred students on 11 November 1940 to the Arc de Triomphe which led to physical conflict with the German police. There was therefore no *a priori* distinction between intellectual and physical struggle, rather the dynamic of ideas was seen as an activity in itself, as it had been in pre-war situations. The passage which vehemently denounces those who were making political capital out of the defeat in the corridors of Vichy starts by brandishing opinion, 'Know that the country despises you' but concludes with the physical threat, 'At the first breath of liberty you will be swept away'.[21] The transition is natural: though produced by intellectuals whose business was words, there is nothing abstract in the arguments of *Liberté*. It was addressed to a middle-class intelligentsia but was not removed from the problems of action, as the difficult mechanics of production and distribution from a base in

[19] *Liberté*, no. 1 (25 Nov. 1940).
[20] Ibid.
[21] Ibid.

Marseille confirmed. It was hoped to publish it once a fortnight but it was impossible to realize such regularity.

By the end of 1940 the role of the Christian Democrats in the protection of diversity of thought and open-ended inquiry was firmly established, even if only in a small circle of like-minded people. The circle was not even coextensive with the whole Christian Democratic movement. The elected members of the P.D.P. in the Assembly were no less responsive to the arguments of 'realism' than members of other parties and on 10 July only Champetier de Ribes, a senator, and two deputies Paul Simon and Pierre Trémintin voted among the eighty. Among those who voted with the majority three had signed a manifesto on 9 July calling for a single national party, to which Tixier-Vignancour's name was also appended,[22] and the votes of most P.D.P. politicians in favour of Pétain make it clear why de Menthon, Teitgen, and others restructured themselves round tracts, publications, and discussion groups and did not attempt to revive the old party. Unlike the politicians they had no responsibilities to a constituency and were not subject to pressure within the Assembly which met at Vichy, and they thus found it easier to maintain their independence from the pervading submissiveness of public opinion. Similar freedom to think and write, detached from day-to-day pastoral concern, helps explain why Dominicans and Jesuits featured more prominently in the continuation of anti-Nazi ideas in 1940 than did parochial and diocesan clergy. Maydieu, Fessard, Chaillet, and other regulars who congregated round *Temps nouveau* and *La Voix du Vatican* were exceptions within their own orders, but were not such a small group, relatively speaking, as Saliège, de Solages, the curés Alvitre and Sigala, and the handful of other clergy who stood out against the vast majority of bishops and local priests.

The factor which lies behind the action of most, if not all, of the Christian Democrats mentioned here is their thorough acquaintance with the issues of Nazism and Fascism before the war. It has become a historical platitude to say that few people actually read *Mein Kampf* or Rosenberg's *Myth of the Twentieth Century*, even with Hitler in power, but among these Christian Democrats it appears that these books were not

[22] They were Reille-Soult, Goussus and Saudebroy.

only read but answered before war began. After the defeat they stuck to their opinions and deliberately broke the ranks of Catholicism neatly ordered within the *attentisme* of Vichy, although this did not at first entail opposition to the figure of Pétain himself. They either considered Pétain was an innocent in the hands of wilful and scheming politicians like Laval, or considered it prudent to avoid an open confrontation with his image, however much they rejected the Armistice and its consequences. De Menthon's position is symptomatic of this apparently ambiguous attitude which did not seem ambiguous at the time. In the hospital to which he was sent on 19 June he heard one of the early broadcasts of de Gaulle from London and he opposed the idea of an armistice from the moment Pétain announced it.[23] Yet in the first number of *Liberté* he decided not to mention de Gaulle's name when reporting the student demonstration of 11 November, but wrote that the students were crying 'Vive de . . .', and when exposing German pressure on the inhabitants of Alsace-Lorraine he adds that Pétain, in resisting the advice of Laval to meet German demands, has 'once more saved more than honour.'[24] The allusion is to Pétain's broadcast on 30 October 1940 after meeting Hitler at Montoire, in which he claimed that it was 'in honour and to preserve the unity of France . . . that I have set out on the path of collaboration'.[25] The word 'collaboration', though containing few of its later connotations, was clearly suspect to de Menthon, but he could do no more than refer to Pétain's 'human weakness' when reporting Montoire, and he thus preserved the hope, shared by Saliège in his episcopal reflections and evident in the pages of *Temps nouveau*, that Pétain had kept himself intact from the compromises in which his regime was progressively involved.

Such a distinction between Pétain and his advisers did not emerge from Pétain's public statements alone, but was encouraged by rumours of secret negotiations between Pétain and Churchill, which by their very nature could not be made

[23] Evidence given by de Menthon in Marie Granet and Henri Michel, *Combat* (P.U.F., 1957), p. 58 n. 1.

[24] *Liberté* (25 Nov. 1940).

[25] *Les Paroles et les écrits du Maréchal Pétain* (édité par la Légion française, n.d.), p. 90.

public. When the word 'Resistance' later gained currency, Pétain was how many people imagined the official Resister must look to the occupying forces.[26] Furthermore, there were the facts, variously used, of Pétain's concern for refugees, prisoners of war, and the people of the annexed provinces, Alsace and Lorraine. The Christian Democrats had no monopoly of welfare work among these groups, but they were well represented and there was a natural reluctance to question the intentions of Pétain while he stood at the moral centre of this activity. Financial support was also needed. For example, Edmond Michelet, although he never personally accepted Pétain,[27] was in 1940 a member of the organizing committee of the Secours national and to that extent needed to co-operate with the Vichy ministry which controlled the budget for national assistance. For well over a year considerations such as these weighed heavily with many who were otherwise vehemently opposed to the Armistice and the notion of collaboration, accepted by Pétain at Montoire.

Not all Christian Democrats were Catholics. René Courtin, whose influence at Montpellier was considerable, was a Protestant, and in Lyon the Protestant Pasteur de Pury preached a strong attack on defeatism on 14 July 1940 from his pulpit in the rue Lanterne, extolling those who continued to fight and insisting on the just cause for which France had declared war.[28] He became a close associate of the Catholic circle round *Temps nouveau* and a colleague of Père Chaillet. This ecumenical element in Christian Democracy was particularly evident in welfare work where the Protestant movement CIMADE (Comité inter-mouvements auprès des évacués), animated by Madeleine Barot, worked closely with Catholics such as the Polish abbé Glasberg in camps to which *emigré* Spaniards, Jews, East Europeans and political refugees from other parts of Europe were sent, located mostly in the departments bordering on the Pyrenees. Throughout most of 1940 the CIMADE, formed in September 1939, could be said to be working within the canon of Vichy welfare, but once the

[26] e.g. Jean Texcier, *Lettres à François* (published clandestinely Apr. 1941), second letter, 17 Jan. 1941, p. 19.

[27] Michelet, p. 48.

[28] P. Mouterde, 'La Résistance chrétienne dans la région lyonnaise' (unpub., Diplôme d'Études Supérieures, Faculté des Lettres, Lyon, 1946), p. 15.

regime began to legislate against the Jews its work gained a new significance.[29] In 1941 its continuity of care for the dispossessed and persecuted became, like the continuity of anti-Nazism among Christian Democrats in 1940, an element contesting the values of the Vichy regime and keeping open the possibility of other solutions.

At the end of July 1940 in Sainte-Maxime on the Mediterranean near Saint-Tropez, Captain Henri Frenay sat down in a room in his mother's house to write a personal reaction to the events of the war, the defeat, and the Armistice. In common with Père Maydieu, de Menthon, Teitgen, and others he had the experience and commitment of escape from a prisoner-of-war camp behind him, and like them he had taken an ideological position against Nazism before the war, though couched in the military language which was his *métier*. Lecturing in Toulouse in September 1938 to a group of reserve officers he had warned them of the danger in the Nazi myths which lay behind the German army, a danger impressed on him by the teaching of René Capitant in Strasbourg, where Frenay had attended the Centre of German Studies. In 1939 he had toured a number of towns with another lecture on the National Socialist ideology, and in 1940 the experience of the war and defeat did everything to reinforce the conclusions of that lecture: 'What we will have to defend is more precious than our lives, our homes, and the soil of France: it is our spiritual freedom, our concept of the world and of life itself.'[30] It was this that he sat down to recapitulate in July, refusing to accept that the defeat was final or involved him in the general quietism of the French army. Frenay was a mixed product of family and social conditioning among the Lyon bourgeoisie, which stamped him as militaristic and paternalist, and of intellectual conditioning before the war, not just in the lectures of René Capitant, but also in left-wing circles in Paris to which he had been introduced by Bertie Albrecht, a friend with an English husband and a Protestant upbringing whom Frenay greatly admired and to whom he was indebted for much of his political education.[31]

[29] See below, pp. 181–2.
[30] Henri Frenay, *La Nuit finira* (Laffont, 1973), pp. 27–8.
[31] Ibid., p. 42.

The army to which Frenay reported after his escape had been reduced to 100,000 men under the terms of the Armistice, in ironic imitation of the restrictions imposed on Germany by the Treaty of Versailles. Of these only 3,768 could be officers, so that a special dispensation known as the *congé d'armistice* was introduced to allow those officers, who wished to do so, to withdraw temporarily from their jobs. Regiments were stationed in provincial towns and the military schools rehoused; Saint-Cyr at Aix-en-Provence, Saumur at Tarbes, the artillery at Nîmes, and the engineers at Avignon. Alongside this Armistice Army the Vichy Government created a number of organizations infused with military spirit and incorporating varying amounts of military training: the Chantiers de la jeunesse, obligatory for all those at the age when previously they would have done their military service, the Compagnons de France, an official but voluntary scout movement for those between the ages of 15 and 20, the Légion française des combattants, a single organization grouping together all old soldiers of World War I and those of the 1939–40 war, and two staff colleges, one at Uriage near Grenoble and the other at Opme.[32]

In all these institutions, as in the army itself, loyalty to Pétain was paramount and there was a general acceptance that the current war had been lost and that any preparations would be for the next one, but anti-Germanism was far from excluded. Several officers maintained uncompromisingly anti-German positions and throughout 1940 it was easy for these to contact each other, some openly, others with more circumspection. Frenay was one of the latter, and in Marseille, where he was given a job on the garrison staff, he plied his views carefully, gaining a positive response from a medical officer of the reserve, Marcel Recordier, a close friend from before the war, and from Maurice Chevance, a lieutenant of the colonial infantry who knew nothing of Nazism but was convinced that Germany could not win the war. Frenay conveyed to them not only sentiments but preliminary plans for a military reorganization to continue the war. He envisaged the formation of an intelligence service (Service de renseignements: S.R.) and of paramilitary units, organized in groups of six and thirty, and from the start he deliberately exaggerated the extent of his recruitment to add

[32] See Delperrié de Bayac, *Le Royaume du Maréchal*, pp. 151–200.

the argument of numbers to that of ideas. Strategy, tactics, and plans being as natural to an officer as ideas and publication to an academic, Frenay's initiative was as much a mark of his career training as *Liberté* was of de Menthon's. Both initiatives were developed in Marseille in the last months of 1940 without any connection, though Frenay saw an early copy of *Liberté* in December, adding to his confidence that his organization, staffed as yet by no more that a handful, had the capacity for rapid growth.

Also circulating in the Mediterranean towns as elsewhere in the southern zone were tracts written by a senior officer of the French air force, General Cochet, who told his men at the time of the Armistice to continue the war by dissimulation if necessary. On 6 September 1940 he issued a typed page signed openly by himself calling on the French to 'watch, resist, and unite' and telling them to create a new order not on the Nazi model but on the basis of French traditions and spiritual values. In this very first tract he made much use of the word 'resistance', signifying action not an organization, but the succession of tracts which followed, called *Tour d'horizon*, did produce an embryo organization of small groups of sympathizers, though they remained uncoordinated and without specific aims. Rémy Roure, a journalist from *Le Temps*, evacuated to Lyon, belonged to a 'General Cochet group' before becoming involved in the publication of *Liberté*,[33] and in Marseille and Nice C. L. Flavian, an officer who had served in the Foreign Legion, said that Cochet's tracts were a formative influence among military men like himself who felt disinclined to sit back and do nothing.[34] They began to gain a sense of purpose by distributing *Tour d'horizon*, its influence among soldiers increased by Cochet's expressed loyalty to the person of Pétain, enthusiastically worded in each of his tracts. At first this loyalty offset the rest of his position but as the fact of *attentisme* began to crystallize in the passive role of army personnel in a society which believed life was returning to normal, Cochet's arguments for continuing the war looked increasingly subversive and the openness of his statements made him conspic-

[33] André Roure, *Valeur de la vie humaine*, Œuvre posthume (Sfelt, 1946), p. 14.

[34] C. L. Flavian, *Ils furent des hommes* (Nouvelles Éditions Latines, 1948), p. 31.

uous. Frenay, by contrast, argued privately and could exploit the residue of anti-Germanism within the army with some ease to obtain both support and information. What they had in common was the conviction that the defeat made no difference in principle to a soldier's behaviour: his function was in no way abrogated by the collapse of 1940.

This was also the attitude of Georges Loustaunau-Lacau. It was the duty of a soldier, he declared in his memoirs, to fight to the very end and in doing so in 1940 he was only doing his job.[35] His own understanding of this job, however, was not so normative as this statement implies, though his activities from the pre-war period into the Occupation have a tenacity of direction which makes him almost a model for the continuity elements of 1940. He had a distinguished war record in 1914–18 and in 1934 was in the Ministry of War under Pétain whom he came to know well. From 1936 he was convinced that the army was internally collapsing owing to outmoded ideas and the sabotage of Communists, and he devoted himself to exposing this danger using clandestine means. The first group he set up had the underground name of Corvignolles, the family name of the Maréchal de Vauban, whose life he was writing, and it infiltrated itself throughout the army carrying its slogan 'Alerter, nettoyer' into action until 1938 when it was publicly denounced as part of the secret, anti-communist movements, known collectively as the Cagoule. Loustaunau-Lacau lost his office but not his determination. From 1938 to 1940 he waged a Press feud with *L'Humanité* in papers which he founded and ran himself, *Barrage*, *Notre prestige*, and finally *L'Ordre national*, while continuing his predictions of doom for the army. His alarm was increased by the *drôle de guerre* and justified by the defeat and he found himself a prisoner of war after a campaign in which he had almost been court-martialled for his criticisms of those in charge of the war. In August he bluffed a German commander into giving him a *laissez-passer* to return to Paris 'under the terms of the Armistice' on account of his age, and crossed the demarcation line to Vichy.[36]

[35] G. Loustaunau-Lacau, *Mémoires d'un Français rebelle 1914–48* (Laffont, 1948), p. 205.

[36] Ibid., p. 194.

Here his political reputation earned him visits from Eugène Deloncle, leader of the Cagoule, and Jacques Doriot, head of the Fascist P.P.F. (Parti Populaire Français), but to both he made opposition to the Germans the condition of any co-operation and thereby lost their interest. On 29 August Pétain created the Légion française des combattants to replace the plurality of veteran groups which had existed since World War I and appointed Loustaunau-Lacau as General Delegate with special concern for propaganda. His passion for subterranean activity was instantly indulged and within two months he had used the Légion to establish information and escape routes from the occupied zone to the Spanish border through his native province of the Béarn, where local leaders for the Légion were personally recruited by Loustaunau-Lacau and secretly detailed for work of this kind. Frenay in Marseille envisaged a reorganization of men, mostly from the army, into a movement to continue the war: Loustaunau-Lacau at Pau and Vichy believed that just such a movement existed ready-made in the Légion, purified as it was to his approval by the absence of Communists, and capable of camouflaging the work of retraining and re-equipment. Assisted by Marie-Madeleine Méric, he created an ostensible youth centre at the Hôtel des Sports in Vichy, for which he was provided with an initial financial subsidy by Pétain, and using this as the hub of his operations he launched what he called a new 'crusade', the term by which he had defined his efforts to purify the army in the 1930s. In October he drew up a manifesto of La Croisade which he hoped could be dropped from English aeroplanes across France. Rebellious against the foreign policy of Vichy, La Croisade looked for close relations with London and the first special envoy sent by de Gaulle to France, Captain Pierre Fourcaud, was well received by Loustaunau-Lacau. But when de Gaulle began to assume that any movement within France should be dependent on his own this initial cordiality ceased. Loustaunau-Lacau and de Gaulle had been contemporaries at the École de Guerre, they had both been impressed by Pétain, and they both reacted to the defeat with a vigorous continuity of pre-war attitudes. They were both strong, idiosyncratic personalities and as their separate authority developed, each came to suspect the other's position.[37] This did not, however, draw Loustaunau-Lacau closer to Vichy where his ambitions for the Légion were opposed by Xavier Vallat, the politician and war veteran who, as Secrétaire-Général des Anciens combattants had initiated the Légion's constitution. Vallat intended the Légion for a more political future as a substitute party and at the beginning of November he dismissed Loustaunau-Lacau. Pétain acquiesced and Loustaunau-Lacau lost his ready-made structure. La Croisade, which had been an ambitious project for the military reorganization of unoccupied France was forced to become a tighter and more specific escape and information network and in the winter of 1940–41 took the name of Alliance.[38]

It is often assumed that the anti-German continuity of Cochet, Frenay, and Loustaunau-Lacau was assured at a purely individual level without the help of any army institution. But within the truncated and demoralized French army which settled down to wait for better times, one institution, comprising the departments of espionage and intelligence, continued much of its wartime function, tempered to the service of Vichy and Pétain. In December Frenay was appointed to this section, the 2e Bureau, at Vichy and on his arrival he found that its chief Colonel Louis Baril was not only anti-German in spirit but was already involved in constructing routes to enable information to flow out of France through the American Embassy in Vichy and the British Consulate in Switzerland. In Lyon the 2e Bureau set up its German section behind the façade of a commercial enterprise, and here its clandestine activity was even more defiant of the terms of the Armistice, securing information which Frenay was able to use

[37] In January 1941 Loustaunau-Lacau met Colonel Rémy, sent by de Gaulle to sound out potential networks of escape and information. Rémy wrote of the meeting, 'He talked at great length about his projects. According to him he disposed of ten thousand men in the Béarn. He wanted to stage a *coup*, starting no less with the capture of Sardinia. . . . This curious man with a brilliant intelligence made me think of a wild boar and charmed me at the same time as he made me anxious. I left him with an indefinable feeling of embarrassment.' (Rémy, *Mémoires d'un agent secret de la France libre 1940–42*, Aux Trois Couleurs, 1946, p. 128. Rémy's memoirs for the whole period of the war were published later by France-Empire. See Bibliography, p. 291.)

[38] Loustaunau-Lacau, op. cit., pp. 215–16. See also the memoirs of Marie-Madeleine Méric published under her married name, Marie-Madeleine Fourcade, *L'Arche de Noé*, Fayard, 1968, pp. 15–157.

even after he himself had resigned from the army, a decision he made in January 1941.[39] In Marseille an innocuous plaque advertising 'Travaux Ruraux' on the villa Eole hid the work of a counter-espionage branch under Captain Paillole, a family friend of Dr. Recordier and a junior contemporary of Frenay's at Saint-Cyr, and the information gained was placed without reserve at Frenay's disposal.

For Frenay therefore and for Loustaunau-Lacau, who also made use of Colonel Baril's services at Vichy, the alternative actions which they prescribed for France in 1940 were not launched in a total vacuum of military support, though not all the operations of the espionage and intelligence departments could be said to be mounted solely against the Germans. Baril also had the official task of protecting the Vichy regime against 'antinational' activities, mainly interpreted as those involving communist and, later, Gaullist forces, but in 1940 there seemed little contradiction in this work. To be pro-Pétain and yet attempt to undermine the terms of the Armistice, to be anti-German yet suspicious of de Gaulle's breakaway movement in London, and to be involved in clandestine activity yet opposed to the underground operations of the Communists was a position easily justified by more than a few members of the army. There was a certain amount of paradox in this position and an uncertainty as to how it might develop, but in Vichy at the time schemes for preserving some sort of military presence in defeated France fed on the atmosphere of paradox and uncertainty and produced a level of intrigue which was well suited to certain personalities, of whom Loustaunau-Lacau was one and Georges Groussard another.

Groussard was an officer on the General Staff of the military government of Paris when the Germans arrived in June 1940. He was briefly imprisoned by the Germans and showed non-cooperation by means of a hunger strike. On release he crossed to Vichy where he obtained a post in the Sûreté nationale and met Loustaunau-Lacau through de Gaulle's agent Pierre Fourcaud. Before the war Groussard had investigated the Cagoule for Marshal Franchet d'Espérey to see if it could be of positive use to the army, but had found that its mystery was greater than its power and reported that it could be of little

[39] Frenay, op. cit., pp. 55–65.

value in protecting the army from any internal dissension. He himself was accused of being a member of the Cagoule and not just an outside investigator, but he always stringently denied this although he came to know many of the members including Deloncle and his assistant François Méténier both of whom were imprisoned for their Cagoulard activities. When Groussard met Loustaunau-Lacau at Vichy their familiarity with this world produced mutual sympathy and they closely agreed on the need to restructure and retrain the army to redeem the failures of its recent past. While Loustaunau-Lacau developed his ideas of using the Légion, Groussard, with the secret agreement of General Huntziger, Minister of War, and the implicit support of Marcel Peyrouton, Minister of the Interior, set up a special police force divided into regions and subjected to rigorous military training. His aim was to build, clandestinely, a network of military units, specializing in the camouflage of arms, espionage, and parachute operations and to do this he recruited leaders from those he had known before and during the war as active nationalists. As second in command he chose Méténier who was introduced first of all to his ostensible role as head of a police force to hunt down Communists and dissidents and then to his subterfuge role at the centre of a potential military élite. As a police head he soon attracted attention. In November the communist section of the Michelin works at Clermont-Ferrand warned the workers that any efforts to recruit them would be a calculated diversion from the facts of unemployment and stated that it was Méténier 'the Cagoulard, the tool of Michelin . . . who is directing recruitment for this mercenary force.'[40]

There is no external evidence of his progress as a clandestine military leader but Groussard maintains that his organization was well under way when it was halted abruptly by events in December 1940.[41] On 13 December Pétain dismissed and arrested Pierre Laval, as a result of successful pressure by other Vichy ministers who resented Laval's close relationships with the German occupying authorities and objected to his influence over Pétain. Groussard was personally involved in the intrigue which led to this dismissal and his

[40] *Bibendum*, N.S. no. 1 (23 Nov. 1940).
[41] *Service secret*, pp. 76–135.

police force was given the task of detaining Laval's entourage while he was arrested. The Germans reacted by obtaining Laval's release and Groussard's police were strongly criticized. Their dissolution was demanded and Vichy agreed. Groussard's pattern of military and political activity dating from 1936 was broken. At Vichy he had not submitted to the inactivism dictated by the Armistice but had found ways of continuing the combination of nationalist assertiveness and political intrigue which made him an immediate friend of Loustaunau-Lacau. Together they stretched the possibilities of Vichy, and their failure to create the institutions they envisaged illustrates the growing rigidity of the regime by the end of 1940. In the first half of 1941 Loustaunau-Lacau departed for North Africa and Groussard for London; Frenay, having left the army, became increasingly clandestine while General Cochet was arrested. The activities of the 2e Bureau continued but the margin left for alternative solutions within the army had narrowed.

In a remarkably shrewd essay on Pétainism the Marquis d'Argenson explained the army's general passivity under Vichy not by reference to the military failures of May and June and subsequent loss of morale, but by a comment on the place of the army within society. The army, he claimed, submitted to the Armistice not because it was a separate caste of isolated aristocrats and nationalists, but because it was very much part of the country as a whole. It had been 'assimilated' and shared the views of the bourgeoisie in general. There was thus no purely military response to Vichy.[42] An inquiry into the attitudes and activity of the regiments stationed in the provincial towns would almost certainly bear out this point, but those who have defended the Armistice army from accusations of defeatism and inactivity argue that the army in general did the one thing within its power: it secretly hid arms and ammunition in defiance of the Armistice regulations.[43] The orders to hide arms were given and carried out by several high-ranking officers during the early months of the Vichy

[42] Marquis d'Argenson, *Pétain et le pétinisme* (Éditions Créator, 1953), p. 109.

[43] Cf. Étienne Anthérieu, *Le Drame de l'Armée de l'Armistice* (Éditions des Quatre Vents, 1946), *passim*. Raymond Sereau, *L'Armée de l'Armistice* (Nouvelles Éditions Latines, 1961), pp. 31 ff.

administration, in particular by General Colson, Minister of War in July 1940, General Picquendar, head of the General Staff, General Frère, military chief in Lyon, General Weygand, Minister of Defence, and Commandant Mollard, who was attached to the General Staff. In Marseille Mollard set up the first in a network of camouflage operations disguised as a transport business called 'Les Rapides du Littoral', whose aim was to remove army vehicles and hide them. According to one author the network was successful, hiding over 46,000 vehicles,[44] and several sources testify to secret depots of arms across the southern zone such as those made by men from the 26th Infantry Regiment in Bergerac[45] and by the 5th Dragoons in Mâcon.[46]

This activity, claims d'Argenson, was no more than a symptom of the *attentiste* spirit, preparing for better days and another war,[47] whereas the apologists maintain that the operation C.D.M. (Camouflage du matériel) was the practical side of a combative mentality which continued to envisage a renewal of the conflict at any time. Together the two views point to the realities of 1940. The hiding of materials was a reflex action of an army deprived of its fighting identity and humiliated by the terms of the Armistice. For some officers and men it was the first step in clandestine activity, an initiative which committed them to further action against the official *attentisme* of Vichy. This was certainly the case in Bergerac and Mâcon. For others it was a gesture without consequence though this could not necessarily have been foreseen in 1940. In so far as it was anti-German any camouflage of material served to link the army to its wartime operations. It was a thin strand of continuity.

No one in France in 1940 knew of all these elements which, among a scattered minority, kept alive the possibility of choice. Most people knew nothing at all of either the Christian Democrats or the military figures whose obstinate adherence to their own ideas and continued expression of their personality questioned the uniformity of public opinion on which Vichy

[44] Sereau, op. cit., p. 33.
[45] Bergeret, *Messages personnels*, p. 13.
[46] André Montaron, *Le Maquis de Corlay* (Jobard, Dijon, 1950), p. 25.
[47] Marquis d'Argenson, op. cit., p. 111.

relied. In no sense did these various elements in 1940 constitute a single movement which a shopkeeper in Toulouse or a peasant in the Ardèche could decide to join, or even a coherent movement of opinion with which they could identify. The sense of isolation which most of these separate elements felt from the rest of society was acute and formed one of the constituent factors in their activity. They felt a desperate need to inform people, not just of their own ideas or, as in General Cochet's case, of their own identity, but of the basic facts of the situation, facts about the ongoing war, the Occupation, or the German treatment of Alsace-Lorraine, which did not appear in the authorized Press. It was this which gave these different individuals and groups a unity of purpose, even when they were not aware of each other's existence, and it was this which corresponded most closely to precedents in French history when struggle for public opinion had issued in a flood of publications. This was to happen in 1941 as it had in the Dreyfus Affair of the 1890s, the last years of World War I, and the middle years of the 1930s, and those who created newspapers or information sheets were perpetuating patterns of behaviour which extended well beyond their own individual or group experience. Precedents were fewer for those with a propensity for escape routes, intelligence networks, or subterfuge retraining, though Groussard was well versed in the success of General von Seeckt in by-passing the restriction of Versailles under the Weimar Republic and Seeckt's achievement was much discussed in Vichy when the youth and veteran organizations were created.

The peculiarity of the southern zone in 1940 was that alternative attitudes could be cautiously expressed without fear of immediate arrest. An English artist living near the Italian and Swiss border wrote of late 1940, 'Almost every day during my journeys to and from Lyons there occurred violent quarrels between partisans of the old and new regimes.'[48] The Jesuit Père R. P. Dillard was still permitted to preach at Vichy during 1941 on the theme 'France Continues' and to protest from the pulpit against the anti-Semitism of Vichy,[49] and as late as December 1941 in a lecture in Montpellier Pierre-

[48] Neville Lytton, *Life in Unoccupied France* (Macmillan, 1943), p. 34.

[49] G. Rougeron, *Le Département de l'Allier sous l'État français 1940–44* (Typocentre, Montluçon, 1969), pp. 404–5.

Henri Teitgen was able to salute the entry of America into the war with the words, 'We must wish for an American victory, the triumph of civilization over barbarism.'[50] This relative freedom allowed ideas to gain more substance and assume more ideological proportions than in the occupied zone. On the other hand, the fact that Germans could only be seen in the south in their minor role as overseers of the Armistice in the major towns, and not at all elsewhere, made it difficult for opponents of the Armistice to generate a sense of urgency or immediacy in public opinion: they could not play on the urge, increasingly common in the occupied zone, to do something, however trivial, to irritate the occupying forces.[51]

People in Vichy France were quick to interpret any opinion that actively regretted the *status quo* as an attempt to undermine Pétain, as a wish to throw the country back into the confusion of May and June or as an effort to play the kind of politics renounced on 10 July. These were the three pillars on which Vichy was built: the mystique of Pétain, the fragility of the Armistice settlement, and the renunciation of party politics. In exposing the second of these, in attempting to inform people of its dangers and in creating alternatives to *attentisme*, the actions of those mentioned in this chapter did not specifically threaten the image of Pétain or seek to end the moratorium on party politics. There were, however, other continuity elements which did.

[50] G. Bouladou, 'Contribution à l'étude de l'histoire de la Résistance dans le département de l'Hérault' (unpub. Thèse 3e cycle, Montpellier, 1965), p. 95.

[51] Armand Maurice, who began in the autumn of 1940 to help people escape across the demarcation line in the Jura, gave as his reason for becoming a 'passeur', 'The urge was stronger than I was. It gripped me like the wish to catch a pike or trap a hare. I just had to get across. Time and time again just to irritate the Germans.' (André Besson, *Une Poignée de braves*, Nouvelles Éditions Jurassiennes, Poligny, 1965, p. 58.)

III. Continuity II

THE persuasive argument of realism which led most French people to accept the Armistice as the only viable alternative open to France in the summer of 1940 made it difficult to envisage ways in which a better settlement might have been established. Pierre Laval was one of the few politicians who started from the conviction that the Armistice could and should have been better negotiated, and that there was still considerable room for diplomatic manoeuvre towards a more acceptable peace. Throughout his first period in office from July to December 1940[1] he cultivated the belief that the Germans would respond to tactical advances from Vichy and would establish France as a favoured nation within the new Europe. His policy was opportunistic and he had neither a preformed image of peace to present to the country nor an organized section of public opinion to support him. He lived by the native intelligence said to be a feature of the Auvergne and quickly enlarged his reputation as the most skilful of *maquignons* (horsedealers). This reputation and his isolation point less to the probity of other politicians than to the degree of paralysis which affected most of French political life after the defeat. Laval stood out as a political operator because the vast majority of his colleagues from the Chamber of Deputies stopped their political operations and in many cases stopped thinking politically altogether.

The group exception to this was the Communist Party, excluded from the official political scene since September 1939, but clandestinely alive and actively engaged in working out its own alternative solution to the predicament of defeated France. The P.C.F. was never very detailed about the settlement it came to propose in 1940, nor very certain about how to achieve it, but after some hesitation it was certain that it

[1] From 12 July to 13 December 1940 Pierre Laval was officially Deputy Prime Minister since Marshal Pétain was both Head of State and Prime Minister. In his second period of office, 18 April 1942 to 17 August 1944, Laval was Prime Minister as well as Minister of Foreign Affairs and Minister of the Interior.

did not want the settlement achieved by the Armistice, or those proposed by Laval, and utterly certain that it did not want the Vichy regime itself.

The hesitation found voice in *L'Humanité* between 24 June and the end of July in a series of demands to the German Propaganda-Staffel for the legalization of the paper, and in three articles praising the fraternity of French workers and German soldiers in occupied Paris.[2] These articles, in their context, suggest an absence of policy towards the Occupation rather than wilful co-operation with the Germans, though it is in this light that they are usually quoted to exemplify what has often been called the party's development from defeatism to collaboration.[3] Had collaboration been a determined policy of the central committee it is difficult to understand why they did not persist in it, and why by mid-August *L'Humanité* was protesting vigorously against the persecution of Communists in both zones and by September had launched a campaign to denounce the 'traitors of Vichy' for their part in reducing France to a condition of slavery through the defeat and Occupation.[4] It seems that the communist leaders in June and July nursed several illusions about the role of the party in defeated France and that having opposed the war since September 1939 expected to be able to publish openly when the war appeared to be over.[5] By the end of August, in the face of continuing persecution and the favour shown by the German authorities to Jacques Doriot, particularly hated by the party as a renegade, these expectations were reconsidered and the applications for legal publication withdrawn. The P.C.F. could in no circumstances allow itself to be even marginally identified with Doriot's policies and to this extent the long-standing feud with Doriot led the central committee to be circumspect in its overtures to the Germans. In a period of internal doubt this negative force was far from insignificant.

[2] *L'Humanité*, no. 59 (4 July 1940); no. 61 (13 July 1940); no. 65 (27 July 1940).

[3] e.g. A. Rossi, *Les Communistes français pendant la drôle de guerre* (Iles d'Or, 1951), ch. XXV.

[4] *L'Humanité*, no. 73 (28 Aug. 1940); no. 75 (10 Sept. 1940).

[5] The best treatment of the negotiations is in Claude Angeli and Paul Gillet, *Debout, partisans* (Fayard, 1969), pp. 61–6.

Throughout July *L'Humanité* continued to dissociate the Communists from the 'Imperialist War' but there was no explicit condemnation of German imperialism to equal the attacks on English city finance and French imperialism, signifying an imbalance in the party's neutralist position while the applications for legal publication were pending.[6] But by August there was a growing awareness among the party leaders not just that it was Doriot and his Fascist P.P.F. who were benefiting from the German presence but also that individual Communists had been placed at risk when they emerged into the open. Charles Tillon, in July 1940 responsible for the party in the south-west, has been particularly severe in his strictures on the central committee for their lack of caution during the summer and believes that the arrest of several party members was facilitated by the attention they drew to themselves.[7] The renewed coverage given by *L'Humanité* at the end of August to persecution, and the disappearance of demands for legality, suggest that this connection was eventually acknowledged by the party and that attitudes changed in the face of hostile events.

As the change took place and the party settled more firmly into its clandestine operations, it recovered the sense of direction which it had gained in the months of persecution during the *drôle de guerre*. In place of the hesitation initially induced by the Occupation and the temptation to argue the party into an open and legal position, there returned the old pride in opposition and the language of outrage and hostility towards the rulers of France, increasingly defined to include the German Occupiers as well as the Vichy regime, coupled all the time with continued denunciation of British city finance still held to be as guilty for the war as any other imperialist factor. The solution which the party proposed for France was a product of this renewed policy of opposition, and the number of communist underground publications in the autumn of 1940 testifies to the recovery of the party's political vigour. In August a five-

[6] *L'Humanité*, no. 58 (1 July 1940); no. 65 (27 July 1940).

[7] This criticism was launched in general terms in *Les F.T.P.*, p. 83, written well before Tillon left the party. Since he left he has made his accusations more specific, stating in oral evidence to the author that Gabriel Péri, who was arrested and executed as a hostage at the end of 1941, was one of the major casualties of insufficient party caution.

page appeal 'Peuple de France' bearing the names of Jacques Duclos and Maurice Thorez began to be disseminated; in September a separate edition of *L'Humanité* for the southern zone was firmly under way; young Communists were producing *L'Avant-Garde*, and communist trade-unionists, who had been expelled from the C.G.T. because of the Nazi–Soviet pact, restarted *La Vie ouvrière*. At the end of the year a long pamphlet called *Le Parti a vingt ans* celebrated the history of the party since 1920, while in the course of the early winter there was a considerable expansion of local papers and tracts appealing to regional or sectional interests.

The appeal 'Peuple de France' belongs more to the July period than the subsequent phase, though it points the way to the latter. In the southern zone it was typed and stencilled and carried various dates, the most frequent being 15 August, but according to Victor Joannes who was working with the Jeunesses communistes in the south, he had seen a draft well before that date and had used it for a similar appeal to the youth of France.[8] In an interview he referred to it, as it is often known, as the Appeal of 10 July, though Auguste Lecœur, one of the party leaders in the Nord and Pas-de-Calais area, says that it cannot have emerged before September.[9] Two details in the content point to an earlier rather than a later date, the claim to the right of open publication and the specific mention of British rather than German imperialism, but there is much in the appeal which shows crystallization of policy rather than the vacillations of July. There is, above all, a forceful statement of the wish of the French people to be 'free and independent' and a call by the party for a 'front de la liberté, de l'indépendance et de la renaissance de la France', while the denunciation of Vichy as a cut-throat dictatorship is a pungent one. The final summary of all the points is not misleading:

Down with capitalism, bringer of misery and war.
Long live the Soviet Union of Lenin and Stalin, hope of the world's workers.
Long live the unity of the French Nation.

[8] 'Souvenirs de l'année 40', *Notre musée*, no. 29 (6 Nov. 1968), 1.

[9] Evidence from Victor Joannes. Auguste Lecœur, *Le Parti Communiste Français et la Résistance 1939–41* (Plon, 1968), photocopy between pp. 48 and 49.

Long live a Free and Independent France.
Long live the French Communist Party, hope of the People of France.
Long live the Government of the People, in the interests of the People.[10]

The main polemic of this appeal was directed against all those responsible for the misfortunes of France and all those who were benefiting from the defeat and the Occupation. In broad terms this meant all capitalists and their 'lackeys'. In listed names it included politicians like Daladier from the Radical Party, Léon Blum and Paul Faure from the Socialists, Déat, Doriot, Laval, Flandin, and Marquet grouped as representatives of the Right, and Jouhaux, Belin, and Dumoulin from the C.G.T. which had expelled the Communists in late 1939. Laval was singled out as the sinister power behind the Vichy regime but the ease with which Pétain was able to nominate himself as dictator was attributed to the complicity of the Radical Party and the Socialists, which could be seen as an implicit reference to the support for Pétain given by the majority of both these parties on 10 July. But the fact that Léon Blum, who had voted against Pétain on 10 July, and Paul Faure, who was sympathetic to Vichy, were linked together in the list of those culpable for the misfortunes of the country, suggests that they were opposed by the P.C.F. more for their part in promoting the war and the persecution of the Communists after the Nazi-Soviet pact than for their relationship to Vichy. The party was not looking for political allies in its opposition to Vichy: it regarded its position as totally isolated, as indeed it was in the particular combination of its policies. For a tract so vehemently opposed to Vichy as a capitalist dictatorship exploiting the miseries of defeat and Occupation 'Peuple de France' was remarkably silent about the Occupiers themselves, yet on the other hand, for a party said by its detractors to be involved in defeatism and collaboration, the tract was remarkably forthright in its use of the emotive words *liberté* and *indépendance*.

[10] 'Peuple de France', *L'Humanité* (zone sud), 15 Aug. 1940.

Published from the centre, the appeal integrated closely with the Paris-based *L'Humanité* and as the first major policy statement since the defeat it was aimed at giving Communists throughout France a political programme round which to regroup. The solution it offered for France was twofold: internally a government of the people forged by the P.C.F. and externally a free and independent France linked by a pact of friendship to the Soviet Union, which would secure a true peace: 'There is no true peace unless the people of each country are independent, and the Communists, who claim for France the right to its independence, proclaim also the right to independence for colonial people enslaved by the imperialists.' When this point is put beside the recurrent denunciations of capitalism in the tract it looks as if the solution was a faithful piece of Marxism-Leninism; but the Leninist conclusion that the imperialist war should be transformed into a revolutionary class war was not drawn for reasons which had already been given during the *drôle de guerre* in the *Cahiers du bolchevisme*.[11]

On this issue another negative force was operative in the formation of communist policy. Since mid-September 1939 the party's position had veered sharply in the direction of Trotskyist policy as given by *L'Étincelle*, the French organ of the Fourth International. On 15 November 1939 this paper had announced 'This war is not ours' and had called for a class struggle to transform the imperialist war into a revolutionary one, while a month later it quoted the historic words of Karl Liebknecht during World War I, 'The enemy is in our own country', and urged its readers to fight for peace through revolution.[12] With statements such as these it looked as if Trotskyists and Stalinists might almost converge after the Nazi–Soviet pact, but *L'Étincelle* kept the old conflict in the forefront of its propaganda. It accused the P.C.F. of having supported a policy of national defence in the late 1930s and therefore of culpability for the outbreak of the imperialist war; it interpreted the Nazi–Soviet pact as an alliance between Stalin and Hitler which involved the Communists in positive collaboration with Germany, and it proclaimed its own policy as the only pure

[11] See above, p. 10.

[12] *L'Étincelle* (15 Nov. 1939); no. 2 (15 Dec. 1939).

version of Marxist–Leninist theory.[13] The paper had a small circulation compared with *L'Humanité*, which was printing an average of 140,000 copies, and appears to have managed only four numbers between October 1939 and September 1940. But through *L'Étincelle*, and another Trotskyist paper *La Vérité* which began in August 1940, the arguments of the Fourth International were well enough known to the P.C.F. to constitute the same sort of negative factor as Doriot's arguments for collaboration: keeping the party uncontaminated by either set of arguments meant not over-emphasizing revolutionary war on the one hand and not pursuing the initial demands for open publication on the other.

For French people living in the southern zone the most contentious aspect of communist party policy in the autumn of 1940 was the claim that France would be better served in the crisis of Occupation by a people's government rather than the government of Marshal Pétain. This ran directly counter to the mythology which had been woven round the figure of Pétain as a providential leader, and perpetuated the divisions between Communists and others which had become so bitter during the *drôle de guerre*. Initially the reaction of many Communists in the southern zone to the Vichy regime was almost as confused as the reaction of the Paris leaders to the arrival of the Germans. Certain approaches were made to the Vichy authorities by individual party members, some of whom signed declarations of good intent in order to gain release from the prisons to which they had been sent by the Daladier Government. In the Vichy regime's hostility to those who had led France to its catastrophe Communists found common cause, but in practical terms this never became the basis for an agreement. Anti-Communism was deeply entrenched in the Vichy Government and on the communist side the experience of being ostracized and persecuted during the *drôle de guerre* was ineradicable. They had understood it as the revenge of Fascists and capitalists for the gains of the working class in the 1930s and the Vichy ministers were seen by the average party militant to be the incarnation

[13] Nevertheless, its slogans could still read like ones from *L'Humanité* or the appeal 'Peuple de France', notably its call on 15 September 1940, 'We want a Free France in a Europe liberated from capitalism'.

of these revengeful forces. Whatever the initial confusion the base was firmly laid for conflict and when the central committee in August and September put anti-Vichy propaganda at the hub of its policies it merely intensified a confrontation which was already growing in the south.

Any lingering illusions the Communists might have held were dispelled in October 1940 when the Vichy police carried out a series of raids against Communists suspected of restarting party activity. In the Allier, the *département* in which Vichy was situated, 47 raids were made in 19 communes leading to 38 arrests. Those found guilty were sent to the political concentration camp at Mons in the Puy-de-Dôme.[14] A third of the communist membership in the Allier, which totalled some 3,000 in 1938,[15] lived at Montluçon, centre of engineering, chemical, and rubber industries, and in November a police official of the town reported that 'Communist propaganda, abandoned during the war and hesitant in the first months after the Armistice, has, since October, become organized once again in our *département*. From being discreet and individualistic it has become general and open. Raids and imprisonment have had no effect on those responsible for the Communist Party . . .'[16] Wherever local archives have been investigated, evidence such as this has been found of intensive communist persecution from October onwards. In the Hérault arrests were made mostly for distributing tracts;[17] in the Corrèze about twelve members of the clandestine party were imprisoned between November and January;[18] in the Dordogne sentences of up to five months' imprisonment were served for any communist propaganda including the singing of The Internationale,[19] while communist sources of the time talk of '100,000 workers suffering in prison',[20] '500 internees from Marseille, mostly in the

[14] G. Rougeron, *La Résistance dans le département de l'Allier 1940–44* (Typocentre, Montluçon, 1964), p. 7.

[15] Jean-Francois Viple, *Sociologie politique de l'Allier* (Pichouet, 1967), p. 99.

[16] Rougeron, *Le Département de l'Allier sous l'État français*, p. 390.

[17] Bouladou, 'Contribution à l'étude de l'histoire de la Résistance', p. 65.

[18] Martine Chateau, 'Contribution à l'étude du maquis corrézien' (unpub. Mémoire de Maîtrise, Poitiers, 1969), p. 30.

[19] From the files of René Larivière, based on local archive material. Kindly made available by M. Larivière who holds the files as Correspondant départemental du Comité d'Histoire de la Deuxième Guerre Mondiale.

[20] *L'Humanité* (zone sud), no. 84 (30 Nov. 1940).

camp at Chibron',[21] numerous arrests in Grenoble on the night of 29–30 November,[22] and the internment of Communists in each town that Pétain visited on his tour of the provinces in the late autumn and early winter.[23] It was widely assumed that Communists would naturally be against the government. The reputation they had gained among their opponents for 'anti-patriotic' behaviour during the *drôle de guerre* was perpetuated into the Occupation, and after the Armistice anti-patriotism was co-extensive in most people's minds with anti-Pétainism. The party was thus labelled as hostile to Pétain even before its policy had fully developed in that direction. By the grass-roots logic of French politics it was impossible to believe that a Communist could also be a Pétainist and by an extension of such logic it was possible for *Gringoire*, the collaborationist paper of Henri Béraud, noted in the 1930s for its Anglophobia, to accuse Communists in Toulouse not only of anti-Pétainist propaganda but also of fostering illusory hopes in de Gaulle.[24]

Throughout October and November the communist papers in the southern zone developed the case against the government, and *L'Humanité* used the meeting of Pétain and Hitler at Montoire on 24 October as the occasion for an attack on Vichy's external relations. Until then the paper, like its Paris edition, had carried no clear article on Germany, Nazism, or Hitler, except for references to the cost of the Army of Occupation, so that this issue was something of a departure. 'The Communists', it began. 'are fighting for peace and for the national and social liberation of France' and it went on to ask what sinister event was being prepared by Hitler, Pétain, and Laval. Referring to Pétain's speech after Montoire, when he said he had entered on the path of collaboration, the paper declared,

[21] *L'Humanité* (région marseillaise), no. spécial (26 Oct. 1940).

[22] *Le Travailleur alpin*, no. 5 (2 Dec. 1940).

[23] e.g. *Rouge-Midi* (région vauclusienne), no. spécial (Dec. 1940).

[24] Noted by Jean Duhamel in the diary he kept in his retirement in the Périgord on 21 November 1940 (*Le Journal d'un Français moyen*, p. 91). Cf. Marcel Déat writing in *L'Œuvre* on 6 November: 'Our Communists have become nationalists once more. Their clandestine tracts contain conclusions exactly parallel to the Gaullist ones. It's now a question of the liberation and independence of France, and they assure us that Communism alone will restore its full sovereignty.'

The people do not believe in a collaboration for peace. Its first consequence is the opening of hostilities in Greece and the extension of the imperialist war on to a world scale. . . . History has known other agreements between victors and vanquished, always made on the back of the people: Bismarck and Thiers to crush the Commune of 1871, Clemenceau and Noske against the German workers in 1918.

And today, the paper concluded, the profiteers of defeat are ready to declare the 'most shameful alliance with the hereditary enemy of yesterday'.[25] In the circumstances of November 1940 with Vichy's external and internal policy beginning to gain some coherence in its increased co-operation with Germany and growing dictatorship at home, this issue of *L'Humanité* was subversive on both counts, and particularly so for its open inculpation of Pétain, something which de Menthon's first number of *Liberté*, which was also suspicious of Montoire, was not prepared to embark on.[26] At the end of the month the attack on Pétain was sharpened and personalized. The Marshal had begun his tours of the provincial areas where he was fêted to the point of worship and his charismatic appeal mythologized by René Benjamin in terms comparable only to Béranger's poems on Napoleon Bonaparte.[27] But even without the hagiography Pétain was undoubtedly popular, a fact sacrificed by *L'Humanité* in its headline 'Pétain vomi par le peuple!' It went on to address Pétain directly: 'You and Laval represent the policy of the 200 families repudiated by the nation: you are not even embarrassed by a shameful collaboration which puts France at the mercy of Germany. . . . In you stirs the assassin of soldiers who mutinied in 1917, the old Cagoulard, the military brute in the service of capital. France hates you for its misfortunes.'[28] In no other publication of similar date is there an attack on Pétain of equal violence, and throughout the winter *L'Humanité* continued to inculcate this hatred of Pétain, holding him personally responsible for a 'reactionary alliance with the Church', 'total servility to Germany', the shortage of food, and the persecution of Communists. On 9

[25] *L'Humanité* (zone sud), no. 80 (2 Nov. 1940).
[26] See above, p. 30.
[27] See René Benjamin, *Le Maréchal et son peuple*.
[28] *L'Humanité* (zone sud), no. 83 (25 Nov. 1940).

January 1941 it stated that the 'government of Pétain is the most dictatorial regime France has known since the Second Empire',[29] on 6 February it nicknamed him 'Pétain-la-Faim',[30] and on 20 February it distorted his famous remark 'Je hais les mensonges qui ont fait tant de mal' to read 'Pétain qui "est" le mensonge'.[31] The vilification was persistent and unbridled and there was no other attack in the paper on any other person, institution, or country to match it in its rigour. A regular reader of *L'Humanité* in the southern zone was in no doubt, well before the end of 1940, that as a Communist he was expected to be in total opposition to everything for which Pétain and his government stood.

The context of this opposition made it more complex. In external affairs the paper did not relinquish its claim to be neutral in the imperialist war and opposed to any subservience to Britain, though the coverage given to this aspect of neutrality was small. The slogan 'Ni Londres, ni Berlin' dates from early November and is repeated at intervals, changing on 23 January 1941 to 'Ni Dominion Britannique, ni Protectorat Allemand'.[32] Subservience, the paper claimed, was just one of the characteristics of Vichy France which compared so badly with the virtues of Soviet Russia where there was 'no unemployment, no ration cards, and no restrictions'.[33] An assessment of the old year on 2 January 1941 contrasted the sufferings of France with the 'year of victories for the motherland of socialism' in which the U.S.S.R. 'had welcomed into its arms the people of the Baltic States, Bessarabia, and Bukovinia . . . joining the Bielorussians and the liberated Ukrainians'.[34] With such a country, it was argued, France had a duty to conclude a commercial treaty, the presumption being that only a people's government would conclude this treaty and therefore France needed such a government of the people.

Even after the confusion and doubt caused by the Nazi–Soviet pact it can have been no surprise to the communist militant to see Russia still paraded as the model country to

[29] Ibid., no. 90 (9 Jan. 1941).
[30] Ibid., no. 94 (6 Feb. 1941).
[31] Ibid., no. 96 (20 Feb. 1941).
[32] Ibid., no. 92 (23 Jan. 1941).
[33] Ibid., no. 81 (10 Nov. 1940).
[34] Ibid., no. 89 (2 Jan. 1941).

which all communist eyes were turned. But after a war in which Communists had fought as French soldiers, after a defeat in which France had been defeated, and under an occupation in which half of France was subjected to enemy rule, there was an understandable sensitivity among party members to the accusation that they were not really patriots of France. *L'Humanité* produced a telling footnote on this subject in November. 'In 1789 the word patriot was inseparable from the notion of revolutionary struggle against the agents of feudalism: in 1940 the word patriot is inseparable from the notion of revolutionary struggle against the agents of the capitalist regime.'[35] The nuances in the communist position are as faithfully caught in this and other references to the past of France as in any other way. With allusions to the great Revolution, the Commune of 1871, and the mutineers of 1917, *L'Humanité* re-emphasized the communist claim of the 1930s that the P.C.F. was the legitimate heir of revolutionary patriotism in modern France, a claim which asserts that the interests of the French working class are the real interests of France itself. In pursuit of this claim the clandestine *L'Humanité* carried several articles on traditional republican and revolutionary themes, keeping alive conflicts specifically French and still capable of dividing opinion as they had done during the Dreyfus Affair and before. In October the paper called on Communists to defend 'secular education' and attacked the Vichy government for 'replacing good, capable lay teachers, who come from the people, with Jesuits from occult religious orders' and on the same page condemned the anti-Semitism of followers of Doriot in Lyon.[36] This anti-Semitism, it said, at several points during the late months of 1940, was a traditional way of diverting the people's anger from the whole capitalist class on to merely a section of it, a point made powerfully during the 1890s by French Socialists, while in December there was a further return to the preoccupations of the early Third Republic with Vichy portrayed as 'the dictatorship of Army and Church'.[37]

These attacks by historical reference were not gratuitous

[35] Ibid., no. 84 (30 Nov. 1940).

[36] Ibid., no. 76 (4 Oct. 1940).

[37] Ibid., no. 86 (12 Dec. 1940). Pétain was rumoured to be going to Paris at the time and the paper wrote 'Pétain à Versailles, les Jésuites à l'École, les communistes en prison. C'est la dictature du sabre et du goupillon.'

polemic, but the response of Communists in the southern zone to Vichy legislation which restored the right of religious orders to teach in state schools and degraded the Jews to inferior citizenship, legislation which was as reactionary in its historical consciousness as it was divisive in its political effect.[38] The reaction of *L'Humanité* was couched in equally historical terms and among the regional communist Press the stirring of old French passions was clearly a theme which rallied local militants. In Marseille a local edition of *L'Humanité* drew attention to anti-Semitism in the town and repeated the interpretation that it was a diversionary tactic;[39] in the *département* of the Loire a special number of *Le Cri du peuple* stated that in the munition works at Roanne 'workers are forced to declare whether they are Jews or not. If they are they will be sacked. Vichy in the service of Berlin! Down with Racism!'[40] and in March 1941 *Le Travailleur du Languedoc* declared,

> In a period which greatly resembles the one in which we live, in 1851, the Languedoc forcefully opposed the *coup d'état* of Napoléon le Petit. . . . The Commune and the Dreyfus Affair reasserted the old fighting tradition, a flame never extinguished. And it was the people of the Languedoc who passionately upheld the Spanish Republic. This people, ardently republican, are said to be acclaiming Pétain, grave-digger of the Republic, purveyor of prisons and concentration camps. Come now![41]

Communists were not the only ones to react in this way to the traditional right-wing doctrines of the Vichy Government, but the fact that they identified so clearly with French republican aims, wider than the economic interests of the working class, shows that the Nazi–Soviet pact had not separated them so entirely from their recent past as is sometimes alleged. The slogans of the old French Left had been revamped by the Popular Front and had been seen to be relevant not just to a continuing conflict with an equally old French Right but also to the new struggle against Fascism. In defining patriotism in terms of 1789 and recalling the conflicts of the last hundred

[38] See Ch. V.

[39] *L'Humanité* (édité par la région marseillaise), 12 Oct. 1940.

[40] *Le Cri du peuple* (Organe régional du P.C.), no. spécial (Jan. 1941).

[41] *Le Travailleur du Languedoc*, no. 1 (Mar. 1941).

years, the P.C.F. in the southern zone was continuing to express a belief, central to both Communism and the Popular Front of the 1930s, that internal enemies were enemies of the people and for that reason enemies of France.

By the end of 1940 it was clear from *L'Humanité* and other papers that the Communists in the southern zone were anti-Vichy, both for its internal and external policies, anti-collaboration with Germany, anti-Pétain, suspicious of de Gaulle and Britain, opposed to any further involvement in the imperialist war on any side, vigorous in their defence of French republican values, and as vehemently anti-capitalist as at any other time in their history. In the first few months of Occupation the party Press had succeeded in producing a policy of peace, people's government, and opposition to the 'usurpers and traitors of Vichy', in which the local federations could find both national and local relevance. For the *militants de base* the party stood nationally for a 'real peace' rather than a 'servile armistice' and for a government of the people of France rather than one in the interest of Occupiers and capital. More important for their own sphere of activity it also stood for the continuation, by clandestine methods, of party organization and politics in the defence of the working class. Keeping the party alive, regrouping its scattered members and giving them a renewed sense of identity and purpose was, according to almost all oral evidence, the main preoccupation of Communists at the local level in the autumn and winter of 1940, and the difficulties in doing this provided the militants with hard experience in underground operations and a certainty that they were politically alone in resisting the forces of Fascism and capitalism which they saw as enslaving the people of France. 'Inform, educate, clarify', said M. Pavoux, a railway-worker talking of party activity in 1940 at the Oullins factories near Lyon, 'that was the role of the party at the beginning.' M. Pavoux had joined the party late in 1939 to identify himself with the victims of government persecution, and a year later found himself one of those in charge of the local reorganization of the party. He could not exaggerate, he said, the importance of tracts and publications in convincing fellow workers of the reality and origins of the repression.[42] For Roger Pestourie, a

[42] Evidence from M. Pavoux.

young peasant farmer near Gignac in the Lot, the production of tracts was also the first active sign of continuing party life in his rural area. They showed, he said, that the party existed, and the distribution made it easier to form a reliable inventory of militants who were still loyal. The tracts were stencilled at Brive where he had been a member of the local Young Communists in 1938–9, with whom he had continued his contacts after he returned to run the family farm.[43] The inital process of regrouping was a difficult one and Pestourie, and other witnesses, agree that the confusion caused by the Nazi–Soviet pact had disturbed the harmony within local parties, making a careful reassessment of members all the more necessary. On top of this, mobilization had put members of the party out of touch with the local leadership which itself had often been decimated by arrest and imprisonment, while after the Armistice Communists who had fought in World War I, or the families of Communists who were taken prisoner in the fighting of May and June, proved particularly susceptible, like others of similar experience, to the appeal of Pétain.[44] As a result the number of Communists in the southern zone actively involved in restructuring the party and producing its literature in the autumn of 1940 was small. A fraction within the zone as a whole, they were also a minority within their own party. On this the oral evidence is also agreed.

The disruption of liaisons during the *drôle de guerre* and the war itself and the inexperience of party members in clandestine activity made it possible for the Vichy police to infiltrate certain local groups as they were reorganizing. This happened in December 1940 within the Young Communists at Brive, leading to arrests and the seizure of their roneo machine which had been supplying Pestourie and his colleagues in the Lot,[45] and it happened in Marseille where it poisoned relationships within the party. Joseph Pastor, a member of the party since 1930, imprisoned briefly in the autumn of 1939, mobilized then demobilized, destined for a French concentration

[43] Evidence from Roger Pestourie. Cf. his book of memoirs: *La Résistance, c'était cela aussi* (Éditions Sociales, 1969), pp. 29–36.

[44] Roger Pestourie made this point, but had himself been free from this influence even though his elder brother was a prisoner of war.

[45] Evidence from Pestourie, and his memoirs, op. cit., p. 36.

camp but successful in evading the police, had reconstituted the party in the south of Marseille between January and July 1940. In September he was finally caught and sent to the camp at Chibron but not before he had entrusted his operation to a new party official from the communist sector of Saint-Loup in the suburbs of Marseille who later turned out to be a member of the Vichy police. As a wave of arrests broke out in Marseille at the end of October, Pastor escaped from Chibron and avoided recapture. His hiding-place was raided but when this failed to secure his arrest he was systematically undermined by police rumour that it was he, Pastor, who was the police agent and he who had betrayed his colleagues. The party in Marseille believed this, not least because Pastor had been critical of the Nazi–Soviet pact, had reconstituted his sector with no concern for the party's neutralist position, and went on to edit his own communist tracts in the spring of 1941 calling for a broad-based working-class alliance and activity against the Germans.[46]

Other examples of sharp conflict within the party are easier to find in the occupied zone,[47] but in several areas in the south Communists were forced to act as individuals, owing to the difficulties of communication, and examples of the individuality or particular emphasis of certain local groups is visible in their publications. The visit of Pétain to Avignon occasioned a special edition of *Rouge-Midi* for the Vaucluse in which the language of attack was unequivocally anti-Fascist and anti-Nazi. Pétain's security, it began, had been assured by numerous arrests of local Communists but the party would not be silenced. The Vichy Government 'profiting from the defeat which they themselves prepared . . . are working towards the enslavement of our people to Fascism. They encourage the French Hitlerians of the P.P.F. and the P.S.F. who are preparing the "Révolution nationale", a revolution which strangely resembles that of Hitler and Mussolini . . .' This government, the paper concluded, 'is subject to the power of the Führer and the Duce.'[48] In the Puy-de-Dôme *La Voix du peuple* carried an article on 20

[46] The feud between Pastor and the party in Marseille surfaced in the summer of 1941. Information on the 'Affaire Pastor' from Joseph Pastor; Madeleine Baudoin, *Histoire des groupes francs des Bouches-du-Rhône* (P.U.F., 1962), pp. 259–62; and evidence from Louis Gazagnaire.

[47] See Lecœur, op. cit., esp. pp. 63–101.

[48] *Rouge-Midi* (région vauclusienne), no spécial (Dec. 1940).

December which was equally outspoken within the party confines of neutrality:

The military power of the Germans is not eternal. The submission of the German people—like that of the French people—to their Hitlerian executioners has its limits. No one has forgotten that it was the Spartacist revolt which compelled Germany to capitulate in 1918. The disintegration of the Hitlerian Moloch will sound the knell for the French bourgeoisie to which the government of Pétain–Laval has yoked its fortune. Then the German, French, and Italian workers will together free themselves from Hitlerism, Fascism, and capitalism with the help of the Soviet Union. . . . It is to that end that Communists are working.[49]

Statements such as these signify both the existence of anti-German pressure groups at the local level and the breadth of expression possible within the loose party organization of 1940. The party leaders of the southern zone, operating from a house with several access routes near Lyon, included Jean Chaintron, Georges Marrane, Victor Michaut, Félix Cadras, and Claudine Chomat. They directed *L'Humanité* and re-established the party structure throughout the Vichy zone, but were forced to leave a great deal of initiative to local party secretaries with the result that the redevelopment of the party was extremely uneven. Personalities were particularly important and it was during the autumn and winter of 1940 that Pierre Georges emerged in Corsica and the south-east as the epitome of party activism using every kind of public event from cinema-shows to the visit of Pétain to Marseille as an opportunity for propaganda, and moving on to the accumulation of arms in the spring of 1941.[50]

It will be impossible to produce a satisfactory summary of the communist position in 1940 until the variety of local attitudes has been fully researched. Undoubtedly Communists were

[49] *La Voix du peuple* (Organe de la région communiste du Puy-de-Dôme), 20 Dec. 1940.

[50] On the morning of Pétain's visit to Marseille, 3 December 1940, red flags were found flying from the suspension bridge and the Protestant church. In cinemas, it was not only Communists who used the galleries as places from which to scatter tracts at the moment when the lights were switched off. In many towns authorities tried to combat the propagandists by showing films with the lights on, only provoking a different form of audience hostility.

a force of opposition to Vichy France which the authorities saw as dangerously subversive, and this in itself was of vital importance in keeping political alternatives open within the rigid framework imposed by the defeat, the Occupation, and the values of the Pétain regime. But the party's position was far from internally coherent. Whatever individual Communists were doing, there were no overt suggestions in the central party Press for activity against the German occupiers, and the selective news reporting, which neutralism induced, made it a poor guide to international events of the period. Communists who heard of the Battle of Britain and other developments in the war did so not from their own pages but directly or indirectly from the BBC broadcasts, the Swiss radio or clandestine news-sheets prepared by sources other than their own. On the other hand, no sources in Vichy France were as detailed and determined as the communist Press in their questioning of Pétainism, and this, as shown in the reaction to Montoire and Pétain's 'collaboration', overlapped considerably with external relations. No conclusion can be reached which suggests that Communists were enlightened on the war issues of 1940 but neither can a judgement be sustained that their heads were totally buried in the sand, for the party's continuity of political conflict with the established powers meant an attack on Vichy and its growing dictatorship which made many Communists into forceful dissenters within the France which had overwhelmingly submitted to Marshal Pétain.

IV. Resistance and Relativism

THE threat posed to the Armistice settlement, to Pétainism, and *attentisme* by the forces so far mentioned was not a unified or coherent one in any sense. Those Christian Democrats, military officers, and Communists who offered alternative ideas and action to the French of the southern zone in 1940 were more marked by their differences than similarities. They form a historical unit not because they inter-related in 1940 but because they were forces of continuity which refused to curb their ideas and activities to fit the pervading attitude of defeated France or to accept the orthodoxy of those who kept their hopes of change to themselves and concentrated on survival. To this extent these disparate forces, whatever their standing in pre-war France, were subversive in the new circumstances. By continuing to express attitudes which had developed well before the outbreak of war they rejected the psychology of defeat which appeared to sever France from her recent past and make previous concerns and interests irrelevant. They intensified previous patterns of behaviour and undermined the uniformity of stunned reaction on which the Vichy regime depended.

For many others who resisted the norms of 1940 it was less a question of continuity than of change. The passivity of Vichy France was rejected not only by the forces so far mentioned but also by individuals and groups with little or no experience of what opposition might involve and marked by a determination to do something without always knowing what it was they could, or should, do. Acting in individualistic ways they stood out against the *attentisme* of Vichy in defiance of the specific events of 1940 and often in apparent contradiction to their own political positions or public image before the war. They frequently surprised others of similar situation and not infrequently surprised themselves. If there was continuity in their actions it was one of personality, but in most other respects the effect of 1940 was to change, if not revolutionize, their patterns of behaviour.

In November in Marseille Pierre Henneguier, aged 27, who had been a volunteer for the Seine commando unit in the Battle of France, conceived the dramatic idea of a fleet of lorries which would attack German convoys and capture their arms. With Ernest Gimpel, originally from Alsace and badly wounded in the same unit as Henneguier, Marcel Meyer, who was half Swiss, and Robert Lynen, aged 20 and already something of a film star, he set up a transport business called 'Azur-Transports' to act as a cover for the more belligerent enterprise. The idea had much of the fantasy of Robert Lynen's film world, and during the winter of 1940 they did little more than build up a fleet of vehicles and divide clients into those who asked why there was no portrait of Pétain in the office and those who approved of a poster showing British and French flags intertwined. The former they charged 3,000 francs for a lorry to Aix, the latter they charged 300. With little success they tried to recruit members for what they called their 'conspiration' but after several months the conspiracy was still confined to a very small group. In early 1941 they met Maurice Chevance, partner to Henri Frenay in his ambitious design to create a secret army, and Chevance needed lorries eventually to transport the arms they intended to collect. The enterprise at 40 rue Saint-Bazile began to look less whimsical and from that moment what had previously seemed a gesture became a functional activity.[1]

In the west of the Dordogne in the small village of Saint-Antoine-de-Breuilh Louis de la Bardonnie created his conspiracy among friends who were fellow landowners in the vicinity, and he, like Henneguier, admits to an initial period of illusory expectations. De la Bardonnie, aged 38, whose family had been in the area for over 600 years, had monarchist sympathies, read *L'Action française*, and had volunteered for the war but was refused on account of his eight children. In his house called Château la Roque, high above the village, he heard one of de Gaulle's first broadcasts from London and promptly invited seven friends whom he had known since childhood to meet and discuss what to do. Mostly men with right-wing political attitudes, but differing widely in the status and size of their

[1] Pierre Henneguier, *Le Soufflet de forge* (Éditions de la Pensée Moderne, 1960), pp. 14–20.

property, they shared de la Bardonnie's sense of outrage at the Armistice and were united in respect for his powerful personality. With little idea of what it might entail they decided to collect information about the occupied zone, which started only a few kilometres away, and send it to London. As early as July they took information across the southern zone into Switzerland, entrusting it to the British Embassy in Geneva, a journey repeated several times in the late summer without any reply from London. They had envisaged a rapid contact and instant recognition of their group and the lack of response dampened the early enthusiasm even though the group continued to expand. In mid-October almost as a desperate gesture they sent a 71-year-old priest, the abbé Dartein, through Portugal to London with photographs of the occupied harbour of Bordeaux. The mission was successful and in November Gilbert Renault, called Rémy, arrived in the Dordogne as the envoy of de Gaulle and France Libre. In December the group, over thirty strong, became known as the intelligence network Confrérie Notre Dame (C.N.D.).[2]

The months of expectation and uncertainty between the formation of the group and its recognition in November were also the months in which the pull of Pétainism in right-wing circles was at its strongest. Charles Maurras and Maurice Pujo had pledged the support of *L'Action française*, the paper most assiduously read in de la Bardonnie's household, to Pétain and the Vichy regime in terms of unquestioning faith. Maurras, the apostle of monarchism as a secular religion, had settled for Pétain as a substitute godhead, and lavished extravagant praise on the 'saviour of France'. From the start this was totally unacceptable to Louis de la Bardonnie. He stopped taking *L'Action française* and wrote an open letter to Maurras dissociating himself indignantly from the paper's position regardless of the possibility that this would attract the attention of the Vichy police.[3] He was not the only angry reader of *L'Action française* in the Dordogne. M. le Moal, a professed militant of the movement, was told by the police in August to

[2] Evidence from Louis de la Bardonnie. Typed manuscript on the origins of C.N.D. kindly lent by M. de la Bardonnie; and Rémy, *Mémoires d'un agent secret*, pp. 93–7.

[3] 'Je les attends de pied ferme', he said. Rémy, op. cit., p. 97.

remove a chamberpot which he displayed in his window containing the masks of Hitler and Mussolini,[4] and the aristocratic Choiseul-Praslin, a wounded veteran of 1914—18 and a lifelong monarchist, made an anti-German speech at Périgueux shortly after the Armistice in which his coolness towards Vichy was not well received. While his son Charles joined the Pétainist youth movement, Compagnons de France, Choiseul-Praslin, who was an Anglophile with friends in England, wrote several letters to Maurras arguing that the anti-German doctrines proclaimed over the years in *L'Action française* led to entirely different conclusions from those drawn by Maurras and Pujo. In 1949 he wrote of Maurras: 'His own anti-German feelings and doctrines cannot be doubted, but from June 1940, for reasons which were illusory, he hid them from the public at large, putting all the emphasis on hatred of England, with fatal results for the numerous Frenchmen who followed him. This was unforgivable, for Maurras could plead neither ignorance nor stupidity.'[5] Despite his opposition Choiseul-Praslin did not break with Action Française in 1940, hoping to out-argue Maurras from within, though his arguments were not new to the movement. Several militants had left in the mid and late 1930s in protest at its dwindling nationalist vigour and its support for appeasement.

In Nice the writer and journalist Guillain de Bénouville, who had left Action Française in 1934 because Maurras had not shown sufficient leadership to turn the riots of 6 February into a nationalist revolution, started to group right-wing friends into a volunteer force which would leave for the colonies or England. His aim was to disprove the Vichy propaganda which said that only corrupt politicians, followers of Béla Kun, and Jews had joined de Gaulle. In December he made contact with the most colourful defaulter from Action Française, Jacques Renouvin, and informed him of his project, but Renouvin was already involved in action of his own.[6] A Parisian barrister and, like Bénouville, a militant of the Camelots du Roi until 1934, Jacques Renouvin had signalled his personal hostility to the diplomacy of appeasement by publicly striking

[4] From the files of M. Larivière.

[5] Choiseul-Praslin, *Cinq années de Résistance*, p. 36.

[6] Guillain de Bénouville, *Le Sacrifice du matin* (Laffont, 1946), pp. 63–77.

the ex-minister P.-E. Flandin who had sent a telegram of congratulation to Hitler and the other signatories at Munich. In the war he opted for a low rank in a fighting unit rather than a commission in the judicial department of the army, was wounded and escaped from hospital, crossed into the south and settled at Montpellier, rejecting the decision of Pétain to end the fighting. In Montpellier he was surprised to hear that Pierre-Henri Teitgen and other Christian Democrats held views on the Armistice similar to his own, the first time he had confronted the possibility that anyone on the political Left could be interested in the welfare of France. Albin Tixador, a long-standing member of the Socialist Party in Montpellier and a veteran of World War I, in which he lost a leg, expressed the same surprise about Renouvin and the political Right when they met in November.[7] By then Renouvin had established a close understanding with a right-wing journalist in Montpellier, Ferdinand Paloc of *L'Éclair*, who was also a wounded veteran of the First War.[8] In September Paloc had helped refugee Belgian officers escape to England from Sète, the main port of the Hérault, and together he and Renouvin decided to continue such activities and to combat the 'collaboration' announced by Pétain after the meeting with Hitler at Montoire. Renouvin, tall, outspoken, and immensely active, quickly became an unmistakable figure in local groups which rejected the Armistice, not only because of his background in Action Française and his public gesture against Munich, but increasingly because of his influence on students and his determination to use violence against the overt supporters of collaboration. Alongside him, Paloc, as a notable veteran of the area, was under pressure both to join Pétain's Légion française des combattants and to organize celebrations for Pétain's visit to Montpellier. He did neither, but he did continue to work on the strongly Pétainist *L'Éclair* in order to keep informed of the oral and written instructions which came to the Press from the Vichy authorities.[9]

[7] Evidence from Albin Tixador.

[8] Renouvin had been sent to see Paloc by Henri du Moulin de Labarthète, Pétain's *chef de cabinet*. Evidence from Ferdinand Paloc. For the attitudes of *L'Éclair* during this period, see Gérard Astier, 'La Révolution nationale d'après la presse languedocienne, *Éclair* et *Petit Méridional* 1940–44' (Mémoire de Maîtrise, Montpellier, 1973).

[9] Evidence from Ferdinand Paloc.

Henneguier, de la Bardonnie, and Renouvin all created small circles of like-minded people with special action in mind. Structurally insecure, the groups tended to gravitate towards more solidly based organizations. 'Azur-Transports' became attached to the designs of Frenay with his labyrinth of established military connections, de la Bardonnie's intelligence service became one of the earliest networks of France Libre with its established base in London, while Renouvin, once he had met P.-H. Teitgen, gradually became part of the group which produced *Liberté* with its support among Christian Democrats. It was argued in all three groups by one or more members that the only really practical solution was to leave France and go to England, but resistance to this argument soon gained a status of its own. Renouvin argued to Guillain de Bénouville that action was more desperately needed in France and Henneguier dissuaded Ernest Gimpel from going to London by making the same point.[10] Among those in the southern zone who approved of de Gaulle and the British war effort it became increasingly accepted that contact with London did not necessarily entail, and in some circles should not entail, leaving France. The challenge of staying seemed to many to be a greater one.

The decisions which were made by these individual opponents of the Armistice were rarely made in a cautious, calculated manner. The emphasis on activism which most of these personalities produced seemed to be almost in inverse proportion to its practicality and the schemes envisaged in 1940 were as grandiose as any that later materialized. With a refusal to admit defeat went a fertile imagination of what was possible. Emmanuel d'Astier de la Vigerie elevated this quality of adventure to a point where fantasy and reality were indistinguishable. Described by Colonel Groussard as an 'impassioned intransigent man, a sort of Saint-Just',[11] d'Astier described himself as the black sheep of his aristocratic family, with a weakness for left-wing politics and an abhorrence of class distinctions.[12] He had married an American divorcee,

[10] Guillain de Bénouville, op. cit., p. 77. Henneguier, op. cit., p. 17.

[11] *Service secret*, p. 142.

[12] Marcel Ophuls, 'Le Chagrin et la Pitié' (script of the film), *L'Avant-Scène*, nos. 127–8 (July–Sept. 1972), 54.

was something of a writer and journalist after leaving the navy, but in June 1940 was back in the navy as an intelligence officer at Saint-Nazaire on the Atlantic coast. As the Germans approached the town he took his place with five assorted colleagues in the *exode* to the south, and on the Mediterranean coast at Port Vendres near the Spanish border laid histrionic plans for the future, impelled by 'anger and disgust . . . to do something different from everyone else.'[13] Once demobilized he went to Marseille and elsewhere in the south, talking to friends about a 'Dernière Colonne', a unit which would go on fighting in France, rather than abroad, and in November at Clermont-Ferrand a meeting took place at which d'Astier discussed such ideas and talked of a broad-based movement, with a small group including Jean Cavaillès, a philosophy professor evacuated from Strasbourg, Georges Zérapha, who had been a close collaborator of Emmanuel Mounier on *Esprit* but who opposed Mounier's plans to restart the journal under Vichy,[14] and Raymond and Lucie Aubrac, the latter a history teacher at a *lycée* in Lyon.[15] The 'Dernière Colonne' at that stage was still more theoretical than actual, but theory of that kind counted for much in 1940. Frenay in Marseille had embellished the nature of his organization, when first introducing it to potential colleagues, and Alban Vistel, an engineer in Lyon who formed a group of workers and artisans in his factory to discuss events and the possibilities of action, claimed contact with London when none existed. 'I had to say that, otherwise it would all have seemed useless.'[16] Similar exaggeration alongside similar ideas and discussion can be found in many places in the southern zone in late 1940 when the actual numbers involved were extremely small.

To the qualities of spontaneity and inventiveness one can add the importance of self-expression for those who opposed the norms of 1940. Particularly among journalists and academics the ideal of self-expression as well as free expression was a motivating force which in certain individuals led directly to

[13] Emmanuel d'Astier, *Sept Fois sept jours* (Éditions 10/18, 1961), p. 17.

[14] See below, p. 197.

[15] Jacques Eschalier, 'Le Journal *Libération* (zone sud) 1941–4' (Diplôme d'Études Supérieures d'Histoire Contemporaine, Paris, 1962), p. 6.

[16] Evidence from Alban Vistel.

conflict with the control and censorship of Vichy, while both professions had a high degree of access to methods of publication and communication, necessary for the expression of alternative views. Cerf-Ferrière, himself a journalist in the 1930s on *La Flèche*, organ of Gaston Bergery's Front commun, which had tried to unite the disillusioned of Right and Left, started producing his own tracts at Brive, his first stop in the *exode*.[17] In Lyon, where he settled, he was introduced by the journalist-artist Pavil of *Paris-Soir* to a number of other journalists, mostly evacuated from Paris, who supported each other in obstructing and bypassing Vichy censorship.[18] In Saint-Étienne another refugee journalist, Jean Nocher, the son of a schoolteacher and an immediate critic of Vichy's support for private, catholic schools, continued to work for the local newspaper, *La Tribune républicaine*, of which he had been a Paris correspondent before the war.[19] He used the paper and its columns to establish contacts in the area and to criticize Vichy by satire, verbal innuendo, and often outright opposition which earned him a series of official reprimands during 1940–1. Like Paloc on *L'Éclair* in Montpellier, Nocher found his access to official propaganda through *La Tribune* invaluable, and in Lyon this was true of Rémy Roure on *Le Temps* and Georges Altmann and Yves Farge in the editorial offices of *Le Progrès de Lyon*. They are just a few examples of the many journalists whose dissidence in 1940 was expressed through their professional skills, and among other individuals mentioned so far a high percentage were familiar with the world of journalism and used its connections to develop their activities, not least Guillain de Bénouville, Emmanuel d'Astier, Loustaunau-Lacau, and the Catholic writers Maydieu, Fumet, Fessard, and Chaillet.

Journalists, it might be assumed, with their professional understanding of the limitations of the Press, would be fairly sceptical of the capacity of marginal tracts to correct the majority opinion of the time. But among the individuals who started tracts and news-sheets in 1940 there was a balancing idealism which believed that the facts of the situation, clearly

[17] See above, p. 8.

[18] Cerf-Ferrière, *Chemin clandestin*, p. 49.

[19] Faure, *Un Témoin raconte . . .* p. 89.

stated, would carry a conviction of their own.[20] This belief was evident in the group called France-Liberté started in Lyon, which contained little initial journalistic experience, but which in later 1940 decided to combat the Vichy Press, item by item, and to send copies of its tracts to the senior personnel at Vichy.[21] The group had grown from several smaller groups of friends who began meeting independently of each other in the summer of 1940 to discuss what could be done to present an alternative to the dominant Pétainism of the town. The Marshal made a triumphant visit to Lyon on 18 November when an estimated 150,000 received him with something close to religious ecstasy, and it was during November that the groups combined to meet regularly at the Café de la Poste in the Place des Terreaux with a smaller meeting at the home of Noël Clavier.[22] The regulars included Élie Péju and J.-J. Soudeille, both ex-Communists who had left the party in the early 1930s, Antoine Avinin who was a member of Marc Sangnier's left-wing Catholic movement Jeune République, Auguste Pinton, a Radical who was one of the municipal councillors dismissed by Vichy, and Noël Clavier, whose political attitudes were largely formed in the circle which grouped itself round Georges Valois. Valois was living near Lyon in 1940 and was a total opponent of Pétain and Vichy, having moved steadily towards an individualist position on the trade-unionist Left, after early years in Action Française and in his own Fascist movement Le Faisceau. Through his friends and followers he became a powerful stimulus to opposition in 1940, while remaining independent of the dissident groupings, including France-Liberté itself.

With this mixed political background France-Liberté proclaimed its freedom from Vichy propaganda and set out to influence the circles of small business men and middle-class professions from which its members were mostly drawn. Their unifying concern was to defend republican ideals against the

[20] See below, pp. 119–27 for the news-sheets of General Cochet and the group created by Henri Frenay.

[21] N. Clavier, 'Franc-Tireur. Tel que je l'ai vu naître', *Bulletin des AMUR*, no. 6 (June 1947), 4.

[22] I am greatly indebted for information on France-Liberté to Mme Dominique Veillon whose thesis on Franc-Tireur is a pioneer work of analysis and reconstruction (D. Veillon, 'Le Mouvement Franc-Tireur', Thèse 3e cycle, Paris, 1975).

authoritarianism of Vichy, particularly as it gained the submission of such large sectors of their own social class in Lyon. To this was added a wider aim and a new range of adherents by the arrival of Jean-Pierre Lévy, a Jewish refugee from Strasbourg, along with the small commercial business in which he was employed, which continued its operations from the Croix-Rousse in Lyon. Introduced to France-Liberté by an Englishman called Robertson, Jean-Pierre Lévy brought to the group his refugee and business contacts outside Lyon and his anger against the fate of fellow Alsace-Lorrainers. He was younger than the other members of the group and was unmarried, with a job which allowed him to travel freely across the southern zone, and by the spring of 1941 he had enlarged the compass of France-Liberté to the point where it was an embryo movement of opposition, with its tracts penetrating other big towns of the south-west and attracting the support of Alsace-Lorrainers by a vigorous indictment of the victimizations and expulsions from the annexed provinces.[23]

The margins of freedom which still existed in the southern zone in 1940 were not difficult for journalists, or amateur publicists, to exploit if determined to do so. The academic world in this respect was similar to that of journalism, knowledge being under the same censorious scrutiny as news, but in universities there were even wider margins for individual expression. The bond between Christian Democrats which had resulted in *Liberté* was strengthened by the academic links between the Facultés de Droit in which several of them worked.[24] In Montpellier alongside the university courses of Teitgen and Baumel in law and Courtin in political economy, there were those of the medieval historian Marc Bloch and the German specialist E. Vermeil, both from Paris, all of which provided a forum for critical opposition to any kind of compromise with the Germans. In Grenoble the mathematician René Gosse, Dean of the Faculty of Science, a Socialist and a vigorous anti-Fascist of the 1930s, used every aspect of his university

[23] Veillon, op. cit., pp. 52–7, 314. Mme Veillon indicates that Lévy's contacts with the exiled communities were immeasurably strengthened by a fellow exile from Strasbourg, Pierre Eude, who had been Secretary-General of the Strasbourg Chamber of Commerce and knew large numbers of small business men and their employees who were desperately trying to find homes and jobs in Lyon.

[24] See above, p. 30.

position to produce hostility to the Armistice, which was easier to achieve on the undefeated Italian front than in most other areas in the south. In December he was replaced as dean, though he was allowed to continue as professor, and together with the local socialist deputy Léon Martin, whose vote had been cast against Pétain on 10 July, he was one of those largely responsible for the judgement sent to the Prefect by the Ministry of the Interior that 'Grenoble is the centre of a propaganda which is anti-government, Anglophile, and Gaullist, whose protagonists seem to be members of the university, municipal council, and prefecture.'[25] University teachers who used their positions to subvert the policy of Vichy did so with little, if any guilt about the 'detachment of scholarship'. The tradition of intellectual involvement in political and ideological issues, though strongly condemned in the classic *Trahison des clercs* by Julien Benda, was well entrenched in French academic behaviour, and to encourage it there was the equally long tradition of lecture courses featuring not just the scholarship but the personality of individual professors. At Clermont-Ferrand Jean Cavaillès used his philosophy courses to build a following among students without any departure from normal practice. His popularity in the legitimate exercise of his profession made it difficult for Vichy in its early months to find reason for intervention, though his criticisms, like those of most dissenting academics, were well known.[26]

Only a wealth of biographies could begin to satisfy the search for motivation among the individual opponents of 1940. No single factor was an absolute determinant, not even personality. Because they were exceptions to their class, locality, or profession it has been tempting to imagine they were already outsiders or misfits, rather as Sartre interpreted the personality of those who became collaborators.[27] Two of

[25] Lucienne Gosse, *Chronique d'une vie française: René Gosse 1883–1943* (Plon, 1962), p. 333.

[26] Vichy's limitations in making academics conform was publicly exposed at the end of 1941 when the government ordered all academics to swear an oath of loyalty to Pétain. Gosse and others at Grenoble said they would refuse as did professors elsewhere. Vichy withdrew the order.

[27] J.-P. Starre, 'Qu'est-ce qu'un collaborateur?' *Situations III*.

the most colourful opponents of the Armistice and Vichy policy, Emmanuel d'Astier and the poet and art-historian Jean Cassou, have provided some support for those who favour this approach. D'Astier, giving evidence to Marcel Ophuls for the film *Le Chagrin et la Pitié*, said 'I'm going to stick my neck out and say that I believe one could only be a Resister if one was maladjusted'.[28] Jean Cassou, who continued his anti-German activities in Toulouse in the spring of 1941 after a period of imprisonment in Paris, wrote in 1953:

I myself had always been someone without possessions, without inheritance or title, with no fixed home, no social status, no real profession, putting on a series of masks and pretending, for the gallery, to believe in these arbitrary masks. Finally I found myself in a situation where . . . it was the norm not to give your own name, where it was the rule not to have a social position and no longer to look for one. . . . And life in prison was also to my liking, giving me the feeling of being at home. At last society had found me the social position I wanted, at last it had understood me and at last I was living, adequately and harmoniously as I wanted to live.[29]

The generalization of d'Astier is both as bold and provocative as his own personality, of which it was largely a projection, while the self-analysis of Jean Cassou is specific to himself, even though there were undoubtedly many others who experienced the same kind of self-realization in clandestine activity. Both the 'maladjustment' of d'Astier and the 'anonymity' of Cassou indicate certain types of individuals in 1940 but they cannot be of more than relative value. If there was one quality which can be generalized it was that most of the opponents of 1940 had an unusually strong conviction that they were right, even when faced with arguments which appeared more realistic, and behaviour which seemed more practical. Such a conviction points to a degree of obstinacy but does not necessarily indicate the personality of an outsider. It can equally well suggest that the individuals were people within their own society or grouping of whom a lead was expected. Several individuals like Michelet, Cavaillès, de Menthon, Jean-Pierre Lévy,

[28] Ophuls, op. cit. 54.

[29] *La Mémoire courte*, pp. 53–5.

Frenay, de la Bardonnie, Joseph Pastor, Pierre Georges, and others exhibit just that quality. In the circumstances of 1940 the lead they gave forced them outside the current norms, since all opposition in 1940 was an exception, but it does not mean that they always had been, or always would be, outsiders. The possession of a strongly self-determining, independent, and combative personality is not inevitably synonymous with maladjustment, either personal or social. To say that it is, is to miss the important variable of circumstance.

It is equally important to note that many of the individuals who rejected the Armistice and its consequences made their first contacts within the coherent if loose grouping of colleagues and friends who shared similar values and who were leading similar lives. It is easy to miss this point because the total picture of opposition in the southern zone in 1940 shows a mixture of almost all aspects of French society. A more detailed picture shows that the separate groupings were not always so mixed or heterogeneous. The extent of an individual's isolation or 'outsiderness' is exaggerated in the total picture which juxtaposes such different people as Renouvin, Cerf-Ferrière, d'Astier, the curé Alvitre, Joseph Pastor, and Jean-Pierre Lévy, but in the situation of 1940 they were not juxtaposed, and although of those six Renouvin and d'Astier did make heterogeneous relationships, the others made fairly predictable and coherent ones, Cerf-Ferrière with other ex-Parisian journalists, Jean-Pierre Lévy with fellow *emigrés* from Alsace, the curé Alvitre with other left-wing Catholics, and Joseph Pastor with like-minded Communists in his area of Marseille. De Menthon, Teitgen, Michelet, and de la Bardonnie also developed an understanding within the groupings to which they naturally belonged, and these initial contacts provide evidence that many of the individual opponents of 1940 did have a group identity, even though the scope and nature of their activity eventually took them well outside it.[30]

A far more generalized reason for acts of opposition in 1940,

[30] Mme Veillon, in her thesis on Franc-Tireur, op. cit., p. 56, emphasizes that the individuals comprising France-Liberté in 1940–1 each worked consciously and effectively among their own socio-political groups in order to build up the membership of the movement: e.g. Antoine Avinin among fellow members of Jeune République, Auguste Pinton among Radicals and ex-municipal councillors, and Noël Clavier among friends and followers of Georges Valois.

and one which long pre-dates the idea of 'outsiderness', is that provided by the idea of patriotism, a concept which runs throughout the history of Resistance, turning the wheels of explanation. Many who use it unthinkingly forget that patriotism in 1940 was the justification for many points of view, not least support for Pétain, and that while Pétain was widely thought to be a security against the concessions which others wished to make to Germany, this patriotic trust had the appearance of good sense. Despite this there is no need to contest it as a motive for Resistance or to try to explain it away, for it was a powerful emotion among most Resisters. But what is unacceptable in the explanation of patriotism is the way it has been used to produce a notion of Resistance as an almost mystical phenomenon, or Aristotelian essence. This notion is expressed with fervour in the memoirs of Guillain de Bénouville, but it can be found in numerous other writings and in the oral inheritance handed down since the war. Talking of France at the moment of the defeat and Armistice, de Bénouville wrote,

> Already the Resistance was present and the destinies of those who were about to enter it were already linked. Thousands of men who did not as yet know each other, took a step which, without their knowledge, would bring them together. Already at this desperate hour France was saved. And they knew it. . . . The Fatherland is not an abstraction. It is a living reality which moves in men's hearts, and these men were obeying its command. . . . Everywhere already the Army of Liberation existed.[31]

There is an implicit assumption in this 'essentialist' approach that the defeat and Armistice of May–June 1940 carried, or should have carried, the same emotional charge for all French people; and that it was possible for individuals of totally different backgrounds and interests to react in the same patriotic manner. The variety of individuals who did react with anger and opposition is taken as proof that no sector of society was excluded from such a reaction and that other individuals might have reacted in the same way had they been perhaps more clear-sighted, less submissive, less concerned with day-to-day

[31] Op. cit., p. 38.

survival, more imaginative, or more independent. The small minority of dissidents in 1940 are seen as those who first realized the latent or potential patriotic reaction of all French people, and are called the 'First' Resisters, *les Résistants de la première heure*. They were joined, it is said, by a larger number in 1941 and a still larger one in 1942 and 1943 until sympathy with the Resistance became as widespread in 1944 as support for Pétain in 1940, even if the proportion of activists remained relatively small. With this approach a hierarchy of Resisters is built up according to 'date of entry' as if the Resistance was something that could be 'joined' at any stage after June 1940 because, in some essential way, the Resistance was born at the same moment as the Armistice as its patriotic alternative; 'Déjà la Résistance se dessine . . .'[32] Those who 'joined' in 1940 or 1941 occupy a place in the hierarchy superior to those who 'joined' at a later date. Such a hierarchy is not openly vaunted in France but it is widely assumed and tacitly acknowledged.[33]

A much more relative position is reached, and one nearer to the complexities of the period, when it is understood that the great majority of French people needed something other than the emotional charge of defeat and Armistice to provoke the kind of anger and defiance necessary for opposition. This is not a judgement on their patriotism but a realistic acceptance that the events of May–June 1940 did not, and could not, affect all French people in the same way. It was not so much a lack of imagination and foresight or an excess of self-concern as a highly disaggregated reception of the events, leading to a diffusion of anger and a confusion of interpretations. Those who protested with emotional or intellectual anger against the defeat and Armistice and initiated acts of opposition in 1940 did so for reasons which were largely specific to themselves, reasons which are as yet beyond categorization. Some were influenced by family or educational connections with England and America, others by their personal experience of the war, by injury or captivity; some were anti-authoritarian and rebellious; some had written or fought against Fascism in the 1930s

[32] Ibid., p. 38.

[33] The most explicit defence for this 'date of entry' approach is provided by the Association nationale des résistants de 1940, an organization with its offices in the Palais de Chaillot in Paris.

with particular personal investment; some were just obstinately optimistic. There were also the variables of family situation, locality, group membership, jobs, and communications, which, if not determining factors, often made it easier for the initial defiance to be expressed in action. The explanation of patriotism can be added to these motivating forces but it cannot stand as a substitute for them.

Those who resisted at a later date did not start with the same specific reaction to defeat and Armistice, but the same kind of anger and defiance was often produced by a subsequent event or experience which made them react in ways similar to those in 1940. When they did so the similarity of their reaction to that of the 'first' Resisters in 1940 makes it clear that a relative chronology of Resistance is needed. Many individuals and groups who started to resist in 1941 or 1942 went through many of the same initial moves and experienced much the same sense of isolation as those in 1940. They were often impelled by the same urge to do something without any clear idea of what to do, and although the defeat and Armistice were a year or more in the past, their anger and defiance often had the same kind of immediacy and urgency as that of 1940. It is true that in 1941 it became possible for French people in many areas of the southern zone to 'join' an existing organization and therefore respond to the initiatives of other, earlier, Resisters. In no sense can this be denied; it is crucial to the history of Resistance. But at the same time there were areas, jobs, or communities in which an individual could be a *Résistant de la première heure* even as late as 1942. It cannot therefore be said that something called 'The Resistance' began in the southern zone in 1940: it can only be said that resistance to the German Occupation and to the values and behaviour accepted as normative in Vichy France began at various times and in various ways between 1940 and 1942 and that resistance to the ideas and practice of Nazism and Fascism had begun even earlier. By 1942 there had emerged a consciousness of collective action and collective identity and in that year one can begin to talk meaningfully of The Resistance. Even then it remained, and still remains, subject to relative interpretations according to political and other criteria.

What this entails for the historian is not just a description of how the initiatives of 1940 developed but also a search for the events and experiences subsequent to the defeat and Armistice which had a similar motivating force in producing Resistance. When these have been found and the groups and individuals affected by them presented, it will be seen that the trauma of defeat and Armistice is only one of many starting-points for an explanation of French Resistance.

V. Political Reassertion

THE main achievement of opposition in 1940 was to keep the situation open and to remind French people that the possibility of choice still existed. Most of the individuals mentioned so far were involved in what some Resistance writers have called a 'refus absurde', a refusal to accept what was offered in 1940 against all the apparent force of reason, common sense, and self-interest.[1] Between 1940 and the end of 1942 the opportunities for such a refusal steadily increased. The events of the continuing war and the growing pressure of the Occupation re-established the defeat as a dynamic factor in the southern zone, and not one that had been successfully dealt with at the Armistice, while the increasingly open activities of those sympathetic to the Germans forced the French more and more into a position of choice. As the alternatives became more apparent so the *refus* became less *absurde*, even in some cases becoming all that it had not been in 1940, rational, sensible, and conforming to the needs of self-interest. In this process no factor played quite such an ironic role as the internal policies of Vichy itself.

There is no validity for talking about the Vichy regime as if it were a united, monolithic, and unchanging phenomenon. Too many studies have now shown how fissiparous it was. But in 1940 it did possess a single image which, if not substantiated by subsequent analysis, was its proclaimed rationale, and was responsible for much of the early submission of the southern zone. This image was one of being 'above politics', a concept perfected by that most political of French ideologues, Charles Maurras, and one that only carried conviction because of the widespread illusion that politics meant the activity of political parties. Maurras claimed that Action Française was not a party, in the sense of something that is a part of the nation, but rather that it represented the whole nation, was above parties and therefore above politics. In similar language Pétain had no party following, came from outside parliament,

[1] e.g. Cassou, *La Mémoire courte*, p. 57.

and was therefore not a political person. In the mood of guilt and penitence in 1940, which meant finding others guilty and being penitent because they had been allowed to perpetrate their crimes with impunity, the Third Republic as the *régime des partis* was accused of dividing the French through politics. By contrast, Vichy claimed to be apolitical. This apolitical image was ostensibly preserved for most of the period of the southern zone's independence, but in reality it was quickly lost and the way in which it was lost points to a major ambiguity in the situation of Vichy. Just how far Vichy was constrained by the German Occupation is still a matter of debate and will continue to be so even when the archives are fully available. The ideological constraint will always be a question of interpretation. But even at this stage it is possible to offer the paradox that Vichy had too much, and not too little, freedom of manœuvre. The government, caught in a diplomatic vice, was unable to establish more than a small element of choice in its negotiations with Germany, but in home affairs its autonomy was relatively unimpaired. Most Vichy ministers, lacking Laval's dedication to diplomatic bargaining, tended to compensate for their loss of freedom in external matters by an assertive display of legislation at home. In this area the Vichy regime between July 1940 and November 1942 did not see itself, and should not be seen, as a puppet government. Its freedom was considerable, and by using its freedom in a massive programme of legislation it perpetuated or recreated the deepest political divisions in the country.

It is difficult to imagine how it could have been otherwise. The defeat was, in a sense, the justification of the right-wing opposition to the Third Republic. It was a long-term vindication of Charles Maurras, who before World War I had prophesied that the weakness engendered in the Republic by the political parties would lead to military disaster. The result of 1918 was his failure as a prophet. The result of 1940 was his success. In so far as he and the nationalist Right had consistently predicted the collapse of the parliamentary regime they had a vested interest in it when it occurred. Having vigorously opposed the parties of the Third Republic they had an apparently unquestionable right to dispose of them. Political gestures of a sectarian kind were thus the natural extension of an ideology which had moved from opposition into power. Only for a brief period of little more than a month was this sectarianism restrained, then from August 1940 the legislation, known collectively as the 'Révolution nationale', progressively defined the political nature of the Vichy regime and in so doing progressively defined its political opponents.

The 'National Revolution', or 'Renovation', as Pétain preferred to call it, was the term applied to a series of legislative innovations beginning in the late summer of 1940, and to the ideology which they embodied. More loosely it referred to the moral aims of the government, or more often to the declared intentions of Pétain, announced to the nation on radio and in public appearances on his provincial tours. For this reason members of the youth or veteran organizations created during 1940 could claim to be 'workers for the National Revolution', merely by their loyalty to Pétain. The National Revolution was, in this sense, more of a creed than a programme, but as the legislation increasingly detailed the aims of both Pétain and his government so the disciples of the creed were expected to become instruments of the programme. This change in character can be seen, for example, in the development of the *Légion française des combattants*.

Created by the law of 29 August 1940 the Légion was intended to be the single organization for all French veterans of 1914–18 and, after initial hesitation, those of 1939–40. A month after its creation the German authorities refused to allow it in the occupied zone, authorizing instead the continued existence of four separate associations,[2] and the Légion was therefore confined to the southern zone. From the start it was seen as coextensive with Pétainism, Pétain being at its head and each Légionnaire being 'l'homme du Maréchal', although the oath of loyalty which he swore on entry did not mention Pétain in person.[3]

[2] Union fédérale, Union nationale des combattants, Fédération nationale des grands invalides, and Union nationale des mutilés et réformés.

[3] Pétain was head of the Légion not as Chef de l'État but in his capacity as Marshal of France and 'doyen des médaillés militaires'. The oath was as follows 'Je jure de continuer à servir la France avec honneur dans la paix comme je l'ai servie sous les armes. Je jure de consacrer toutes mes forces à la Patrie, à la Famille, au Travail. Je m'engage à pratiquer l'amitié et l'entr'aide vis-à-vis de mes camarades des deux guerres, à rester fidèle à la mémoire de ceux qui sont tombés au Champ d'Honneur. J'accepte librement la discipline de la Légion

The monolithic simplicity of the Légion did not mean that its origins were free from conflict. Several notable leaders of old veteran associations, particularly Jean Goy, President of the Union nationale des combattants, and Maurice Randoux, President of the Union fédérale, repudiated it as an attack on the self-determination of the separate groups, and Xavier Vallat, its chief progenitor and Secrétaire-Général des Anciens combattants in the Vichy Government, dismissed one of his first appointees Loustaunau-Lacau within a few weeks after disagreements over the future of the Légion.[4] But the reception of the Légion among veterans themselves was overwhelmingly positive. Of those eligible to join a vast majority did so.[5] Leaders were easily found among local notables and the enthusiasm generated at public functions where the Légion was on display showed that the movement was considered by most people in the southern zone as a sign of patriotic rejuvenation. It lifted morale and appeared to justify the apolitical claims of Pétain by unifying the rival factions of the inter-war years.[6] The Légion was received, as was intended, as an attempt to give authority to a natural grouping of the community and to delegate power from the government to the people without involving them in narrow political activity.[7] At least, this was how it was easily interpreted at local level. But among the aims of the movement a distinct political purpose was wrapped in the language of consensus in so far as the Légion was expected to provide moral and patriotic support for the decisions of the administration. During 1941 the pressure

---

pour tout ce qui me sera commandé en vue de cet idéal'. Most noticeable is its reference to the state of France following the Armistice as a state of 'peace'.

[4] See above, pp. 38–40.

[5] Percentages were particularly high in the Alpes-Maritimes, the Rhône, the Dordogne, Savoie, and Haute-Savoie. (J.-P. Cointet, 'La Légion française des combattants', in *Le Gouvernement de Vichy 1940–42*, Fondation Nationale des Sciences Politiques, Colin, 1972, p. 134.)

[6] Much of the fragmentation of the veteran movement in this period was, however, due less to party politics than to disparate ideas about methods, rights, pensions, and status. Nor was Pétain the first to attempt a unification. The movements themselves had moved towards such a position in 1939 when two large groupings had emerged, the Légion des combattants français and the Légion française des combattants. These tentative moves were superseded by the Vichy legislation. (Lynette Chaffey, 'The Mouvement combattant in France in the 1930s', unpub. Univ. of Sussex D.Phil. thesis 1972.)

[7] Cointet, op. cit., pp. 128–9.

grew within the Légion and at Vichy itself for this support system to be made more positive, enabling the Légion to initiate measures in the *départements* and even, if necessary, to supersede the authority of the prefect. Initially the Légion was answerable through Vallat to the Ministry of War but a few months after its inception Vallat succeeded in moving both the Légion and his own office into the sphere of the Ministry of the Interior. In February 1941 the Légion was given more precise instructions to collaborate in the work of the administration at all levels, and a few months later was brought even closer to politics when, on the initiative of Paul Marion, Secrétaire-Général d'Information et de Propagande, it was opened to all Frenchmen over 20 in the southern zone whether they were war veterans or not. Membership of the Légion became a required qualification for certain jobs, offices, and privileges and the movement looked increasingly like a *parti unique* in the eyes of those who saw Fascist tendencies in Vichy legislation.

From the Légion itself strong pressure in this direction had come from several local branches, particularly Nice and Toulouse, and it was in Nice that the politicization of the Légion was most fully advanced under the leadership of Joseph Darnand whose much-respected reputation for bravery in both 1914–18 and 1939–40, his influence with Pétain, and the distance of Nice from Vichy gave him the freedom to use the local Légionnaires for militant activity far exceeding their formal duties. In September 1940 at the municipal casino the Légion of Nice elaborated a programme containing the aim to fight against Communists, Freemasons, and Jews, described as 'gangrenous and leprous', as well as against the capitalist trusts described as 'Jewish plutocracy'.[8] This specific orientation was crystallized in action during 1941 when the Légionnaires provided a propaganda unit for the German anti-Semitic film *Jud Süss* and tried to prohibit André Gide from giving a public lecture on Henri Michaux.[9] In the summer of 1941 Darnand created an élite of activists from within the Légion and pressed Vichy to recognize this departure. It did so in January 1942 and élites under the name Service d'ordre

[8] Flavian, *Ils furent des hommes*, p. 28.
[9] The lecture was due to take place on 21 May 1941. See below, pp. 194–6.

légionnaire (S.O.L.) were officially sponsored with the task of vigorously promoting the National Revolution and rooting out all opponents of Vichy. The Légion in Toulouse, Lyon, and Marseille quickly followed Nice in this direction and the S.O.L. confirmed the inner mutation of an apolitical organization into an agent of political power.

The effect of this development among the mass of veterans was a steady decline in membership. In one area, the Haute-Savoie, where recruitment had been among the highest in the southern zone, this decline was associated with a specific event but one that was seen as typical of the new political militancy which had been encouraged within the Légion during 1941. Initially the Légion in this area, as in others, was only marginally involved in political gestures, most of which concerned the 'unmasking' of mayors and other local officials who criticized the government, and the replacement of republican street names with names more in keeping with the new regime.[10] But with the creation of the S.O.L. and the growth of authority of Vergain, the *chef départemental* of the Légion, the politicization increased to a point where veterans who had joined for general patriotic reasons, particularly pride in the Alpine regiments which had not been defeated by the Italians, resented the more narrow commitment to the specifics of Vichy policy.[11] In April 1942 this commitment was displayed by the S.O.L. in Annecy after a tree planted to commemorate Pétain's visit had been cut down, and red paint thrown over the statue of St François de Sales, the S.O.L.'s patron saint. Rising to the provocation, a group of Légionnaires belonging to the S.O.L. picked on François de Menthon, who had never joined the Légion and whose opposition to Vichy was widely known, lured him to the *mairie* and threw him into the fountain outside.[12] The action was in itself a

[10] In Annecy the rue de la République was changed to rue de la Légion. Such substitutions occurred all over the southern zone.

[11] In the small commune of Petit Bornand in the Haute-Savoie the curé, abbé Jean Truffy, and the schoolmaster, M. Pinget, advised the local Légionnaires against joining the S.O.L. since the Légion had proved not to be the instrument of national regeneration which it had appeared to be in 1940. (Truffy, *Mémoires*, pp. 11–12.)

[12] For de Menthon's opposition see above, pp. 30–2. In the area of Annecy, regardless of his attitudes to Vichy, he was widely respected as a war veteran, head of a large family, and a local notable.

minor one but the consequences were considerable. Vergain congratulated the group and dismissed the incident, but protests from within the Légion gained momentum and the issue became a test of where authority lay. One of the communal leaders of the Légion, Édouard Pochat of Thônes, condemned the assault in a letter to his section and so eventually did General Cartier, Mayor of Annecy and Honorary President of the Légion in Haute-Savoie. But Vergain had the support of Darnand who wrote, 'I congratulate you warmly. By seizing this opportunity, the S.O.L. of the Haute-Savoie has proved its civic courage and its shrewd political sense.'[13] This support weighed sufficiently at Vichy to obtain the dismissal of General Cartier as mayor of Annecy, and the exoneration of Vergain, but from the Légionnaires came hundreds of resignations. The apolitical image of the Légion was permanently broken in the area. The result, concluded Paul Viret, who documented the event, was a massive increase in local Resistance.[14]

The François de Menthon affair in the Haute-Savoie, like the anti-Semitism of the S.O.L. in their strongest towns Nice, Toulouse, Lyon, and Marseille, was a far cry from the patriotic displays of the Légion at the visit of Pétain to the provincial centres, or the welfare work undertaken by the Légionnaires, though the two kinds of activity existed side by side. From Limoges came a pamphlet at the end of 1943 summarizing the achievements of the local Légion in the work of helping prisoners of war and their families, listing some 137,000 parcels sent to the camps in one year alone and concluding 'We are united in a spirit of complete national solidarity. Faithful to its motto, under the emblem of absolute union of all Frenchmen, the Légion offers you its help.'[15] But well before the publication of this pamphlet the descent of the

[13] Viret, *L'Affaire François de Menthon*, p. 33

[14] In the same month, April 1942, the communist paper of the Bouches-du-Rhône carried an article on the Légion, reporting a number of resignations, particularly at Périgueux, but counselling its readers to remain in the Légion, though not in the S.O.L., in order to exploit its potential: 'Légionnaires, écœurés, sincères patriotes français ne démissionez pas. Dénoncez les profiteurs, les mauvais Français qui nous mènent à la ruine totale. Amenez votre organisation au service du peuple, au service de notre malheureux Pays'. (*Rouge-Midi*, Apr. 1942.)

[15] *La Part de la Légion de la Haute-Vienne dans l'aide aux prisonniers de guerre* (Imprimerie Nouvelle, Limoges, n.d.).

Légion into the political arena had made the conclusion a hollow one. The Légion had become divisive.

The history of other Vichy institutions reveals much the same pattern as the Légion, but in most cases the original legislation was more explicitly aggressive. The Légion in 1940 could justifiably be seen as an attempt at unity. This was not true of legislation discriminating against Jews, dissolving trade unions, and prohibiting the Freemasons; it was not true of decrees dissolving socialist and radical local councils nor of educational laws designed to upgrade the private, Catholic sector and to reintroduce a greater degree of religious teaching into the state system. Yet all were advanced as measures to unite the country, since by the logic of the nationalist position the declared aim of Jews, Freemasons, trade-unionists, Marxists, and anticlericals, all those under legislative attack, had been to divide and fragment the nation. It was two years before the Légion produced widespread resignations. It took less time for these other aspects of the National Revolution to create opposition, but even here there was an initial readiness among some of those affected to credit the regime with good intentions. Jews were found who were prepared to co-operate in a separate administration of Jewish affairs, there were Freemasons who willingly dissolved their own lodges, trade-unionists who favoured the Vichy style of corporatism, and local councillors who submitted to being replaced without protest. This degree of conciliation was mostly due to the exigencies of 1940, the charisma of Pétain, and the wide agreement that unity was better than disunity in the crisis, but much of it was also due to the peculiar potential of Vichy, compounded as it was of highly traditional social and political interests on the one hand and hopes of change and innovation on the other.

Many of those who have been called the nonconformists of the 1930s, those who looked for change in France through new departures or a synthesis of previously antagonistic positions, responded in 1940 to the possibility that Vichy would embody their heterodox ideas.[16] Even as the regime appealed predictably to the peasantry, the upper bourgeoisie, the army, the traditionalist elements in the Church, and the nationalist

[16] Cf. Jean-Louis Loubet del Bayle, *Les Non-Conformistes des années 30* (Seuil, 1969).

Right, there were also dialectical hopes from René Belin that it would serve trade unions, from Gaston Bergery that it would produce a synthesis of political Left and Right, and from Emmanuel Mounier that it would forge a new Catholicism based on the inner strength of the individual. Belin, Deputy Secretary-General of the C.G.T. since 1933, had led a breakaway pacifist group of trade-unionists in 1938 which produced its own paper *Syndicats*; Gaston Bergery had pioneered a Front commun antifasciste in 1933, a form of neo-Communism which set out to link dissidents of any party who felt a new initiative in politics was necessary, while Emmanuel Mounier, editor of the Catholic journal *Esprit*, with its doctrine of *personnalisme*, had supported the Spanish Republicans in the Civil War against the weight of the Catholic hierarchy. In 1940 Belin became Minister of Labour and Industrial Production in Pétain's first Cabinet. Bergery was largely responsible for drafting Pétain's speech of 10 October 1940 on the principles of the National Revolution, and Mounier restarted *Esprit* in Lyon in November in the belief that the National Revolution and the ideals of *personnalisme* were compatible or capable of being made so.

The three were not isolated exceptions in 1940, but even from them alone there emerges a complex view of Vichy in 1940 as a regime which created expectations of change among many who could not be identified with the nationalist Right, and these expectations meant a broad base of tolerance for Vichy policies in their initial period. It was Vichy's own determination to pursue the sectarian ends of its programme with rigour and persistence that destroyed this broad base. Starting, if not from an apolitical position, at least with a multipolitical potential, it failed to fulfil its promise of being above politics and developed instead a narrow image as a right-wing dictatorship whose only difference in content from the programme of the traditional nationalist Right was the technocratic ambitions of its experts.[17] Against all its declared intentions, the Vichy regime, by its internal policy alone, caused dissent and created Resistance, steadily in 1940–1 and rapidly in 1942.

[17] See R. Paxton, *Vichy France: Old Guard and New Order, 1940–44* (Barrie and Jenkins, London, 1972), pp. 259–73. For material on one of Vichy's most professional economic experts, Jean Bichelonne, see Milward, *The New Order and the French Economy*, pp. 149 ff.

The particular hostility of the Vichy regime towards political parties was met head on by the reorganization of the Communist Party, as we have already seen. In the southern zone the appearance of *L'Humanité* (zone sud) and its local offshoots coincided with the elaboration of the National Revolution, and the difference between the two programmes of revolution, communist and Vichy, provided permanent material for the party Press. In the document 'Peuple de France', already discussed, which was distributed in August and September there was a call for Communists to create Comités populaires de solidarité et d'entr'aide in each town and village, to organize welfare for refugees, unemployed, the sick, and the wounded, and to provide an equitable distribution of food. The committees stood in clear rivalry to Pétainist organizations, and the principle underlying them, 'Un pour tous, tous pour un', had a distinct flavour of moral regeneration, comparable to the proclamations of Vichy.[18] By the end of September 1940 this generalized moral principle had disappeared, though there were still calls for communist welfare work, particularly to help prisoners of war.[19] What replaced it was a campaign of denunciation directed against specific items of Vichy policy, in which the language of class conflict and historical struggle against right-wing politics was uppermost. On 26 September the Chantiers de la jeunesse were attacked as 'camps d'esclavage'[20] and on 4 October the Légion française des combattants was denounced as the tool of the 'Cagoulard Xavier Vallat' to divide the anciens combattants of 1914–18 from those of 1939–40 and thereby to control them.[21] In the same issue the Vichy plan to indict the leaders of the Third Republic at a trial in Riom was dismissed as nothing but a comedy. If there is to be a trial, the paper states, it should at least include Pétain and Laval who are equally responsible for the country's disasters.

Throughout the winter the personal attacks on Pétain increased, and he was several times accused of having sold France to the financial and industrial trusts, which he had

[18] 'Peuple de France', *L'Humanité* (zone sud) (15 Aug. 1940).
[19] e.g. *L'Humanité* (zone sud), no. 79 (27 Oct. 1940); no. 84 (30 Nov. 1940).
[20] Ibid., no. 75 (26 Sept. 1940).
[21] Ibid., no. 76 (4 Oct. 1940).

publicly denounced, by including in his government Bouthillier, an Inspector of Finance, Pucheu of the Comité des forges, and Lehideux, nephew of Louis Renault, the car magnate.[22] In April 1941, as different editions of *L'Humanité* multiplied, the conflict with Vichy was focused on preparations for 1 May. Editions for Clermont-Ferrand and the Gard both called for large local demonstrations to reclaim the date from Pétain's Fête du travail, a festival which *Le Semeur*, a party pamphlet distributed on either side of the demarcation line in the Franche-Comté, called a cynical gesture by the 'valets nazis de Vichy'.[23]

Cynicism was an attitude held to be at the root of most of the National Revolution by the communist Press. *L'Humanité de la femme* began in the southern zone with an attack on Pétain's campaign to keep women at home. 'What cynicism to speak of the "woman at home" when the husband is a prisoner of war, is unemployed, wounded, or killed in the war and when her older children from 14 to 20 can find no work.' A report follows of women sent to prison for demanding the release of their communist husbands, and the article concludes, 'France is transformed into a vast concentration camp'.[24] Appearing monthly in the winter of 1940–1, *L'Humanité de la femme* was the first publication in the southern zone to register hunger and shortage of provision, holding the Vichy regime responsible for the dearth of potatoes and other staple foods. Two issues called for militant action by housewives, in the form of demonstrations at the local *préfecture* where it was claimed vast stocks of provisions were hoarded.[25] Calls for protests by women against the Chantiers de la jeunesse also appeared in *L'Humanité de la femme*, though the organ of the party's youth, *L'Avant-Garde*, carried the most detailed indictments of this aspect of the Vichy programme. A special issue in the spring of 1941 listed six deaths at the Camp Bayard in the Hautes-Alpes and referred to forced marching, epidemics, and hunger in Camp Bayard, in group No. 3 in the Jura, No. 4

[22] Ibid., no. 82 (17 Nov. 1940); (6 Mar. 1941).

[23] *L'Humanité* (édition de Clermont), 12 Apr. 1941; ibid. (édition du Gard), 18 Apr. 1941; *Le Semeur* (Organe régional du Parti Communiste) [n.d.].

[24] *L'Humanité de la femme* (Dec. 1940).

[25] Ibid. (Dec. 1940 and Mar. 1941).

at Cormatin, and No. 9 in the Isère. By unity, *L'Avant-Garde* concluded, 'we can achieve the suppression of the Chantiers which are not getting France back to work, but which are organized unemployment with its attendant misery and despair'.[26] A further issue in June holds the camps responsible for military preparations to throw French youth into the war to defend imperial interests in Syria and East Africa, and calls on the inmates of the camps to fight against the government. The call is completed by a line of music in the treble clef 'Vive la vie, vive la joie, vive l'amour', the song of the Soviet youth, 'la plus heureuse du monde'.[27]

The policy which *L'Avant-Garde* opposed to the Vichy youth programme was based on an extension of basic educational opportunities, together with a system of technical schools in which a trade would be taught and from which employment would be assured. This technical apprenticeship would replace the Chantiers de la jeunesse, and in the earlier schooling there would be no religious education, the private religious schools would be abolished, and grants would be made freely available for any child needing financial help.[28] The emphasis in this programme on technical, industrial training contrasted not only with the rural location of the Chantiers, but with the entire bias of the Vichy mentality towards agriculture, the peasantry, and the countryside. But the P.C.F. did not merely abandon the peasantry to Vichy and concentrate on the towns. Special editions of *L'Humanité des paysans* called on peasants to be worthy of their ancestors of 1789, by fighting against the requisitions, the forced contracts, and the controlled production of Vichy. 'The collectors of the Gabelle tax have returned', claimed the first number in December 1940, but in this case the requisitions were not held to be a purely Vichy affair, as was the dearth of provisions by *L'Humanité de la femme*, but were described as requisitions 'pour l'étranger'. Vichy is represented as 'agents working for the colonizers of France', paying 400 million francs every day to

[26] *L'Avant-Garde*, no. spécial des Chantiers de la jeunesse (édité par la Fédération des jeunesses communistes), Apr. 1941. Cf. *L'Humanité* (zone sud), no. 82 (17 Nov. 1940), which carried the first claim that the camps were 'killing young people'.

[27] *L'Avant-Garde*, no. spécial des Chantiers. no. 3 (June 1941).

[28] *L'Avant-Garde* (zone sud), 12 Jan. 1941.

the 'invader' while refusing indemnities to the French peasant.[29] A subsequent edition for the Corrèze headed 'Ceux de la terre' continued the peasants' cause against Vichy 'oppression', mentioning in particular the constant inspections to control the peasants' marketing and the regular investigations into holdings of wheat, potatoes, wood, and poultry. Quite as much as government economic controls, the communist peasants resented the discrimination against them during the hunting season. As food rationing began to take effect, hunting permits were jealously sought and guarded. The prefect had the right to refuse a permit to anyone who could be deemed a threat to security and order, under which all Communists, as members of an illegal organization, were instantly included. At the end of October 1940 in the area of Lunel in the *département* of the Hérault numerous posters appeared protesting at this discrimination. Ten arrests followed.[30]

The communist attacks on the National Revolution in the southern zone belong primarily to the period October 1940 to May 1941. There is little doubt that Vichy legislation and policy in this period intensified communist opposition, though, as we have seen, open conflict with Vichy existed before the full details of the National Revolution became known. In May 1941, and particularly after the German invasion of Russia on 22 June 1941, the emphasis in the communist Press was transferred to the wider conflict of the war and protests purely against Vichy's internal policy become less frequent, the link with German policy and Nazism being consistently and forcefully made, where before June 1941 it was made only occasionally and less explicitly.[31] What is clear is that the P.C.F. overtly supported exactly the kind of party politics repudiated by Vichy and that it did so by propaganda and organization both before and after June 1941. It was a central confrontation between two incompatible systems in which the Communists responded item for item to the specific innovations of Vichy. The legislation and institutions of the National Revolution provoked a coherent articulation of communist

[29] *L'Humanité des paysans* (Dec. 1940); cf. the publication of the same period *Le Parti a 20 ans*, in which indemnities were demanded in detail for all peasants adversely affected by the events of 1940 (p. 57).

[30] Bouladou, 'Contribution à l'étude de l'histoire de la Résistance', p. 54.

[31] See Ch. VI below.

attitudes, so that by May 1941 the P.C.F. had a more integrated position than at any time since August 1939.[32] In respect of the Communists Vichy policy achieved the opposite of its intentions: it led to an actual increase in party-political activity.

The P.C.F. was the party most heavily persecuted by Vichy, but in the eyes of Vichy supporters the Socialist Party was, if anything, more symptomatic of the Third Republic, mainly because its leader Léon Blum had been Premier of the Popular Front Government in 1936, when, according to official Vichy history, the decline of France had sharply accelerated, He was also a Jew, and, on 10 July 1940, was one of the thirty-six Socialists among the eighty politicians who voted against full powers for Pétain. Ostensibly for his political part in the events leading to war and defeat, he was arrested on 15 September 1940 and imprisoned first at Chazeron and then at Bourassol where he was held to await trial at the nearby town of Riom with others accused of responsibility for the disaster.[33] His arrest, like the sectarian legislation of the National Revolution, was in the logic of the situation. Blum had been the object of both vilification and attempted assassination by the Action Française in the 1930s and he was an obvious scapegoat demanded by the nationalist supporters of Vichy to right the wrongs of the previous decade and to place the blame for the defeat beyond Reynaud and Daladier on to the Popular Front. Compared with his standing in 1936 he was an isolated figure after the vote of 10 July, for the vast majority of his party had defied his leadership and voted in favour of Pétain, while his former associates in the Popular Front elections, the Communist Party, had few qualms about his fate, for he had been in the forefront of those who called for harsh measures against the P.C.F. after the Nazi–Soviet pact.[34]

But Blum's arrest, along with other socialist leaders, together with the purge of socialists from local councils and *mairies*, the attack on Jews, and the dissolution of Freemasonry to which fourteen out of the thirty-six socialist voters on 10 July belonged, meant that the minority Socialists of July 1940 stood as no less

[32] This position was also expressed in trade union terms. See below, pp. 108–12.

[33] The details of his arrest and imprisonment are given in Blum's memoirs: *L'Œuvre de Léon Blum 1940–45* (Albin Michel, 1955), pp. 129–219.

[34] He himself felt his isolation keenly. (See ibid., pp. 98–9, 129–31.)

victimized than the Communists, with equal motivation for Resistance on the internal level alone, regardless of their individual attitudes to the war. These thirty-six provided the basis for party continuity, it being agreed by Blum, Marx Dormoy, and others of the minority that the party could not be reconstructed across the divide of 10 July. In the three months that followed the vote this agreement was crystallized by visits to each other's homes: Marx Dormoy at Montluçon, Léon Blum at Colomiers near Toulouse, Jules Moch in Toulouse itself, André Blumel in Antibes, Félix Gouin in Marseille, Édouard Froment near Val-des-Bains, Léon Martin in Grenoble, and Lucien Hussel at Vienne. The minimal survival of the party assured by these contacts under the eye of the Vichy police was strengthened and promoted by the activity of other socialist militants who were neither deputies nor senators and therefore less under observation. Throughout the autumn and winter of 1940 Henri Ribière, the close assistant of Marx Dormoy in the Allier, travelled between Bordeaux, Paris, and Moulins, where he was temporarily attached to the *mairie*, and across the southern zone, compiling lists of Socialists who were in agreement with the thirty-six, a political test which could easily be applied to any member of the party. Daniel Mayer, a journalist on the party paper *Le Populaire* which had been evacuated to Clermont-Ferrand and had ceased publication after an attempt by the majority of 10 July to refloat it, engaged himself in the same activity as Ribière.[35] With his wife Cletta, he kept in touch with Léon Blum and Marx Dormoy and with their agreement began to salvage what was left of the party organization. A third militant with the same incentive was Suzanne Buisson, Secretary-General of the women's organization within the Socialist Party, who had contacted Léon Blum from Sète and worked closely with Daniel Mayer and the deputy André Blumel in the regional search for a viable party basis.

The tight, if limited, liaisons established by these various initiatives suggest that the concept of party allegiance was still of importance among Socialists. The memoirs of Léon Blum and Daniel Mayer substantiate this but those of J.-Pierre Bloch, Socialist Deputy for the Aisne, are ambiguous in this

[35] Daniel Mayer, *Les Socialistes dans la Résistance* (P.U.F., 1968), p. 11.

respect. An artillery officer in the Battle of France, he had been taken prisoner, had escaped via Nancy, and had crossed the demarcation line to his home at Villamblard in the Dordogne, too late to take part in the vote of 10 July. 'My party', he wrote ,'offered me no hope. In one nearby village, the socialist schoolteacher, a supporter of Paul Faure, flirted with the most notorious members of Action Française'.[36] In fact, he continued, party politics were no longer of any meaning, yet, in contrast to this, he records that in November 1940 the Socialist Party in the person of Daniel Mayer visited him at Villamblard and that Mayer had thrown himself fully into the reconstitution of the party. At the end of December Bloch and Mayer visited Félix Gouin in Marseille, but *en route* he found that 'most of the party had cautiously retired into their shells'.[37] The ambiguity continues, for in 1941 Bloch became one of the activists in creating the Comité d'action socialiste (C.A.S.) which proclaimed itself as the official extension of the Socialist Party in the fight against Vichy and the German Occupation.[38]

The story of the creation of the C.A.S. in the occupied zone at the end of 1940 and in the southern zone through meetings in March 1941 at Nîmes, at Lyon in May, and most conclusively at Toulouse in June, has been told by Daniel Mayer, whose contribution was as central as any. Among other details he draws attention to the significance of local party members in Toulouse in making the meeting of June a success. [39] These members stood in a minority to the socialist notables in the town and *département* who, with the exception of Vincent Auriol, had voted for Pétain on 10 July or had endorsed the consequences of that vote, and their conflict with a passive, *attentiste* socialist majority can be paralleled elsewhere in the southern zone. In the Basses-Alpes Jean Vial records that the revocation of Freemasons, Socialists, and Jews from public offices in 1941

[36] Bloch, *Mes jours heureux*, p. 99. Paul Faure, Secretary-General of the Socialist Party, had been deputy leader of the party under Léon Blum. A lifelong pacifist, he supported all the moves for peace in the late 1930s and had broken with Blum over this issue. In 1940 he supported the Vichy Government and was an adviser to Pierre Laval .

[37] Ibid., p. 100.

[38] Bloch goes on to state that when he finally reached London in 1942 he greatly surprised de Gaulle by saying that in the Dordogne Resisters grouped together according to political affinity (ibid., p. 269).

[39] Their names are listed by Daniel Mayer (op. cit., p. 36).

led to a regrouping of socialist militants around the person of Louis Martin-Bret, and he notes that one of their activities which made the group aware of both its tightness and its isolation was the distribution of copies of Léon Blum's speeches at his trial in Riom. The reproduction involved was costly and known republicans in the *département* were approached for contributions. Some, Vial wrote, were enthusiastic but many others 'replied in a cowardly manner, alluding to the firing squad and the madness of the enterprise.'[40] At Montélimar in the Drôme a group of Socialists met at the home of Charles Bertrand at the end of 1940 but remained a small, isolated group throughout 1941.[41] At Albertville in the Savoie the abbé Ploton credits the Socialist Party in the person of Monsieur Gaudin, assistant mayor revoked by Vichy, with 'the honour of having first gathered together a number of volunteers in 1940',[42] and in the Corrèze at Tulle a Socialist, Martial Brigouleix, formed a group in 1940 with the specific intention of defying the socialist deputies of the *département*, all three of whom had voted for Pétain on 10 July.[43]

Compared to the party ostracism inflicted locally on most of these dissidents, the experience of socialist opponents to Vichy in Grenoble and the Allier was considerably less isolated. Although in the Allier only one of the four socialist deputies, Isidore Thivrier, had voted against Pétain, he had the support of the local socialist senator Marx Dormoy, a figure of stature in the party who had been Minister of the Interior in 1936 and 1938, had taken action against the right-wing and Fascist leagues, and had opposed the growing pacifism in the party both nationally and locally.[44] Dormoy's vote against Pétain on 10 July and his strong personal influence over those who worked with him were enough to give confidence to Henri

[40] Jean Vial, *Un de l'Armée secrète bas-alpine* (Imprimerie Villard, Marseille, 1947), pp. 18, 23.

[41] Alban Vistel, MS. on the origins of Resistance in ten *départements* of the south-east, p. 644, kindly made available by the author in typed form, since published as *La Nuit sans ombre. Histoire des mouvements unis de Résistance, leur rôle dans la libération du Sud-Est* (Fayard, 1970). Further references below to the unpublished manuscript are given as Alban Vistel, MS. on origins of Resistance.

[42] Romain Ploton, *Quatre années de Résistance à Albertville* (Ploton, Albertville, 1946), p. 16.

[43] Chateau, 'Contribution à l'étude du maquis corrézien', p. 31.

[44] Cf. Viple, *Sociologie politique de l'Allier*, p. 70.

Ribière, Daniel and Cletta Mayer, René Ribière, and Georges Rougeron in the *département*, even though his own attitude to events was strangely fatalistic. Asked by Daniel Mayer for instructions on 26 July 1940 he replied, 'In a year I shall be a minister or I shall be shot.'[45] In September he was arrested but his colleagues in the Allier continued to provide much of the initiative for the reorganization of the party.[46] The situation in Grenoble was comparable. Here Dr. Léon Martin, one of the socialist thirty-six, kept much of the working population faithful to the Third Republic. Together with René Gosse, the Dean of the Faculty of Sciences, whose socialism derived from Jean Jaurès, he was largely responsible for the conviction held at Vichy that Grenoble was the centre of anti-government propaganda.[47]

The problem for the historian is to know just how far the motivation of any or all of these Socialists who opposed Vichy in 1940 was due to political reaction to Vichy's internal policy and how far to a more personal reaction to the defeat and the Armistice. The obvious answer and one given orally by Albin Tixador, an early socialist Resister in Montpellier, is that the two were indivisible or at least not mutually exclusive.[48] René Gosse, for example, did not hide the fact that he was a Socialist when he said to his students at the start of the academic year in 1940, 'You must acknowledge only one cause, the Liberation of France'.[49] But the answer should not obscure the fact that Socialists at the time were themselves worried about the relationship between party politics and the wider opposition to Vichy and the Occupation. They were particularly conscious of the fact that Communists in 1940 were being accused of putting their party before the national interest, and did not want to gain the same reputation. For that reason many of their statements at the time and their memoirs since have stressed the acceptable 'patriotic' motivation and played down the less acceptable one of party politics. Daniel Mayer's memoirs

[45] Mayer, p. 12.

[46] Cf. G. Rougeron, *Le Mouvement socialiste en Bourbonnais 1875–1944* (Éditions du Beffroi, Vichy, 1946), and *La Résistance dans le département de l'Allier.*

[47] See above, p. 75.

[48] Evidence from Albin Tixador.

[49] Gosse, *Chronique*, p. 333. René Gosse was revoked as Dean on 6 December 1940, though he remained a Professor.

were something of a corrective to this in so far as his detailed descriptions of the way in which the C.A.S. was created show the determination of socialist opponents to Vichy in 1940–1 to band together not just locally but nationally to keep the Socialist Party alive as a political movement. This determination was at its strongest in the period when the National Revolution was elaborated and the image of Vichy as anti-republican firmly established. In 1941–2, with the events of the war and collaboration growing in significance, the emphasis on party continuity through the Comité d'action socialiste was replaced by a wider stress on socialist Resisters, meaning Socialists not just from the Socialist Party but from the two trade union movements, the Confédération générale du travail (C.G.T.) and the Confédération française des travailleurs chrétiens (C.F.T.C.) and from individual socialists with no party or trade union allegiance. This wider grouping was established within the movements of Libération-Nord in the occupied zone and Libération-Sud in the south, and in joining these movements the Socialists of the C.A.S. made the conscious decision not to keep themselves separate as a Resistance organization.

The decision was made possible and easy in the southern zone by the socialist sympathies of Emmanuel d'Astier, whose ideas of a 'Dernière Colonne' to continue the struggle against the Germans took more concrete shape during 1941 and led to the first number of *Libération* in July, published from Clermont-Ferrand.[50] D'Astier had secured the confidence of Léon Jouhaux, and Jouhaux's assistant as Secretary-General of the C.G.T. was Georges Buisson, husband of Suzanne Buisson. The link between d'Astier and the C.A.S. was therefore both ideological and personal and the integration of Socialists into Libération was rapidly recommended to socialist opponents in the southern zone. Of those individuals we have mentioned, Gaudin in Albertville, Édouard Froment in the Ardèche, Charles Bertrand and his group at Montélimar, Georges Rougeron and René Ribière in the Allier all moved into Libération, but there was nothing automatic about the move. Martial Brigouleix in the Corrèze, René Gosse and Léon Martin in Grenoble, Martin-Bret in the Basses-Alpes, and Albin Tixador in Montpellier all rallied to different movements,

[50] See below, pp. 137-8.

though this did not necessarily indicate a rival preference, more normally the accidents of early Resistance contacts.

As a counter to this dispersion of socialist activity, the Comité d'action socialiste was strengthened by the outrage at the assassination of Marx Dormoy and the revival of republican sympathies during the trial of Léon Blum. Marx Dormoy's arrest came shortly after Léon Blum's in September 1940, and he was interned with Jules Moch and Vincent Auriol at Pellevoisin in the Indre. In February 1941 Darlan, Vice-Premier of the Vichy Government, removed them, confining Auriol to his house at Muret south of Toulouse, and sending Dormoy to house arrest at Montélimar, away from his area of regional influence in the Allier. Five months later he was murdered there by members either of Doriot's P.P.F. or of the old Cagoule, both organizations having pre-war reasons for revenge against Dormoy, who, as Minister of the Interior, had removed Doriot from his position as Mayor of Saint-Denis and had prosecuted the Cagoule. The fact that the assassination occurred exactly a year after Dormoy's fatalistic statement to Daniel Mayer gave it added emotional effect. Protests to Pétain and Darlan incriminating Pierre Pucheu, the Vichy Minister of Interior, as an accessory to the murder, came from most leading Socialists, headed by Félix Gouin, one of the lawyers preparing the defence of Léon Blum. Vichy did nothing. The incident was technically regretted, that was all. Its main consequence was to give the newly formed C.A.S. its first martyr, to reinforce the political conflict between the Socialists and Vichy, and to reanimate the fundamental conflict of ideologies which had polarized France in the 1930s. The Riom trial accentuated this still further.

The confrontation between Léon Blum and Vichy at Riom is one of the strangest events in the history of the Occupation, illustrating the peculiarity of the southern zone, with its unpredictable mixture of authoritarianism and freedom. No such opportunity for rhetorical debate could possibly have been given to a defendant in the occupied zone and yet Blum was condemned before he even appeared. In August he had been warned by Henri Ribière that he was likely to be arrested and, like Auriol, Jules Moch, and Marx Dormoy, he did nothing to avoid it. Once transferred to Bourassol to await his trial he settled down to write his memoirs and was allowed visits from socialist colleagues, visits which played a significant role in the elaboration of the C.A.S.[51] Throughout 1941 the High Court prepared its dossier against the three main defendants, Blum, Daladier, and Gamelin, but in the autumn Pétain and the Vichy Government grew tired of the delay and created a special 'Conseil de justice politique' which suggested, without any judicial hearings, that the three were guilty of betraying France in the pre-war period and should be given life-imprisonment. Pétain accepted this 'verdict' and announced on the radio on 16 October that he was implementing these sentences. The trial at Riom was, however, to continue, and it was expected by Pétain that its verdict would surpass that of the Conseil de justice politique in its severity. 'The sentence which will close the Riom trial must be given openly. It will condemn individuals, but also . . . the [republican] regime itself. There will be no appeal. There will be no further discussion. It will mark the end of one of the most tragic periods in the life of France.'[52] As a result of this 'verdict before the trial' Blum, Daladier, and Gamelin were incarcerated at Portalet in the Pyrénées and were only brought back to Bourassol when the Riom trial finally opened on 20 February 1942.

The terms of Blum's indictment expressed the intention of the trial. He was accused of having instigated the forty-hour week, having created a secretariat for sport and leisure and paid holidays, having allowed strikes and the occupation of factories, having disorganized production by nationalizing the arms industries, and having tolerated extremist propaganda against rearmament. The entire trial was conducted on this level of polemic against the Popular Front, with the rationale that the Popular Front Government was mainly responsible for French unpreparedness for war.[53] Blum had no difficulty in

[51] Mayer, pp. 22–5.

[52] Philippe Pétain, *Les Paroles et les écrits du Maréchal Pétain*, message of 16 Oct. 1941.

[53] Originally in 1940 it was presumed that the Riom trial would hold pre-war leaders responsible for *causing* the war. This was what the Germans expected. In the event the High Court of Justice during 1941 altered the basis of accusation, charging Blum, Daladier, Gamelin, Guy la Chambre (Air Minister 1938–9), and Jacomet (General Secretary at the Ministry of War 1938–9) for failures in the preparation for war. When this became clear in February 1942 the German authorities began their pressure for closing the trial.

refuting this, and the spectacle of Blum, and to a lesser extent Daladier, gradually turning the accusation against Pétain who had been Minister of War before the Popular Front and had reduced expenditure on arms, and against Laval, one of Blum's predecessors as Premier, became the only talking point of those who were allowed to attend at Riom. Under pressure from the Germans and in defence of the Vichy image both in France and abroad, Pétain intervened again, this time to suspend the trial on 11 April, though with characteristic obstinacy he insisted that the investigations should continue. Blum was returned to Bourassol and a month later the Socialist Party organ *Le Populaire* appeared as a clandestine paper, a sign of strengthened party confidence, the clearest result of Vichy's most disfunctional act of propaganda.[54]

Sub-titled 'Organe central du parti socialiste (S.F.I.O.)' and numbered 'Nouvelle série, no. 1, 26e année', the first issue of *Le Populaire* announced that it might soon be the great daily paper of the 'Fourth Republic'. It listed socialist deaths at the hands of Vichy, called on Socialists to regroup themselves, and mentioned the heroism of the English and the Russians against Germany. It ended with the slogan 'La Patrie et la liberté'. This balance between the call to party politics and the call to liberate France was forcefully tipped towards the latter by the second number on 15 June, which was twice as large as the first and was printed where the first had been stencilled. It contained a manifesto from the C.A.S. stating, 'The Comité d'Action socialiste is not the old party. Several of the old militants have betrayed the party: many others have taken refuge since June–July 1940 in a cowardly abstention. By contrast numerous Frenchmen who had never joined its ranks are now working within the C.A.S. in the task of purging the party to bring about the rejuvenation and renovation that are necessary'. The C.A.S., it went on, has fought from the very first against the men of Vichy and it 'remains the resolute enemy of the capitalist regime . . . but in

[54] Vichy's handling of the whole affair had also drawn continued criticism from the Fascist collaborators in Paris. On 2 February *Les Nouveaux Temps*, directed by Jean Luchaire, wrote, 'We will never regret enough that today's accused were not tried in twenty-four hours over a year ago, and were not put in front of a firing-squad and buried deep in a forest somewhere.'

France today all activity in the interests of Socialism is subordinated to the liberation of the country'. As a result the C.A.S. promised co-operation with all Resistance groups including the Communists, adding the hope that after liberation Russia would become democratic, and that relations between the various working-class parties would improve.[55] There was nothing here that could be called narrow party politics, nor in the numbers that followed, though an awareness of the paper's political origins is never absent. In no. 3 the C.A.S. states its pride in having been among the first to shake the public out of its torpor by distributing tracts in July 1941, stating simply '14 juillet 1941, Liberté, Égalité, Fraternité, Vive la République', tracts which, wrote Daniel Mayer, he received from Emmanuel d'Astier and spent a night posting all over Marseille with his wife and Gaston Defferre.[56] The message could have been relevant at any period of internal threat to republican France and to that extent it spoke for the civil-war situation between Vichy and the French Left. In the light of the Occupation it spoke for more. The Socialist Party neither succeeded, nor even attempted, to keep the two separate, but it would be missing the plurality of Resistance motivation if the element of party loyalty to the thirty-six voters of 10 July, to Dormoy, to Blum, and to all socialist victims of Vichy legislation was ignored. Vichy set out to destroy the record and reputation of the Popular Front and with it to destroy its major constituent party. In so doing it provoked the opposition of those Socialists who felt threatened or victimized and thus created political conflict.

With the forces of organized labour, Vichy's role in producing conflict and opposition was similar. There was the same move from a much-proclaimed unity to the reality of division that marked Vichy's political history. From the start Vichy declared itself hostile to elements of capitalism, particularly the power of money and the growth of large cartels and trusts which were seen as alien to the workshop tradition in French industry. This degree of anticapitalism was not just paper rhetoric, for in the first Vichy Government René Belin, former Assistant Secretary-General of the C.G.T., accepted the posts of Minister

[55] *Le Populaire*, N.S. no. 2 (15 June 1942).
[56] Ibid. N.S. no. 3 (15 July 1942); Mayer, pp. 30–1.

of Labour and Minister of Industrial Production. Before the war Belin had been the leading influence among pacifist trade-unionists who grouped round the journal *Syndicats*, and, according to his own statement, had seen French trade-unionism alternatively 'under anarchist and Stalinist influence' degenerate into powerlessness and irrelevance by the end of the 1930s.[57] His aim in joining the Vichy Government was to produce a new form of trade-unionism based on the principles of unity and co-operation within industry, rejecting both the doctrines of class struggle and the political motivation of the Communists. He had good reason to believe that he was not totally isolated among trade union leaders in this aim. The C.G.T. had expelled its communist members after the Nazi–Soviet pact and in the first two months of the Vichy Government there were statements emanating from the trade unions at a national level suggesting co-operation between workers and employers and a reassessment of the place of unions within the state.[58] These statements alone are a testimony to the disarray of public opinion after the defeat, and an indication that some sympathy for national reconciliation under Pétain extended into the organized labour movement. It is difficult to imagine how Pétain or his ministers might have held on to that sympathy, but it is clear that with every project on labour relations after the summer of 1940 the goodwill was progressively dissipated. On 16 August 1940 a law prepared by Belin dissolved both workers' and employers' unions at the national level, and set up Comités d'organisation in each branch of commerce and industry. It quickly became apparent that the only losers by this law were the trade unions, for the committees were monopolized by the employers with the more than tacit agreement of Belin who was ultimately responsible for their composition. Again according to his own statement, he had every intention of regulating this by a more permanent settlement of labour relations which was promised in the law of

[57] *Le Gouvernement de Vichy 1940–42*, pp. 195–7.

[58] E.g. on 20 July 1940 a meeting of the National Federal Committee of the C.G.T. at Toulouse adopted a text which suggested that trade unions could be incorporated in a new structure of workers and employers, 'c'est-à-dire le syndicat libre dans la profession organisée'. The meeting was under-represented but not unrepresentative of the views of the C.G.T. leadership in the immediate crisis of defeat (ibid., pp. 158–9).

August.[59] Such a settlement was not finally produced until October 1941 in the *Charte du travail*, by which time the long period of interference with union activity had substantially undermined the possibility of labour co-operation.

The dissolution of the unions had been enacted without the consent or consultation of either the C.G.T. or the C.F.T.C. and it occasioned the first collective opposition of labour. On 21 August a rigorous letter protesting at the measure was sent to Pétain by Jules Zirnheld, President of the C.F.T.C., and on 15 November a combination of trade union leaders from both the C.G.T. and the C.F.T.C. published a *Manifeste du syndicalisme français* from Paris. It was the result of deliberations in a 'Comité d'études économiques et syndicales' which had been formed between the two national confederations after the law of 16 August and it was signed by three ex-C.F.T.C. and nine ex-C.G.T. leaders. Though its intention was to inquire into the possible role of unions in the new situation, it made it initially clear that no rejection of trade union history was acceptable. As for the present, the signatories refused to accept any union organization which was unfree or not democratically structured. They also rejected any accusation that trade-unionism was responsible for the present crisis. All the blame for the defeat is directed against the financiers and the international trusts who 'are more responsible for the defeat of our country than any politician, however inept and incapable he might have been'. As to relations with the state, the manifesto accepted that the state had an economic role, but maintained that this role must not be confused with that of the unions, nor must the two functions be compounded. To this extent, it claimed, the suppression of the national union bodies was an error. Finally, French trade-unionism was proclaimed as a movement opposing any attack, including anti-Semitism and religious persecution, on the dignity of the human person, and founded on the principle of liberty, including the liberty to choose which trade union to belong to, or not to belong to any. Compared to these clear affirmations of trade union principle the only discernible concessions to the crisis of 1940 were an omission of any specific reference to the class struggle, a rele-

[59] Ibid., pp. 195 ff.

gation of the question of strikes to a marginal reference, and an admission that the unions had become too involved with party politics, though this latter point was more a restatement of trade union purity dating from the *Charte d'Amiens* of 1906 than a gesture towards Vichy.[60]

From the southern zone Léon Jouhaux, General Secretary of the C.G.T. since 1912, had been in touch with the Comité d'études, and the manifesto spoke clearly for trade union opponents of Vichy across both zones, though it did not attempt to represent the Communists. After the Nazi–Soviet pact, the Communists, whose unions had merged with the C.G.T. only three years before, were subjected to the same punitive exclusion from organized labour as from parliamentary politics. In reply, the party Press attacked Léon Jouhaux and other C.G.T. leaders in the same language as they used against Léon Blum and the Socialists. By December 1940 *La Vie ouvrière*, the communist trade union paper, had its own clandestine edition in the southern zone but the problem for the party was to know whether Communists should attempt to reconstruct their old union organization, the Confédération générale du travail unitaire C.G.T.U., whether to attempt to rejoin those unions from which they had been expelled, or whether they should join the labour organizations proposed by Vichy. There was an anomaly here which made the whole union scene extremely confusing, not just the communist side of it. According to the law of 16 August the national confederations had been dissolved but the local unions were still legal. This was clarified by a circular from Belin and Peyrouton, Minister of the Interior, on 23 December 1940 to all prefects and Inspectors of Labour. All existing unions not expressly banned by government decree, it said, are legal and meetings of their executive councils can be allowed. 'On the other hand, the creation of any new grouping should be met with the greatest suspicion. . . . In particular you must prevent the reconstitution of all groups under communist direction . . . as well as preventing communists from taking over other existing groupings. All workers and employers must confine their activity to their professional area.

[60] The text of the manifesto is reproduced in several places, e.g. Henri Michel and Boris Mirkine-Guetzévitch, *Les Idées politiques et sociales de la Résistance* (P.U.F., 1954).

All political activity is rigorously forbidden . . .'.[61] Local unions were therefore still a permitted area of activity, though because they were legal they could be interpreted as a Vichy device for dividing the working class. In certain regions in the southern zone, particularly Lyon, Saint-Étienne, and Clermont-Ferrand, the Communists had a strong union base and despite the ban by the C.G.T. and the measures of the Vichy police the continuation of communist unions in these areas was a feasibility. In December 1940 one local edition of *La Vie ouvrière* gave specific instructions to its readers to make this potential a reality. Appearing in the Puy-de-Dôme, its heading was 'Tous au Syndicat' and the article which followed explained that it was necessary for people to overcome the natural repugnance at the way the unions had been taken over by Vichy sympathizers and the fact that Communists had been driven out, and to return to the unions as the only means of proletarian defence. The figures of the Syndicat de produits chimiques at Clermont-Ferrand are given as falling from 11,000 to 100 and the paper clearly feels that this had weakened the workers' position. It therefore repeats its call for all workers to join a trade union, and adds 'unity against the employers and the criminal government of Vichy'.[62]

No such clear guidance was given by *La Vie ouvrière* in its main edition for the southern zone, though it is arguable that for reasons of secrecy it kept its advice as general as possible. In its opening issue dated 15 December 1940 it calls for workers' unity against René Belin, against unemployment, and against the inflated cost of living, a unity to be achieved, 'immediately, at all costs, and in all forms, under the flag of June 1936'.[63] The number of 15 January 1941 was no more specific, while that of April was concerned with an attack on the Révolution nationale as anti-proletarian, and a warning that the leaders of the C.G.T., including Jouhaux and Vivier-Merle, had agreed to the co-operation between classes after the 1940 defeat as they had done in 1914–18. In May there was a repeated call to 'Enter the unions' without further detail and on 15 June a paean

[61] *Circulaire de la Ministère de la Production Industrielle et du Travail*, 23 Dec. 1940 (Archives de l'Union Syndicale du Bâtiment C.G.T. Rhône).

[62] *La Vie ouvrière* (Organe de défense des travailleurs, édition Puy-de-Dôme), Dec. 1940.

[63] *La Vie ouvrière* (zone sud), 15 Dec. 1940.

to June 1936 with the conclusion that the triumph of united labour at that date could be repeated in the present crisis, created by the 'Fascist *coup d'état* achieved by Pétain and his crew with the aid of Hitler'. There then followed the paper's first news of union struggles in the southern zone, unspecified action by railwaymen at Oullins and by the steel-workers at Trévoux.

From *La Terre*, a communist publication addressed to the peasant community, there is a hint that the 'Comités populaires' announced by the party in the summer of 1940 were a possible buttress or camouflage for the proscribed communist unions. In May 1941 its first number in the southern zone called on 'peasant comrades' to unite in the 'local trade union' and then specified 'go into your village and join your comrade in arms, the worker, the artisan, and the small trader, within the Comité populaire'.[64] But the second number setting out the demands of the peasants for a freer market, for loans and indemnities against loss, and for the suppression of all state inquisition into peasant life, made the call for unity in traditional union terms, 'Organize yourselves in your agricultural trade unions and your co-operatives. Demand general assemblies to discuss in freedom your claims and to elect democratically the leaders of your organizations which should be run by the peasants and not under orders from the Vichy clique of adventurers.'[65]

Both *La Terre* and *La Vie ouvrière* declared their communist derivation, but other clandestine papers representing union opinion which emerged in 1940–1 kept more rigorously to the old trade union independence from party politics, so that it is difficult to know whether communist party members were or were not involved in their publication. From railway-workers and miners came *La Tribune des cheminots* and *La Tribune des mineurs*, both carrying a strong call for revived trade union activity, with the miners' paper appearing in at least two local editions by mid-1941. They contained no more detailed instructions than *La Vie ouvrière* but the mounting anger of labour against the economic exploitation of a crisis economy and against the discrimination of Vichy policies is more pungently expressed than in the official communist paper. The first number of the railway-workers' paper appeared in De-

[64] *La Terre* (Organe de défense paysanne), no. 1 (May 1941).
[65] *La Terre*, no. 2 (May 1941).

cember 1940, denounced Vichy repression, and gave a list of workers imprisoned at Bourges, Valence, and Puy, mostly names of union leaders of 1936.[66] There followed a series of issues in the first half of 1941 listing the railway-workers' demands, rejecting the worker appointed by Vichy to act as their representative, and claiming, in May, small, unspecified concessions by the railway authorities after union pressure. The same paper carried one of the first references to the projected *Charte du travail*, promised since August 1940 by Belin and the Vichy Government to regulate every aspect of labour relations. The railway-workers rejected it totally as a complete violation of trade union rights and an attempt to undermine national action by splitting them into separate categories of employment.[67] The miners of the Loire and the Gard both ran a *Tribune des mineurs* in the second half of 1941, with an intensity of economic and social demands which virtually excluded the international situation, even though Russia was by now at war with Germany. The July number from the Loire was given entirely to protest following a number of fatal pit accidents at Saint-Louis and the imprisonment of five miners who had refused to work until safety was improved. It called for a massive campaign of solidarity for the victimized workers through the union, not just to pressurize the government but also to enlighten the population of Saint-Étienne.[68] It could be that this issue was drawn up before the invasion of Russia, accounting for the absence of any reference to it, but in the Gard as late as March 1942 *La Voix des mineurs* was no less preoccupied with the internal struggle, giving details of government persecution which had led to the death of a worker Vital in a French concentration camp, and claiming, as throughout 1941, a minimum rise in wages of 20 frs a day, an increase in rations, trade union liberty, and the release of militants imprisoned by Vichy.[69] An earlier publication in November 1941 condemning

[66] Sémard, Tournemaine at Bourges; Midol, Benoist, Mocquet at Valence; Demusois, Prot at Puy.

[67] *La Tribune des cheminots*, no. 4 (May 1941): one of the few clandestine papers which carried a price—75 centimes (dropped in August 1941).

[68] *La Tribune des mineurs* (Organe de défense des mineurs du bassin de la Loire), July 1941.

[69] *La Voix des mineurs* (Organe de défense des revendications des mineurs et similaires du Gard), Mar. 1942. It is possible that this number is wrongly dated.

the *Charte du travail* which was announced in October was also entirely concerned with trade union activity against Vichy though the number that followed shortly after contained a confident article on the Red Army and the headline 'Il nous faut passer à l'action.'[70]

None of these trade union papers mentioned the P.C.F. or the party's conflict with Vichy, though the imprisonment of militant unionists by first the Daladier and then the Vichy Governments gave the political and the trade union sides of French Communism a common experience. What the publications show is that militants in the unions still had their separate voice, provoked into increasingly virulent opposition by the intention and effects of Vichy's labour policy, though the difficulties of creating viable union organizations to translate words into action have been stressed by several workers of the time. M. Pavoux, a railway-worker in Lyon, and Albert Solié, a metal worker from Béziers in the Hérault, have both said that the main problem in 1940–1 was convincing fellow workers that *any* kind of union activity was either necessary or desirable,[71] and the constant exhortations in the union Press to create or return to the unions reflect this. Unlike the occupied zone there was no outstanding strike action to give a lead. In the Nord and Pas-de-Calais the textile and miners' strikes of May 1941 were a catalyst in opposition to both the employers and the German Occupation and a vital affirmation of local communist resistance. There was nothing parallel in the southern zone. Militant trade-unionists, like militant Communists and Socialists in the political sphere, were in a minority among their own colleagues, but Vichy policy towards labour ensured that union opposition was widespread even if fragmented. There is some evidence from Béziers that workers in union positions were less fragmented than those in politics. The traditional separation of trade unions from the political parties meant that communist workers on the factory-floor felt less affected by the party's tribulations after the Nazi–Soviet pact and consequently less divided from their fellow workers.[72] The fact that they were technically

[70] *La Tribune des mineurs*, no. 1 (Nov. 1941); no. 2 (Nov. 1941).
[71] Evidence from M. Pavoux and Albert Solié.
[72] Evidence from Frédéric Montagné and Albert Solié.

banned from the C.G.T. was less significant after 16 August 1940 because from then on the C.G.T. itself was illegal. Local organizations became the only source of activity and to that extent Communists who were strong in the local branch of a union could survive the various acts of exclusion and persecution more easily, keeping the confidence of other workers who were not in favour of the Nazi–Soviet pact yet who respected the trade union strength and experience of their communist colleagues.

For those from the C.G.T. and C.F.T.C. who *were* represented by the November manifesto the dissolution of the national confederations had provided a growth point for opposition, but it could only be exploited at local level and as a result it was individual militants or union branches rather than federated unions who responded to Vichy provocation. This diffusion of protest was similar to that within the Socialist Party and the links between the two were not accidental. In the two months following the defeat Léon Jouhaux was living at Sète with Georges and Suzanne Buisson, Georges Buisson being his assistant in the office of General Secretary to the C.G.T. He was therefore closely involved with the initiatives taken by Suzanne Buisson in contacting the dissidents of the Socialist Party. This involvement continued after the Buissons moved to Lyon in the autumn, where a job had been arranged for Georges Buisson by the C.G.T. Secretary for the Rhône, Vivier-Merle, who, from the moment the C.G.T. was dissolved, started to organize local union opposition to Vichy. The new home of the Buissons in Lyon rapidly became the meeting-place for both socialist and trade union groups, the latter embracing individual militants of the dissolved C.F.T.C. like Marcel Poimbœuf, whose understanding with Vivier-Merle made Lyon a centre of inter-union solidarity—the point of maximum agreement being their hostility to a single union structure under state authority, known to be the object of Belin's labour policy and advocated in moral and ideological terms by Pétain's speeches. It was at Lyon that leaders of the dissolved C.F.T.C. in the southern zone convoked a Regional Liaison Committee in October 1940 to act as a substitute for the old Confederation, and the mark of its widely based hostility to the Vichy programme was the replacement of the

Confederation Secretary Jean Pérès by Marcel Poimbœuf in the spring of 1941, on the basis that Pérès was too compromised with the Vichy administration. In so far as any generalization is possible this action was representative of most branches of the C.F.T.C. in the southern zone and had been anticipated in certain areas like the Savoie where Lucien Rose set up a Collège syndical de formation ouvrière at Chambéry in September 1940 as a cover for union protests against Vichy,[73] and Toulouse where the C.F.T.C. metal workers signified their rupture with Pérès some months before his dismissal.[74] In Toulouse the inter-union situation was similar to that in Lyon, a microcosm of the co-operation expressed in the November manifesto. On 15 December a motion by the Syndicat chrétien des travailleurs de la métallurgie was adopted by the dissolved C.F.T.C. unions in the Haute-Garonne, making it clear that any move towards monolithic state unions would be entirely the individual worker's responsibility.[75] Collective union support went to the anti-Vichy position of Jean Brodier and Paul Vignaux, who had been meeting locally with Julien Forgues, Léo Hamon, and Pierre Bertaux from the dissolved C.G.T. with the knowledge and approval of Léon Jouhaux in the southern zone and Christian Pineau in the occupied zone. In July 1941 Pineau made a tour of union opponents of Vichy in the southern zone, visiting Jouhaux at Sète and Vivier-Merle and Poimbœuf at Lyon, and during this visit links were strengthened between Socialists, trade-unionists, and the movement of Libération in the two zones.[76] A month later Léon Jouhaux met Emmanuel d'Astier, leader of Libération-Sud, and agreed that trade-unionists should be encouraged to join the movement, and the fourth issue of *Libération* in December 1941 carried an 'Appeal to workers' written by Jouhaux, though not signed, arguing that trade-unionism must be free, that Vichy's *Charte du travail* was meaningless, and that only by expelling the invader would union liberties be

[73] André Mollard, *La Résistance en Savoie 1940–44* (Mollard, Chambéry, 1972), p. 16.

[74] Gérard Adam, *La C.F.T.C. 1940–58* (Colin, 1964), p. 20.

[75] Ibid., p. 20.

[76] In the occupied zone Libération—Nord was organized principally by Pineau from the C.G.T. and by Lacoste, Texcier, and Henri Ribière, all from the Socialist Party.

recovered.[77] From this number the paper carried regular articles on 'Workers' Resistance' throughout 1942, and in the movement itself the links were extended and strengthened by the activity of Yvon Morandat, the dissolved C.F.T.C. Secretary-General for the Savoie, who had joined de Gaulle in England after fighting in the Norwegian campaign and was parachuted into France in November 1941 to make contact between the Free French and the labour opposition in the southern zone. After meeting d'Astier in December he quickly became an active leader of Libération, working on the paper, and travelling to the main centres of union Resistance. In Toulouse, Marseille, Clermont-Ferrand, Lyon, and Montluçon he found inter-union groups, solid in their opposition to Vichy and related through individuals to the socialist Resisters in the C.A.S. His own position in Libération in the next few months was vital in giving this socialist and union opposition a tighter organization, and the money he brought from the Free French allowed him to subsidize the clandestine Press, *Libération* in the first instance and *Le Populaire* in April and May 1942.[78]

The publication of the *Charte du travail* in October 1941 was the climax of Vichy's contribution to this growing opposition within the southern zone. The *Charte* established a system of single, compulsory unions within each profession for each of the five categories of personnel, employers, manual workers, white-collar workers, middle management, and technical staff. These unions had no power to strike or conduct collective bargaining and they had no national federated structure. Workers unionized in the railways, for example, could therefore have no official relationship with workers in the iron and steel industry or any other 'famille professionnelle'. Still further, the questions of labour relations, wage structures, insurance, and unemployment were entirely given to special 'Comités sociaux', the main pillar of corporatist thinking, which were to be established in each profession and would be composed of all sides of industry, with the ostensible object of ending the class war and the real effect of isolating the forces of labour which

[77] *Libération*, no. 4 (Dec. 1941).

[78] Morandat's record of this period is given in Henri Noguères, assisted by M. Degliame-Fouché, and J.-L. Vigier, *Histoire de la Résistance en France de 1940 à 1945* (Laffont, 1969), ii. 205–7, 272, 274, 451–3.

would be overwhelmed by the combined representatives of employers and management. Compared with these social committees, the unions were no more than ciphers, harnessing trade union experience to the national enterprise. 'La paix sociale est le but suprême', said the preamble to the *Charte*, dedicated as it was to the realization of Pétain's 'spiritual aspiration' for France, but what followed made it clear that Vichy's idea of social peace was based on the total elimination of the worker's collective power and independence. The arrest of Léon Jouhaux on 26 December at Marseille made it finally impossible for Vichy to hide this underlying purpose.[79]

The *Charte du travail* had been fifteen months in gestation, during which time trade union opposition, both communist and non-communist, both C.G.T. and C.F.T.C., had developed to a point where, most historians agree, Vichy had no chance whatever of realizing its programme. The *Charte* was little more than a fantasy. But it was not just the delay which allowed this opposition to grow. The Vichy programme itself, announced on 16 August 1940, expanded in Pétain's speech to workers at Saint-Étienne on 1 May 1941, and expressed most forcefully in the persecution of union militants, actively provoked and promoted opposition, though the potential unity of this labour Resistance was not fully apparent while the Communists and Socialists were at the lowest point in their relationship since the 1920s. The Nazi–Soviet pact which the P.C.F. had endorsed, and the suppression of the Communist Party and Press, which the Socialists had encouraged, added violent antipathy to the tension created by divisions of policy since 1936. No statement expressed this more forcefully than the attack on Dormoy published by *L'Humanité de l'Allier* in October 1940 at the moment of his arrest. In outspoken language it held him responsible with Blum and Paul Faure for the collapse of the Popular Front, and accused him of joining the bourgeoisie in its action against the Communist Party, in its suppression of *L'Humanité* and the imprisonment of Communists. His arrest is labelled as a clever and transparent manœuvre by the bourgeoisie to raise his prestige.[80] Such a total attack on a leading Socialist was not the norm in the communist Press, but,

[79] The point was made forcibly in *Libération*, no. 5 (20 Jan. 1942).
[80] *L'Humanité de l'Allier*, no. 1 (1 Oct. 1940).

together with the polemic against Léon Blum which was more frequent, it conveys in accurate terms the extent of the hostility between the P.C.F. and the Socialist Party at the time, But the P.C.F. tempered its rejection of the socialist leaders with appeals to the socialist rank and file, recalling party policy in 1934 shortly before the Popular Front. The attack on Dormoy ended with a call to Socialists not to be duped but to join the pressure for a 'government of the people',[81] while *L'Humanité* (zone sud) in December carried a report on four arrests at Bourganeuf in the Creuse, one of which, it stated, involved the local secretary of the Socialist Party, thus drawing readers' attention to the fact that Socialists were also involved in anti-government activities. 'Let us unite', it ended, 'to liberate all victims of the repression.'[82] In February 1941 in the Basses-Pyrénées a local communist paper prophesied an even broader front against Vichy as a result of the National Revolution and Vichy's collaboration. It concluded its news item on further imprisonments by quoting Pétain's speech of 1 January 1941 which promised that he would recognize 'no parties and no classes in France' and then commented, 'Yet today he imprisons the Communists, tomorrow the Socialists, and after that the republicans.'[83]

The suggestion in this local paper is that Vichy itself was responsible for producing the common ground on which left-wing solidarity would be based, and although nothing was more important in achieving this solidarity than the major *external* event of 1941, the entry of Russia into the war, the paper was shrewd in its assessment of the importance of *internal* events in the development of left-wing opposition. There was no rebirth of the Popular Front in 1940–2 but undoubtedly one major result of Vichy legislation and persecution was to lay the basis for a Popular Front mentality among left-wing and labour forces. A still more significant result was to reproduce the classic division of France into those who put the values of the individual first and those who extolled the values of the state, and this can be examined separately.[84] But before that,

[81] Ibid.

[82] *L'Humanité* (zone sud), no. 88 (26 Dec. 1940).

[83] *L'Étincelle des Basses-Pyrénées et Landes* (Organe régional du P.C.F.), 10 Feb. 1941.

[84] See Ch. VII below.

the growing effects of the Occupation and the war must be considered, for the dynamics of opposition in Vichy France demand that the two aspects, anti-Vichy and anti-German, be kept in a state of permanent interconnection.

VI. Reactions to the War

INTERWOVEN with Vichy's claim to be above politics was its claim to have rescued France from the nightmare of defeat and chaos and to have achieved the best settlement that could have been hoped for through the Armistice. They were similar claims, both creating an image of wise and paternal care without the bias of *parti pris*. *Attentisme* was the equivalent in external affairs of apoliticism at home. It was also equally misleading. Just as the logic of Vichy's political ideas led to sectarianism in legislation, so the commitment to the Armistice and peace led inexorably to more and more compromising diplomacy with the Germans. The National Revolution provided increasing motivation for opposition, so too did this growing relationship between Vichy and the Germans.

It was opportunity as much as ideology which brought right-wing politics and collaboration together in Vichy. The National Revolution was an authoritarian programme which used the opportunity afforded by a defeated France, while collaboration was mainly an opportunistic policy in the wake of defeat which could only have been carried through by an authoritarian government. The association of the two would have been unthinkable in the first twenty years of the century when the nationalist Right was fervently anti-German; it became more feasible in the 1930s when the links between nationalism and Fascism were developed and it finally became an actuality in 1940—41. It did so clumsily and unsuccessfully, alienating the more determined Fascists in Paris, most of whom settled into a scornful rejection of Vichy for its paternalism, and losing the support of many nationalists who rejected its collaboration with the traditional enemy. Vichy therefore became a special case, *sui generis*, compounded of uncertainties and inconsistencies and failing to carry with it many of those whose attitudes it appeared to incorporate. If anything its main support lay among those who were not particularly political, had no particular ideology, and had no particular feeling about the war. Those who were strongly political, strongly ideological, or strongly committed to a certain view of the war produced for different reasons a large number of opponents, whose opposition grew and thrived on Vichy's stumbling progress towards a more defined and involved position than the one it initially held in 1940.

Among many of those who had rejected the Armistice in 1940 and envisaged a continuation of the war effort there was a confusion about the direction of Vichy's foreign policy, which lasted for well over a year. During that time there was a tendency to look to events in the war outside France for justification and stimulus, and to use these events in an attempt to recreate a commitment to the war. But to most of the French in the southern zone the war seemed more a matter of the past than the present and the absence of Germans gave the news from the occupied zone an air of unreality. The rhythm of life which resumed after the *exode* and after the demobilization of the army seemed to most of the population to be as near normal as could be expected. Even food shortages and rationing, the main subject of everyday conversation in the winter of 1940–1 were discomforts more to be assimilated than resented. This relative contentment was underlined by the propaganda of Vichy, so that the problem for the opponents of the Armistice was to formulate a counter-propaganda which would reawaken the urgency of the war without recreating the anxieties of the defeat and *exode* from which Vichy had so obviously benefited.

The formula developed by General Cochet was to combine news of the war, which Vichy censored from the public Press, with a high degree of optimism to match the kind of confidence radiated by Pétain, in fact to use Pétain as if he were, without question, identified with the alternative views put forward. Inevitably this involved an element of strain and by May 1941 Cochet's *Tour d'horizon* was finding it increasingly difficult to rescue Pétain from the consequences of Vichy policy. On 15 May Pétain made a short authoritarian broadcast to proclaim his support for the meetings between Hitler and Admiral Darlan, Vice-Premier of Vichy, held in Germany at the Führer's invitation. In this speech he called for unquestioning obedience from the French people. 'If public opinion is uneasy it is because it is badly informed. There is no longer any justification for it to judge our actions, calculate our chances, or measure the risks we run. You, the French people, must follow me on the paths of honour and national interest without any second thoughts.'[1] Cochet's reaction was to point out that if the French were badly informed it was due entirely to official censorship. Blind confidence in Pétain, he stated, was impossible after such a speech, but that was not to say Pétain had betrayed his trust. 'We are sure', he wrote, 'that the Marshal is only waiting for an assertion of the people's will and discipline to drive out the traitors and reassume his total independence.'[2] An element of doubt was there but it was the Vichy Government, not Cochet himself, who confirmed it, by arresting the General and confining him in a requisitioned property near Val-des-Bains with Paul Reynaud, Georges Mandel, and others, shortly to be joined by Colonel Groussard who was arrested on 16 July.

The isolated groups of Cochet's supporters who had come into existence out of a common optimism in the events of the war and who kept together as a distribution network for his *Tour d'horizon* tended to break up after his arrest, and the individuals comprising them made contact with other groupings. Henri Noguères in his *Histoire de la Résistance en France* has collected a great deal of oral and written evidence testifying to the influence and importance of General Cochet, none more fervent that that of Serge Ascher, a young student at the École Polytechnique evacuated to Lyon. Ascher began distributing *Tour d'horizon* in early 1941 with its optimistic interpretation of the war in Yugoslavia, Greece, the Atlantic, and North Africa. 'Cochet', he remarked, 'was frequently wrong about the Germans who were moving from victory to victory but that was of little importance beside the fact that he nurtured among us a confidence in the ultimate victory of the Allies.'[3]

Cochet's optimism about events abroad and his careful avoidance of too much controversy at home were paralleled by Henri Frenay who by early 1941 decided that some form of publication was necessary to speed recruitment for his grand design of a secret army and intelligence network to cover the whole of France. The approach he chose was similar to that of

[1] *Les Paroles et les écrits du Maréchal Pétain*, speech of 15 May 1941, p. 167.
[2] *Tour d'horizon*, no. 129 (16 May 1941).
[3] Noguères, i. 303.

Tour d'horizon only more carefully and widely researched, and in February his first *Bulletin d'information et propagande* was typed in collaboration with Bertie Albrecht and a former military colleague, Captain Robert Guédon, who had sustained serious injuries in Holland during the German offensive and who had ideas close to Frenay's for an intelligence service in the occupied zone.[4] From the moment of his personal manifesto in July 1940 Frenay had called his projected organization Mouvement de libération nationale (M.L.N.), but there was no disclosure of this fact on the news-sheet, nor any suggestion that a structured movement of opposition was either contemplated or desired. The *Bulletin* was a factual presentation in catalogue form of events in the war and in the occupied zone, taken from BBC broadcasts, Frenay's contacts in the German section of the 2e Bureau in Lyon and from the *Tribune de Genève*, a source openly acknowledged in the *Bulletins* and one which was relatively accessible in Lyon.[5] An air of optimistic belligerence was contained in the quotation from Napoleon which stood at the head of several issues, 'Vivre dans la défaite c'est mourir tous les jours', as also in the repeated call which concluded the items of news, 'France, France, libère-toi'. The fate of Alsace-Lorraine was a frequent subject and the other internal emphases were on the suspicious policy of Darlan, the collaboration of Doriot and others in Paris, and the bleeding of French industries by the Occupation. There was no hint of political enmity towards Vichy nor a mention of the National Revolution.

Typical of the comment and intention of the *Bulletin* was the issue of 13 May 1941 which gave a brief résumé of the war since September 1939 pointing out that Hitler had failed to win the two most decisive battles, that of the Atlantic and that of the Mediterranean, and for this reason the French had every reason to be hopeful. 'The German victory curve is at its highest point. We are now about to watch its steady decline.

[4] The origins of Frenay's publications and his initial contacts are clearly presented in Granet and Michel, *Combat*, pp. 28–68. Cf. also Frenay's own memoirs, *La Nuit finira*, pp. 29–65.

[5] Cf. Duhamel, *Le Journal d'un Français moyen*, p. 189. Arriving in Lyon in April 1941 from the Dordogne the first thing Duhamel noted was the ease with which reliable reports on the war were available there in the Swiss Press.

Let us prepare for that radiant day when France will resume charge of its own destiny. This has been written on 11 May, Joan of Arc's birthday, and we interpret that as a symbol, a symbol of deliverance.'[6]

No surprised reader of the *Bulletin*, discovering it inserted into an illustrated magazine such as *Signal* or *Marie-Claire*, would have doubted the strong anti-Germanism of the authors, nor the serious quality of the news. Most aspects of the war were covered including one of the doctrinal manifestations of Nazism, 'the odious creation' of breeding camps in Alsace where by forced mating the 'best specimens of the Aryan race are to be produced'.[7] The news-sheet's conclusions about Vichy policy were not clear, however, and to this extent the avoidance of internal controversy left the *Bulletin* with a rather distant, academic flavour, providing only fragmented answers to the problem of how far to trust the Vichy Government or to believe in the integrity of Marshal Pétain. There was nothing dishonest here: the lack of a clear line reflected the ambiguity within the attitudes of Henri Frenay himself and his shifting expectations of Vichy in the period after Montoire. The dismissal of Laval on 13 December was widely interpreted as a firm stand by Pétain against concessionary negotiations with Germany, but it did not have the sequel that the optimists had hoped for. Flandin succeeded Laval but resigned within two months, and his successor, Admiral Darlan, looked for a diplomatic relationship with Germany and was no less prepared than Laval to offer working collaboration on terms to be progressively negotiated.[8] Frenay had close contacts at Vichy, he knew the disarray of attitudes within the various institutions, and also knew the degree of anti-Germanism among many Vichy officials. He therefore had some reason to speculate on an eventual clash between Pétain and Darlan on the question of collaboration, and even to hope that Vichy might unofficially give a free hand to publications such as the *Bulletin* if it refrained from attacking Pétain in person. There was a complex series of hypotheses to work through in this situation, and the

[6] *Bulletin d'information et de propagande* (13 May 1941).

[7] Ibid. (6 May 1941).

[8] Admiral Darlan was Deputy Prime Minister and Minister of Foreign Affairs from 10 February 1941 to 17 April 1942.

Bulletin, followed by its sequel *Les Petites Ailes* in June, shows the calculations at work.

After Pétain's speech confirming his support for Darlan, to which Cochet had replied in his *Tour d'horizon*, the *Bulletin* made similar observations. Public opinion will not be reassured, it stated, not least because one of the so-called advantages proclaimed by Darlan as the result of a close relationship with Germany was already largely a fiction: instead of the 100,000 prisoners of war returned by Germany as stated in the official Press only some 43,000 had been released, totalling no more than 2 per cent of all prisoners of war. Doubt about the bargains available from negotiations with Germany 'is at the very least permitted', the article concluded. As for Pétain, 'we wish to believe that such a great soldier will be able to keep the negotiations, to quote his own phrase, on the path of national honour, without alienating or diminishing the sovereignty of France'.[9] There was no call here for all negotiations with Germany to cease, but rather a scepticism about their outcome and a certain reserve of judgement. This was not the case shortly after in mid-June when *Les Petites Ailes* gave one of its eleven pages to a discussion on collaboration, arguing that true collaboration was always two-way and voluntary, whereas Darlan's version did not have this quality. 'Let us remove this word from our vocabulary. Under its deceptive cover Germany is merely exercising the will of the strongest. . . . For Germany collaboration is colonization.'[10] But this was not the last word, for the next issue, treating the problems in the annexed province of Lorraine, maintained that the facts on the government's negotiations to protect large numbers of Lorrainers from expulsion were too obscure to allow a conclusion. A letter from General Doyen to von Stülpnagel within the Armistice Commission is published, containing official protests against expulsions, and the paper cautiously states, 'We wish to refrain from emotional positions and remain objective.' Two pages later Pétain's 'opposition to further concessions to Germany' is again mentioned, so that the issue of Vichy policy *vis-à-vis* Germany is still largely unresolved. Frenay's publications up to this point were as clear as they could be that no concessions

[9] *Bulletin d'information et de propagande* (27 May 1941).

[10] *Les Petites Ailes* (Journal hebdomadaire. Tirage de zone libre), 10 June 1941.

to Germany were acceptable, but taken as alternative news media to the official Press they did not give a fully alternative picture of what Vichy was doing.

Exposing Vichy policy was clearly not Frenay's first consideration. Foremost in his intentions was the exposure of Germany and the events of the war. In this the papers of his Mouvement de libération nationale were the most consistent and detailed available anywhere in the southern zone. He started with the belief that to be better informed was already half-way to being committed to the liberation of France, but gradually this was balanced by a realization that the inertia of the southern zone was heavily weighted against him. 'Our leader', ran an article at the beginning of July 1941,

> has just returned from a journey to the occupied zone, full of admiration for the progress being made there . . . where our colleagues, united by a common ideal, are working with a faith and a devotion which are already bringing great results. . . . Alas! Returning to the free zone, the tragic and profound difference between those two parts of France can at once be measured. Here there is no energy, no nobility, only an apathetic fatalism often covering a despicable cowardice. The majority of those in the free zone remain indifferent to external events and the future of France. Their main preoccupation is how to get food, and anxiety over this dominates people's minds.[11]

This realization changed much of the tone of *Les Petites Ailes*. From an assumption that news carried its own power of persuasion, the paper turned to a more argumentative style, confronting public opinion with its own obstinacy and concluding news articles with phrases such as 'This is *not* exaggerated' and 'You *must* realize . . .' Warning the southern zone against complacency, it stated, 'Frenchmen of the so-called "free" zone, do you insist on being less perceptive than your compatriots across the line, just because you are suffering less?'[12]

This forthright challenge was more emotional than the earlier numbers of the paper, bringing it closer in style to the paper which Frenay was most interested in, the clandestine *Liberté*

[11] *Les Petites Ailes* (1 July 1941).
[12] Ibid. (30 July 1941).

which, by mid-1941, was confident enough to be giving the kind of instructions on what to think and how to act that neither the *Bulletin* nor *Les Petites Ailes* attempted. In other respects the paper from Marseille, produced by the group including François de Menthon, Pierre-Henri Teitgen, Rémy Roure, and Paul Coste-Floret, had several points in common with the publications of Frenay's movement. It continued the sympathy towards Pétain displayed in its first number in November 1940,[13] and wrote about the war with the same optimism as the *Bulletin*.[14] It was less uncertain about the eventual outcome of Vichy's negotiations with Germany, although in the issue of 30 May 1941 it credited Vichy with good faith. In this issue it printed a document from Huntziger, French representative on the Armistice Commission, protesting to the Germans about various contraventions of the Armistice. The protest was dated September 1940, but the paper felt it was still relevant news eight months later and it concluded with the comment that 'The people's legitimate anxiety will be relieved by knowledge of this document', an assumption which was not totally in keeping with suspicions of Vichy policy voiced in both previous and subsequent numbers.

The first passage which marked *Liberté* as substantially different occurred in the same issue. Headed 'Instructions for Action', it claimed 'Our movement is growing' and called for the setting-up of small groups in all regions with one person responsible for each region, *département*, town, neighbourhood, and community. Warning was given not to move too quickly as this would attract German attention, and a final statement said 'Beware of double agents'. The aim of these instructions was, the paper said, to recreate national unity against the Germans, something that Vichy could not do since its hands were tied by the Occupiers.[15] The next issue a month later contained more detailed instructions including a list of specific things to do: 'Distribution of *Liberté*. Distribution of tracts. Preparation of demonstrations. Boycott of collaborationist

[13] See above, p. 31. The number of 5 February 1941 spoke of Pétain's 'résistance . . . aux exigences de Hitler et de Laval'.

[14] e.g. the issue of 30 May 1941 admitted the German successes in the Balkans but added that the Germans had lost the wider war in beginning it. The Anglo-Saxons would undoubtedly win and there was no cause for pessimism.

[15] *Liberté*, no. 6 (30 May 1941).

Press. Patriots must *not* read *L'Illustration* or *Gringoire*.'[16] These basic lessons in what was later taken for granted in any Resistance organization are a reminder of the novelty of clandestine activity, just as the uncertainty towards Vichy in the *Bulletin* and *Les Petites Ailes* is a reminder of the complexity of the period. People in the southern zone no more adopted a clandestine role as if it were a known activity than they moved into a simple and total opposition to Vichy. Naïvety in underground operations, like confusion in attitudes to Vichy, was common among dissidents of 1940–41. Only the Communists had both experience in clandestine activity and a position of total opposition to Vichy, their complexity, however, lying in their party's ambivalent attitude to the war, the issue on which the *Bulletin*, *Les Petites Ailes*, and *Liberté* showed no equivocation.

It is difficult to find precise evidence on the effect of these early clandestine news-sheets. There is much to suggest that distribution was more important than content and that extending a network of contacts was the major achievement of both *Les Petites Ailes* and *Liberté*.[17] What was actually written probably exercised the authors more than the readers, but this is not to say that the items of news could have been replaced by mere exhortation and polemic. Getting the facts right, filling the gaps in the Vichy Press, and countering the German propaganda which influenced cinema news-reels and radio broadcasts, were among the most powerful of all motivations to opposition and Resistance. The 'facts' of 1940, defeat, *exode*, Mers-el-Kébir, German 'correctness' of behaviour, the popularity of Pétain, had mostly told in Vichy's favour and thus in favour of the Armistice settlement. If a viable alternative to *attentisme* was to be developed, then facts which told against the Vichy settlement had to be found. Printing important news which Vichy ignored or refused to publish was a vital activity if the image of reasonableness and good sense was to be wrested from those who had accepted the Occupation and divisions of France. The *status quo* of 1940 had to be made to

[16] Ibid., no. 7 (30 June 1941)

[17] Writing about the later paper *Combat*, René Cerf-Ferrière acknowledged that what was written about the war and collaboration was important to Resisters but what really interested them was distribution as a means of recruitment. (*Chemin clandestin*, p. 78.) Oral evidence from many Resisters tends to confirm this opinion as a general one.

appear unnatural, irrational, and reversible if opposition was to appear normal, rational, and practical. The absurdity accredited to those who were in opposition had to be shifted on to those in power, and this could not be done by exhortation alone. Every new fact which undermined the propaganda of Germans, collaborators, and *attentistes* confirmed the Resisters in their opposition. News-sheets were a major way in which they gave a rationale to their actions. Only those who have forgotten the difficulties of 1940–1 would deny that such a slow and cumulative case for Resistance activity had to be made.

In making this case, Frenay's movement and Liberté were obviously dependent on developments in Vichy policy and in the war in the same way as those more involved with internal and political opposition were dependent on the developments in the National Revolution. On 22 June 1941 Hitler invaded Russia, the biggest event in the war since the Battle of Britain and one that had major repercussions on all forms of opposition within France. The invasion was not a complete surprise to those producing the news-sheets. Already in May, over a month before the invasion, General Cochet had stated that German victories in the Mediterranean and the Balkans would never be acceptable to Russia,[18] and the *Bulletin* had headlined a subsection of news, 'L'Attaque contre la Russie', relating German propaganda to the effect that Ukrainians were welcoming Germans as liberators.[19] On 20 May the paper quoted *Pravda*'s warning that the Russian army must be ready for all eventualities, and added that Russia seemed to anticipate a conflict with Germany.[20] There was no hint in either paper that such a conflict would help the opposition movements in France, and later in May the *Bulletin* gave a clear indication of how it regarded the Communists. In an article on the communist-led strikes in the Nord and Pas-de-Calais it acknowledged that the strikers were expressing a growing hatred of the Germans but it nevertheless regarded the strikes with suspicion if not hostility. The article was headed 'L'Occupation allemande et le danger communiste dans le Nord de la France' and it claimed that the 'violent communist movement' was

[18] *Tour d'horizon* (15 May 1941).
[19] *Bulletin d'information et de propagande* (6 May 1941).
[20] Ibid. (20 May 1941).

led by the 'same men as in 1936'. The strikes, it said, are directed against both the Germans and the employers, who are accused of eating much better than the workers and of being in collaboration with the Germans. 'In the event of the Germans evacuating this region', it concluded, 'a highly violent communist movement is to be feared.'[21] This was the most explicit comment of a political nature contained in the *Bulletin* during its four months of publication, and the anti-Communism of the M.L.N. which it revealed was still strongly present in the reaction of *Les Petites Ailes* to the German–Russian conflict when it finally broke out. On 1 July the paper stressed Hitler's duplicity in once more breaking a pact. 'Although we are delighted at this war which will exhaust two nations who are enemies of France, we must remember that we can have no confidence in Hitler.' Later in the issue the paper returned to the effects of the war and opposed the formation of a French division to fight with Germany against Russia. The reason it gave was that there was no danger from the Russian army. 'Germany, provisionally master of Europe, remains the only real danger at this moment.'[22] This coverage of the invasion was no more than a first reaction, for it was followed by an article of much greater length and prominence in the next issue. The attitude was still the same. Over six pages there was a summary of German–Soviet policy up to 1939, with the conclusion that 'hand in hand Nazi and communist propaganda have slowly undermined the morale of our country'. After 1939, it argued, Stalin relied on the duplicity of the Nazi-Soviet pact to seize the Baltic States, but became anxious when Germany began its victories in the Balkans. Now there is war between them, but 'one fact remains incontestable and of tangible importance. It is not the Red Army which occupies two-thirds of France, but the German army', and no intelligent Frenchmen will be taken in by Hitler's talk of a new crusade. 'France', it continued, 'has the rare opportunity to sit in the balcony and watch a superb combat between her two principal

[21] Ibid. (27 May 1941).

[22] *Les Petites Ailes* (1 July 1941). The French division referred to, the Légion des volontaires français contre le bolchevisme (L.V.F.), was initially recruited in the occupied zone, before being endorsed by the Vichy Government in the southern zone where it was known as the 'Légion tricolore.'

enemies. Her interest is in strict neutrality.' Finally on page twelve in a summary of the issue the paper concluded, 'France has no interest in the German–Soviet war. She neither wants nor favours the victory of either Germany or Russia. Her interest is obviously in a long war which will exhaust both the adversaries who, for different reasons, are both enemies of France.'[23]

The beginning of a retreat from this position of strict neutrality was signalled in the following issue. Churchill's speech of 22 June, the evening of the invasion, was reproduced with its distinction between tactical support for Russia and continuing hostility to Communism. The paper endorsed this distinction, and *Les Petites Ailes* fell into line with the British policy.[24] So too did *Liberté*, which reached the same point by a slightly different route. It published two long articles on the invasion of Russia, the first at the end of June with a particularly subtle piece of reasoning. 'What really delights us', it read, 'is that if Hitlerism commits suicide in this venture, official Bolshevism will also disappear', the argument being that if Russia wins, Stalin will be strong enough to get rid of the last remaining communist elements, and if Russia loses, the regime will be held responsible and will be repudiated. 'One could say, therefore, that M. Hitler is doing Europe a service. Without meaning to, of course.' Not that he should be helped, the article continued, since he is not fighting Bolshevism, but looking for corn and petrol. The conclusion is that he will not find them, because the Russians will destroy everything. 'The one thing that Communists are really good at is destruction.'[25] Nearly a month later the next issue of the paper disclaimed this article as 'not corresponding exactly to the ideas of the Central Executive on the subject'. There followed a more sympathetic article with the statement that 'one condition of our liberation is that the Russians should resist as long as possible' and the conclusion reiterated this: 'The Russian soldiers . . . are not defending a doctrine. They are defending their country, the land of their ancestors. Their resistance . . . contributes to the triumph of liberty and law over the imper-

[23] Ibid. (8 July 1941).
[24] Ibid. (16 July 1941).
[25] *Liberté*, no. 7 (30 June 1941).

ialism of Hitler and Mussolini. That's the real truth.'[26] This second article not only contained this sharp shift of emphasis but also an implicit realization that to be anti-communist after the invasion carried the risk of being seen as sympathetic to Germany. The Vichy Government, stated the paper, suddenly 'without protest allows Eugène Deloncle to raise a Legion in Paris to fight the Germans'. Why it asked, had Vichy become so hostile to Moscow at this point when Communists were no less of a danger a year ago? The question is asked rhetorically, and whatever the mistakes of the authors in imagining that Vichy's anti-Communism only began in June 1941, the implied answer is that Vichy policy towards the Communists and Moscow is a further sign of growing collaboration with Germany.[27]

The impact of the German invasion of Russia is worth extended analysis, partly because it is often presented as an event which affected only the communist position in France. Its importance in that respect is unquestionable, but seen through *Les Petites Ailes* and *Liberté* it is also a moment when the assumptions of these two movements are revealed. The invasion of Russia was one of those vital events in the war which gave both *Les Petites Ailes* and *Liberté* an opportunity to distinguish themselves radically from the official Press. *Les Petites Ailes* responded negatively on the whole, *Liberté* with contradictions but with a greater sense of the import of the event. Both rejected the idea of French volunteers to fight against Russia, which was an important departure from the Vichy Press, but neither saw the event as bringing the P.C.F. out of its isolation or showed any sign that this would be welcome. Despite the assertion in *Les Petites Ailes* that Hitler's involvement in Russia marked the beginning of the end of Germany,[28] the event clearly did not provide a great deal of encouragement to these papers, nor did it make them reconsider the value of communist opposition within Vichy France. The embryo organizations of Liberté and the M.L.N. derived their concepts of opposition from the conviction in 1940 that the Armistice was wrong and that the war effort should be continued by all

[26] Ibid., no. 8 (25 July 1941).
[27] Ibid.
[28] *Les Petites Ailes* (23 July 1941).

relevant methods. Political opposition to Vichy and hostility to Pétain were not considered relevant since neither movement had reached any certainty about the regime. The M.L.N. had started from a military position with the fundamental aim of producing a secret army and an intelligence network. Liberté, coming from a political and academic background, was more interested in ideas and propaganda than military initiatives. But neither movement had a subversive attitude to the political *status quo*, and because of their sympathy for Pétain they were doubtful about what kind of opposition they should encourage. For both movements the Communists were at best suspect and at worst anathema and in either case not the kind of opposition that Frenay or de Menthon had conceptualized. Even trade union and socialist opposition, if it stemmed from the internal situation rather than from commitment to the war, lay outside the concept and was included only if the political motivation was strictly subordinated to the non-political.

This distinction between two kinds of opposition was developed in the paper *Vérités* which the M.L.N. launched in the southern zone in August 1941 as the sequel to *Les Petites Ailes*. On 12 August Pétain had delivered a full statement of Vichy policy, both internal and external, in an attempt to cure the *malaise* which he saw growing among the French people. It reiterated many of the principles of the National Revolution and reaffirmed Pétain's confidence in the foreign policy of Admiral Darlan.[29] In an article headed 'Your opinion and ours', *Vérités* addressed itself to Pétain, and, without questioning his over-all intentions, found the internal policies of Vichy more or less acceptable but rejected the external statements as leading France further into collaboration. 'The interior difficulties met by the government', the article ran, 'have been courageously underlined by the Marshal. We are on his side when he attacks the power of money, Freemasonry, and bureaucracy . . .' The paper also lent its support to the suppression of political parties in the southern zone, with the reason given that it meant the disappearance of parties led by Colonel de la Rocque and Doriot, and the section on internal politics concluded, 'Without doubt, excellent interior reforms have

[29] *Les Paroles et les écrits du Maréchal Pétain*, message of 12 Aug. 1941, pp. 213–22.

been announced and we approve them, but the future of France will not be determined by these, however judicious they are. . . . Monsieur le Maréchal, we beg you, do you want French veterans to become the allies of the German army? If that's what you want say so! If you do *not* want it make it quite clear that you don't! You have understood that France needs a firm line. You must give it to us. . . .'[30] Even more forcibly on 5 September 1941 the paper made it clear that opposition to the Germans and the Occupation was one thing but political opposition to Vichy another. 'The French people must not be faced with the dilemma of being for the government and therefore for the Germans or against the Germans and therefore against the government. If the French are forced to choose we fear that since the majority of the country are anti-German they would by this logic become anti-government.'[31] Had the M.L.N. approved of such an indivisible opposition it would have responded to Hitler's invasion of Russia in a different way. As it was, neither this movement, nor to a lesser extent Liberté, saw anything to be gained from the German–Soviet conflict in terms of their own ideas of Resistance. It was an event in the war which gave grounds for optimism purely on the external basis that Germany now had one more front on which to fight.

For the Communist Party the invasion was anything but an external event. It was central to their day-to-day propaganda and activity within France and had immediate consequences on the scope of their opposition. This effect was more obvious in the official party Press than in the actions of various individuals and local groups, some of whom experienced little need to change the nature of their action. At the very least the invasion was a stimulus to existing anti-Germanism within the party, expressed as it had been in such major events as the textile and mining strikes in the Nord and Pas-de-Calais, and on numerous, if disconnected, occasions in the local Press of the southern zone.[32] At the most it changed the character of *L'Humanité*'s propaganda and directives to the extent that non-Communists have seen it as yet another volte-face, but

[30] *Vérités*, no. 9 (25 Aug. 1941).
[31] Ibid. (5 Sept. 1941).
[32] See Ch. III above.

a far more acceptable one than that of August–September 1939.[33]

In *L'Humanité* (zone sud) there was both continuity and change between the issues of May and June and those of July and August. Like *Tour d'horizon*, *Les Petites Ailes*, and *Liberté* the paper had reacted with considerable hostility to the negotiations between Darlan and Hitler, accusing Vichy of preparing an extension of the imperialist war, of throwing France into the arms of the Nazis, and of making France an even more inferior vassal of Germany. 'La collaboration c'est la nazification de la France', it stated on 10 May.[34] On the twenty-ninth it opposed any action by Vichy in defence of the French colonies:

> The 'reconquest' of the colonies will cast France once more into the wars to the profit of the rival imperialist powers. On one side fighting behind de Gaulle, agent of the City of London, and on the other behind Darlan, valet to Berlin, French soldiers are led to the slaughter for a cause which is not their own. Vichy is the grave-digger of the nation. The only patriots are the workers and peasants of France, heirs of the French Revolution and the Paris Commune.[35]

Two days later in another reference to patriotism the paper attacked Pétain's association with the Fête of Joan of Arc. 'How dare he do this! Joan of Arc put herself at the head of an army to drive out the invader. Compare Pétain!! Joan of Arc, a national heroine, was the victim of the forces of obscurantism to which the miserable Pétain is enslaved.'[36] In the same month therefore *Les Petites Ailes*, *Liberté*, and *L'Humanité* (zone sud) had all identified with Joan of Arc in the context of the latest moves linking Vichy and the occupying power,[37] but *L'Hu-*

[33] In July 1941 a socialist publication of the occupied zone called *Jaurès*, Organe des jeunesses et étudiants S.F.I.O., contained a long column attacking the Communists for their volte-face in 1939 in the light of their 'recent change of policy in June 1941'. If Stalin had allied himself to the democracies in 1939, the paper argued, Hitler could have been halted and the working classes would not have been 'so cruelly misled'. Criticisms in similar style have become a permanent part of non-communist history.

[34] *L'Humanité* (zone sud), no. 105 (10 May, 1941).

[35] Ibid., 29 May 1941.

[36] Ibid., no. 109 (31 May 1941).

[37] *Liberté* had carried a short statement on 11 May 1941 stressing the heroism of Joan of Arc against intrigue and treason and concluding that such heroism could occur again.

manité's opposition to Darlan's negotiations was not just directed against compromises with Germany, but was part of its rejection of any part in the European war. This was repeated on 20 June with further attacks on warmongers from the City of London and followers of 'Darlan-le-Nazi', but the headline on that date marked a new departure as well as an old emphasis, 'A bas la guerre impérialiste. Unissez-vous dans un large Front National pour l'indépendance du pays.'[38] The decision of the party to create a Front National to fight for French independence dated from May 1941, was mentioned in the northern *L'Humanité* on 9 June, and repeatedly stressed during the rest of the month before the invasion of Russia. No details of the Front were given nor any indication of how it would enlarge communist action, but the use of the word 'national' took it beyond the concept of the 'Front de la liberté, de l'indépendance et de la renaissance de la France' which had been announced in the late summer of 1940.[39] It coincided with the increase in anti-German action among Communists in the north and in Brittany during May, and crystallized the growing references to communist patriotism in the party Press. The Front National was a ready-made concept, already known to party members, on which to hinge the new policy after the invasion of Russia. In the southern zone the issues of 2 and 7 July carried *L'Humanité*'s reactions to the war, the first accusing Vichy of anti-Soviet policy and support for Hitler, and the second calling for a full-scale struggle by workers, peasants, civil servants, intellectuals, and all French people against the invader: 'Unite and refuse to serve Fascism.'[40] The full flavour of the new situation was contained in the issue a month later which carried the claim that '999 Frenchmen out of 1,000 are against the Occupier. All are friends of the U.S.S.R. and friends of those who, like England and the United States, are fighting the Hitlerian enemy.'[41] This marks one of the most significant shifts in party propaganda. From October 1939 to June 1941 the action of England had been labelled imperialist and subject to city finance: now it was

[38] *L'Humanité* (zone sud), no. 109 (20 June 1941).

[39] See above, p. 50.

[40] *L'Humanité* (zone sud), no. 111 (7 July 1941).

[41] Ibid., no. 114 (12 Aug. 1941). The headline of this issue read 'Tout pour la France. Tout contre Hitler et ses complices.'

endorsed as a genuine conflict with Nazism. With Russia in the war there was an immediate end to all references to 'the imperialist war' and the P.C.F. fell into line with the new international situation, accepting the need to support England despite its previous hostility to city finance. This bears some comparison with the way in which *Les Petites Ailes* and *Liberté* after June 1941 accepted the need to support Russia despite their hostility to Communism.

One obvious problem for the communist Press after June 1941 was how to refer, if at all, to the period *before* the invasion of Russia. For a party so historically conscious the question of continuity was raised in an acute form. The campaign against the imperialist war had still been at the forefront of party propaganda in mid-June, and little or no information on the state of the war had been given to communist readers. A sudden flood of information about the evils of Hitler's war and the course of German expansion would clearly raise the question 'If these were evils in July 1941, why were they not recognized as such in 1940?' One local edition of *L'Humanité* in August 1941 risked such a reaction when it wrote 'Those who pillage our land and our goods now are those who, a year ago, killed our sons and wives on the roads, who kept 1,800,000 Frenchmen as prisoners of war, who drove out the Alsace-Lorrainers and who annexed our provinces . . .'.[42]

But this kind of retrospective look at the events of the war was not a common one in the party Press. On the whole there was a discernible break in the language and content of the communist papers, with no attempt to put the policy of 1939–41 into any perspective or even to allude to it. It disappeared without a backward glance, though one local paper in the Cher, more realistic than most of the party Press in admitting the first defeats of the Red Army, used these defeats to justify previous Soviet policy, arguing that they were a substantial proof that Russia had not taken the offensive but 'had genuinely wanted peace'.[43] More typical in tone was *Le Travailleur alpin* which devoted a special issue to the invasion and, with forward-looking assertion, claimed that 'The formidable Red Army . . . has taken up the fight not just to defend the independence of

[42] *L'Humanité* (édition d'Agen), Aug. 1941.
[43] *L'Émancipateur du Cher* (Aug. 1941).

their own socialist country, but also to liberate the people of Europe from the Fascist and capitalist brigands.'[44] It was this kind of international messianism which dominated the party newspapers in the months after June 1941 and which contrasted most sharply with attitudes before the invasion. In other respects continuity posed no problems. The antipathy to all aspects of Vichy, the call for 'Comités populaires', the demand for a government of the people, and the historical references to previous periods of communist struggle, were all continuous elements of propaganda from 1940 to 1942. In the papers representing the trade unions it was often impossible to sense that anything fundamental had changed. Social and economic claims still predominated and the call to return to the unions was still the central rallying cry. To these were added the call to sabotage the transport of goods to Germany and a general appeal for the liberation of France, but the hard core of the papers consisted in the kind of trade-unionist arguments that had been developed well before June 1941.[45] It was of course important that the *Charte du travail* was enacted within a few months of the German invasion. Taken together the two events greatly escalated the labour opposition for which there was no need to find a new structure. Trade union activity, proscribed, harassed, and victimized since August 1940 or even earlier in respect of the Communists, was a form of Resistance which adapted to the new situation after June 1941 with an ease which suggested natural progression, even though it was still only a small minority of militants who were fully involved.

There was no other war event in 1941 comparable in its impact to the invasion of Russia, even if the effect of this event on the Communists was not registered as a step forward by such papers as *Les Petites Ailes*, *Vérités*, and *Liberté*. For Frenay's movement in particular the Communists remained a suspect if not hostile force. At the end of September *Vérités* carried a serious warning to the French people not to join the Front National offered by the Communists since the Communists have always 'worked for Moscow' and not for France. 'We do not want any sectarian politics, either of Left or Right. When

[44] *Le Travailleur alpin*, no. spécial (June 1941).

[45] Cf. *La Tribune des cheminots*, no. 3 (Nov. 1941); *La Vie ouvrière*, no. 33 (15 Sept. 1941); *La Tribune des mineurs* (Gard), no. 1 (Nov. 1941).

our country needed defending, Thorez deserted it and his propaganda joined that of Dr. Goebbels to demoralize the French. We shall not forget that. And now his tactic is to exploit French patriotism for the greater benefit of the Soviets.'[46]

In fact, for *Vérités* as already for *Liberté* the events of the war outside France were becoming of less and less value in priming the forces of opposition and by late 1941 it was clear that the combination of war information and optimism, established by Cochet's *Tour d'horizon* and Frenay's *Bulletin*, was being abandoned. With it eventually went the caution and ambiguity towards Vichy. From this period onwards the drive to expose the Vichy Government as inimical to French interests gains gradual ascendancy in all the opposition Press, registering the fact that Vichy's growing collaboration with Germany had become a provocation to Resistance, far stronger than anything else since the Armistice, and approached only by the provocation of the National Revolution with which it became identified. The realization that underground action against Germany involved a form of civil war against Vichy is the central development in Resistance history during 1941. It paralleled the development within the Communist Party which added war against Germany to civil war against Vichy. In both cases there had been individuals and groups who had anticipated the synthesis well before the middle of 1941 and who had been anti-German and anti-Vichy with equal vigour, but it was not until these groups became the norm among opposition movements that Resistance in the southern zone began to lose some of its bewildering complexity. In a zone where there were only a handful of Germans in each *chef-lieu*, it was vital to find a more accessible enemy. Increasingly from mid-1941 onwards Vichy came to fill this role, completely against its own intentions. Through its collaboration, Vichy itself was a major factor in bringing some coherence to a fragmented opposition, in provoking Resistance, and providing new motivation across an area where *attentisme* was still the reasoned position of the vast majority.

It was the first two numbers of *Libération* in the southern zone

[46] *Vérités* (25 Sept. 1941).

which firmly established the synonymity of Vichy and collaboration. Before that, *Liberté*, in November 1940, had accused Laval of a 'politique de collaboration' and in June 1941 had warned that if Darlan's negotiations brought France into any closer collaboration the country would be a totalitarian fief under German influence.[47] There had also been the discursive article on collaboration in *Les Petites Ailes*, already mentioned, which had rejected German collaboration as colonization.[48] But the paper started by Emmanuel d'Astier and his group in July 1941 went much further. It identified the day-to-day administration of Vichy with collaboration, and claimed that the ordinary process of business and agriculture was geared to the German war effort. Since June, and Darlan's negotiations, it declared, France had become the ally of Germany and was already envisaged as the bastion of Germany against an Anglo-American attack.[49] A month later the second number made it clear that *Libération* saw no distinction between Pétain and the rest of Vichy. 'For over a year he (Pétain) has staged the most grotesque and odious of comedies in this town of petty operas. He has dishonoured himself by infamous legislation, by the statute against the Jews, by concentration camps, by his snivelling Légion, and by all the filth in which he looks for his ministers, and into which he periodically rejects them.'[50] No paper outside the communist Press had carried such an unequivocal attack on Pétain, and *Libération*'s subversive approach to Vichy on all levels allowed it to propose a public charter of Resistance activity, going beyond the only comparable set of instructions issued by *Liberté* at the end of June.[51] In a list of points it called for: a boycott of the papers most under German influence, *Signal* and *Gringoire*, of all German films, and of all places used by the Germans; go-slow and sabotage in any industry and business working for the Germans; identification of collaborators by marking their houses with a swastika; reproduction and diffusion of all anti-Nazi and anti-collaborationist tracts; the celebration of the anniversary

[47] *Liberté*, no. 1 (25 Nov. 1940); ibid., no. 7 (30 June 1941).

[48] *Les Petites Ailes* (10 June 1941). See above, p. 123.

[49] *Libération* (Organe du Directoire des forces de libération francaises), no. 1 (July 1941).

[50] Ibid., no. 2 (Aug. 1941).

[51] See above, pp. 125–6.

of the victory of the Marne on 6 September by flags in the streets; and finally the diffusion of *Libération* itself.[52] The range of proposed activity was wide, but the main difference from *Liberté*'s instructions was that it did not suggest a structured organization for those who adopted the proposals. This was not an accidental omission. Not until late in 1941 did Libération in the southern zone begin to have a coherent structure, though its contacts particularly in the socialist and trade union circles were many. In August it was geared as much to provoking the resistance of anybody and everybody as to building an organized movement. It assumed at this point that the more people who protested against collaboration, the more effective the protest would be. To this extent it was openly indiscriminate in its appeal for support, it encouraged notions of civil resistance and industrial defiance and thus acknowledged the existence of a latent civil war in which all Frenchmen were involved.

In 1940–1 opponents of the Armistice had tried to enlighten the French people on facts and events which mostly lay outside their day-to-day lives. In 1941–2 opponents of Nazism and collaboration appealed increasingly to the people's own experience, within their immediate reach. *Libération* in August 1941 was in the forefront of this more tangible propaganda, which began to exploit rumours, emotions, and prejudices as well as the facts of the situation. In the second half of 1941 an increasing number of people began to react to rumours of a military alliance which Vichy was said to be planning with Germany, to rumours of official hoarding and discrimination in the allocation of goods and provisions, to the half-known facts of economic exploitation by Germany, and to the suspicions that Vichy police were helping German authorities in their acts of persecution. There was the official support given by Vichy to the Volunteer Legion raised in Paris to fight in Soviet Russia, the growing incidence of arrests in the southern zone, the dominance of German newsreels in the cinemas, and the Vichy broadcasts against 'terrorists', all of which gave substance to the rumours. Gradually the word 'collaboration' was becoming known and used as a derogatory term without the need for explanation. From a concept in diplomacy describing

[52] *Libération*, no. 2 (Aug. 1941).

co-operation with Germany it was beginning to be used in some circles to describe those who co-operated with Vichy, a far more subversive and disturbing usage for the southern zone.

This was the usage implied in *Libération*, and it carried with it a perspective which had not been developed outside the communist Press, a perspective of opposition as *total* opposition, of Resistance against Vichy as much as against Germany. This entailed planning for a new regime not just for the defeat of the Occupiers. The future of France, said the third number of *Libération*, is not yet defined but 'we want no more class privileges, no more social injustice, no more restrictive paternalism, just as we want no more disorder. We know only too well who provided the money for Hitler's success *and* for the Cagoule.'[53] The argument in this issue was that France had to fight for its own regeneration regardless of what any other country might do, and that in this fight the French were acting to protect universal values as well as national ones. If Frenay's aim of constructing an underground army to liberate France was grandiose, this was even more so, though far looser in conception. But it was an aim which faithfully represented a degree of anger against the *status quo* and idealism about the future, found in many individuals who opposed both Germany and Vichy. It gave Resistance a function of its own, almost separate from the war, and opened its possibilities to all categories and kinds of people. Secret operations against the Occupier risked being seen as a specialist enterprise, of a military nature, however unorthodox. But working for a new society was something from which no one was excluded for lack of skill or experience. It was a familiar, but in the circumstances uncharted enterprise involving the whole nation. 'It is only together and by working in common that we can save ourselves and hang on to our values.'[54] Finally in the language of *Libération* there was the implication that action against Vichy would be violent. In December two long articles accused Vichy of treason and elaborated the growth of collaboration under Darlan. The belligerence and provocation of these articles showed that the absence of Germans in the southern zone was no longer such

[53] *Libération*, no. 3 (Sept.–Oct. 1941).
[54] Ibid.

an inhibiting factor as it had been in the first year after the Armistice.[55]

The new voice of opposition heard in *Libération* between July and December 1941 contrasted strongly with the tone of *Liberté* and *Vérités*, though by the end of the year the difference was less marked. The most vigorous attack on Vichy mounted by *Vérités* was in October when it revealed that Darlan was negotiating the cession of naval bases in North Africa to Germany, but the paper still divorced Pétain from any responsibility. 'We hope that the Marshal will know how to defend the interests of the country against his ministers. But if the latter overrule him we invite all Frenchmen to show their shame and their anger by writing a letter to the Marshal and to Admiral Leahy.'[56] This was the nearest the paper came to a call for public action, though its extensive coverage of anti-German resistance in Poland, Czechoslovakia, and Greece carried a clear implication for France. There was also the news of the first assassinations of German soldiers in the occupied zone in Paris and Bordeaux during August and September, and in October the shooting of hostages in retaliation, twenty-seven at Châteaubriant and fifty at Bordeaux. The Vichy Government preferred to take part in the selection of the hostages rather than leave the process of retribution solely to the Germans and so became an immediate collaborator in the shooting of political prisoners, most of whom were Communists. In both zones posters declared that it was the 'Jewish–Marxist–plutocratic alliance' which lay behind the assassinations and on 21 September and 22 October Pétain broadcast against what he called the 'criminal acts' of the assassins.

The assassinations were not particularly popular,[57] but the shooting of hostages horrified people, and the failure of Vichy to protest was widely criticized. The communist Press led the denunciations, and the other clandestine papers expressed their own anger, but without mentioning the overt political

[55] *Libération*, no. 4 (Dec. 1941).

[56] *Vérités*, no. 15 (25 Oct. 1941).

[57] Charles Tillon, in *Les F.T.P.*, pp. 110–11, describes the reluctance among Communists in certain areas to accept the assassinations. Some militants called them 'individual acts' and at Nantes a party official went so far as to recommend that the assassin of a German officer should give himself up to prevent the shooting of hostages.

discrimination in the selection of the hostages. *Vérités* paid homage to the martyrdom of the hostages and attacked the Vichy Government for not having protested against the violation of justice and the Catholic Church for not having celebrated an official requiem for the dead. It reported that Pétain had sent a wreath to the most recent German victim at Nantes rather than to the French who were shot in reply.[58]

Liberté, always nearer to a complete break with Vichy than *Vérités*, contained a hint in its October issue that a campaign against Pétain might be necessary. It quoted Clemenceau's statement about the battle of Verdun that he had preferred the 'madness' of Foch, who had argued for the fight to continue, to the 'sanity' of Pétain who had said there was no hope, and on the back page it printed a letter to Pétain from a Professor Basdevant from the Faculté de Droit in Paris carrying his resignation in protest at the servility of Pétain's government towards the Germans. The German authorities, said the paper, were now very pro-Pétain due to Darlan's collaboration which had exceeded that of Laval.[59] Given Pétain's reputation as the 'victor of Verdun' which went unchallenged in public opinion, the use of Clemenceau's verdict was a substantial piece of polemic against him. But *Liberté* ran into difficulties before it could develop the case any further. A year after its first number the group in Marseille involved in its publication was discovered by the Vichy police and François de Menthon's brother-in-law Guy de Combault and his colleague on the paper Roger Nathan were among those arrested. Due to these arrests the November edition of the paper never appeared, nor did any further issue, but this was due to other causes. During November the two movements represented by *Liberté* and *Vérités* were merged by their leaders, François de Menthon and Henri Frenay, and in December 1941 the first number of the combined movement appeared with the new title *Combat*.

The progress of the two movements which led to *Combat* had been uneven, but there had always been points of close similarity, as seen in their total hostility to the Armistice, the

[58] *Vérités*, no. 16 (5 Nov. 1941).

[59] *Liberté*, no. 10 (1 Oct. 1941). The quote from Clemenceau ended: 'J'ai laissé aller cet homme sensé, plein de raison qu'était Pétain; j'ai adopté ce fou qu'était Foch. C'est le fou qui nous a tiré de là'.

Occupation, and Nazi ideology, their readiness to see Pétain as a patriotic buttress against the collaboration of his ministers, and their mutual suspicion of Communism. Frenay had strong links in the occupied zone, particularly through Robert Guédon, and access to the military personnel of Vichy, and these contacts gave his Mouvement de libération nationale more apparent credibility as a potential underground army, likely to mount an operation against the Germans. He had also succeeded, as detailed by Marie Granet and Henri Michel, in realizing an embryo structure and chain of command for the members of his movement, though the idea of a secret army still lacked the practical ingredients of numbers, money, and material, besides a strategy for action.[60] François de Menthon, who met Frenay occasionally during the summer of 1941,[61] acknowledged the larger size and more advanced organization of the M.L.N. but his movement had two points of strength which recommended themselves to Frenay. The first was Liberté's intellectual capacity and its close contacts within the universities across the southern zone and the second was the action initiated by Jacques Renouvin in Montpellier to expose government collaboration with Germany and to harass those who locally supported it.

Renouvin has been much talked about in Resistance history. Like Emmanuel d'Astier he has been the object of romantic attention, and stories about his idiosyncracies proliferate. The portraits suggest a tall, myopic Don Quixote, or the angular figure in Feininger's early cartoons, stalking the streets of Montpellier with a bundle of explosive under his coat. The curé Alvitre from Brive tells how he borrowed his cassock to pose as a priest when delivering a time bomb to a particular collaborator, and how he disappeared down the street on his mission with the cassock reaching no further than his knees.[62] The stories are important for they introduce an aspect of opposition in the southern zone which had been largely absent until late 1941. In the occupied zone the most commonly heard acceptance of the need for protest was couched in the phrase 'il faut narguer les allemands'. Anything qualified. Giving

[60] See Granet and Michel, *Combat*, pp. 5–68.
[61] Frenay, op. cit., pp. 103–4.
[62] Evidence from curé Alvitre.

wrong directions in the street, upsetting a German's wine glass, delaying services, refusing to talk or understand, as well as the more calculated acts of provocation, through tracts, newspapers, scrawled inscriptions, and the placing of wreaths on war memorials and other public monuments. None of these largely *ad hoc* actions had the same potential in the southern zone until Renouvin began to give them an alternative focus. From the late summer of 1941 he started organizing action units called *groupes francs*, with the aim of striking at the names and property of those who supported Germany, particularly the local members of Doriot's Parti populaire français and those who were publicly in favour of Darlan's foreign policy. The action also envisaged sabotage of goods going to Germany, an important inclusion, enabling Renouvin to recruit among industrial workers at Sète and agricultural workers in the country regions. The prime function was to demonstrate that responsibility for the easy progress of German demands both at government level and in society at large lay with specific Frenchmen. Inevitably much of the early action was of little more than nuisance value, but even this was not insignificant. Whether walls were daubed with paint, statues covered in slogans, or flats and houses blown open by explosive, the effect was to show that means of protest were available to anybody. To the constant question 'What can *we* do?' Renouvin provided answers which could at first be shrugged away but which had to be taken more and more seriously as they began to bite into the consciousness of Vichy supporters and opponents alike. It was hardly a state of urban terror, but it forced people to argue and take sides, and was a permanent reminder that the issues of the war and Occupation were still alive. The very simplicity of some of the gestures defied the fatalism which had confirmed people in their inertia. Something *could* be done, by anybody. This was the effect on public opinion of Renouvin's activity and as such it paralleled the verbal effect of *Libération*, which had also 'democratized' opposition in the southern zone, by restaging the conflict between France and Germany as a local conflict between the French who opposed collaboration and those who supported it.

The actions of the *groupes francs* undermined confidence in Vichy and eventually in Pétain, though Renouvin himself, like his first colleague in Montpellier, Ferdinand Paloc, had begun by trusting Pétain and avoiding any criticism of Vichy's internal policies. By the time the *groupes francs* were organized this trust had evaporated, and the two men had little of the residual respect which *Liberté* and still more *Vérités* were prepared to show. It was impossible for street action against collaboration to draw fine distinctions between Pétain and others: slogans and explosive had a simplifying effect. Nor would the volunteers to the *groupes francs* have tolerated an uneasy combination of subversion and respect. Several of the students involved had already taken part in anti-Vichy demonstrations within the University, not only in response to the lectures and influence of Teitgen, Courtin, and Baumel, but also in defiance of the group which published a paper *L'Écho des étudiants* in January 1941 with a strong Pétainist call for moral purpose among the French youth.[63] Other recruits had a socialist background and a recent history of commitment to the Left in the Spanish Civil War. Albin Tixador was typical of this political formation. He had a close acquaintance with refugee republicans who had settled in large numbers in the Hérault, and he had made the journey several times to Toulouse to take part in meetings which prepared the way for the Comité d'action socialiste. He was a wounded veteran of World War I and his contact with Ferdinand Paloc and thus with Renouvin lay in the local group of anciens combattants. Both as a Socialist, he declared, and as a patriot he rallied to Renouvin's initiative because it was action in which the people could directly participate.[64]

The new paper *Combat* did not move as fast in the direction of civil conflict as the *groupes francs*, but the tone of its first number in December 1941 was considerably more rebellious than *Vérités* had been. In the closely argued justification of the paper on page 1 the word 'collaboration' is used in its full derogatory sense, with a category of its 'deplorable effects': territorial and spiritual division of France, systematic

[63] *L'Écho des étudiants*, no. 1 (26 Jan. 1941). Its editorial included the words: 'Nous voudrions que résonne dans l'Écho la voix de ceux d'entre nous qui se sentent "gonflés", ceux en qui vit le courage, la foi en eux-mêmes, l'amour de la vie, la confiance, l'espoir. Le devoir de ceux-là est de lutter contre la résignation, le je-m'en-foutisme, l'indifférence. Et aussi contre la tristesse.'

[64] Evidence from Albin Tixador and Ferdinand Paloc.

spoliation of the nation, lowering of the standard of living, destruction of the French currency, exploitation of the French economy, propaganda in the colonies, and servility or degradation of French culture with the aid of the so-called 'national' Press and radio. 'Our combat', stated the paper in its one reference to a possible civil war, 'is primarily against Germany, but it is also against anyone who makes a deal with Germany and, consciously or not, becomes an accessory in our misfortunes.'[65] The second issue in the same month was a great deal more explicit: 'Being opposed to collaboration we are therefore opposed to the government which admits that it was freely chosen to collaborate.' There followed the first sign that a break with Pétain was contemplated. 'Our attitude to the Marshal is clear. In him are two men. The man of World War I whom we respect and the man of collaboration whom we refuse to follow.'[66] It was a telling sentence, but in the next few months the criticism of Pétain remained at that level. *Combat* could not bring itself to mount a full denunciation of Pétain until May 1942.

This reluctance within *Combat* gave a particular sting to the taunts of another paper which started in December 1941, *Le Franc-Tireur*. In its second issue it stated:

> We reject the current hypocrisy which consists of shouting that Laval, Darlan, and Pucheu are the traitors and that the Marshal can do nothing about it. . . . No! No! If Laval and the others have found it easy to give themselves to treasonable activity it is because Marshal Pétain covers all their actions, even the worst, with his name and reputation, stifling French Resistance.[67]

Le Franc-Tireur was the product of the group constituted in late 1940 which had called itself France-Liberté.[68] 'By our new title', wrote Noël Clavier, one of the founders of the group, 'we wanted to mark our determination to be independent',[69] and the name itself recalled the Francs-Tireurs of 1870–1, volunteers

[65] *Combat*, no. 1 (Dec. 1941).

[66] Ibid., no. 2 (Dec. 1941).

[67] *Le Franc-Tireur* (Jan. 1942). 'Mensuel dans la mesure du possible et par la grâce de la police du Maréchal.'

[68] See above, p. 73.

[69] Clavier, 'Franc-Tireur. Tel que je l'ai vu naître'.

to the Republican army who had no set uniform or place within the established military structures. Clavier and Élie Péju organized the paper, though Jean-Pierre Lévy was seen as the leader of the movement, which spread rapidly once the paper strengthened and extended the lines of communication to other main towns of the south. Within Lyon itself it recruited the strong professional abilities of Georges Altmann and Yves Farge, both journalists on the local paper, *Le Progrès de Lyon*, whose editorial staff produced numerous Resisters for the movements centred in Lyon, together with technical knowledge and access to censored news and information. Altmann had known Élie Péju when they were both members of the P.C.F. in the 1920s and when both had been involved with *Clarté*, the organ of intellectual Communists which was deeply affected by the Stalin–Trotsky conflict, leading to the resignation of many militants from the party including Altmann and Péju themselves. On the outbreak of war in 1939 Altmann was working in Paris on *La Lumière*, a left-wing weekly which had taken a strong stand against the Munich agreements, and he was also employed in the Paris offices of *Le Progrès de Lyon*. Once the Armistice terms were known, *Le Progrès* moved its Paris staff to Lyon and Altmann took up residence there, quickly becoming a close friend of Yves Farge, head of the Foreign Affairs Department at the paper's headquarters in Lyon. Farge at the time was fundamentally a pacifist, but he had written consistently against the dangers of Fascism and had been as critical of the Munich agreements as Altmann and *La Lumière*. Together they turned the editorial offices of *Le Progrès* into what Georges Bidault called a 'den of conspiracy' and when Péju approached them and asked them to write on *Le Franc-Tireur* their response was immediate.[70] The paper also gained the influential voice of Jean Nocher at Saint-Étienne who had finally been banned from his profession as a journalist on *La Tribune* after numerous suspensions during 1941, and had come into contact with the group of France-Liberté through a member of Jeune République who had introduced him to Antoine Avinin.[71]

The January edition of *Le Franc-Tireur* was printed in 10,000 copies, equalling the average run of *Combat* in its early stages,

[70] Veillon, *Le Mouvement Franc-Tireur*, pp. 87–92.
[71] Ibid., p. 65.

and the movement behind the paper, though smaller than the combined forces of Frenay's and de Menthon's organization, successfully recruited among radicals, anticlericals, and Freemasons who were not particularly attached to party politics but whose independent republicanism stood strongly against Vichy's brand of right-wing authoritarianism. Bolshevism was also firmly rejected in the opening paragraphs of the paper's first issue,[72] and in February the stigma was spread to Communists within France, accused of submission to the frequent changes in Stalinist policy.[73] The paper was adamant that its opposition should not be categorized in any terms which suggested political dogma, and its strength within the unstructured but interconnected groups of Alsace-Lorrainers in Clermont-Ferrand, the Dordogne, and Limoges was essentially non-political in the party sense of the word. The same was true of its expansion into working-class circles in the winter of 1941–2 through the work of Benjamin Roux.[74]

Le Franc-Tireur, both as paper and movement, reinforced the great change which had happened in non-communist opposition during 1941. The war which a small number of people, both inside and outside France, had wanted to continue in June 1940 had not been continued. A new kind of war had had to be started. In what now seems an obvious causal relationship, but was far from predictable at the time, the nature of this new war was closely dependent on the actions of the Vichy Government. The assumption of General Cochet's *Tour d'horizon* and of Frenay's *Bulletin* in 1940–1 was that the war outside France and the facts of Occupation would carry their own conviction and create more and more Resistance. The assumption of *Libération* and *Le Franc-Tireur*, and increasingly of *Combat*, was that evidence of collaboration by the Vichy Government and its sympathizers had become the main dynamic for Resistance. The extent of Vichy's collaboration thus progressively defined the extent of Resistance. The Germans were still there in the occupied zone and their everyday presence continued to create Resistance. They were still absent from the southern zone but their absence had grown steadily less impor-

[72] *Le Franc-Tireur* (Dec. 1941).
[73] Ibid. (Feb. 1942).
[74] Veillon, op. cit., p. 62.

tant. The focus had settled on Vichy's collaboration, with results that encouraged an even greater campaign against the Marshal's regime, a campaign of an overt political nature. The Communists were already well established in that area. *Libération* and *Le Franc-Tireur* also acknowledged political motivation to varying degrees, but with a good deal of caution. *Combat* was more hesitant. In 1942 the caution and hesitations progressively disappeared.

VII. Towards an Ideology

By the end of 1941 reluctance to jeopardize the fragile stability of the southern zone was no longer the dominant emotion that it had been in the summer of 1940. It was still a majority sentiment, and the clandestine Press in the winter of 1941–2 provides plenty of evidence of the difficulty experienced by the various movements in convincing the public that action was necessary. But the Vichy France of that second winter of Occupation is far from showing the homogeneous respect for the Pétain regime which so many writers had observed in 1940. The inroads into consciousness made by Vichy's political sectarianism, by the extension of the war into Russia, and by the growing association of Vichy with collaboration, had been deep. The effect was to reopen discussions which had been closed in 1940, to revitalize ideas and points of view which had looked dead and lifeless, and to reassert the meaning and importance of the past which had been discarded. Vichy's main contribution to this was its continued polemic against the values of the Third Republic, leading, in March 1942, to the long-prepared trial of Riom.[1] But it was no longer so easy to persuade people by the rhetoric of propaganda, and Riom was one more way in which Vichy scratched open the wounds of the past which it claimed to have healed.

Much of the early Occupation period can be seen as France in pursuit of its past as well as its future. Every month some new group of French people rediscovered for themselves the relevancy of their past ideals and politics, which the paralysing effect of defeat, *exode*, and the Vichy consensus had covered like a heavy blanket. As the corners were lifted, and the Popular Front, the Dreyfus Affair, the revolutions of the nineteenth century and of 1789, and a multiple memory of French traditions revealed, the ideological debate was restarted. Its reference points were as wide as they had ever been, but the debate itself was more anguished and less academic. It was the urgent need to adopt a clear position in response to the growing

[1] See above, pp. 101–3.

ideological aggression of Vichy and the occupying Germans that acted as yet another dynamic in Resistance motivation.

In his first open letter from Vichy on 15 January 1941 Jean Texcier, socialist writer and journalist, described the government as reactionary, and asked 'Are we going to rally to the regime praised by Charles Maurras? Certainly not.'[2] Texcier had already started the paper *Libération* in the occupied zone which anticipated by several months the related development under Emmanuel d'Astier, and his question was reiterated in socialist and republican circles in the southern zone as the National Revolution confirmed his description of the regime. Jean Cassou, whose activity in Toulouse was intended from the start to subvert the government, saw Maurras as the 'Enemy Number One of the French people'. In his memoirs he accused the leader of Action Française of fifty years of lies, betrayal, and corruption which had sapped the morale of the French and undermined their values and their energy.[3] In the Lozère, Henri Cordesse, a schoolteacher of left-wing views but attached to no political party, said that Resistance in his area was a slow 'prise de position' against the events of 1940–1, which became heavily orientated to the political Left especially in the Cévennes where the peasants were mostly Protestant and socialist and steeped in the history of the Camisards, the Calvinists of the Cévennes who fought against Louis XIV after the revocation of the Edict of Nantes.[4] In this 'prise de position' the internal repression organized by Vichy of all political opposition played a major role and Cordesse quotes a number of prefectoral decrees and ministerial decisions which particularly antagonized the Left of the region, prompting a solidarity which embraced republican, socialist, and communist sympathies in a broad alignment. They resented the ban on all duplicating machines, the official circular claiming that 'Communists were in the pay of the Jews', the dissolution of the Conseil Général and its replacement by an appointed Commission, the victimization of Freemasons, and the constant fawning of the local authorities before the image and

[2] *Lettres à François*, p. 11. Typed and circulated in Vichy while Texcier was there on an extended visit from Paris. These letters reached Clermont-Ferrand and Lyon.

[3] *La Mémoire courte*, p. 34.

[4] Evidence from Henri Cordesse.

person of Pétain.[5] Cordesse himself, who as a *normalien* in 1927 had taken part in a local demonstration against the execution of the two trade-unionists Saccho and Vanzetti, was angered in 1940–1 by the victimization of Communists, Freemasons, Jews, and teachers. By 1942, he claimed, people in his town of Marvejols knew not only what his attitudes to Vichy were, but where everybody stood, and the rival positions had long roots in the politics of the past.[6]

In the Haute-Savoie Jean-Marie Saulnier, Catholic, Socialist, and republican who ran a restaurant at Annecy, resented the anti-republican propaganda of Vichy and the values of the New Order and began to see himself in 1941 as a 'modest actor in the return to the Republic.'[7] In the Drôme Commandant Pons said the choice between Pétain and de Gaulle was no problem for most people of the political Left. 'For sincere republicans the choice was quickly made, as it has been at all points in our recent history when the people of France have felt the Republic was in danger.'[8] On 14 July 1942 he organized a demonstration at Crest south of Valence in front of the monument to local 'Victims of the *coup d'état* of 1851', republicans of the Drôme who had risen against Napoleon III and, armed with primitive weapons had been crushed by soldiers from Valence, and either killed or deported.[9] Further to the east in the Basses-Alpes Jean Vial, who had found many local republicans less than enthusiastic about openly supporting Léon Blum during the Riom trial,[10] was linked to the rebels of 1851 through his grandfather who had been one of those who marched to the *préfecture* at Digne to defend the Second Republic, a link which had created a strong personal identification with the idea of the Republic.[11] In Marseille L.-H.

[5] Henri Cordesse, *Histoire de la Résistance en Lozère* (Cordesse, n.p., 1974), pp. 16–20.

[6] Evidence from Henri Cordesse, and MS. of the book quoted above, kindly lent by the author, pp. 6–7.

[7] Alban Vistel, MS. on origins of Resistance, p. 709.

[8] Commandant Pons, *De la Résistance à la Libération* (*Défense du Vercors Sud*) (Imprimerie Passas et Deloche, Valence, 1962), p. 12.

[9] Ibid., pp. 15–16. Demonstrations for 14 July 1942 were co-ordinated by France Libre through the BBC as well as by Resistance organizations within the southern zone. See below, pp. 217–8.

[10] See above, p. 98.

[11] *Un de l'Armée secrète bas-alpine*, p. 31.

Nouveau was a dissident within a bourgeoisie which was overwhelmingly Pétainist, and ascribed this isolation to the legacy of his father who had been a passionate Dreyfusard, almost equally alone among his social group at the time.[12]

In Lyon the initial success of Franc-Tireur led its members to make the republican patriotism of the movement more explicit. Early in 1942 Élie Péju suggested the reincarnation of *Le Père Duchesne*, the father of all revolutionary papers started by Hébert in 1793, and recreated in 1848 and 1871. In April 1942 the first number was launched with a pungent, epigrammatic style, readable and easily memorized, with a section on internal enemies, both local and national, headed 'A la Lanterne', an outraged attack on Philippe Pétain with no prefix of 'maréchal', and parodies of Vichy slogans: 'Travail, Famille, Patrie. Mothers you are cold. Your children are shivering. Don't worry. The brothels are well heated' and 'National Police, National Revolution. If after that you don't understand . . .'[13]

Le Père Duchesne was more than a relic from the revolutionary past. It stood as a direct rival to the paternal image of Pétain. Compared with Pétain's 86 years, the revolutionary paper was 151 years old, symbolizing greater historical wisdom and continuity and pointing to republicanism as the true tradition of modern France. It did this with panache, arrogance, and sarcasm, promising vengeance in the name of the 'true people of France'. It left no doubt that Vichy had plunged France into civil war, though the struggle against Germany was not forgotten, and in its second number it combined both causes in its report of demonstrations in Lyon, Marseille, and Toulouse on 1 May when the slogans had been 'Vive la République, Vive de Gaulle, A bas Hitler, Vive la Liberté'.[14] The next issue did not appear until September 1942 and the fourth, and last, a year later, but its success was considerable not least for the humour in its first issue which provided Resistance in France with its first stock joke: 'A Boche has made the following

[12] L.-H. Nouveau, *Des capitaines par milliers*, p. 12.

[13] *Le Père Duchesne*, no. 1 (Apr. 1942). Its leading slogan was 'Haine aux tyrans, la Liberté ou la Mort' and its first internal enemy was named as Paul Charbin, a Lyonnais accused of buying up declining businesses since the defeat, making a fortune of others' misfortunes, and eating well while others starved.

[14] Ibid., no. 2 (May 1942).

accusation "I saw a Jew, with my own eyes, eating a German's brain. It was exactly 9.15 p.m." Now this accusation is false on three counts: 1. A German has no brain; 2. Jews do not eat pigs; 3. At 9.15 p.m. everyone is listening to the BBC.'[15]

It was not the only paper of its kind. At Saint-Étienne a small group led by *lycée* teachers Maurice and Laporte and recruited among students, intellectuals, and anticlerical teachers started *93* in May 1942 with the sub-title 'Journal des héritiers de la Révolution française'. The French triumph in 1793, it said, was due to the conviction that they were instituting a new justice and a new truth. 'Frenchmen of 1942. Republicans! To you, who must lead the country against the invader, against traitors, and against famine organized by the government, to you we offer this paper.' Short epigrammatic statements condemned the financial and industrial trusts, run by the government of Gauleiter Laval,[16] condemned anti-Semitism and made one further historical reference, this time to the period of republican struggle in 1873–4. 'The New Order of Marshal Pétain is the Moral Order of Marshal MacMahon.'[17]

Four numbers of *93* appeared before its printer was arrested, and its circulation is said to have been about 20,000, mostly in Saint-Étienne itself.[18] It appeared alongside the republican journalism of Jean Nocher, who had started his opposition by criticisms and innuendos in the authorized Stéphanois paper *La Tribune*, and then wrote overtly in the clandestine *Espoir*, while the group who produced *93* also distributed the whole range of Resistance papers which came from Lyon. *Le Père Duchesne* had made a point of listing all the clandestine Press

[15] Ibid., no. 1 (Apr. 1942).

[16] Laval had returned to the premiership of Vichy on 18 April 1942.

[17] *93* (May 1942). Marshal MacMahon succeeded Thiers in 1873 as President of the newly created Third Republic. For two years he presided over a regime of 'moral order' in partnership with the Prime Minister Duc Albert de Broglie and with the support of monarchists and clericals who were still looking for a restoration of the Bourbons. The regime dismissed militant republicans from all local government positions, suspended a large number of teachers, censored the Press, and controlled public morals. Faced with mounting republican opposition in the Chamber of Deputies, he dissolved the Chamber in 1877, but elections returned a republican majority and he eventually resigned in 1879. The image he projected to the country as a soldier who was 'above politics' led to frequent comparisons with Pétain during the Occupation.

[18] Alban Vistel, MS. on origins of Resistance, p. 620.

including *L'Humanité* in its first number, *Combat* had welcomed the birth of *Le Franc-Tireur* and the latter had acknowledged the reference with gratitude. In April 1942 the socialist organ *Le Populaire* reappeared,[19] preceded by *L'Insurgé* from a socialist splinter group, and followed by *Le Coq enchaîné* from a Lyonnais group dominated mainly by radicals. This in turn was followed in July by *Libérer et fédérer* published in Toulouse with a programme which was revolutionary, internationalist, and socialist but strictly non-party. 'The more clandestine papers there are,' said *Le Franc-Tireur*, 'the more chance that *one* will be read.'[20]

It was a policy to which most Resisters against Vichy and the Germans subscribed with some notable exceptions like Georges Groussard and Guillain de Bénouville who both believed that the popularization of Resistance was in inverse proportion to its effectiveness. More, for them, meant worse, or in more specific terms, less disciplined and therefore with less military potential, though de Bénouville later came to see the need for a massive campaign of propaganda. Both were from the political Right, whereas the overwhelming tendency of the papers which mushroomed in 1942 was to the Left, with references to popular struggles from the Revolution to the 1930s and attempts to make more distant figures like Joan of Arc and Vercingétorix into popular heroes consonant with the tradition of revolutionary patriotism.[21]

The title *L'Insurgé* was taken directly from the novel by the Communard Jules Vallès, and it carried two leading slogans, one from 1792 and the other from the *canuts* of Lyon, silk-workers who had rebelled for higher wages and better conditions at several points in the early nineteenth century.[22] The group which published it had a more recent history, dating from 1938 when Marceau Pivert, L. Vaillant, and Socialists from the Fédération de la Seine broke away from the Socialist Party and formed the Parti Socialiste Ouvrier et Paysan (P.S.O.P.),

[19] See above, p. 103.

[20] Feb. 1942.

[21] Cf. *Libérer et fédérer* (1 Sept. 1942), which attacked the Légion for celebrating its second anniversary at Gergovie which Vercingétorix had defended against Caesar in 52 B.C., and concluding 'Vercingétorix est le héros de la Résistance'.

[22] 'Liberté, égalité, mort aux tyrans' (1729), and 'Vivre en travaillant ou mourir en combattant' (les canuts de Lyon).

having demanded from Blum a more socialist stand against Fascism, capitalism, and war. In its journal *Juin 36* it had condemned war as a diversion from the class struggle, but when France was invaded and defeated, Pivert, who was on a visit to America at the time, wrote to de Gaulle in London expressing support for his stand against Hitler and Fascism, but adding that the only way for Socialists to fight Fascism was by a socialist revolution.[23] By the end of 1940 members of the P.S.O.P. in Lyon led by M. Fugère, who worked for the Compagnie Electromécanique, and a lawyer Pierre Stibbe, had decided to reconstitute the party on a programme of opposition to Vichy and Fascism, and by mid-1941 there were branches reorganized in Bourg-en-Bresse, Montpellier, Toulon, Nîmes, Narbonne, Clermont-Ferrand, and later Saint-Étienne. In an analysis of these groups Robert Fiat has stressed their working-class basis and their continuity with the pre-war P.S.O.P. which counted about 26,000 members at its first congress in May 1939. He also underlined the importance of their contacts outside France with Marceau Pivert and the International Workers' Front created in 1938 against Fascism and war.[24] The newspaper first emerged in March 1942, founded by contributions from members of the National Committee of the movement and printed in Lyon by Martinet who was also printing *Combat* and *Libération*. It established a moderate circulation of about 25,000 and gave itself almost entirely to promoting the social struggle against Fascism, the word used to cover Vichy, the capitalist system, the German Occupation, and every aspect of collaboration, particularly economic. Like other papers, including *Le Franc-Tireur* and *Combat*, it utilized Clemenceau's method of attack in 1898, 'J'accuse', to arraign the guilty, but like few papers outside the communist Press it arraigned first and foremost the world of high finance and economic monopoly, holding it responsible for a conspiracy to undermine France, to achieve its defeat, to instigate Fascism before the war and collaboration since, and to destroy the

[23] Robert Fiat, 'L'Insurgé. Un Mouvement de Résistance. Un Journal' (Diplôme d'Études Supérieures d'Histoire, Lyon, 1961), p. 8.

[24] To which the following, among others, belonged: Independent Labour Party (I.L.P.), the Independent League of America (I.L.A.), the Spanish Partido Obrero de Unificación Marxista (P.O.U.M.), the Italian Maximalist Party, the German Opposition Communist Party. Fiat, op. cit., pp. 12–24.

resistance of the people of France by organized starvation.[25] Its relationship to the local scene in Lyon was a close one, carrying news of local demonstrations and featuring local collaborators and black marketeers as candidates for public vengeance. In August it made it clear that it would also support the assassination of Pétain.[26]

When *Le Franc-Tireur* justified the growth of the clandestine Press, the implication was that one paper was almost interchangeable for another, in that all were supporting the liberation of France. This may have been the common point of propaganda, but it did not insure a common political, social, or ideological programme. This appeared to be regretted by *Libérer et fédérer* whose first number in July 1942 made a strong call for an end to all divisions, factions, and parties, in the interests of a united effort to win both the war and the peace.

> The old parties are dead. Their outdated formulas have failed. From the extreme Right to the extreme Left none of these parties knew how to give France the unity, vitality, and idealism which it so badly lacked in the crisis . . . common hatred against the invader and the traitors who have collaborated has united us and we saw at once that our divisions were only factions . . . and that we had the same need for liberty and the same aspirations for justice.[27]

But the timing of the issue, to emerge on 14 July, the use of the word 'revolutionary' in the sub-title, the call on page one for the suppression of capitalist exploitation of the workers and for the management of factories by elected assemblies of all those involved in production, gave the paper a distinct political colour if not a party identity. It could have little appeal to the conservative Centre, and, because of its federal vision, none to the traditionalist Right; for it claimed to be sketching the basis for a totally new, federal alignment not just of all French people but of all the people of Europe, once they were liberated from 'the tyranny of the Moloch State.'[28]

[25] *L'Insurgé*, no. 4 (June 1942).

[26] 'Si un homme levait sur toi [Pétain] la main pour te tuer, la France entière dans un soupir de soulagement, serait unanime à dire Amen!' (Ibid., no. 6, Aug. 1942.)

[27] *Libérer et fédérer* (Organe du mouvement révolutionnaire pour la libération et la reconstruction de la France), 14 July 1942.

[28] *Manifeste de Libérer et fédérer* (14 July 1942).

Two of the group behind the movement Libérer et fédérer, Jean Cassou and Georges Friedmann, had been involved since 1940 in a wide range of opposition and Resistance activities, Cassou starting in left-wing intellectual circles in Paris and contacting Socialists and trade-unionists, and Friedmann joining him in Toulouse in the information and escape network organized by Pierre Bertaux, as well as in discussions with Archbishop Saliège and Mgr. de Solages. The main orchestrator of the group, Silvio Trentin, had an even wider association, being an anti-Fascist exile from Mussolini's Italy. In Toulouse he had found a post in the Faculté de Droit and also ran a bookshop in the Place Rouaix where many of the early meetings of Libérer et fédérer took place in the summer of 1942. It was also one of the centres for the network 'Bertaux', and Pierre Bertaux's own connections with the syndicalist opposition in Toulouse further widened the basis of the group in which intellectuals, teachers, and lawyers were prominent.[29] Both the first number of *Libérer et fédérer* and the accompanying manifesto published on the same day show that the group regarded its own collective existence as a symbol of the federalism which it was demanding. But it was a federalism of a kind, not of any kind, and its assumption that the liberation of France should have consequences of a broadly socialist nature was more political than its rejection of parties and factions would seem to suggest. It was using highly politicized language without the framework of party or the language of parliamentary divisions. In its second issue it made two major demands of the French. 'We must cease to be a nation of *petits bourgeois*' and 'We must once again become a revolutionary people'. If these two conditions were successfully met then France would be a great nation and the French a great people.[30] The meaning of the word *petit bourgeois* was spelt out, but the desired alternative was not given in any detail. What exactly 'revolutionary' meant is unclear in terms of party-political programmes. The word was more evocative than descriptive and its vagueness was an expression of the open-ended quality of rebellion against Vichy, Fascism, and the Germans which

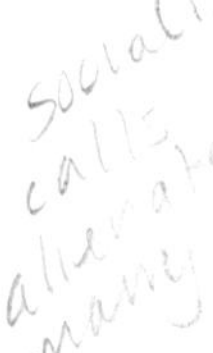

[29] I am indebted to Alun Evans for much of the information about the composition of the movement Libérer et fédérer.

[30] *Libérer et fédérer* (1 Sept. 1942).

Libérer et fédérer, like so many Resistance papers, was advocating.

References to 1793, the Paris Commune of 1871, republican struggles against Maurrasian doctrines, revolts of Cévennes Protestants, Lyon *canuts*, or the local republicans of many areas against Napoleon III, all these references were gradually creating a political vocabulary specific to Resistance activity. It was the result of confrontation with two different, but increasingly related, phenomena, the Vichy regime and the German Occupation, moulded into one for the purposes of opposition. Just as *L'Humanité* and *Libération*, in their separate ways, had begun the process of simplifying the different attitudes within Vichy into the one term of collaboration, so the papers of 1942 continued the process and forged an even larger composite from the German Occupation, Vichy, capitalism, and the politics of repression and autocracy from the *ancien régime* down to Action Française. Against this composite evil a composite ideal was advanced, and it was this mosaic of republican and revolutionary pieces which was laid out in the clandestine Press of 1942, and which constituted the political ideology of Resistance.

Le Coq enchaîné produced the radical version of this composite ideal. It was published by a group in Lyon including members of the Radical, Socialist, and Catholic Democratic parties as well as other unattached *hommes de gauche*. The printer, Chevalier, was a Radical, and the group kept in close touch with Edouard Herriot, the leader of the old Radical Party who had voted for Pétain's full powers on 10 July 1940, but later returned his Légion d'Honneur to Vichy in protest at its policies. Several of the group, like Antoine Avinin, were also already involved in *Le Franc-Tireur*, and *Le Coq enchaîné* followed the larger paper in pledging full support to de Gaulle in equally enthusiastic terms.[31] But it then went on to be more explicit about its republican position than *Le Franc-Tireur*: 'We are above all *laïcs*, republicans, and democrats. We are not Communists but we absolutely despise the hypocritical anti-Bolshevism which has done us so much harm. The enemy of the Republic has never been on the Left.'[32] This reference to Gambetta's

[31] See below, pp. 213–4.

[32] *Le Coq enchaîné* [Mar. 1942] (given as '631 jour de la lutte du peuple français pour sa libération').

cry 'No enemies to the Left' firmly indicates the radical inheritance of *Le Coq enchaîné* and the last two pages were full of further historical allusions ending with a speech in the style of Cyrano de Bergerac affirming the values of the Republic against Cagoulards and traitors, and a final quotation from Goethe extolling the values of liberty and equality.[33] In May the paper continued the elaboration of its political position with a call to 'republicans and *laïcs* of all kinds', exhorting each reader to 'join with whoever handed him the paper and form a Ligue d'espoir humain which will bind itself to no group and no doctrine in its desire to retain a total independence.' There followed quotations from Foch, Victor Hugo, Napoleon I, and Jaurès, to which the next issue added others from Chateaubriand and Verhaeren.[34] To detail the *laïc* ideas of the paper there was a long article on the educational reforms of the National Revolution, accusing them of attacking secularism (*laïcité*), favouring the private, Catholic schools, and dismissing teachers who are 'trop républicain'. As a result, 'the old passions of anticlericalism, which had died among the primary school teachers, have now been brought back to life'.[35] Of all the policies defining a broad republican position the defence of secular education was one of the most recurrent, and in this rehearsal of the issues *Le Coq enchaîné* was blatant in its intention of stirring those passions which Vichy had rekindled. It was not seen as a trivial motivation to start Resistance because Vichy had victimized the militant *laïcs* in the schools.

The broadly left-wing papers of 1942, with their fund of historical quotations and allusions, were quite clear on this point. The struggle to which they were committed was a wider one than the liberation of France from German Occupiers, though that was the unifying objective. In this wider struggle motivations were justified which had only contextual connections with the Occupation, and which had figured frequently

[33] Ibid. The 'Cyrano' speech included the lines

> Puis la République en triomphant plus tard
> Pourra dire aux Français 'Huez les Cagoulards'
> Vis-à-vis de soi-même bien garder le mérite
> De brimer, jusqu'au bout l'occupant parasite . . .

[34] Ibid. (10 May 1942; given as '686 jour . . .'); (1 June 1942; the '708 jour . . .').

[35] Ibid. (10 May 1942).

enough in previous French history to appear the stock-in-trade of republican resistance to forces of repression and autocracy since the eighteenth century. In everyday terms this gave a familiar purpose to large numbers of French who had felt uneasy about the defeat, the Armistice, and the Occupation but not angry enough to protest, yet who became increasingly angry between 1940 and 1942 at such recognizable oppressions as economic exploitation, victimization of political militants, persecution of free-thinkers, Freemasons, and the Jews, censorship, and police control. Against these there was a known and well-tried response in republican and revolutionary activism, and it was this response which gave a familiar shape to the more unfamiliar task of underground activity against enemy occupation. The Communist Party had reached this point from the other direction. Between 1939 and 1941 it had nurtured and deepened all the traditional socialist and republican responses to oppression. It had protested against clericalism, anti-Semitism, police tyranny, economic exploitation, and political persecution and had been active in organization against these oppressive features of Vichy France. Political and social motives for opposition were never discarded by the P.C.F. and therefore did not have to be rediscovered. What the party did have to rediscover was the continuing importance of its pre-war policy of national defence. The Germans had to be *driven* out. They would not succumb to political, social, and economic protest. It needed the outbreak of war against Russia to convince the party hierarchy of this, a conviction already held by many individual Communists and several regional groups well before then. By contrast, among non-Communists it was the importance of social and political opposition which was rediscovered in pungent terms by steadily increasing numbers in 1941–2.

What made this social and political opposition so different from previous periods was the link with military or quasi-military activity and what made the military Resistance so unique was its gradual incorporation into the wider political struggle. By mid-1942 it was possible to talk of The Resistance in the southern zone, meaning not just a range of military activity to liberate France, but a combination of different activities, military, political, social, and ideological. They had never been completely distinguishable from each other. After two years of Occupation and experience of the Vichy regime they were even less so, though the different elements within the combination were more clearly articulated and the disparate motivations for Resistance more obvious and more accepted. By definition The Resistance had to include activity or propaganda directed in some way towards the liberation of France. But due to the growing necessity of fighting Vichy as well as the Germans, it also meant a defence of human and political values long identified with the left-wing republican tradition of France.

An individual example of this Resistance in 1942 comes from the town of Cahors in the Lot in the history of a schoolmaster, Jean-Jacques Chapou. Before the war he had been Secretary of the Union of Secondary School Teachers in the Lot, affiliated to the C.G.T., and in 1938 became a Freemason. His father had died of war-wounds in 1914 and Chapou developed a strong personal hatred of war. He was a vehement supporter of Munich in 1938 and a reluctant soldier on the Alpine front in 1939–40. With his daughter born in April 1940 he was far from disappointed when the war ended and he was able to return home to his family, his job at the *lycée*, his trade union activity, his fishing, garden, and rugby. *Il est rentré chez soi.*

In the winter of 1940–1, after the dissolution of the C.G.T., he found he had time to attend the University of Toulouse once a week where he was influenced by Julien Forgues, the C.G.T. Secretary for the Haute-Garonne, and Professor Naves of the Faculté des Lettres into reassessing his relative contentment with the *status quo*, and in 1941 he decided to explore the possibilities of reviving trade union activity in Cahors. Then in October 1941 he was given the powerful motivation he had previously lacked when the Minister of Education ordered his dismissal from the *lycée* because he was a Freemason. He refused to send an appeal to Vichy, found a job in a transport business, and throughout the winter of 1941–2 devoted himself to the clandestine reorganization of trade-unionism in the Lot. With a friend, Marcel Metges, and with the help of Léon Jouhaux, who arrived in Cahors under house arrest in January 1942, he reconstituted the C.G.T. at local level beginning with railway and post-office workers. 'Thus', states Georges Cazard, 'the first core of the Resistance in the Lot was established under the aegis of the C.G.T.'[36] In September 1942 Chapou became the representative of Libération for the Lot, and groups belonging to the movement were established at Cahors, Figeac, and Puy-l'Évêque.

While J.-J. Chapou is no more the 'typical' Resister of the southern zone than any other individual, his history illustrates the way in which people became angered by the political orientation of Vichy to the point of rejecting their quietism of 1940 and restarting a political activism which had seemed out of place in the national crisis of defeat and Occupation. Victimized by a government whose peace policy in 1940 had not stirred him into opposition, he became, in late 1941, one of the 'first' Resisters in his area largely for political reasons, though his action quickly became part of the composite Resistance, and from an organizer of trade-union protest he became one of the pioneers and martyrs of military Resistance in the Lot.[37]

In 1941–2 victimization by the Vichy Government and its authoritarian assault on elementary freedoms became as fundamental a reason for Resistance as any other during the whole period of Occupation, though among the victimized the initial decision to resist was more often individual than collective. Chapou as a victimized Freemason did not act as part of a collective opposition by the Masonic community. Freemasons in the National Assembly had split in their vote on 10 July 1940 and were uncoordinated in their reaction to the decree dissolving secret societies a month later on 13 August. A week before the decree Masons Groussier and Villard had written to Pétain to inform him that the Grand Orient and all its lodges had voluntarily closed, and to affirm their respect for Pétain, a gesture which did not stop Vichy itself from dissolving the Grand Orient on 19 August and the smaller lodges in February 1941. The Masonic funds were officially forfeited and, to make sure there was no attempt at reorganization, a special administration of Masonic affairs was attached to Pétain's Cabinet, headed by Bernard Fay. His staff identified over 60,000 Freemasons, but when it was decided by Admiral

[36] Georges Cazard, assisted by Marcel Metges *Capitaine Philippe 1909–44 (J.-J. Chapou)* (Imprimerie A. Coueslant, Cahors, 1950), p. 76. The whole story of J.-J. Chapou is taken from this source.

[37] He became a captain in the *maquis* unit 'France' and avoided capture by killing himself when caught in an ambush on 16 July 1944.

Darlan and the Minister of Interior Pierre Pucheu to publicize the names of office-holders in the *Journal officiel* so that they could be dismissed, only 14,000 were named.[38] In the admission of Maurice Gabolde, Garde des Sceaux in the Vichy Government, 'the number who had occupied high office under the Third Republic was, contrary to expectations, extremely small. The lists revealed the names of unknown men, small administrators, traders, chemists, and lawyers in small towns.'[39] Of these it was mainly teachers like J.-J. Chapou of Cahors and Martial Brigouleix of Tulle, or local administrators and mayors like Lucien Hussel of Vienne who reacted by starting Resistance, and their opposition was a minority action. It was not until 1943 that a Resistance movement claiming to speak for Freemasonry, 'Patriam Recuperare', was formed, though one of its founders, Roig, had started a small group in the Dordogne before then which led to a Comité d'action maçonnique.[40] On the whole Freemasons as a group benefited from the *laissez-faire* policy of many local prefects, and after April 1942 from the undisguised hostility of Pierre Laval to the entire anti-Masonic campaign, but that did not prevent the earlier victimization from adding significantly to the anger and resentment which prompted individual Resistance.

Far more serious both as victimization by Vichy and motivation for Resistance was the persecution of the Jews, a policy which epitomized the Maurrasian ideology against which so much of the Resistance was directed. The persecution deepened the social and political conflict, intensified the situation of civil war, and extended the ideological opposition to Vichy into a passionate struggle for basic human values. In defence of the Jews the republican tradition of France reached one of its highest points of moral protest, yet as with every element of protest in 1940–2 it was not a general response, but the reaction of a minority, both of Jews and non-Jews, in the face of hostility, indifference, and submissiveness.

When Charles Maurras in *L'Action française* welcomed the

[38] J.-A. Faucher and A. Ricker, *Histoire de la franc-maçonnerie en France* (Nouvelles Éditions Latines, 1967), p. 433.

[39] Ibid., p. 432.

[40] Roig was captured, imprisoned at Fresnes, and shot by the Germans. The movement published its own paper *La Nouvelle République* with four issues at the end of 1943 and nineteen in 1944.

government of Marshal Pétain as something approaching his monarchist ideal it was in terms which were relatively unchanged since the Dreyfus Affair of the 1890s. Nor were the Popular Front deputies who voted overwhelmingly for full powers to Marshal Pétain on 10 July 1940 unaware of the traditional right-wing policies which such powers could enact. Within three months the kind of anti-Semitic measures for which Maurras had campaigned and against which the Popular Front had solidly united were a central feature of Vichy legislation and official propaganda. Protected by the Third Republic against numerous attempts to reduce their citizenship the Jews were abandoned to a right-wing government at a point when the most virulent racialist regime had occupied half of France. Such was the dislocation of political life and the extent of public withdrawal from major issues that the anti-Jewish law of 3 October 1940, which would have consolidated republican forces at any time between Drumont's *La France juive* of 1886 and 1940, occasioned little protest.

The law, together with a series of anti-Jewish decrees from July 1940 onwards, reduced all Jews to inferior citizenship and on 2 June 1941 was replaced by an even harsher law which became the main *Statut des juifs* for the southern zone. The Vichy Government made strenuous efforts to have it applied in the occupied zone rather than allow the Germans a free hand, but in doing so found themselves more compromised with German racialism rather than less.[41] In its first article the *Statut* defined a Jew as anyone with three grandparents who 'belonged to the Jewish race' or anyone belonging to the Jewish religion on 25 June 1940 and having two Jewish grandparents. According to the former definition, which was the racial one, a man or woman with three Jewish grandparents yet converted to Christianity or any other religion was still considered as Jewish. Under the Articles that followed Jews were forbidden to hold certain offices including Chef de l'état, any government post, any job in the Court of Appeal or in any of the other major administrative bodies and inspectorates, any post in regional administration, particularly prefect and sub-prefect, any diplomatic position, any post connected with

[41] See Paxton, *Vichy France*, pp. 169–85.

the police, any teaching post in state education at all levels, any officer rank in the armed services, or any job in an industrial, financial, or commercial company benefiting from public subsidies. In other jobs and professions Jews were to occupy no more than a percentage of the jobs available, a *numerus clausus* usually fixed at 2 per cent by subsequent decrees covering such professions as medicine, law, dentistry, pharmacy, journalism, theatre, and film in all of which Jews had always had a substantially higher percentage than the one now permitted. The loss of livelihood, as well as the inferior status, was therefore a major feature of these Vichy laws which went well beyond the first anti-Jewish restrictions imposed by the Germans in the occupied zone. It was, in fact, the incidental decrees as much as the *Statut des juifs* itself which expressed the full anti-Semitic intentions of the government. By decrees on 4 and 8 October 1940 the prefect of each *département* was allowed to intern all foreign Jews in 'special camps' and was given total freedom in the operation of finding them and transferring them from wherever they were living. Before the war there were about 300,000 Jews in France, half of whom were of foreign nationality, and to this figure must be added an unknown number who arrived during the *drôle de guerre*. On 14 May 1940 Reynaud's government had ordered all German refugees to be interned, many of whom were Jewish, but the internment decrees of Vichy were specifically aimed at the Jews, particularly those who had fled from Germany and Eastern Europe in the face of Nazism since 1933. During the night of 22 October 1940 the Nazi Government, still at this time envisaging deportation as their 'answer' to the 'Jewish problem', deported over 6,000 Jews from Baden and the Palatinate into the southern zone, without informing the Vichy Government in advance, and this action gave the government extra justification in their eyes for the internment decrees. Camps had been opened in both zones, two becoming quickly notorious, Drancy in the occupied zone and Gurs in the southern zone in the Basses-Pyrénées. Gurs had started as a camp for Spanish Republicans who escaped from Franco's advancing armies, but in the autumn of 1940 it received between 15,000 and 16,000 Jewish men, women, and children, most of them without any possessions or money. In the first winter 1940–1 there was a severe shortage of food and over 1,000 died of starvation, dysentery, and typhoid.[42] Other camps in the southern zone included Rivesaltes and Argelès in the Pyrénées-Orientales, Noé and Récébédou in the Haute-Garonne, Le Vernet in the Ariège, and Les Milles in the Bouches-du-Rhône. All of these camps were overcrowded and in all there was serious undernourishment, but Gurs became a by-word in Vichy inhumanity within a few months of its new usage.

French Jews in the southern zone were not interned, unless arrested for opposition activity, but they were forced to be registered as Jews, the first administrative task undertaken by the Commissariat général aux questions juives established by Vichy on 29 March 1941 under one of the main nationalist spokesmen against Jews and Freemasons of the 1930s, Xavier Vallat. His nationalism eventually proved stronger than his anti-Semitism and he incurred the hostility of the German authorities for slowing down the process of arrest and internment of Jews in the southern zone, and in April 1942 he was replaced by a venemous racialist, Darquier de Pellepoix, who had spent three months in prison in 1939 for articles of racial hatred in his paper *La France enchaînée*. Under his more energetic direction the Commissariat co-operated with German demands in the summer of 1942 when the mass deportation of Jews was launched from Paris in July and from the southern camps in August and September. Witnesses of the indescribable scenes at Gurs and other camps are emphatic that it was the French authorities who both gave the orders and carried them through, filling the deportation trains by force, despite the pleadings and terror of the victimized Jews. Even some of the police involved were shocked by the brutality of the event, wrote the chaplain of Les Milles, Pasteur Henri Manen.[43]

Like the first legislation against the trade unions, the early laws and decrees against the Jews were a straight imposition by Vichy. But later, in November 1941, a month after the *Charte du travail* had attempted to gain the co-operation of labour in its own fate, the Commissariat général aux questions juives attempted the same with the Jews. It established a Jewish body,

[42] The figures are from a Protestant welfare worker at the camp, Jeanne Merle d'Aubigné, 'Souvenirs de quelques camps en France 1940–47', *Quelques actions des protestants de France en faveur des Juifs persécutés sous l'occupation allemande* (édité par la CIMADE, 1965), pp. 29, 48.

[43] Ibid., p. 20.

called the Union générale des Israélites de France (U.G.I.F.), with the aim of grouping all Jews together to facilitate registration and to take over the administration of Jewish concerns. French trade-unionists had been found to bury the traditional freedoms of the labour movement , and French Jews were found to run their own loss of citizenship. The U.G.I.F. counselled Jews to be passive and non-resistant through its publication *Informations juives*, and it attempted to take over most of the Jewish social and welfare organizations. Above all it compiled extensive lists of Jews in the southern zone with jobs and addresses, an index which the Germans found of inestimable value when they invaded and occupied the southern zone in November 1942.

The *Statut des juifs*, the internment decrees, the U.G.I.F., and eventually the deportation of foreign Jews in the summer of 1942 were all measures consonant with Vichy's nationalist ideology, and did not depend on either suggestions or coercion from the Germans in the north. Nor did the Vichy Government oppose the showing of the German anti-Semitic film *Jud Süss* throughout the southern zone in 1941, but on the contrary allowed it to be promoted as *Le Juif Süss* with French credits and sound-track as if it were an authentic French product. The final passage in the film in which a proclamation was read banning all Jews from Württemberg in 1738 concluded with the exhortation to future generations to learn from the drama which had just unfolded, and the Vichy Government clearly approved of its 'educational' potential since the strong official patronage given to the film in the major towns included the organization of transport to bring children in from outlying schools to the cinemas. It seems that the only area of disagreement between the French and German authorities over the foreign Jews was about who should supervise the deportations from the occupied zone, but there was more disagreement as the Occupation intensified over the fate of French Jews, and it appears a reasonable conclusion that Pierre Laval in the summer of 1942 began to trade the foreign Jews against the lives of those whose nationality was unmistakably French.[44]

[44] Paxton, op. cit., pp. 184–5; Warner, *Pierre Laval and the Eclipse of France*, pp. 304–7, 374–7. See also René de Chambrun's defence of Laval's policy towards the Jews in *Le Monde* (11 Sept. 1971).

Anti-Semitism, in France as elsewhere, was nurtured on fantasies of Jewish subversion and conspiracy. The absurdity of these had been proved at the time of the Dreyfus Affair when the French Jews had shown a dominant preference for assimilation within French society, despite the nascent Zionism and Jewish cultural assertiveness of Bernard Lazare and, later, the followers of Theodore Herzl.[45] In 1940–2 assimilation was equally pronounced and the fantasies no less absurd. Not even the blatant provocation contained in the anti-Semitic decrees and laws of 1940–1 could produce anything approximating to a co-ordinated Jewish opposition, and it was not until the mass deportations began in the summer of 1942 that the optimism of the French Jews in the southern zone turned to a more general anxiety, fear, and anger. As with French society at large, only a small minority of Jews responded initially to the Vichy regime with outright opposition. For the majority it was important that the synagogues were still open, that isolated exceptions were made to the laws preventing Jews from holding public office,[46] and that the Jewish youth organization, Éclaireurs israélites français (E.I.F.), was protected by Vichy's own scouting philosophy of healthy, outdoor youth and by the personal support of General Lafont. Prohibited in the occupied zone by the Germans, the E.I.F. increased its centres in the southern zone from two to over twenty, with an estimated membership of 3,000 by the end of 1941. Of these centres Moissac in the Tarn-et-Garonne became the most celebrated within Jewish circles, the hub of rural activities at such places as Charry, Viarose, and Lautrec, where a return to the land was worked out as a potential solution for the Jews.[47] At Charry the leader, I. Pougatch, and his wife Juliette created a commune of young Jews with origins in all countries, and developed a pattern of rural life which was both idyllic and remote from the events of the period, until after the German occupation of the south, when Pougatch was forced to escape to Switzerland and the commune was closed. In the recollections of Charry which he wrote from Switzerland, Pougatch

[45] See M. Marrus, *The politics of assimilation. A study of the French Jewish community at the time of the Dreyfus Affair* (Clarendon Press, Oxford, 1971).

[46] e.g. the historian Marc Bloch was allowed to teach at the University of Montpellier.

[47] Anny Latour, *La Résistance juive en France 1940–44* (Stock, 1970), pp. 32–7.

produced a manual for youth leaders which could have come from any of the Vichy leaders of the Chantiers de la jeunesse.[48]

Yet despite the clear acceptability of the E.I.F. and its leaders to *scoutisme français* and to both the rural and youth programme of the Vichy Government, the summer of 1942 brought not only the indiscriminate deportation of foreign Jews, young and old, from the southern camps, but also by a law of July 1942 the exclusion of all Jewish youth from the Chantiers de la jeunesse. The regime was determined on confrontation with the Jews and on a policy of victimization, in the crude pursuit of ideological purity and in defiance of the facts of Jewish assimilation. By the time the Germans invaded and occupied the southern zone even the E.I.F. had realized that it was no longer secure from persecution, and from late 1942 there was a steady move of Jewish youth into Resistance.

The Jewish hierarchy in France was no more intent on subversion than its youth, although it protested against the first laws and decrees of 1940 and continued to protest as they became more openly vindictive. The central consistory, the main religious body of the Jewish community, reconstituted itself in 1941 to incorporate a voluntary body which had started a system of Jewish Defence Committees from Marseille,[49] and later in the year opposed the creation of the U.G.I.F., condemning it as alien to Jewish interests.[50] Letters went from the Grand Rabbis to the Vichy Government but the replies they received merely rationalized the persecution. When the Grand Rabbi J. Kaplan wrote to Xavier Vallat on 31 July 1941 pointing out his war service as a chaplain and the war record and losses of French Jews in general, a reply from the Commissariat général aux questions juives mentioned the 'invasion of our country by a mass of Israelites with no connection to our civilization' and said 'We must point out that there is no anti-Semitism in the government's policy, merely the

[48] I. Pougatch, *Charry. Vie d'une communauté de jeunesse* (Chant Nouveau, 1946).

[49] *Activité des organisations juives en France sous l'occupation* (Éditions du Centre, 1947), p. 21.

[50] Among other strong denunciations of the U.G.I.F. were those by the Socialists Daniel Mayer and Marc Jarblum, the latter as President of the Fédération des sociétés juives. He was asked to join the directorate of the U.G.I.F. but refused and was then forced to escape into Switzerland, from where he sent money to Jewish Resistance. (Anny Latour, op. cit., p. 23.)

application of *raison d'État*.[51] As the number of Jews in the internment camps continued to grow from the figure of 25,000 early in 1941, an organized chaplaincy system was needed, rather than one based on the voluntary efforts of individual rabbis, and by the winter of 1941–2 the Grand Rabbi of Strasbourg, René Hirschler, was in charge of such an organization with an area of pastoral oversight divided into the regions of Marseille, Montpellier, Toulouse, Limoges, Lyon, and Clermont-Ferrand, covering over twenty camps, thirty groupings of foreign workers, and a multitude of separate residences specially assigned for Jews.[52]

The Jewish chaplaincy, operating in a situation of official inhumanity and persecution, inevitably came to involve opposition to Vichy whether the chaplains were personally hostile to an authoritarian government or not. The same was true of the other Jewish welfare organizations, which found their welfare merging into opposition due to the provocation of Vichy rather than to a general intention to conspire and subvert.

With mobility in the 1930s at such a high level and a mentality which was forced to consider the problems of poverty and statelessness as a norm, Jewish welfare organizations were already experienced at both national and international levels by the time Vichy added its own persecution to that of Nazi Germany. In the southern zone the most skilled and tenacious of the welfare units was the Œuvre de secours aux enfants (O.S.E.), originally founded, like most Jewish self-help organizations, after the Russian pogroms under the last Tsars. Reconstituted for France in June 1940 with its centre at Montpellier its action in rescuing hundreds of children from the southern camps was personified in the work of Andrée Salomon and Dr. Joseph Weill, the latter a well-known doctor from Strasbourg. Other centres at Limoges, Marseille, and Lyon operated in the same way, removing children into the remote villages of the Lozère and the Haute-Loire, from where some were found visas to the United States, some smuggled into Switzerland, and others hidden by peasant families to protect

[51] David Knout, *Contribution à l'histoire de la Résistance juive en France 1940–44* (Éditions du Centre, 1947), p. 58.

[52] *Activité des organisations juives en France*, pp. 34–6.

them from the periodic round-ups by first Vichy and later German authorities.[53] The O.R.T. (Organisation, reconstruction, travail) was founded even earlier than the O.S.E., reaching back into the 1880s, and during the period between the wars had devoted itself to finding work and training in France for the Jewish immigrants from the east. Within the internment camps it set up workshops and classes in mechanical and electrical trades and in such crafts as weaving and basketry. It also tried, like both the O.S.E. and the Comité d'assistance aux réfugiés (C.A.R.), which operated from Marseille, to free the internees for work outside, to reintegrate them into society, or to hide them in unprejudiced and generous communities.

Much of the financing of Jewish welfare in France came from the American Joint Distribution Committee known as 'Le Joint' which moved its French centre from Paris to Marseille in 1940. The European centre was at Barcelona and from there money from American Jews was sent to Marseille to fund the activities in the internment camps.[54] Like the welfare organizations themselves, Le Joint did not start under Vichy as either political opposition or military Resistance. Its policy was not to provide money for any form of armed or violent protest, but the evolution of Le Joint, like all Jewish organizations, towards first a clandestine mentality and finally into outright Resistance was marked by the appointment of Dika Jefroykin on to the controlling body of Le Joint in 1942. Jefroykin was an ex-army officer who had accepted the need for armed Resistance over a year before. The man who had convinced him was David Knout, a poet whose family was of Russian origin and whose wife Ariane, the daughter of Scriabin and the niece of Molotov, had been converted from Russian orthodoxy to her husband's militant Zionism. Living in Toulouse in 1940 David Knout had reacted to the French defeat by circulating typed pages suggesting that the Jews should do something, but unsure of what exactly could be done. He had already set up a secret organization called Main forte to

[53] David Diamant, *Les Juifs dans la Résistance française 1940–44* (Roger Maria, 1971), p. 57; Anny Latour, p. 41; see also Dr. J. Weill, *Contribution à l'histoire des camps d'internement dans l'anti-France* (Éditions du Centre, 1946).

[54] Other money came from Vaad Hatzalah (Fonds palestinien de sauvetage) established at Istanbul and distributed through Switzerland. (Anny Latour, pp. 120–3.)

pursue his Zionist aims against Britain, the main imperialist obstacle in the Middle East to the creation of an independent Israel, and he found it possible to imagine that the defeat of Britain by Germany would promote his ideal. The occupation, the anti-Semitic legislation of Vichy, and the showing of *Le Juif Süss* at Toulouse convinced him that the immediate threat was in France and he spoke to Jefroykin in Marseille of organizing an armed struggle. A group was developed in Toulouse with Knout, Jefroykin, and later Abraham Polonski at its head, the latter also of Russian origin and with some experience of underground activity when his part of Russia was conceded to the Poles in 1920. The group eventually took the name L'Armée juive (A.J.), but the armed struggle did not really materialize until 1943 after the German invasion of the southern zone.[55] Until then the group contributed to the activity of rescuing victimized foreign Jews, and to the development of Zionism in the south. In May 1942 there was a Zionist Congress in Montpellier at which the Mouvement de la jeunesse sioniste was founded, becoming rapidly another network endeavouring to save some of those condemned to deportation from the internment camps.

Unlike most opposition and Resistance groups, the active Jewish movements from O.S.E. to L'Armée juive did not publicize themselves or their cause in clandestine publications. In this respect they were much closer in operational terms to the escape and intelligence networks like C.N.D.-Castille, Alliance, and Brutus, rather than to movements such as Liberté and Libération. Among communist Jews there was more concern for publication and the southern zone received copies of the Yiddish paper *Unzer Vort*, published in French as *Notre parole* or *Notre voix*, which started in Paris in July 1940, taking the place of the previous Jewish communist paper *La Presse nouvelle*, which had been suppressed after the Nazi–Soviet pact.[56] Noted by the French police in October 1940 for its incitement to Jewish and communist opposition against the repression in both zones, *Unzer Vort* was backed by the state-

[55] Diamant, op. cit., pp. 26–7; Latour, pp. 91–100.

[56] Anny Latour argues that relations between Jewish Communists and the party hierarchy were strained after the pact and that *Unzer Vort* was restarted independently (op. cit., p. 29).

ments condemning anti-Semitism which came from *L'Humanité* and the local party Press,[57] and in May 1941 a special tract, calling for unity of the French people against anti-Semitism, was published by the party.[58]

Communists and Jews were closely integrated in the activity aimed at subverting the occupying forces, which the Germans called specifically *Wehrmachtzersetzung* and the French more generally Travail allemand (T.A.). In the summer of 1940 Ernst Melis, a journalist on the anti-Nazi *Deutsche Volkszeitung*, which had moved from Prague to Paris in 1937, created a clandestine centre of the German Communist Party in Toulouse. In the area were the aerodromes of Blagnac and Francazal used by the German air force under the Armistice regulations, and the Travail allemand of the small communist centre started with tracts left in trams going to and from the aerodromes, calling on German personnel to desert or to demand the kind of peace advocated by the Communists as part of their polemic against the 'Imperialist War'. In April 1941 Otto Niebergall was sent by the Toulouse centre to Paris to assume responsibility for all T.A. work in France, Belgium, and Luxembourg, and he became part of an international collective, comprising French, Germans, Austrians, Czechs, and Poles. Their activity, which brought little response from German soldiers until after the Battle of Stalingrad, was mainly confined to the distribution of anti-Nazi literature in German barracks, and in theatres and cafés frequented by Germans, but the importance of the communist T.A. lay less in its sabotage results than in its grouping of Jews into purposeful activity and the network of communication it established.[59] *Unzer Vort* was largely distributed through this network which was manned almost entirely by Jews, and by 1942 it had its own edition in the southern zone. In September it published an urgent warning to French Jews in the zone that the deportations were

[57] See above, pp. 58–9.

[58] *Brisons l'arme de l'antisémitisme* (P.C.F., May 1941). It condemned in general the motivations behind anti-Semitism, and expressed outrage against the recent internment of 5,000 foreign Jews in the northern camps of Pithiviers and Beaune-la-Rolande.

[59] Florimond Bonte, *Les Antifascistes allemands dans la Résistance française* (Éditions Sociales, 1969), pp. 130–9; Knout, op. cit., p. 99 (Knout dates the beginning of T.A. at the end of 1941, not before).

not just affecting Jewish immigrants since 1933. 'People who have lived in France for over 20 years and whose children were born here are being deported from the camps.' Jews in every town 'must set up a Defence Committee . . . to awaken public opinion to the persecution . . . and above all to fight the lassitude amongst ourselves. We must not become sheep led to the slaughter.' Jewish families, threatened with arrest, were told to barricade themselves in their houses, to fight and to make as much noise as possible in order to 'alert your French neighbours'. By these means, the paper concludes, the Jews will gain the respect of the population.[60]

Measured in terms of public reaction, the only short-term success of Vichy's brand of racialism was that no Jewish rising against the deportations occurred, either inside or outside the camps. Its much greater failure was that it provoked a humanitarian reaction which transcended religious and political barriers and gave an unassailable moral strength to the Resistance.

Nowhere was this more evident that in the inter-religious groups in Lyon, epitomized by the Jesuit Père Chaillet. Ever since his return from Hungary in January 1941 Chaillet had not merely volunteered to help the Jewish immigrants and refugees, but had from the start schemed to find homes for Jewish children and escape routes from France for whole families. He had immediately put himself into an illegal and subversive position by procuring false identity papers, and he was adept at concealing the full extent of his activities from some of his more ambivalent colleagues. Few individuals in the southern zone in 1941 had such a developed ideological antipathy to Nazism combined with such an acute sense of underground organization. With increasing urgency after the definitive *Statut des juifs* of 2 June 1941, Chaillet ran a circle called Amitié chrétienne to provide cover for his help to the Jews. One of the principal activists within the circle was a literary student Germaine Ribière, and it worked in co-operation with the vicaire of Saint-Alban in Lyon and with a priest evacuated from Strasbourg, abbé Glasberg, who set up centres to receive Jews 'liberated' from the camps. Glasberg's

[60] *Notre voix* (zone non occupée), Sept. 1942. No figures have been found to indicate how widely this warning was circulated.

Polish origin gave him access to immigrant groups from Eastern Europe and he operated closely with the Lyon committee of O.S.E., with which Chaillet also became increasingly associated in 1942. The Amitié chrétienne, like the Jewish welfare groups, did not start with a wholly underground mentality. It was known to the religious and civil authorities and was supported in its philanthropic aims by the Archbishop of Lyon, Cardinal Gerlier, and the leader of the Protestant churches in France, Pastor Boegner. Gerlier's image was a poor one in the Resistance Press. Rumours were reported by *Le Coq enchaîné* in March 1942 that he was the self-appointed heir to Pétain, a new Richelieu,[61] and *L'Insurgé* in June denounced him as a 'supporter of collaboration who has prostituted his soul'.[62] Certainly throughout 1941 Gerlier was preaching the virtues of Pétainism, but it is an index of Vichy's capacity to alienate its initial supporters that it forfeited Gerlier's loyalty by its overtly racialist decisions in 1942.

In the summer of 1941 Chaillet was entrusted with an essay by his fellow Jesuit dissident in Lyon, Père Fessard, who had responded to the suggestions of two colleagues and had written a searing indictment of collaboration which he hoped to publish for the suppressed Fête nationale of 14 July. The date arrived and no means of publication had been found, and Fessard was forced to leave Lyon on business. Chaillet's own experience with the clandestine Press had been growing during the year by his contributions to Frenay's papers *Les Petites Ailes* and *Vérités*, for which he had provided a 'chronique religieuse' under the pseudonym Testis, stressing the fundamental antipathy between the Nazi idolatry of the state and Christianity, and using his pre-war knowledge of Nazi literature to illustrate his arguments.[63] In August 1941 the Catholic weekly *Temps nouveau*, which had perpetuated the pre-war emphases of Catholic Democracy, was finally suppressed by Admiral Darlan, and in the same month *Esprit*, which had been restarted in 1940 by Emmanuel Mounier with high

[61] 'Après le militaire-traître, pourquoi pas l'ancien avocat, affairiste en soutane': *Le Coq enchaîné* (17 Mar. 1942).

[62] *L'Insurgé*, no. 4 (June 1942).

[63] e.g. in *Les Petites Ailes* (16 July 1941) he quoted a number of *Schwarze Korps* which had said that Christ was great but Hitler was greater, and on 30 July 1941 he quoted from Rosenberg's *Der Mythus des 20. Jahrhunderts*.

hopes that the National Revolution would embrace the spiritual revolution of *personnalisme*, was also forced to stop publication, with no appeal from Mounier himself who was moving into active opposition.[64] With encouragement from these two sources and with financial help from Frenay, Chaillet decided to start a paper of his own for which Fessard's essay provided instant copy with the pungent style necessary to launch a new publication. In November 1941 it emerged as the first number of *Cahiers du témoignage chrétien*, the title borrowed from a small edition of spiritual tracts published from the Jesuit centre on the hill at Fourvière in Lyon, and substituted for the initial idea of *Témoignage catholique* owing to Chaillet's close understanding with Protestants in the Amitié chrétienne.

Fessard's essay appeared as the warning to France he had intended it to be four months earlier. Headed *France, prends garde de perdre ton âme*, it analysed the methods of seduction, compromise, perversion, and destruction by which Nazism was killing the soul of France, after stifling its liberty, an operation in which, he claimed, Vichy and its leader Pétain were collaborating. Under 'seduction' he mentioned the pre-war visits of anciens combattants to Nazi Germany, the pre-war collaboration in the Comité France–Allemagne of de Brinon and Abetz, and the Fascist writings of Brasillach and Alphonse de Chateaubriant. The mentality which made the Armistice acceptable was therefore well prepared, and since then the National Revolution had continued the seduction and had involved the French in one compromise after another, culminating in the anti-Masonic and anti-Semitic legislation which had played on the prejudices of the Catholic Church and the public alike. 'How could the Catholic Church refuse its support for a programme headed Travail, Famille, and Patrie?', he asked, only to add that in so doing it was collaborating in the construction of the Nazi New Order, and in the practice of anti-Semitism 'condemned by the Vatican.'[65] In November 1941 only the communist Press and *Libération* had linked the Vichy internal legislation so unambiguously to Nazi and Fascist principles, a fact which was not lost on the Vichy authorities nor on the Church hierarchy, which, in the vast majority,

[64] See below, pp. 196–205.

[65] *Cahiers du témoignage chrétien*, no. 1 (Nov. 1941), 33–8.

condemned the *Cahiers* as totally unacceptable to the Catholic position. Among the bishops and archbishops in the southern zone only Mgr. Saliège of Toulouse and Mgr. Théas of Montauban received the first *Cahier* as expressing their own views, the norm in episcopal circles being to disown it as communist-inspired, despite the overt rejection of Bolshevism by Fessard as an evil second only to Nazism.[66]

The second and third *Cahiers*, in a combined issue, were written by Chaillet himself and were published with the dates December 1941–January 1942. They further attacked the pro-Vichy sympathies of the Church, in particular its support for the anti-Bolshevik 'crusade' of the Légion des volontaires français contre le bolchevisme (L.V.F.) articulated by Cardinal Baudrillart of Paris and, more locally, by *La Croix du Rhône*.[67] Chaillet's rejection of this 'crusade' was not because of its anti-Communism but because of its collaboration with Nazism, the criterion with which he proceeded to build an unanswerable case against Vichy's racialism in the next eight issues of the *Cahiers*, with the help of his co-Jesuits Père de Lubac, Père Ganne, and Père Fessard and with contributions from Joseph Hours, history teacher at the Lycée du Parc whose influence in Catholic and intellectual circles in Lyon was as considerable as that of Chaillet himself. These eight issues provided a sustained and intensive moral indictment of anti-Semitism which the Church could only refute by endorsing the principles of Nazism, an argument doctrinally blocked by the papal encyclical *Mit brennender Sorge* of March 1937. As such the *Cahiers* were a vital dynamic in the relationship of Catholicism to the phenomenon of Fascism which ranged well beyond the issue of the Jews, while within France itself they were the most potent countercharge to Vichy's anti-Semitic propaganda which was preparing public opinion for the deportation of foreign Jews in 1942. By careful quotations, skilfully used, the *Cahiers* undermined the distinction made by Vichy between

[66] Ibid. 29. In contrast to the episcopal rejection of the *Cahiers du témoignage chrétien*, Alban Vistel suggests that much of the lower clergy responded favourably, particularly in 1942, and he cites two priests in the Ardèche, abbé Sanial at Tournon and abbé Rignol at Silhac, as examples of this support (MS. on origins of Resistance, pp. 631–3).

[67] 'Notre Combat', *Cahiers du témoignage chrétien*, nos. 2–3 (Dec. 1941–Jan. 1942), 113–17.

foreign Jews and French Jews, to show that any anti-Semitism was not only inhumane but anti-Christian. In 'Les Racistes peints par eux-mêmes', published as the fourth and fifth *Cahiers* in March 1942, there were extensive quotations from Hitler and Rosenberg to show that anti-Semitism and anti-Christianity were interwoven into the basic fabric of Nazi ideology, and in the following issue, 'Antisémites', the facts of Jewish sufferings in Germany, Czechoslovakia, Poland, Greece, Hungary, and Lithuania were compared with the facts of the Vichy camps and the legislation behind them.[68]

The massive documentation of the theory and practice of anti-Semitism provided in these two issues was not accompanied by any practical suggestions for revolt or Resistance. They were primarily intended to convert opinion, a task which the next issue in July 1942 admitted was particularly difficult in the southern zone. In the occupied zone, it said, at least all right-thinking people were against the measures persecuting the Jews. Will it be 'the privilege of the unoccupied zone to sit back and allow the poisoning of men's minds?' The anti-Semitism in Nice was specified as an example of public apathy and police connivance in so far as the synagogue could be ransacked on 3 June without any protest, or without any attempt to bring the assailants to justice.[69] Finally, the issue following the deportations of September left no doubt that it was the French who were responsible, though the *Cahier* showed that Vichy's anti-Semitism was at last alienating the Church hierarchy in considerable numbers. Even Mgr. Delay, the Bishop of Marseille, who had publicly rebuked the *Cahiers du témoignage chrétien* for their subversion, was quoted as protesting to Vichy against the deportations.[70]

In the first year of the *Cahiers* their circulation rose from 5,000 to 25,000 and in 1942 to 50,000,[71] and, due to elaborate

[68] In 'Antisémites', ibid., nos. 6–7 (Apr.–May 1942), Jacques Maritain is quoted to summarize the argument of the previous issue, 'La haine antisémite est une frénésie antichrétienne', and Charles Péguy, much valued by Vichy apologists for his nationalism, is quoted as the overriding example of Catholic opposition to anti-Semitism. The issue ends with the couplet, 'L'antisémitisme triomphe, par la grâce de Hitler. La voix de Péguy fait défaut à la France.'

[69] 'Droits de l'Homme et du Chrétien' ibid., nos. 8–9 (June–July 1942).

[70] 'Collaboration et fidélité', ibid., nos. 10–11 (Oct.–Nov. 1942).

[71] Jean-Pierre Gault, *Histoire d'une fidélité. Témoignage chrétien 1944–56* (Éditions T.C., n.d.), p. 29.

organization, its geographical coverage was wide. François and Renée Bédarida, who have analysed the original contacts and distribution networks of the *Cahiers*, show how the Amis de Temps nouveau, the substructure of the prohibited Catholic paper, was placed at the service of the new publication.[72] At its head was Louis Cruvillier, aged 24 in 1941 and a militant of the Catholic Youth Movement (Action catholique de la jeunesse française), and together with fellow students Fernand Belot and Alphonse Drogou his energies were directed to strengthening the network across the southern zone and co-ordinating the mainly middle-aged volunteers who were members of democratic and Christian Democratic circles which had been prominent in Lyon for over half a century. Catholic girls were important in the local diffusion of the *Cahiers* and the Lyon Protestant Pasteur de Pury was just one of the Protestants involved in the network of support and distribution. It was essentially an organization of the southern zone, with the occupied zone barely affected. In this respect the *Cahiers*, like the rest of the clandestine Press in the south, both created and reflected the specific climate of Vichy France in which the development of ideas were a central part of Resistance activity. Such a determined effort to persuade by argument could not be termed a luxury when the majority of the southern zone, in the opinion of most Resisters, was still Pétainist in 1942, and when the welfare and escape organizations which were dedicated to helping the Jews desperately needed at least the passive collusion of the public.

The activity of Chaillet and Amitié chrétienne did not cease under the pressure of running a periodical. On the contrary, Chaillet's success in sheltering and placing Jews grew throughout 1942 to the point where he was arrested by Vichy in September for refusing to surrender fifty Jewish children to the authorities. Abbé Glasberg also moved into open defiance of Vichy and eventually into armed Resistance, and the events of 1942 carried a number of Protestant welfare workers in the same direction.

[72] F. and R. Bédarida, 'Une Résistance spirituelle' 22–5. This excellent article is particularly useful for its details of the interconnection of left-wing Catholic groups within Lyon and their œcumenical co-operation with Protestants.

Since September 1939 the Protestant Comité inter-mouvements auprès des évacués (CIMADE) had been working in refugee and prisoner-of-war camps, particularly among refugees from Alsace-Lorraine in the Limousin and Périgord, and after October 1940 among immigrant Jews interned in the south. The organizer for the southern zone was Madeleine Barot, assisted by Pasteur J. Delpech, and at her request Jeanne Merle d'Aubigné arrived at Gurs in December 1940 to work for the CIMADE. She consistently protested to Vichy at the conditions in the camp and for a period in the winter of 1941–2 a certain leniency prevailed. Abbé Glasberg was allowed to install groups of internees in the countryside as agricultural units and in early 1942 the camp directorate permitted the transfer of several hundred Jews to a centre created by the CIMADE in the Protestant regions of the Haute-Loire. From there they were smuggled into Switzerland. But in mid-1942 the directorate was changed, the co-operation stopped, and the CIMADE along with all welfare groups, was harassed by the Vichy authorities. In October after the deportations Jeanne Merle d'Aubigné was forced to leave, and she moved eventually to a smaller camp near Châteauroux where she co-operated with the military Resistance in the Indre-et-Loire.[73]

The choice of the Haute-Loire by the CIMADE was determined by the siting of the old Huguenot fortress town of Chambon-sur-Lignon which dominated a plateau at the foot of Mont Lisieux. From there it was possible to be well warned of approaching police or military patrols, and, during and after the deportations, the communes of Chambon, Mazet, and Fay-le-Froid, almost entirely Protestant, hid and fed convoys of Jews arriving particularly from Gurs but also from Marseille where a Jewish Socialist Joseph Bass who had escaped from the camp at Argelès set up a network called 'Service André' to channel foreign Jews from the camps into the Haute-Loire. From this Protestant locality, where the local gendarmes were closely involved in the subterfuge activity, lines of escape lay through Catholic convents of the Savoie to crossing points into

[73] Jeanne Merle d'Aubigné, 'Souvenirs de quelques camps en France 1940–47', *Quelques actions des protestants de France en faveur des Juifs*, pp. 28–48.

Switzerland organized by the CIMADE, Amitié chrétienne, and the Jewish welfare agencies.[74]

The CIMADE and the Protestant pastors of the Haute-Loire received official endorsement in their activities from Pasteur Boegner, at Nîmes, whose respect for Pétain and Vichy had been publicly preached in 1940 but who in 1941 became increasingly critical of the regime because of its anti-Semitism. In March 1941 he protested to Admiral Darlan on behalf of the Conseil national de l'église réformée and confirmed Protestant support for the Jews in a letter to the Grand Rabbi. Darlan made it clear that he was concerned to protect the French Jews but that he wanted foreign Jews out of the country. There followed further remonstration by Boegner to Pétain which finally took the form of a full indictment of Vichy's inhumanity during the deportations of 1942. As a result of this criticism he was received by Laval at Vichy who informed him that not one foreign Jew must remain in France. The deportation of foreign Jews, he said, was a 'policy of prophylaxis' ('Je fais de la prophylaxie').[75]

The *Cahier du témoignage chrétien* of October–November 1942 mentioned Boegner's protests alongside those of Cardinal Gerlier of Lyon, Mgr. Delay of Marseille, Mgr. Kolb of Strasbourg, evacuated to Clermont-Ferrand, Mgr. Théas of Montauban, and Mgr. Saliège of Toulouse. It was the words of the latter which soon came to symbolize the depth of the humanitarian response to Vichy's collaboration in Nazi racialism. Read aloud in the churches of his diocese at the end of August his letter declared,

> In our diocese, horrifying scenes have taken place in the camps of Noé and Récébédou. Jews are men and women. Foreigners are men and women. You cannot treat these men, these women, these mothers and fathers in any way you like. They are part of the human race. They are our brothers like so many others. A Christian must not forget this.[76]

[74] An account of this organization is given by one of the CIMADE workers on the border, Geneviève Pittet, in ibid., p. 67.

[75] 'Rapport de M. le pasteur Marc Boegner à l'Assemblée Générale du Protestantisme. Nîmes 24 octobre 1945' (ibid., pp. 4–16).

[76] *Un Évêque français sous l'occupation*', pp. 81–2.

The letter was taken up by the clandestine Press and published in full or in extract by *Le Franc-Tireur* and *Combat* with coverage of the event by *Le Populaire*, and a mention in the Jewish *Notre voix* and in *L'Insurgé*, the latter stating that all sections of the community had joined in protest against the deportations, 'even Catholic priests'.[77] It was not the first time that a paper with its politics on the republican Left had drawn attention to Catholic protests. In March 1942 *Libération* had printed a letter from the Catholic playwright Paul Claudel addressed to the Grand Rabbi of France containing the words, 'I am writing to you to express the disgust, horror, and indignation which all good Frenchmen, especially Catholics, have experienced at the iniquities, confiscations, and harsh treatment of which our Jewish compatriots are victims. I have had frequent relationships with Jews of all nations . . . and I am proud to have them among my friends.'[78] Claudel had written a paean of praise to Pétain in 1940. The anti-Semitism of Vichy forced him to revise his opinion.

The solidarity among Catholic and Protestant action groups in 1942, and the labyrinth of interconnections, mutual assistance, and common escape routes, had more than a functional character. Among the Catholic protesters there was a democratic respect for the liberty of the human individual, and a social concern for exploited and victimized classes, which had their roots in the social and liberal Catholicism of the nineteenth century, as well as in the more recent ideological stand by left-wing Catholics against Fascism in the 1930s. Protestants equally found themselves conditioned by the past, using the rural areas where the legacy of Huguenot rebellion had permanently marked the population, a legacy in the Cévennes which was strong enough to affect even the *haute-bourgeoisie* in Pasteur Boegner's congregation at Nîmes, where pro-Vichy sentiments were initially no less pronounced in 1940 than in any other section of French society. There was thus a common historical struggle for the rights of minorities and the individual, which in 1942 joined with the political heritage of the Revolution, the Commune, the Dreyfus Affair, and the Popular

[77] *Le Franc-Tireur*, no. 11 (Sept. 1942); *Combat*, no. 34 (Sept. 1942); *Le Populaire*, no. 6 (15 Oct. 1942); *Notre Voix* (Sept. 1942); *L'Insurgé*. no. 8 (Oct. 1942).

[78] *Libération*, no. 8 (1 Mar. 1942). The letter was dated 24 December 1941.

Front, to form something approaching an ideology of the Resistance.

Anger against the anti-Semitism of Vichy was one more motivating force leading to opposition where there had been none before, or leading to a more active and subversive Resistance among those already in opposition. It was also a force which invoked a system of values with which most Resisters identified, the defence of individual rights, for whatever the political or moral starting-point of Resistance activity in the southern zone, it was highly conscious of its minority status, and acutely aware of the isolation of the individual.

VIII. Open Expression

To talk about an ideology of Resistance is to suggest a structure of ideas and values which had some independent existence and could be transmitted from one person to another like a body of knowledge. By the end of 1942 this was to some extent in evidence. The historical references in the clandestine Press to ideological struggles of the past, together with the reassertion of republican values in direct response to Vichy and Nazi Germany, did form a loose, organic structure which remained fairly constant for the rest of the war. The struggle for the liberation of France came to be seen by most Resisters within France as involving something more than victory over Germany, while outside France General de Gaulle responded to this growing consensus in his message of June 1942, published widely in the Resistance Press.

Everyone has the sacred duty to do everything he can to help liberate the country by crushing the invader. There is no way out and no future without victory.

But this gigantic effort is already revealing that the danger menacing the nation is not just from outside. Victory will be no victory at all unless it brings a courageous and profound rebirth within. . . . The French people are not only uniting for victory, they are preparing for a revolution.[1]

The precise nature of this 'revolution' remained open to dispute but a wide agreement on the values of a republican ideology can be discerned in most of the Resistance papers of the southern zone and the occupied zone whether they published de Gaulle's message or not, and this ideology was infinitely strengthened by the outrage against the deportation of the Jews.

And yet there can be something misleading in the term 'ideology' as an independent structure of ideas, however loosely it is presented and however often the disparate origins and nature of the Resistance are stressed. It misleads if it moves

[1] 'Déclaration du général de Gaulle, publiée en France dans les journaux clandestins, le 23 juin 1942': Charles de Gaulle, *Mémoires de guerre* i. 678.

away from the element of self-discovery and self-expression which was a major constituent in both the activity of Resistance and the formulation of its values and ideas. Individual Resisters, discussing their motivations, invariably emphasize the strength of feeling which marked their reaction to a particular event or experience and which was significant in their decision to resist. Yves Farge, the Lyon journalist who wrote extensively for *Le Franc-Tireur* and *Père Duchesne*, dates his commitment to opposition and Resistance to the anger he experienced in June 1940 as the Germans entered Lyon:

> The trolley-bus from Tassin stopped to let a German motorized column pass, and some type on the bus dared to say in a loud voice 'The French are at last going to learn what order really is'. I nearly hit him. Then in front of the Grand Hotel there were women waiting to see the German officers emerge. To one of them I said 'Too old for prostitution'. It all began in ways like that.

Such an incident or such an experience of anger and revulsion can be multiplied endlessly through the memoirs and oral evidence of other Resisters, and it was in such reactions that they both discovered and expressed the values of justice, patriotism, individual freedom, human dignity, democracy, and equality that eventually formed the composite ideology of the Resistance. It was something discovered and expressed as if for the first time, even when there was a long background of commitment to the same or similar values. To this extent the values of Resistance were felt rather than learned or adopted, they were expressed in the language of the emotions rather than the language of the intellect and, as a result of this, they were embodied more easily in the imagery of a poem than in the arguments of a political treatise.[2]

[2] In his poem 'Gabriel Péri', celebrating the communist writer who was killed in December 1941 as a hostage, Paul Éluard gave everyday words a new emotional charge, creating a language of Resistance and a language of poetry at one and the same time. The central lines were these:

> Il y a des mots qui font vivre
> Et ce sont des mots innocents
> Le mot chaleur le mot confiance
> Amour justice et le mot liberté
> Le mot enfant et le mot gentillesse
> Et certains noms de fleurs et certain noms de fruits

This is not to say that Resistance was a purely emotional reaction; no such suggestion is intended, but rather that even the most intellectual Resisters found themselves using words and ideas which in other circumstances would have seemed too general, too highly coloured, too emotional, too mystical, even too picturesque. They did so because they accurately expressed their experience of events and their reaction to them.

In the early years, 1940–1, just such a language and ideology had emanated from Vichy in the cult of Pétain: not the same language, and certainly not the same ideology, but a similar depth of commitment, a similar level of emotional content, and a similar correspondence to personality and the feelings of individuals. The expectations aroused by the image of Pétain in 1940 can best be compared not so much with the later cult of de Gaulle but with the image of Liberation as it came to embody the hopes of the Resistance. The promises contained in both were boundless. By the end of 1942 the emotional balance which had told heavily for Pétainism in 1940 was tipping towards the ideas of Liberation, and the ideology of Resistance began to assume a life and structure of its own.

In the history of this development a particular ambiguity is still attached to the self-expression and self-discovery of those who continued after 1940 to publish in the open as opposed to those who moved at once into secret and underground operations. It is not an ambiguity forced on to the period in retrospect but one that existed at the time, though without the cut and dried judgements that have followed. With newspapers there was little cause for ambivalence. The principal source of information for the Press, L'Agence Havas, was taken over by Vichy and renamed Office français d'information (O.F.I.).[3] Repeated instructions and *notes d'orientation* were sent out from

---

Le mot courage et le mot découvrir
Et le mot frère et le mot camarade
Et certain noms de pays de villages
Et certains noms de femmes et d'amis
Ajoutons-y Péri . . .

[3] *Havas-Information* was nationalized in November 1940 and the O.F.I. came into existence by the law of 25 November. See M. B. Palmer, 'L'Office français d'information (1940–44)' *Revue d'histoire de la Deuxième Guerre Mondiale*, no. 101 (1976).

the O.F.I. not only telling newspapers what not to print, but also telling them how they must refer to the government decisions and in particular to the person of Pétain:

In referring to the Head of State the expression 'old gentleman' must be avoided, even when preceded by a well-disposed adjective like 'illustrious' or 'valiant'. Terms which evoke his military past such as 'illustrious warrior' or 'valiant soldier' should be used as little as possible, though in certain circumstances it is permitted to employ the term 'victor of Verdun'. On the other hand, frequent mention should be made of the Marshal's moral and physical vigour, his generous disposition, his lucidity, and the interest he takes in every problem. Such qualities do not have to be directly described, but should be shown in action, as if incidentally. For example:

'The Marshal came forward with a quick and decisive step.'
'He takes the liveliest interest in explanations which are given to him.'
'He welcomes the delegations with warmth and consideration.'[4]

The Vichy Government did not initiate Press censorship, since it already existed under Daladier and Reynaud, but by adding compulsory propaganda to negative censorship it made it necessary for all newspapers to submit to government control or to cease publication altogether.

It was different for the range of publications which were not strictly related to the news media or to political comment. Censorship was less predictable for literary, philosophical, and critical writing, and usually confined itself to prohibiting certain passages rather than enforcing publication of others. Some guide to the cultural maledictions of Vichy was given in the German-inspired *Liste Otto*, a list of prohibited authors which Vichy endorsed and allowed to be distributed to publishers and bookshops in the south. Among those French authors banned to the public in 1940 were: André Maurois, Joseph Kessel, Léon Blum, Julien Benda, Romain Rolland, Pierre Loti, Marcel Prévost, Wladimir d'Ormesson, Paul Claudel, Henri Barbusse, Georges Duhamel, André Malraux,

[4] Quoted by J. Polonski, *La Presse, la propagande et l'opinion publique sous l'occupation*' (Éditions du Centre, 1946), p. 66.

Ève Curie, Charles de Gaulle, Père Chaillet, and Tristan Bernard. The list was periodically updated and names were added in increasing profusion as the Resistance ideology developed.

There was no collective protest from the official body of publishers, the Syndicat des éditeurs, and most publishing houses in the south continued to operate, though in narrow and straitened circumstances. The question for publishers who valued independent expression was to what extent publication in these circumstances was a loss of independence and whether a certain loss was tolerable providing it ensured *some* expression of independent thought and culture. Writers submitting work faced the extra problem of not knowing in advance what the position of the publishers would be at the time of publication. For example, in the winter of 1940–1 the *Nouvelle Revue française* (*N.R.F.*), which had gained a reputation for independent writing of high quality under the editorship of Jean Paulhan, was penetrated and finally taken over by Drieu la Rochelle and other Parisian intellectuals sympathetic to the Occupiers. This change of direction was not fully apparent to intellectuals in the south until the spring of 1941 or even later. Some continuity with the pre-war period seemed to be assured by the appearance in the journal of Gide's *Feuillets*,[5] and even if Drieu la Rochelle's name appeared as director of the periodical there was still the open question of whether the publishing house, Éditions N.R.F., which had grown out of the journal, would be able to remain independent or not.[6] The ambiguity of the situation was exposed in April 1941 when the Éditions N.R.F. published the first collection of poems by Louis Aragon since the defeat, in a volume called *Le Crève-Cœur*. Aragon, who was living in Carcassonne at the end of 1940 when he wrote most of the poems, had been vehemently attacked by Drieu la Rochelle in the journal *N.R.F.* and could in no way be seen as sympathetic to the intellectual collaborators in Paris. Yet the appearance of his poetry under the suspect label of the N.R.F. was none the less an equivocal event in the eyes of those

[5] *Nouvelle Revue française*, no. 322 (Dec. 1940); no 324 (Feb. 1941).

[6] The periodical was founded in 1909 by André Gide, with Gaston Gallimard as its first business manager. It was the publishing house of Gallimard which then ran the Éditions N.R.F.

committed from the outset either to silence or to clandestine publication only.[7]

A precedent arguing in favour of open publication of *Le Crève-Cœur* had been created by the poetry review edited and published by Pierre Seghers, *Poésie 40* and *Poésie 41*, which had begun in November 1939 as *Poètes casqués 39*, bringing together the work of French poets mobilized and cut off from each other in the army. This was the immediate rationale for the review, but its roots went back to the confluence of literature and anti-Fascism in the Spanish Civil War, and its first adopted martyr was the Spanish poet Garcia Lorca, shot by Spanish nationalists in 1936.[8] It was also imbued with republican patriotism and the first issue in 1939 was dedicated to Charles Péguy.

After the defeat Seghers decided that the voice of French poetry needed to be heard even more than during the war itself, and that the original intention of his review, to bring the work of scattered poets together, could be doubly justified in the demoralized isolation of 1940. In Algiers the literary review *Fontaine* had carried the signed affirmation by Fouchet in July 1940 that 'Nous ne sommes pas vaincus'. The police seized the copies after publication but the review was allowed to continue its open existence. In October 1940, after meeting Aragon and Elsa Triolet at Carcassonne in September, Seghers published *Poésie 40* from his home near Villeneuve-lès-Avignon, adopting the stance of Fouchet with an editorial entitled 'Maintenir':

> This is the 5th number of *Poètes casqués*, founded during the war. Should we give up? The idea has not even been suggested. We have created *P.C.40* in defence of Poetry. More than ever Poetry needs to be defended . . . In December 1939 our first issue paid homage to Péguy. His faith, his tenacity, his courage were our example. His independence also. With his 'Cahiers' he met every kind of difficulty. Who would have offered to help him among those who praise him today? . . . We are poor, as Péguy was, but our aims are the same—to present, as craftsmen, work that is indepen-

[7] For an essay on the journal *N.R.F.* during the Occupation see L. Richard 'Drieu la Rochelle et *La Nouvelle Revue française* des années noires', *Revue d'histoire de la Deuxième Guerre Mondiale*, no. 97 (1975).

[8] Pierre Seghers, *La Résistance et ses poètes* (Éditions Seghers, 1974), p. 19.

dent, the best affirmation of those who believe. . . . After a period of bewilderment, fear, and waiting, hope is reborn. The French spirit and its poetry are still alive. No one would dream that they could be crushed . . . Poets and artists can still work independently as we are doing ourselves. Without lies. Our duty is to write our poetry and to build on it.[9]

It is difficult to imagine that such a passage would have passed the censor in a daily newspaper. But the fact that it passed in *Poésie 40* was an encouragement to Seghers to believe that open publication of poetry involved little or no compromise with the authorities. In issue no. 2, published with the dates December 1940–January 1941, he published an obituary homage to the poet Saint-Pol Roux, who died, aged 79, after wounds inflicted by German soldiers who attacked his home in Brittany on 23 June 1940, killing his daughter and a family servant. News of the atrocity, which the German authorities claimed had been a mistake, only reached poets in the south some months later, and the obituary, written by Aragon, was strongly charged with spontaneous indignation and emotion. The censor allowed it to appear, but rejected a poem by Saint-Pol Roux which was to be used alongside. Seghers left the space blank and inserted the word 'censuré', the first of several such insertions which drew the reader's attention both to the fact of censorship and the editor's implicit disapproval.[10]

Two months later *Poésie 41*, no 3 published open contributions by André Gide, Louis Aragon, Elsa Triolet, André de Richaud, Loys Masson, and Pierre Seghers among others, and contained several pages of notes and news about poetry and poets, writers and reviews, acting as a 'Where is who?' and 'Who has written what?' to form links between writers, mostly in the southern zone, but also across the demarcation line. Éluard in Paris received copies of *Poésie* with some regularity, and news of writers who had stayed in Paris was of vital interest to the exiles in the south. The links were not just on paper. Aragon and Elsa Triolet had not been the only writers to settle initially at Carcassonne. Julien Benda, once the pro-

[9] *Poésie 40*, no. 1 (Oct.–Nov. 1940). The review carried the names of five editors: Pierre Seghers, André Blanchard, Alain Borne, Pierre Darmangeat, and Armand Guibert.

[10] *Poésie 41*, no. 2 (Dec. 1940–Jan. 1941).

tagonist of the uncommitted intellectual in *La Trahison des clercs*, was there in 1940, expressing hostility to all things German and angry at the Vichy *Statut des juifs* which had reduced him to inferior citizenship; André Gide stayed there with the crippled writer Joë Bousquet before moving to Nice; and Jean Paulhan came from Paris to visit this enclave of exiled contributors to his *N.R.F.* Not far away was Jean Cocteau at Perpignan, visited in September 1940 by the young Jewish writer and critic Roger Stéphane, whose detailed diary for this period, chronicling visits to intellectuals across the southern zone, and their long, relaxed meals and conversations, is a powerful reminder that in 1940–1 it was still possible for some well-known figures in Vichy France to meet and discuss without risk of subsequent search or arrest.[11]

In the winter of 1940–1 Aragon and Elsa Triolet stayed at Villeneuve, close to Pierre Seghers, before moving on to Nice, where they became the hub of intellectuals in opposition to Vichy and the Occupation during the years 1941–2. Aragon had been decorated in 1940 with the Croix de Guerre and the Médaille Militaire for bravery in crossing enemy lines to retrieve the wounded. He had also received the Croix de Guerre during the 1914–18 War and was therefore a formidable veteran, resenting the accusations against the Communists for defeatism in the wake of the Nazi–Soviet pact, yet unsure in the period immediately after the defeat what to do or how to deal with the disorientation of living in a double exile, both as Communist and as Parisian. *Le Crève-Cœur* contained the poems 'Zone libre' and 'Richard II Quarante', which reflected a mixture of despair, nostalgia for Paris, and finally, at the end of 'Zone libre', the suggestion of hope:

> J'ai perdu je ne sais comment
> Le noir secret de mon tourment
> A son tour l'ombre se démembre
> Je cherchais à n'en plus finir
> Cette douleur sans souvenir
> Quand parut l'aube de septembre
> Mon amour j'étais dans tes bras
> Au dehors quelqu'un murmura
> Une vieille chanson de France

[11] Stéphane, *Chaque homme est lié au monde.*

Mon mal enfin s'est reconnu
Et son refrain comme un pied nu
Troubla l'eau verte du silence.[12]

The poetry of *Le Crève-Cœur* had the same effect on its readers in 1941 as the 'vieille chanson de France' on Aragon himself, disturbing the silence and questioning the inertia of the southern zone. In *Poésie 41*, no. 5 there was lyrical praise for Aragon, elevated to the position of spokesman for France in its crisis, bringing hope, fighting despair, and 'defending man and his freedom'.[13] Shortly before the German invasion of Russia Roger Stéphane visited Aragon in Nice and discussed the Nazi–Soviet pact. Aragon refused to condemn it, arguing that without the pact war would still have broken out, only Russia would have suffered the full German onslaught without any help. Russia, said Aragon, is the country of 'true liberty', but, added Stéphane, 'Aragon has lost none of his patriotism: he always speaks with affection of "his country", and never allows it to be said that the French soldiers were defeated. "They were betrayed", he maintains.'[14]

From Lyon came another open appreciation of Aragon in the monthly journal *Confluences* restarted in July 1941 and edited first by Jacques Aubenque and later René Tavernier. Its opening editorial placed it 'above all political issues', an intention not fulfilled, unless the narrow definition of politics meaning 'party politics' is applied. In the first issue a short review of a book containing a portrait of Pétain declared, 'For the first time in recent years we have a leader of France who not only commands respect but whom we can admire, love, listen to, and follow',[15] and in December 1941 Tavernier gave an enthusiastic review to Pétain's speeches, published under the title *Paroles aux Français*.[16] Nevertheless, the reception of

[12] 'Zone libre', *Le Crève-Cœur* (Éditions N.R.F., 1941). Reprinted in London by Éditions Horizon–La France Libre, 1942, with introductions by André Labarthe and Cyril Connolly.

[13] *Poésie 41*, no. 5 (Aug.–Sept. 1941). The reviewer admits that he has not yet seen a copy of *Le Crève-Cœur*, but knows of its publication and reviews it on the basis of poems already published in *Mesures*, *N.R.F.*, and *Poètes casqués*.

[14] Stéphane, op. cit., p. 69 (entry for 11 June 1941).

[15] *Confluences*, no. 1 (July 1941). The book in question was *Cité nouvelle* by Père Doncœur.

[16] Ibid., no. 6 (Dec. 1941).

Aragon's *Le Crève-Cœur* in issue no. 4 was eulogistic, the reviewer, Marc Barbezat, declaring that, '*Le Crève-Cœur*, whether a song of despair or hope, will remain one of the most irresistible cries that man has ever uttered'.[17] *Confluences* was clearly more submissive in its attitude to Vichy than *Poésie*, but it was read by the same circles and *Poésie* welcomed it openly after the first issue.[18] *Confluences* in its turn reviewed *Poésie* with respect, and gave an excellent notice to *Temps nouveau*, the Catholic journal edited by Stanislas Fumet. The notice appeared in August 1941, the month in which Darlan ordered the closure of *Temps nouveau*, after suspending it earlier for its attack on the film *Le Juif Süss*.[19] The timing of the notice may have been coincidental, but its reference to the high intellectual quality of *Temps nouveau* and the praise for its contributors Fumet, Paul Claudel, François Mauriac, Louis Terrenoire, and Jean Lacroix indicated strong support for the attitudes of the journal.[20] With *Temps nouveau* closed by the government this notice could be read as an open criticism of Vichy.

It was difficult at the time, and it is even more difficult now, to decide the exact effect of these open publications, appearing as they did to be both submissive and rebellious in their attitudes to Vichy and its censorship. An event in Nice at the end of May 1941 is perhaps as symptomatic as any of the ambiguity of the intellectuals' position in the southern zone, aware that their voice could still be heard, yet equally aware of the constraints imposed. The occasion was a public lecture by André Gide on the work of the poet Henri Michaux, planned to take place on 21 May. The Légion française des combattants under its local leader Joseph Darnand took the opportunity to attack the idea of the lecture both for its subject-matter, a poet associated with drugs, dreams, and fantasies, and for its lecturer, a novelist known for his sympathy to the political Left, despite his disillusion with Soviet Russia, and for his widest-known novel *L'Immoraliste*.[21] Both were seen by the local leaders of the

[17] Ibid., no. 4 (Oct. 1941).
[18] *Poésie 41*, no. 5 (Aug.–Sept. 1941).
[19] See above, p. 176.
[20] *Confluences*, no. 2 (Aug. 1941).
[21] On 9 July 1940 the liberal, bourgeois daily paper *Le Temps* had blamed the 'pernicious influence of André Gide' for the formation of an 'arrogant and delinquent generation'.

Légion as symbols of decadence, and they interpreted the lecture as a deliberate assault on the new morality of the National Revolution. On the morning of the lecture Roger Stéphane, who was organizing the occasion, received a warning letter from the Légion expressing displeasure.[22] Stéphane wrote in his diary that he telephoned Gide and Roger Martin du Gard who promptly called André Malraux, living nearby at the Cap d'Ail. Malraux arrived and was adamant that the lecture should not be given but that Gide should read a few words, as offensive as possible in reply to the Légion's attack. When Gide arrived he was both amused and rather bored by the whole issue, but under pressure from the others agreed to make a short announcement. Just before the lecture was due the Légion telephoned to say that it authorized Gide to give the lecture, 'out of respect for his reputation', but the small group decided to keep to their decision. When Gide arrived at the lecture-hall he was greeted by prolonged applause and his short statement, declaring that he refused the Légion any authority either to cancel or authorize his lecture, caused the audience to break into cries of 'Vive la Liberté' and 'A bas la Légion'. Gide retired to further intense applause and both he and Stéphane regarded the occasion as an epic triumph for cultural independence.[23] Nevertheless, Gide went on to publish the lecture as 'Découvrons Henri Michaux' in Éditions N.R.F., and in no. 5 of *Poésie 41* for August–September he was quoted as saying, 'I would never have dreamed of allowing the lecture to be printed if I had been permitted to read it on 21 May as announced.' The ambiguity of the event continued to the end.

The few words read by Gide to the audience at Nice were a more dramatic equivalent of the word 'censuré' in the blank spaces of *Poésie*, and Seghers gave the event due coverage in his review. In *Poésie 41* no. 4 he wrote, 'Andre Gide was due to give a lecture entitled "Discovering Henri Michaux". But those Frenchmen who whistle tunes from *Tannhäuser* have cultivated a taste for obstruction. An attack was expected and

[22] The account that follows is taken from Stéphane, pp. 63–4.

[23] 'Cette manifestation m'apparaît aussi importante que la première d'Hernani . . .', Stéphane, p. 64. The next day Stéphane was told of 165 resignations from the Légion.

M. Gide decided not to give his talk.'[24] This explicit identification of Gide's opponents with German culture was one of the more overt reminders that *Poésie* had an independent voice, despite its continued appearance under Vichy permission. Seghers insists that the readers were in no doubt about this independence and that they quickly learned how to read the review in order to find the carefully, but not completely, disguised critique of those who accepted the *status quo*. His argument, both at the time and since, is that open, but independent, publication had a role no less important in the formation of a Resistance mentality than the clandestine Press. It showed that defiance was possible.[25]

Retrospectively the same has been said about the reappearance of *Esprit*. In November 1940 Emmanuel Mounier, one of the many Parisian Catholic intellectuals who had settled in Lyon after the *exode*, sought and gained permission from Vichy to restart the journal which had been the leading organ of independent Catholicism in the 1930s. During that decade *Esprit* had taken a clear position against Nazism and Fascism; it had opposed the nationalist rebellion in Spain under General Franco and kept its pages open to Spanish republican intellectuals throughout the Civil War; in 1938 it denounced the Munich agreements as treason, and declared that Hitler was an 'insatiable imperialist'. On the other hand, *Esprit* also attacked the totalitarian tendency which it saw in Communism, allowing Victor Serge and Simone Weil to expose it within the republican government in Spain as well as within Russia. Still more vigorously it opposed the individualism, materialism, decadence, and corruption that it diagnosed in the parliamentary democracy of the Third Republic and in the capitalist system which was its substructure. Against these abuses *Esprit* argued for a revolution which would be both 'personnaliste et communautaire' producing a full person, morally, spiritually, and intellectually, through whom an organic community would be created in which a unity of purpose would in no way threaten the plurality of ideas and the sanctity of the person.[26]

[24] *Poésie 41*, no. 4 (May–June 1941).

[25] Seghers, op. cit., pp. 48, 84, 112, 119.

[26] E. Mounier, *Révolution personnaliste et communautaire* (Éditions Montaigne, 1935).

Repeated references to Renouvier, Péguy, Bergson, Max Scheler, Nicholas Berdyaev, and Martin Buber indicated the pedigree of 'personnalisme', but it was in the pages of *Esprit* and in particular in the writings of Mounier that the philosophy integrating person and community was crystallized. It developed in the 1930s as an alternative to both existentialism and materialist individualism as well as a rejection of the traditional hierarchies of Church and State. It was also advanced as a philosophy of education, to rescue youth from the control of family and state by encouraging self-fulfilment. The journal was read principally by Catholics who were politically on the Left, but it was never the organ of Catholic Democracy or, even more narrowly, of the Parti Démocrate Populaire, whose involvement in the parliamentary mechanics of the Third Republic it severely deprecated.

As Mounier admitted in the first number of the new series in November 1940, the tendency of *Esprit* and its regular contributors was to a form of political anarchism entirely its own, in which the reluctance to formulate a coherent political position gave it freedom to praise and condemn as it wished.[27] The distinction made by Péguy between 'mystique' and 'politique', with his passionate preference for the former, was a distinction, and a preference, which pervaded the political thinking in *Esprit*, priming it for the crisis of 1940 in which every kind of 'politique' appeared to be condemned by events, leaving the country susceptible to the emotional and spiritual pull of a passionate 'mystique'. Mounier's own response, once installed in Lyon with his family after demobilization from the army, was one of excitement at the possibility of spiritual regeneration, and of determination not to let the French youth be corrupted by the Nazi ideology whose revolution would be neither 'personnaliste' nor 'communautaire'. On the other hand, the National Revolution of Vichy appeared to Mounier to promise support for the ideals of *Esprit* by its own stress on spiritual values, youth, and the community. Against the advice of a colleague on *Esprit*, Georges Zérapha, who was already involved with the plans of Emmanuel d'Astier for a

[27] Cf. the statement by Aron and Dandieu: 'La Révolution personnaliste, comme l'être humain, est anti-étatiste par essence' (R. Aron and A. Dandieu, *La Révolution nécessaire*, Grasset, 1933, p. 97).

'Dernière Colonne' to fight the Germans,[28] and against the wishes of Marcel Prélot, Professeur de Droit at Clermont-Ferrand, and the syndicalist Paul Vignaux, Mounier restarted *Esprit* in November 1940 to carry the 'personnaliste' doctrine into the youth and community movements created by Vichy, notably the Chantiers de la jeunesse, the Compagnons de France, and the school created to produce the new society's leaders, the École des Cadres at Uriage near Grenoble. The opposition to his decision came from colleagues he much admired, but he countered their arguments by two reiterated statements about the situation of 1940 as he interpreted it. Firstly, he maintained, like Pierre Seghers in *Poésie*, that the situation was still an open one in which the expression of independent ideas was not only feasible but more necessary than ever before. Secondly, he declared that *Esprit* could exploit the similarity between its values and those publicly proclaimed by Vichy and thereby achieve the essence of its *own* revolution, unchanged since the 1930s. Mounier believed that silence or clandestine publication in 1940 was an admission that the situation was either hopeless or inflexibly polarized. Neither was acceptable to him, least of all the idea of inflexibility, for one of the philosophic achievements of *Esprit* had been to give a positive value to the concepts of ambiguity, potentiality, and flux. All these were present in the crisis of 1940 as Mounier intuitively perceived it, and he placed a supreme value on a continuing open dialogue to protect the virtue of pluralism in a world where the new mystique would be totalitarian if no alternative were made available.

Mounier's editorial article for the first of the new series was subjected to several cuts by the censor, a fact which made him anxious that the article should not be misunderstood, particularly by those in the occupied zone. But he found himself reassured by expressions of support from numerous subscribers and noted in his *Carnets* that 'the immense majority of readers have reacted with delight and have read this first issue without

[28] See above, p. 71. Zérapha was of Jewish origin and was in close touch with Daniel Mayer and other Socialists who were building the Comité d'action socialiste. It was he who introduced Mayer to Emmanuel d'Astier, one of the contacts which led so many Socialists to join Libération. See Eschalier, 'Le Journal *Libération*', pp. 7–10.

any misunderstanding'.[29] The journal, and the censorship, continued. On 20 December 1940 Mounier recorded that over twenty-eight pages had been cut from the second issue, that the main article was substantially altered and criticisms of Laval removed, and in January 1941 he noted that Paul Vignaux and other former colleagues who had opposed open publication believed that *Esprit* was more and more compromised. On the other hand, 'Père de Lubac, Père Chaillet (recently returned from Hungary), Père Fraisse, and Beuve-Méry are enthusiastic'.[30] A month later he sent a letter to Étienne Borne containing an explicit defence of his actions: 'At no moment have those who restarted *Esprit* imagined we were becoming "neutral" towards our beliefs, but on the contrary that we were fighting for them.'[31] He also stated that the review was reaching a wide audience in the very youth and leadership training movements which he wished to influence, and that as a result 'Thousands of people in the "free" zone are reading us as the organ of independence and resistance. Subscriptions in the youth camps have become more and more numerous in the last three months.'[32] To Georges Zérapha he wrote in March 1941 that 'we are selling as many copies in the free zone as we sold in the whole of France before the war' and shortly afterwards in a further letter to his critical colleague he argued that he 'had never accepted any political collaboration [with Vichy] and will never accept any'.[33]

Clearly, Mounier was well aware of the delicate balance he was attempting to strike and during 1941 he grew increasingly certain that his review would soon be forbidden. When the prohibition finally came from Admiral Darlan in August he wrote in his *Carnets*, 'Not a trace of sadness or bitterness. The scenario has been played as I had imagined it and wanted it. It has merely lasted six months longer than I had thought it would.'[34] But to his parents he wrote in a different vein: 'What joy to be no longer on the side of cowardice, and to be made by

[29] *Mounier et sa génération. Lettres, carnets et inédits* (Seuil, 1956), p. 275.

[30] Ibid., p. 284.

[31] Ibid., p. 286 (letter dated 22 Feb. 1941).

[32] Ibid., p. 294 (30 Mar. 1941).

[33] Letters of 9 and 23 Mar. 1941. Reprinted in *Esprit*, 18e année, no. 174 (Dec. 1950), 1025–6.

[34] Ibid., 1029.

an official decree the brother of all the innocents suffering for their faith in concentration camps. . . .'[35] Such an expression of relief and pleasure at the banning of *Esprit* suggests that the uncertainty and anxiety about publication had been more profound than he had allowed himself to admit.

The contents of *Esprit* from November 1940 to July 1941 confirm the change which was personally registered in the notebooks of its director, a change from assertive confidence that the situation was favourable to 'personnalisme', to a realization that the opposite was in fact the case. In the first editorial, entitled 'D'une France à l'autre', Mounier's language was at points indistinguishable from much of Vichy propaganda, whether in Pétain's speeches, the populist prose of René Benjamin, or the journalism of Charles Maurras. *Esprit*, he stated, had underestimated the political evil of liberal democracy: 'We believed that it was parasitic, like dust or lichen; but we failed to realize that it was verminous, eating into France as surely as spiritual evil or social disorder.'[36] In 1940, he continued, this particular form of democracy had been utterly destroyed and 'one must acknowledge in the event a judgement rather than an accident of history'.[37] In the face of this judgement France must inevitably examine itself but, Mounier argued, *Esprit* is not content with a negative breast-beating. With the old France dead and condemned it was the intention of *Esprit* to be present in the creation of a new France and a new Europe. 'France has made its confession, my friends. Let the dead bury their dead. Let the dead France bury the dead France. . . . There is more work to be done than ever before. Let us start on it with a good will'.[38]

Two issues later in January 1941 Mounier called for a new 'national unity' and in his stress on 'purification' reflected the consistent appeal of Pétain, but later in the issue he elaborated a youth programme which emphasized a recurrent value of *Esprit*, the insistence that 'unitaire' should not become 'totalitaire'. For this reason he began to spell out his theory of an organic pluralism, and the word 'pluralisme' figured increasingly

[35] Ibid., 1029.
[36] *Esprit*, 8e année, no. 94 (Nov. 1940), 4.
[37] Ibid. 5.
[38] Ibid. 10.

in subsequent issues.[39] No less recurrent was the word 'crise', and it was Mounier's concept of 'France in crisis', or 'the crisis of 1940', which sustained his arguments in favour of open publication. A crucial editorial in February 1941 was given to this subject, called 'Sur l'intelligence en temps de crise', in which Mounier was clearly writing for his own colleagues who had preferred to be silent in November 1940. Attacking a certain 'fanatical opposition', he declared: 'I am obviously *not* referring to those whose ideals and potentialities were crushed by the crisis: for them the only dignity lies in absolute silence and, if they have the courage, clandestine action.' Rather he is thinking of those who refuse to accept the challenge of the crisis out of 'negative discontent and lack of initiative.'[40]

The encouragement given to 'clandestine action' passed the censor for reasons no more apparent than those which allowed so much of *Poésie 41* to survive, but what is evident is that the censor was faced with an *Esprit* already quite different from that of November and December 1940. In those issues the language of Mounier's editorials, if not the content, could be generally identified with the official propaganda of Pétainism so that only occasional sentences needed to be removed or altered. By February and March 1941 the structure of the language and the content were more closely integrated so that occasional censorship could make little alteration to either the tone or the line of argument. To this extent Mounier was not falsifying the situation when he wrote in August 1941 that he had envisaged a total prohibition six months earlier. The censors must have faced that alternative also. Certainly, from February 1941 *Esprit* contained enough criticism of the prevalent values at Vichy to justify Mounier's claim that the review had guaranteed an expression of independent thought. In February Mounier called for an intellectual dialogue and stated that a monologue is fatal for the intellect, one of the fundamental truths which the National Revolution must understand, and later in the same number he repeated the warnings of Charles Péguy against anti-Semitism.[41] In April the concept of 'flux', in which the creation of a new mystique was possible, was

[39] *Esprit*, 9e année, no. 96 (Jan. 1941), 158–60.
[40] Ibid., no. 97 (Feb. 1941), 205–7.
[41] Ibid. 215, 258–9.

applied not just to France and Europe but to the whole world, and the possibilites widened to include the 'rebirth of reason, moderation, and liberty'. In June 1941 there was a vigorous condemnation by Marc Beigbeder of the film *Le Juif Süss* on its visit to Lyon, ending with an expression of gratitude to the 'young Frenchmen who made their opposition clear in the cinema'. The same issue exactly a year after Edmond Michelet had circulated extracts from Péguy as the first act of defiance in Brive contained an article by Roger Secrétan called 'Les Fiertés de Péguy'. He started with a section of Péguy's *Jeanne d'Arc* and quoted at the head, 'Il ne faut pas céder'. It was the first of several quotes affirming Péguy's determination to defend his values by war if necessary and Secrétan concluded with the statement that Péguy, by defining French patriotism as logically left-wing, 'remained loyal to his republicanism and even to his revolutionary faith'. This was not the Péguy celebrated by the Vichy writers René Benjamin and Henri Massis, and the entire selection constituted an overt defence of Péguy's Dreyfusard values even to the explicit remark that 'Jeanne d'Arc would have made a good Dreyfusard'.[42]

After this June issue came the news of the German invasion of Russia, and Mounier was faced with the compulsive need, as he stated in his *Carnets*, to write something powerful about Communism. The result was the July editorial 'Fin de l'Homme Bourgeois' which started with a total rejection of Stalin and Russian Bolshevism in language which rivalled that of *L'Action française*, but moved into a crescendo of hostility directed against the bourgeoisie, the French *petit bourgeois*, the bourgeois promoters of the 'crusade' against Russia, and the bourgeois fears of Communism. Its argument was that even if Russian Bolshevism were destroyed, and Mounier hoped it would be, the challenge of Communism would still remain as a necessary challenge to the complacent rule of the bourgeoisie. It is this challenge that Mounier takes up, arguing that an 'integral Christianity' which cares about social questions and the problems posed by Communism, can defeat the bourgeoisie more completely than Communism itself. And already, he con-

[42] Ibid., no. 101 (June 1941), 536–50. The extracts were taken from a book by Roger Secrétan which was published as *Péguy, soldat de la vérité*. In January 1942 it was given an enthusiastic review in *Confluences*, 2e année, no. 7.

cludes, the great hopes which Communism raised are being adopted by young workers and young peasants in the Chantiers, in the youth movements, and in private groupings, and 'they do not intend to celebrate the end of Communism without a pledge to continue the revolt which it has started'.[43] Mounier was pleased with this issue. On 25 June he wrote in his notebooks, 'We have a brilliant number for July. I've been able to say my word about the anti-Communist campaign, about bourgeois egoism and blindness. The censor, too, is more and more blind . . . Each month I pull a little harder on the rope and one day it will break. But if I didn't it would just grow longer.'[44] It broke after this issue and *Esprit* ceased to appear. It was not republished clandestinely. Most of its values were incorporated in the new publication from Lyon, *Cahiers du témoignage chrétien*, and the readers changed easily from one to the other.

The final issue of *Esprit* showed an attitude to the Nazi offensive against Soviet Russia almost identical to that of Henri Frenay's publication *Les Petites Ailes* and of *Liberté*, in that it welcomed the possibility that Bolshevism might be destroyed in the conflict, but condemned the crusade against Russia mounted in Paris and endorsed by Vichy.[45] This is just one of the many textual reminders that throughout the period of *Esprit*'s publication in 1940–1, Mounier was an integral part of the circles which provided the political philosophy both of Frenay's movement and of Liberté. There had been a meeting at his house on 30 November 1940 which included François de Menthon, Robert d'Harcourt, Joseph Hours, Stanislas Fumet, André Philip, and others already involved in opposition discussions and protests, and it is clear from Mounier's letters and notebooks that the monthly appearance of *Esprit* did little to separate him from this growing opposition. When the review was finally banned, Mounier did not have to search out opposition groups in which to realign himself. He was already associated with them. In fact he was already seen as a dangerous influence by Vichy loyalists, well before the closure of the review itself. In April 1941 the director

[43] Ibid., no. 102 (July 1941), 609–17.
[44] Reprinted in *Esprit*, 18e année, no. 174 (Dec. 1950), 1028–9.
[45] See above, pp. 130–2.

of the École des Cadres had tried to persuade Vichy to accept Mounier as a member of a 'Bureau d'études permanent' but had been refused, mainly due to the hostility of Henri Massis. It was at Uriage that Mounier believed he was doing most to check the growth of a totalitarian mentality within the Vichy system, and the refusal of Vichy to appoint him on to a permanent committee at the school suggests that he was not overestimating his effect.[46]

There is, none the less, a substantial difference between Mounier's attitude in November 1940 and his position in August 1941, and when he devoted himself entirely to opposition and Resistance activity after the closure of *Esprit* this was in no small way due to the self-discovery involved in publishing the review. He had started with optimism but with a great deal of abstract and confused thought: he ended with much of his optimism intact but with much greater clarity and rigour in his ideas. Publication was important to Mounier because it forced him to face the consequences of his own thinking at an emotional as well as an intellectual level. It carried him in a dialectical direction away from his first assumptions about 1940 and the National Revolution to conclusions almost the opposite. Mounier reached these conclusions through the process of defining his ideas in the open, through the exigencies of censorship, and through the hostility he encountered both from former colleagues on the one hand and from the dogmatic and loyal proponents of the National Revolution on the other. His motivation for Resistance was formed by the discovery that his ideas led in a direction which he did not forsee in 1940, and that they led in this direction with an emotional force which made a complete break with Vichy imperative. He needed the period of self-discovery from November 1940 to at least March 1941 for this motivation to take root, just as others in the southern zone during 1941 needed the experience of victimization, political repression, hardship, or the impact of events in the war for their own Resistance to take shape and develop.

With ideas of flux, crisis, mystique, regeneration, and commitment, Mounier, Jean Lacroix, Marc Beigbeder, and other contributors who took part in restarting *Esprit* believed that open publication would give them an influential voice in the creation of a new France. But the more they talked about

[46] *Mounier et sa génération*, pp. 294–6.

flux the more they discovered that Vichy was polarizing France and that not all alternatives were open to the French; the more they analysed the crisis the more they found that a dialogue did not exist; the more they called for a 'mystique' the more they were aware that the Vichy regime was hardening into 'politique', and the more they spoke of regeneration and commitment the more they found themselves advocating resistance to the *status quo*. And it was more than a gradual *prise de conscience* against Vichy's internal policy. There was also the question of national defence. The review started with no sympathy towards the Germans, Nazism, or the fact of Occupation, but rather with hopes and illusions about Pétain, behind whom Mounier and his co-writers ranged the forces of their Catholic patriotism. By mid-1941 they discovered that these forces were wrongly deployed and that Pétain was no heir to the legendary patriotism celebrated by Péguy. The logic of *Jeanne d'Arc* led in a different direction.

At Uriage the same discovery was made by the director Pierre Dunoyer de Segonzac, aristocrat, tank commander, and Catholic, whose initial prescription for the new leaders of France after the defeat was healthy Christianity, moral vigour, military discipline, and the philosophy of *personnalisme*. 'Without delay', he wrote in March 1941, 'we must choose the intellectuals suitable to lead the National Revolution: our choice will fall on those in good physical condition, who are good husbands and fathers and who can jump on a tram as it is gathering speed.'[47] The metaphor for involvement in something with a growing momentum could be seen as just one of de Segonzac's many ambivalent utterances as he wavered between Vichy and opposition during 1941 after realizing that his panegyrics to Joan of Arc, on whose example much of the moral teaching at Uriage was based, were leading to a total rejection of Vichy's *attentisme*. In a speech to the youth of France, broadcast on Vichy radio on 11 May 1941, he came as close to saying this as analogy would allow:

We are about to celebrate the festival of Joan of Arc. . . . She lived in a France two-thirds occupied by the English, a France terribly

[47] Quoted from *Jeunesse France* (8 Mar. 1941), in Dunoyer de Segonzac, *Réflexions pour de jeunes chefs* (Éditions de l'École Nationale des Cadres, Uriage, n.d.), p. 22.

disoriented, anxious, and impoverished. She could have sat back and waited for better days . . . But she could not bear to see her country dismembered and prey to such moral and physical depression. . . . One fine day she left for Bourges, succeeded in convincing the king, and, followed by a few thousand soldiers, defeated the enemy and drove it out of the country for years to come. The story of her battles is astonishing: little preparation, few armaments, simple actions, against an enemy conditioned to repeated victories . . .[48]

The speech concluded with a passage in praise of Pétain, cast in the role to lead France to a regenerated future, but the precise exposition of Joan of Arc's military achievement was the centre of the broadcast, and the Pétainism at the end was no more than an obligatory piece of moral exhortation. The message was there for those who wanted to hear it, and, as it became increasingly overt in the teaching at Uriage, Vichy moved from suspicion to castigation and finally to suppression in December 1942. Frequent visitors to Uriage in 1941–2 were Chaillet, Henri Frenay, Père Chaillet, Emmanuel Mounier, and Père Maydieu, the Dominican who had greeted the Pétain Government with the clenched-fist salute and who contributed to Frenay's publication *Les Petites Ailes*.[49] His visits from Paris kept de Segonzac and his colleagues closely in touch with the realities of the Occupation and although one account of life at Uriage by a student, who attended there in 1942, fails to give any indication that it might have caused embarrassment to Vichy, de Segonzac had clearly drawn the conclusions of his own patriotic arguments well before the final closure of the institution.[50] Like Mounier during the open appearance of *Esprit*, de Segonzac steadily intensified the ambivalence of his teaching and deepened his contacts with those more firmly committed to clandestine activity before finally taking that direction himself.[51]

The link between *Esprit* and the École des Cadres is not just

[48] Ibid., p. 4.

[49] See above, p. 27. By the end of 1942 he was one of the editors of *Lettres françaises* in Paris, the major clandestine organ of intellectual Resisters.

[50] The account is by Gilles Ferry, *Une Expérience de formation de chefs* (Seuil, 1945).

[51] An analysis of Uriage (1940–2), looking at its relationships with both Vichy and the Resistance, can be found in R. Josse, 'L'École des Cadres d'Uriage', *Revue d'histoire de la Deuxième Guerre Mondiale*, no. 61 (1966).

in the person of Emmanuel Mounier but in the fact that the experience of both journal and school was a central part of the crisis diagnosed by so many Catholics in the southern zone. Mounier, Fumet, Chaillet, Maydieu, de Segonzac, and many other Catholic teachers and intellectuals were agreed that 1940 was a crisis not only for France but for Catholicism, and it was not at all surprising that much of the debate about this crisis should be conducted in the open by Catholics who had placed a premium in the 1930s on bold and uninhibited expression. Lyon was the centre of the debate where all possible shades of Catholic opinion on how to meet the crisis and rise to the opportunity were found, and where the dividing lines between those who favoured clandestine operations and those who favoured open publication were at best indistinct. There was not only *Esprit* and *Temps nouveau* exploiting the ambiguities of censorship, but also *Cahiers de notre jeunesse* which was founded in June 1941 and survived until 1943. Essentially the organ of several young Catholics from the A.C.J.F. and from the student movement Jeunesse étudiante chrétienne (J.E.C.), the *Cahiers de notre jeunesse* were most closely identified with the ideas and personality of Gilbert Dru, a militant student disciple of both the Socialism and the patriotic Catholicism of Charles Péguy. This sympathy for Péguy was crystallized by his reading of *Sept*, *Temps présent*, and *Esprit* as a pupil at the Jesuit college in Lyon during the 1930s. He successively supported the Popular Front, condemned the Fascist leagues and the appeasement of Hitler at Munich, and moved from pacifist internationalism to a conviction that the war of 1939 was necessary to defend justice, Christianity, and Socialism as well as France, his family, and his own integrity.[52] Hurriedly mobilized in 1940 at the age of 20 he was taken prisoner but was surprisingly released by the Germans with the rest of his camp at Surgères after only a month. He returned to Lyon and the Faculté des Lettres after a short spell in the Chantiers de la jeunesse, and at once entered the circle of Catholics whose opposition to Nazism and the Occupation was perpetuating the political debate of the 1930s. His history teacher had been Joseph Hours, whom he continued to see regularly, and he was also in touch with Jean

[52] Jean-Marie Domenach, *Celui qui croyait au ciel. Gilbert Dru* (Elf, 1947), pp. 20–8.

Lacroix who wrote for *Esprit*, and Stanislas Fumet, the editor of *Temps nouveau*. His immediate friends Jean-Marie Domenach and Albert Gortais, the General Secretary of the A.C.J.F., shared his ideas of militant student protest and these led in 1941 to a student boycott of *Le Juif Süss* when it came to Lyon.[53] In June 1941 it was Dru who suggested the title of *Cahiers de notre jeunesse* for a new publication to incorporate the ideals of Péguy and to adapt them to the 'crises of Catholicism, youth, and France' in the situation of defeat and Occupation.[54] Albert Gortais was the first editor, followed by André Mandouze, an assistant lecturer in the Faculté des Lettres who had been dismissed as a teacher in Toulon for mocking the Vichy Minister of Education Abel Bonnard.[55] Dru openly wrote the Press review for the journal, but at the same time he was organizing members of the J.E.C. in Lyon for clandestine Resistance and subversion within the University. There is no evidence that he found these two activities contradictory, even after *Esprit* and *Temps nouveau* were banned and the *Cahiers du témoignage chrétien* had started as a fully clandestine publication. The issue of whether or not to publish openly was clearly not one on which Catholic Resistance in Lyon established a consistent position. Dru's Resistance ideas and action seem in no way to have been hampered by his involvement in a journal which even survived the occupation of the southern zone for several months, and thereby could be said to have appeared with the sanction of the Germans as well as Vichy.[56]

For Gilbert Dru, as for Emmanuel Mounier, the experience of open publication did not lead to a state of collaboration with Vichy but in the opposite direction towards greater independence of mind, and towards opposition and Resistance. In their different ways and to differing degrees the openly published journals *Esprit*, *Temps nouveau*, *Cahiers de notre jeunesse*, as well as *Poésie*, are all part of the history of Resistance in the

[53] It was for reporting this boycott in full that *Temps nouveau* first incurred the full censorship of Vichy.

[54] Jean-Marie Domenach, op. cit., p. 37.

[55] Jacques Duquesne, *Les Catholiques français sous l'occupation*, p. 140.

[56] Gilbert Dru was arrested in 1944, imprisoned at Montluc in Lyon, and publicly shot with four other young Resisters in the place Bellecour on 27 July 1944. His political ideas on the formation of a party based on *personnalisme* were part of the clandestine project out of which the Catholic Mouvement républicain populaire (M.R.P.) emerged after the war.

southern zone, even if their role was neither a central one nor without ambiguity. They are also, of necessity, a marginal part of the history of Vichy, for their very appearance points to a certain level of tolerance by the Vichy regime in its initial phase when the sympathies of the majority of the population were at least passively assured. More particularly, the self-discovery made by de Segonzac and Mounier in the open pursuit of their ideas, though in no sense the common experience of all those who started with sympathy for the regime, was far from unique. The failure of Vichy to meet the expectations of many of its more independent sympathizers was due not just to its record of successive compromises with the Occupiers, but also to its increasing lack of imagination in its internal policy. By the end of 1942 it had little more to parade in front of its audience than a blind confidence in Pétain and a series of legislative measures which equalled the bigotry and narrowness of *L'Action française*, its most faithful daily chronicle and index of decline. That Mounier and de Segonzac could find motivation for Resistance in the elaboration of ideas which started as sympathetic to Vichy, tells us much about the varied origins of French Resistance. It also tells us much about the potentiality of Vichy that was lost or thrown away. The history of *Esprit* from 1940–1 and of Uriage from 1940–2 is the history of an alternative Vichy which might have led to the exclusion of Maurrassian prejudice, the isolation of those wanting compromise with Germany, the resignation of Pétain when the Germans invaded the south, and a greater involvement of Catholics and conservatives in Resistance. It is worth these three lines of speculation to emphasize that Vichy chose *not* to develop in this way, but chose to indulge the prejudices of Maurras, to absorb the collaborators, and to continue with Pétain as a narcissistic cipher after the collapse of his personal domain.

IX. Popular Protest

EDITORS of open, but independent, publications were not the only people to experience the direct effect of Vichy censorship. Nor were they the only ones to gain increased motivation towards Resistance by such a confrontation. For thousands of people the equivalent experience was listening to the English, Swiss, or even Russian radio and participating in open demonstrations in the streets. Both activities were subject to Vichy interference, prohibition, and repression and both led people to discover what their own ideas were, where their sympathies lay, and how committed they wanted to be. For some they were expressions of an opposition and Resistance mentality which had developed in other ways. For many, however, they were the very way in which anger, defiance, and commitment were first aroused.

Many Resisters in their memoirs and oral evidence claim to have heard the first broadcast of General de Gaulle on 18 June 1940. Some doubtless did. Far more read about it or heard one of the subsequent broadcasts in the same month.[1] It soon became common knowledge that a French officer had called from the British capital for continuing action, though first reactions to this were made more than ambivalent by the British attack on the French fleet at Mers-el-Kébir on 3 July, at the very time when the broadcasts were beginning to attract a passively sympathetic public. Incredulity, scepticism, and hostility were then added to the reactions of support, even though de Gaulle himself bitterly regretted the British action in a broadcast five days later. Partly because of Mers-el-Kébir and the resulting Anglophobia, partly because the broadcasts became the object of official Vichy antagonism and technological interference from the Germans, and partly because the general philosophy of a confused and demoralized public was not to upset what little equilibrium remained, it quickly became a sign of opposition to call oneself a Gaullist, whether one

[1] The 'appel' of 18 June was published in full on the front page of *Le Petit Provençal* on 19 June and a number of other papers carried news of the broadcast.

knew anything about de Gaulle or not. The curé Alvitre in Brive mystified Edmond Michelet by announcing 'Je suis gaulliste' after hearing the first or second broadcast[2] and in Grenoble a Mme Gonnet, a mother of nine children, turned the wireless on loud so that it could be heard in the street, and made members of the policeforce sit and listen.[3] Neville Lytton, an English artist living in the southern zone near the Swiss border at the time, claimed that he and French friends went straight out and painted 'Vive de Gaulle' on the village walls after hearing one of the first broadcasts, while Lucienne Gosse, writing about Grenoble, and Georges Rougeron writing about the Allier, are just two among many Resisters who emphasize the early importance of the BBC in orientating individual attitudes and creating a form of fraternity among listeners.[4] In the southern zone it was not at first illegal to listen to the broadcasts, so that it was the reaction to de Gaulle's exhortations rather than the fact of listening that was at first significant. By the end of the year it had been made an offence, and listening became more of a calculation.[5] Nevertheless, the number of passive listeners vastly outran the number of those who felt the need to do something, so that the broadcasts devised ways of promoting moderate degrees of activism. For 1 January 1941 Radio Londres demanded that people should stay in their homes for one hour in the afternoon,[6] and during 1941 specific suggestions for demonstrations in certain towns and regions and general demands for the whole of France proliferated. From Switzerland the broadcasts of René Payot on Friday evenings were highly regarded for their moral and cultural stimulus as he evoked the greatness of France,[7] and Lucie Aubrac, one of the pioneers of Libération, claimed immediately after the war that the Swiss Radio had more

[2] Evidence from curé Alvitre.

[3] Alban Vistel, MS. on origins of Resistance, p. 655.

[4] Gosse, *Chronique d'une vie française*, p. 349; Rougeron, *La Résistance dans le département de l'Allier*, p. 12.

[5] e.g. on 26 November 1940 the prefect of the Hérault decreed a fine and imprisonment for those caught listening to BBC broadcasts. Bouladou, 'Contribution à l'étude de l'histoire de la Résistance', p. 57.

[6] 'A deux heures de l'après-midi la ville [Grenoble] se trouva tout à coup étonnamment déserte', Gosse, op. cit., p. 349.

[7] Henri Picard, *Ceux de la Résistance* (Éditions Chassaing, Nevers, 1947), p. 26.

regular listeners in the southern zone than the BBC.[8] Numerically this may have been true, but even for those who praised Swiss support and encouragement listening illegally to the radio meant tuning in to the BBC at a set hour in the evening as it successfully varied its wavelengths to escape German interference.

The concept of Gaullism rapidly became more elaborate and wide-ranging as the broadcasts continued. The fortuitous reference to the pre-history of France and the struggle of the Gauls against the Romans and the punning imagery of two rods ('deux gaules') which could be carried meaningfully in the streets by any ostensible fisherman gave Gaullism a head start as a popular symbol of Resistance over later contenders like 'Giraudisme'; while de Gaulle's regular access to the BBC created a feeling of familiarity among listeners, vital for turning an unsettling minority attitude in 1940–2 into a comfortable majority position by 1944.

To this inner dynamic were added the effects of the propaganda from Vichy, which attempted to equate Gaullism with Communism and any other officially proscribed subversion. Its success in doing this was double-edged and increasingly counter-productive. Monsieur de la Bardonnie, regular reader of *L'Action française* until its support for the Armistice and Vichy, defiantly accepted the label of Communist when proclaiming his overt Gaullist sympathies,[9] and at Périgueux the abbés Sigala and Bouillon did not protest when denounced indiscriminately as Gaullists and Communists for their 'influence néfaste' at the Collège Saint-Joseph.[10] Such unrefined usage of the term for Vichy's political ends meant that long before de Gaulle himself embraced the possibility that Resistance entailed more than the liberation of France the term 'gaulliste' was widely used as a synonym for all opposition. The less that was known of de Gaulle's own political preferences the more easily the term was adopted. In fact the populist element in de Gaulle's campaign from London was always out of step with its military and professional organization. To the directives

[8] Aubrac, *La Résistance*, p. 29.

[9] Evidence from Louis de la Bardonnie.

[10] Files made available by M. Larivière. Entries for November and December 1941.

in conversation w/ Sweets

issued through the BBC encouraging popular demonstrations was added an embryonic form of referendum. Tracts were circulated in May 1941 inviting a full expression of public opinion:

Send this either to the United States Consulate at Lyon or to the United States Embassy at Vichy, with your name or initials.

President Roosevelt has said: 'I refuse to believe that the French people will freely agree to collaborate with a country which is publicly destroying them economically and morally' (Speech 10 May 1941).

Reply: 'The French people do not want to collaborate.'

Signature . . . . .[11]

As a functional device this was probably less important for the effect it had on President Roosevelt than for its impact on the individuals who were prepared to make their signatures public, though neither result is known. What *is* known is that the non-Communist clandestine Press at the beginning of 1942 was induced to adopt Gaullism not just in the hope of financial and military support from France Libre but because it was a symbol of solidarity which needed no public re-education. It was the symbolic importance of de Gaulle which was stressed by almost all the papers. *Le Coq enchaîné* in its first number in March 1942 claimed that 90 per cent of the French had rallied to de Gaulle in the same way that the people of France had rallied to the First Republic after the Battle of Valmy: 'Republicans, democrats, and syndicalists, we are with de Gaulle because he personifies the fatherland, and because today he has become the symbol of Liberty'.[12] The statistics were wildly optimistic, and were not the claim of other papers, though *Combat* came closest in its evaluation of public support: 'The immense majority of public opinion has, since the beginning, seen in de Gaulle the man who saved French honour and embodied the hopes of the fatherland'.[13] *Libération*, like *Le Coq enchaîné*, asserted the symbolic importance of de Gaulle,[14] and

[11] Tract reproduced in photocopy in Bouladou, op. cit., p. 70.

[12] The headline stated 'Les Faits prouvent: Un traître Pétain: Un patriote De Gaulle'.

[13] *Combat* (Mar. 1942).

[14] *Libération* (15 Feb. 1942).

Le Franc-Tireur accepted his leadership of the current struggle, but warned that there should be no dictatorship after the liberation.[15] In almost all cases Gaullism was adopted with less reference to de Gaulle's initiative of 18 June 1940 than to the status Gaullism had achieved by the end of 1941, and with equal uniformity the papers made direct contrasts between de Gaulle and Pétain, rejecting the symbol of Vichy as a logical step before acknowledging the leadership of de Gaulle. *Le Franc-Tireur* even composed its alternative lyric to the popular Pétainist song 'Maréchal nous voilà':

Général nous voilà
Résolus à lutter pour la France
Car tous les braves gens
Marcheront sous de Gaulle au Combat.
Général nous voilà
Tu nous as redonné l'espérance
La patrie survivra
Général, général, nous voilà.[16]

This recognition of de Gaulle did not make the clandestine Press a subservient organ of France Libre. On the contrary, the independent origins of Resistance in the southern zone continued to mark the character and interests of the various movements. Their Gaullism was an effective way of presenting Resistance as a unifying force and thus answering the accusation mounted by Vichy that their action was further dividing the French. By the end of 1942 this nominal unity had begun to assume organizational strength, a development largely due to the work of Jean Moulin, de Gaulle's influential emissary in 1941–2 whose missions to both zones firmly established de Gaulle as the acknowledged 'leader' of the Resistance.[17]

The adoption of the term 'gaulliste' by sympathetic listeners to Radio Londres and the ensuing recognition of de Gaulle by the non-Communist clandestine Press were the simplest ways in which a common language of Resistance was created. 'Vive

[15] *Le Franc-Tireur*, no. 2 (Mar. 1942).

[16] Ibid.

[17] The achievement of Jean Moulin is rightly highlighted by most Resistance histories. See also Henri Michel, *Jean Moulin. L'Unificateur* (Hachette, 1964), and Laure Moulin, *Jean Moulin* (Presses de la Cité, 1969).

de Gaulle' written on walls or across Vichy and German posters together with the symbol of the cross of Lorraine became the popular iconography of Resistance. Its spread needed no elaborate planning or skill, and in the southern zone far less audacity than in the occupied north. The very simplicity was its recommendation, for every Resistance movement needed a range of simple actions which it could recommend to a public wider than the small core of initiated and militant Resisters.

Equally simple and equally fundamental was the public demonstration on traditional days of holiday and festival, when planning and spontaneity, individual and mass, the defiance of the act and the safety of numbers all combined to make it the ideal public expression of Resistance, local in its structure and national in its ultimate aims. The Vichy regime gave added significance to the traditional holidays by banning the customary celebrations on 14 July and appropriating the first of May as the Fête of St Philippe, the latter only fully apparent as a rejection of the labour movement after the *Charte du travail* of October 1941. The first of May 1942 was therefore the first national occasion on which the forces of labour showed the potential of their massed protest, a rehearsal for the far greater event on 14 July two months later. There had been small demonstrations a year before in some of the main towns and several marches to the local war memorials on 11 November, but few Resisters claim any substantial demonstrations before 1942.

In Lyon the first major demonstration was linked not to a traditional holiday but to a cultural event, the visit of the Berlin Philharmonic Orchestra on 18 March 1942. André Plaisantin, Catholic, trade-unionist, and one of the organizing pioneers of Combat in Lyon, has fully described the event, a description which indicates the nature of many of the subsequent demonstrations also:

Four or five days before the scheduled concert we decided to mark the event by a mass distribution of tracts and a demonstration. We wrote the tracts in a popular style finishing with the statement 'Les Boches de Berlin ne joueront pas' . . . The diffusion, starting at dawn on 18 March went perfectly . . . All day tracts were thrown from trams or dropped from blocks of flats. The day before we had explored all the roofs of the concert-hall hoping to prepare an act of sabotage, but we had to reject the idea . . . From seven o'clock on the evening itself Resisters began to assemble in the place des Terreaux. By eight o'clock a third of the square was full. A police barricade arrived to contain the crowd, and anyone who tried to pass through the crowd towards the concert-hall was jeered and hissed. Very few attempted it. A worker taking a chair into the hall stepped off the pavement and then turned to the demonstrators and shouted at the top of his voice 'I won't go'. Enormous applause greeted his statement. . . . The fervour of the demonstration was such that it spilled down the main streets with cries of 'Les Boches à Berlin'. There was a spontaneous demonstration outside the United States Consulate in the place de la Bourse. Trams were stopped and fights broke out between demonstrators and police. There were numerous arrests.

This was the first great public demonstration of Resistance. The result galvanized our activity. We began to have confidence in ourselves.[18]

The event was reported by *Libération* at the beginning of June,[19] by which time the paper had already given full coverage to the subsequent and larger demonstration of 1 May, printing a photograph of the huge Lyonnais crowd in the place Carnot, and claiming an equal success for demonstrations in Marseille, Nice, Toulouse, Saint-Étienne, Avignon, Montpellier, Sète, Toulon, Clermont-Ferrand, and Chambéry.[20] *Le Coq enchaîné* called 1 May 1942 'the Tennis Court Oath of the present day. Intellectuals and workers assembled fraternally together and swore not to separate until they had liberated France.'[21] It is noticeable that after May all clandestine newspapers, particularly those with a political tendency to the Left, carry greater certainty and assurance, and the results of 14 July further increased this confidence.

Between May and July the Vichy regime indulged in the

[18] André Plaisantin, 'Sur les origines de Combat à Lyon' (May 1949). Unpublished MS. kindly lent by M. Plaisantin. Also evidence from André Plaisantin. The demonstration had its counterpart in Toulouse three months later when a German speaker Dr. Grimm arrived to give a lecture. A crowd assembled in the place du Capitole and sang the Marseillaise outside the lecture-room where Grimm was speaking in front of a huge reproduction of Hitler and Pétain shaking hands at Montoire (*Libération*, no. 15, 14 July 1942).

[19] *Libération*, no. 13 (3 June 1942).

[20] Ibid., no. 12 (18 May 1942).

[21] *Le Coq enchaîné* (10 May 1942).

most direct public overtures to Germany since the meeting of Hitler and Pétain at Montoire in October 1940. On 18 April 1942 Pierre Laval was recalled to office to replace Admiral Darlan and two months later he stated on the radio, 'I desire the victory of Germany, because, without it, Bolshevism will establish itself everywhere'.[22] The speech contrasted starkly with de Gaulle's message broadcast from London and published in the clandestine Press at the end of June in which he extolled the concept of liberation and then accepted the notion of revolution.[23] Undoubtedly this dramatic confrontation gave an extra emotional charge to 14 July 1942, for which the Resistance Press, as well as the BBC, fully prepared the public. The instructions from London, broadcast repeatedly, were specific, giving time and place. Some papers did the same. The communist *Rouge-Midi* in the Bouches-du-Rhône retold the story of 14 July 1789 and called for the same spirit in 1942. 'Demonstrate! Assemble *en masse*. Tuesday 14 July at 6 p.m. in front of the local *mairie*',[24] and *Libération* gave time and place for eleven major towns in the southern zone.[25] Most papers timed a July issue to emerge immediately after the demonstrations, and the tone of all reports was triumphant. *Le Populaire* claimed 100,000 at Lyon, 100,000 at Marseille, 15,000 at Toulouse, and 5,000 elsewhere in many smaller towns.[26] The figures were kept in the next issue except for Toulouse where they were increased to 40,000.[27] *Le Franc-Tireur* was no less euphoric and reported that crowds of some 200,000 in Lyon were shouting 'Death to Laval' and 'Vive de Gaulle'.[28]

The demonstrations were the clearest confrontation between public and authority since the establishment of Vichy, a clash which was only avoided in certain towns either by careful organization or by the reticence of the local police. At Avignon

[22] Broadcast of 22 June 1942. Details of Laval's contacts with the Germans between May and June and the context of this broadcast are given in Warner, *Pierre Laval and the Eclipse of France*, pp. 291–317. The phrase quoted here became one of the main items on which Laval was tried and sentenced to death in October 1945.

[23] See above, p. 185.

[24] *Rouge-Midi* (Organe du P.C., région des Bouches-du-Rhône) [July] 1942.

[25] *Libération*, no. 15 (14 July 1942).

[26] *Le Populaire*, no. 3 (15 July 1942).

[27] Ibid., no. 4 (15 Aug. 1942).

[28] *Le Franc-Tireur*, no. 9 (July 1942).

the parade took place in defiance of a repeated local prohibition, and the demonstrators deliberately placed young children at its head to prevent police repression.[29] By contrast, at Saint-Étienne there was violence between the demonstrators and members of the Légion who had successfully helped to break up the much smaller demonstration of 1941.[30] The conflict was reported in a special edition of the clandestine *Espoir* which congratulated the populace for a demonstration of over 20,000 which it compared to the 'miserable 143 members of the Légion who tried to tear the tricolour from the hands of the crowd. For the first time people felt free to speak their mind.'[31]

This concluding sentence from *Espoir* captures the importance of the demonstrations as well as any statistics. In July 1940 the majority of the French turned in on themselves. *Ils sont rentrés chez eux*. For two years they stayed in their closed world buttressed by the reasoned argument that nothing could be done and that it was best to wait for things to improve. In 1942 they began to emerge, encouraged by the old and acceptable tradition of mass gatherings on festival days, rediscovering collectively what small groups and individuals had rediscovered alone, that past beliefs and actions could not be indefinitely repressed. Acknowledging this was part of the self-discovery which took people into Resistance, and in these two events of 1942 thousands of people began to be themselves again and 'felt free to speak their mind'.[32] The history of Resistance has numerous starting-points at which different people felt, for the first time, more free in opposition than in passive submission.

The significance of the demonstrations was, however, greater than this and they cannot be understood by a stress on political self-expression alone. The social and economic background was vital. During 1941 Vichy had alienated different groups and individuals by its political discrimination, a right-wing authoritarianism which was launched on the assumption of majority support, or at least inaction. Other repressive regimes in modern history have found it possible to survive for a period

[29] Autrand, *Le Département de Vaucluse de la défaite à la liberation*, p. 69.

[30] Faure, *Un Témoin raconte . . .*, p. 73.

[31] *Espoir* [July 1942].

[32] *Le Père Duchesne*, in its edition of May 1942, called the first of May 'Printemps de la Liberté' and, after reporting on the demonstrations, added 'Le Peuple de France retrouvait sa voix. Quel beau moment.'

providing they assured a degree of economic satisfaction in exchange for this support or inaction. Vichy was in no position to do this, and as the economic situation in France rapidly deteriorated so its basis for continuing as a repressive regime narrowed and finally disappeared.

Figures of German expropriation were not made available to the public, whose only guide to the economic state of France was through wages, prices, and rationing.[33] To this *ad hoc* knowledge the clandestine Press added details of goods requisitioned by Germany as random information allowed, though the exact accuracy of the figures was less important than the basic fact of massive German demands, fatally lowering the French standard of living.[34] By late 1941 few housewives were unaware of the rapid price inflation in basic foodstuffs and few workers were under any illusion about the substantial decline in real wages. Money wages had been frozen at the level of 1 September 1939 and although there was one national increase in May 1941 and an increase in child allowances in February, the net improvement in the standard of living was seen as derisory. Local trade union meetings were still permitted until the enactment of the *Charte du travail* and their demands for anything up to a 50 per cent increase in wages occurred with regularity throughout the autumn and winter of 1941.[35] In

[33] Details of the German demands on the French economy are contained in Milward, *The New Order and the French Economy*. Direct requisitioning gave way to a system of quotas in August 1940. Thereafter the development of German involvement in French industry and the expansion of trade between Germany and Vichy meant that by 1943 Germany was directly using at least 40 per cent of French resources. For example, in 1942 only 37 per cent of the work force in the aeroplane industry was working for French purposes, and from December 1940 the Vichy Government successively endorsed various agreements by Vereinigte Aluminiumwerke and the French Compagnie des Bauxites for massive exportation of bauxite to Germany. None of these details was published by Vichy.

[34] e.g. the Communists in the Beaujolais area stated in September 1941 that '70% of all products go to Germany' and that '80% of the Beaujolais wines were requisitioned by the Germans in 1940'. (*La Voix des vignerons beaujolais*, Organe de défense paysanne, édité par la région lyonnaise du Parti, no. spécial des vendanges [Sept. 1941].)

[35] e.g. the Syndicat du Bâtiment et Bois in Lyon sent a list of demands to the government in October 1941 claiming, *inter alia*,

1. A general increase of wages of 50 per cent.
2. A return to free collective bargaining.
3. A minimum of 500 grammes of bread, 2 litres of wine, and half a packet of tobacco per day, per worker.
4. Free replacement of working clothes and shoes.

the early months of 1942 scarcity was added to high prices and the phenomenon of the black market began its ambivalent ascendance in the towns, hated by everyone but widely used. Vichy had grouped *départements* into regions of which there were six in the southern zone: Lyon, Marseille, Montpellier, Clermont-Ferrand, Limoges, and Toulouse. The regional prefects had in practice considerable freedom in determining their policy of *ravitaillement*, competing with neighbouring regions by attempting to keep any surplus within their own borders. Separate *départements* within the region followed this lead so that rural areas where mixed farming was prevalent, like the Dordogne and the Corrèze, were far better fed than *départements* with a large urban population like the Rhône and Bouches-du-Rhône, those with a monoculture like the wine-growing Hérault, or those with little or no arable farming such as the Alpes-Maritimes. By March 1942 working people in the big towns were hungry,[36] and the dynamic of hunger was a powerful motivation for opposition.

Within the clandestine Press it was the local communist papers which gave most prominence to the cost of living, indicating in detail what wages would buy and contrasting this with the minimum food and drink necessary for a working family. Invariably the contrast revealed that families were able to purchase only a half or no more than a third of what was deemed necessary.[37] The urban housewife without friends or

---

5. Payment in advance of the annual holidays.
6. Reconstitution of the C.G.T. and freedom of trade unions.
7. Amnesty for all trade-unionists imprisoned for their opinions.

(Archives de l'Union syndicale du Bâtiment (C.G.T.), Bourse du Travail, Lyon.)

[36] M. Bouladou cites a prefectoral report for Montpellier of May 1942 which read 'La faim règne, sauf chez certains grands propriétaires ou ceux qui peuvent acheter à prix d'or', Bouladou, p. 66.

[37] e.g. *Le Travailleur alpin* (Mar. 1942); *Le Travailleur du Languedoc* (15 Jan. 1942). In November 1942 *L'Insurgé* summarized 'two years of Fascism' with two columns of average prices (fr.):

	August 1939	October 1942
Bread	1·55 per kg	3·70 per kg
Potatoes	0·75 per kg	2·10 per kg
Meat	21·00 per kg	35·00 per kg
Wine	1·70 per l	5·70 per l
Butter	27·00 per kg	64·00 per kg

The quantities of these foodstuffs demanded by *Le Travailleur alpin* in March 1942 for a family of four was: 2 kg of bread per day, 2 l of wine per day, 2·4 kg of meat

family in the country, without a suburban plot of garden, and without the money to buy on the black market, had only one extra access to the food she needed and this was a direct appeal to the local *mairie* or *préfecture*. Such an appeal in the form of a collective demonstration by angry housewives became a regular event in the big towns throughout the early part of 1942, vigorously promoted by the left-wing clandestine Press.[38] *Le Travailleur du Languedoc*, the communist paper based on Montpellier which had upheld the republican tradition of 1848, the Commune, and the cause of Dreyfus,[39] carried a report in January 1942 of successful demonstrations by housewives in the small towns of Frontignan and Bédarieux. Protesting at the *mairie*, the women had succeeded in their demands because, claimed the paper, they had gone there in their hundreds: 'This is the right way to do it. Hitler and Pétain are afraid of the people, which is why sooner or later your protests will be successful.'[40] Subsequent issues kept up the pressure for more organization and more protests from the women of the area, encouraging them with details of the hunger and cold experienced in the months of January and February. On the Languedoc coast at Sète, a fishing port with some of the larger factories of the region, a special hand-written tract called *Le Travailleur sétois* also referred to a successful women's demonstration in January, backed by strikers in the docks,[41] while at Montpellier the prefect was forced to grant an extra three eggs and 300 g of dried vegetables for every ration card after a clash between the police and women demonstrators.[42] At Lyon

per week, 1·5 kg of potatoes per day, and 4 kg of butter per month. According to the prices above this would have meant an expenditure in October 1942 of 1,206·60 fr. per month on these foodstuffs alone, when the average monthly wage of a building-worker in Lyon was 1,760 fr. and in rural communes in the *département* of the Rhône no more than 1,280 fr. (These averages taken from a document in the Bourse du Travail, Lyon, entitled *Borderaux des salaires minima concernant le Bâtiment et les Travaux Publics en vigueur dans la région préfectorale de Lyon, à partir du 16 mai 1942*.)

[38] As early as December 1940 *L'Humanité de la femme* had called on housewives to demonstrate at the local *préfecture* to secure the release of hoarded stocks of potatoes.

[39] See above, p. 59.

[40] *Le Travailleur du Languedoc* (15 Jan. 1942).

[41] *Le Travailleur sétois* (Jan. 1942).

[42] *Libération*, no. 2 (15 Feb. 1942).

the violence was greater after a police charge had provoked the women to seize two policemen and threaten them with strangulation. The result was 200 extra grammes of *choucroute* for each card and the release of women demonstrators who had earlier been arrested.[43] In Marseille *Rouge-Midi* constantly exhorted the women to demonstrate, but the full power of the local housewives was proclaimed separately in a special women's paper circulated in May, June, and July 1942 called *Femmes de Provence*. The content of the first issue was a lengthy polemic against the Vichy stress on the family and its celebration of Mother's Day. 'The criminal government of Pétain–Laval, responsible for our miseries, announce with their usual cynicism that on Mother's Day 300,000 special teas will be offered in the southern zone, when millions of children are hungry *every* day.' The paper called for a demonstration at 4 p.m. in front of the local *mairie* on 31 May, la Fête des mères, and made it clear that it was Pétain's collaboration with the Germans which was at the root of the economic distress.[44] For 14 July the call for a demonstration by the women of Marseille and its region was located firmly in history. 'Women were in the forefront of the 1789 Revolution and contributed to the formation of the Volontaires marseillais who left to defend France. This group distinguished itself in the capture of the Tuileries in August 1792 . . . for which de Lisle composed 'La Marseillaise'. Women of Provence, show yourselves worthy of them.' On the second page a successful women's protest at Aix was claimed to have gained an extra kilogramme of potatoes, and the paper concluded with a militant cry of revolt, encouraging the women to invade all local food stores including luxury restaurants and shops, and liberate the food for their families.[45] By the end of 1942 this was widespread advice in the left-wing papers of the south, though it was more normal to direct the women against the public authorities, the mayor, and the prefect, rather than against the private concerns. *L'Insurgé* in Lyon was adept at provocation of this kind, carrying in its September issue, for example, two lines on the back page

[43] Ibid. The paper's conclusion was biblical: 'Advice to the hungry. Ask and it shall be given to you.'

[44] *Femmes de Provence* (Organe régional d'union et de défense des femmes des Bouches-du-Rhône) [May 1942].

[45] Ibid. (July 1942).

saying 'If you want butter, housewives, go to M. Angeli the regional prefect. He's just had 60 pounds delivered from the black market. Help yourselves to half a pound . . .'[46]

Without an emphasis on this swell of public protest against hunger and cold in the winter of 1941–2, any account of the events of 1 May and 14 July would lack a crucial dimension. The collective discovery of freedom to 'speak one's mind' on 14 July was inextricably linked with the earlier discovery that direct action could bring results; results which were measured not just in terms of extra rations but in terms of motivation to opposition and Resistance. Demonstrations, whether of a handful of housewives or 100,000 Lyonnais, helped to polarize the situation at a local level, undermining the consensus on which Vichy had launched its internal policy and on which it justified its negotiations with the Germans. Conflict with local police drew public attention to the repressive nature of the regime as a whole, and added to the numbers of victimized. To each Press report of a women's demonstration were added the figures of those arrested and in the area itself the arrests gave new reason for protest even if some economic satisfaction had been gained. The cumulative effect was to weaken the hold of Vichy, to politicize increasing numbers of the public, and to focus attention on the reality of being a defeated and occupied country. It was something which the clandestine Press had attempted to do from the first issue of *Liberté* onwards.[47] The combined effect of hunger and cold and the opportunity for protest afforded by traditional days of mass gatherings and public expression helped to achieve a momentum of opposition which the Press alone could never have achieved.

It was not, however, inevitable that hunger would lead to opposition either against the Germans or even against Vichy. Several Resisters have pointed out that in towns like Nice and Marseille, where hunger was far worse than in most inland towns, there was no obvious mass increase in opposition.

[46] *L'Insurgé*, no. 7 (Sept. 1942). In its issue of 26 June 1942 *Le Coq enchaîné* also accused Angeli of benefiting from the black market.

[47] In this first issue on 25 November 1940 the southern zone was called 'La France contrôlée' and news was given of German requisitions in Marseille. On 16 May 1941 *Tour d'horizon*, produced by General Cochet, stated that everyone knew that the Germans controlled the southern zone as well as the occupied zone and that they were using French factories in the south.

Madeleine Baudoin is one who asserts that people in Marseille became more Pétainist as the restrictions and shortages began to bite, since they argued that without Pétain the situation would be much worse.[48] For the majority this was almost certainly the case. Obsession with the problems of *ravitaillement* was a mass phenomenon and yet Resistance before 1942, and even after, was always the province of a minority. And yet this minority was not a static one: it was steadily increasing in size, and although there was no guarantee of a causal relationship between hunger and Resistance, anger against the injustices of food distribution played a substantial part in transforming a small minority into a larger one.

The momentum of public protest achieved in the first half of 1942 was sustained in the autumn by the law of 4 September subjecting all medically fit men between 18 and 50 and all single women between 21 and 35 to work which the government might judge 'beneficial to the over-all interests of the nation'. First announced by Laval in his broadcast of 22 June, a new labour scheme, the *Relève*, was vigorously promoted by Vichy over the late summer. The scheme, said Laval, would enable volunteers to opt for work in Germany and thereby secure the release of prisoners of war. The idea of the *Relève* (relief of prisoners) was given teeth by the September legislation and was advanced with the same arguments as the idea of collaboration in the autumn of 1940, both products of Laval's inventive and activist mind. The public was told that the scheme would further improve the favoured place of France within German-dominated Europe and that co-operation by unemployed, or underemployed, workers would be in their own economic interests as well as in the interests of the country as a whole. The average real wage in Germany was quoted as higher than in France, and the freedom of workers to send parcels and money home to their families was promised as one of several incidental benefits. Posters advertising the *Relève* claimed that each worker would be an 'ambassador of French quality' in the German factories. To discover who the available workers were, the managers and owners of industry were instructed to compile lists of those made redundant or working less than full time. This covert invitation to employers to reduce their work force

[48] Evidence from Madeleine Baudoin.

and cut their employment costs was not something made as public as the rest of the scheme.

The campaign for the *Relève* coincided with the deportation of foreign Jews from the southern camps, and the coincidence was not seen as accidental by the Resistance Press. From the start the *Relève* was denounced as the deportation of workers to slave-labour in Germany, but it is clear from the tone of the arguments that some workers were allowing themselves to be attracted by the scheme. *L'Insurgé*, for example, found it necessary to give a detailed counter image of the fate of workers in Germany to offset the Vichy propaganda:

Journey:	long, little food, under German supervision.
On arrival:	camps where workers treated like cattle.
Later:	sleeping in barracks, herded together.
Work:	12 hours a day, piece-work but no increase in wages.
Wages:	enormous taxes and fines.
Cost of living:	higher than in France.
Food:	not even enough for Italians who are used to low subsistence.
Freedom:	nil.
Conclusion:	exploitation; prisoner's status. Thousands of workers killed by bombing.[49]

In the same issue the subject was pursued by a report on successful strikes in Lyon starting in the railway works at Oullins on 14 October and spreading to metal workers and other industries on the following day. The result was a promise that the departure of workers for Germany would be postponed. Heavy warnings and confident reporting of resistance was the norm in the rest of the Press. *Le Populaire*, the socialist paper, mocked the Vichy propaganda, particularly its claim that the workers were volunteers, and described the scheme as a total fiasco. To workers it advised only one plan of action: 'Disobedience and Sabotage', printed in huge letters across the foot of the

[49] *L'Insurgé*, no. spécial (9 Oct. 1942). Some illusions about the freedom of workers in Germany persisted even among those hostile to the *Relève*. In Toulouse the group Libérer et fédérer published a monthly factory paper which told any worker taken by the *Relève* to pick a contact who would remain in France and to whom the worker could send any useful information from Germany and from whom he could receive news of France and orders from Libérer et fédérer. (*Journal d'usine* [end of 1942].)

page.[50] In Limoges a trade union paper *Le Métallo du Centre-Ouest* reported that a mass strike and demonstration of over 12,000 secured the postponement of a convoy of workers due to leave on 13 November. Out of 830 workers scheduled to leave 826 refused to sign the papers which said they were volunteers.[51] At Tulle, the *chef-lieu* of the Corrèze, a spontaneous demonstration against the *Relève* occurred on 28 October when over 1,500 workers assembled in the streets after the word was passed round shortly after 4 p.m. The local prefect warned the Minister of Interior after this demonstration that the workers were 'ready to follow any lead in order to fight against collaboration'.[52] In the Haute-Savoie Pierre Lamy, a Labour Inspector at Annecy, carefully sabotaged the *Relève* in his area while still acting as a government official. Keeping in close contact with the syndicalist Paul Viret who was one of the local leaders of Libération, he supplied him in advance with the lists of workers required for Germany. By this means Viret claims that less than 3 per cent of those summoned to leave actually went. In addition, Lamy talked to the employers of the area and was largely responsible for their majority stand against the government's scheme. Only one local employer, states Viret, was in favour of the *Relève*.[53]

With the national figures of success and failure of the *Relève* unavailable to the public at the time, the slightest resistance to the scheme at local level was seen as a victory, even though it must have been clear that the recruitment was not the total fiasco that *Le Populaire* claimed.[54] Trains of workers departed from all the big towns in November and the return of prisoners

[50] *Le Populaire*, no. 6 (15 Oct. 1942).

[51] *Le Métallo du Centre-Ouest* (Organe des comités populaires de la métallurgie), no. 2 (Oct. 1942).

[52] Chateau, 'Contribution à l'étude du maquis corrézien', p. 36.

[53] Paul Viret, *Pierre Lamy, Un Héros de la Résistance savoyarde* (Éditions Port-Royal, 1948), pp. 51–3.

[54] With access to information made available since, Paxton puts the demand made by Sauckel, German 'Minister' of Foreign Labour, at 400,000 men, to include 150,000 with special skills. Of these Vichy managed to recruit about half before resorting to an obligatory system of forced conscription (Service du travail obligatoire) in February 1943, by which time Sauckel was demanding double the number. (Paxton, *Vichy France*, p. 368.) See also Milward, op. cit., p. 124, who states that between 1 June and 30 September 1942, 32,530 workers left for Germany and in October–December a further 163,726.

was much photographed and reported in the Vichy Press. Although only one prisoner was returned for every three *skilled* workers, their return could be seen as a tangible sign that Vichy was getting something out of collaboration. In the full euphoria of successful strikes, protests, and demonstrations the realization that French society in the southern zone could still be manipulated by Vichy is there in the clandestine Press. In between their reports and facts of social revolt comes an increasing insistence on the need for organization, a theme by no means new in late 1942 but repeated with a crescendo of urgency as the actual depredations of Vichy and the Germans affected larger and larger numbers of people and areas of public concern. Arrests of Resisters and leading demonstrators, deportation of Jews, and forced recruitment of labour were creating a situation in which the favoured southern zone was beginning to experience the harsher realities of the north. And on 11 November 1942 the differences were finally removed when the Germans occupied the whole of France.

On that day a major demonstration had been planned at Brive in the Corrèze, both against the *Relève* and in traditional celebration of victory in World War I. Despite the entry of German troops the mass demonstration took place in the place Thiers. The Germans were greeted by cries of 'A bas les Boches'; gravel and sand were thrown at them, and the soldiers were jostled by the crowd. The Germans kept fairly calm and left it to the French police to break up the demonstrators and arrest its leaders.[55] It was the last of the big demonstrations of the southern zone and despite the presence of the German Occupiers it produced the same polarization between opposition and Vichy authority as on 1 May and 14 July. There was no sudden solidarity between local police and demonstrators against the invaders. At a higher level the Vichy regime continued to exist and Pétain insisted on remaining as head of a government no longer even ostensibly free. Many Resisters, when asked when the Resistance became a popular phenomenon in the south, reply that it was the German Occupation of November and the continuation of the Vichy regime which formed the

[55] Georges Beau and Léopold Gaubusseau, *R.5. Les S.S. en Limousin, Périgord, Quercy* (Presses de la Cité, 1969), p. 37.

major catalyst.[56] Others point to the institution of forced labour in February 1943 known as Service du travail obligatoire (S.T.O.) which removed the last semblance of voluntarism from the *Relève* and provoked the escape of workers into the woods and hills. Some claim that it was much earlier in June 1941 when Hitler invaded Russia, and there are others who maintain that the Resistance was never either a popular or a mass affair.[57] Inevitably the answer turns on how Resistance is finally described, whether in terms of activism or more widely to embrace passive or semi-active support. If the latter, then the thousands involved in the public protests of 1942 were a sign of a vastly increased opposition and Resistance. If the former, then there is endless work to be done on how many of those in the various demonstrations were subsequently active in the organized movements and networks. Yet even from those who stress organization above numbers it is admitted that the movements of Resistance needed a sympathetic public who would hide men and material, just as much as they needed the safety of place and terrain. The public protests were one way in which Resistance took root among the people.

[56] e.g. the thirty-four *maquisards* interviewed by Annie Viroulaud in 'Contribution à l'étude des maquis A.S. du Secteur-Centre de la Dordogne' (unpub. Mémoire de Maîtrise, Poitiers, 1969), p. 24.

[57] Evidence from Joseph Pastor and Madeleine Baudoin.

X. Resistance Reviewed

By mid-1942 the confusion and fragmentation of life which had typified 1940 and much of 1941 were disappearing and giving way to a much greater clarity of alternatives. The polarization in the towns caused, or expressed, by the big demonstrations was one important sign of this, and among existing Resisters it was marked by a stress on organization, separation of tasks, planned expansion, and a greater awareness of problem and possibilities. Illusions of instant success, sweeping recruitment, widespread popularity, and easy adaptation to circumstance had largely gone, and a sense of hardened reality took their place.

Throughout this study of Resistance in Vichy France there has been an attempt to recreate some of the uncertainties that the southern zone experienced in 1940–1, and to show how Resistance developed as a diffused and inchoate phenomenon, heavily dependent on variables in personality, politics, and place. It could not be known at the time which individual, group, or method would be successful. The very novelty of Resistance was a levelling factor, making it difficult to establish criteria by which to evaluate the different initiatives and developments. By 1942, however, rationalization was possible; there were precedents to draw on and knowledge which could be trusted. Organization could proceed on the rational basis of assimilated experience. This study now reaches the same point: the main features of Resistance can be organized, reviewed, and seen more clearly.

Firstly, Resistance in the southern zone had grown from two kinds of reaction to the facts of defeat, Armistice, the Occupation, and the Vichy regime. Some people continued to act as they had in the pre-war situation and consequently found themselves in opposition. Their recent past remained a significant motivation in defiance of the consensus in 1940 which suppressed the immediate past as an irrelevance if not even worse as a series of fatal mistakes for which France was now receiving due punishment. Others adopted a new form of behaviour in response to the situation and found themselves acting in ways for which their past gave them little or no guidance, though their personality was invariably a constant which united past and present to give an inner credulity to their actions. Continuity and innovation were thus two separate but linked aspects of opposition behaviour, and by 1942 both had received full recognition in the ways in which Resistance was consciously developed.

Secondly, what had started as a national defeat by an *external* enemy had quickly become a civil conflict between *internal* enemies. Had Vichy been less authoritarian, less dogmatic, and less repressive this might have been avoided or at least delayed, but by 1942 anyone involved in Resistance to the national defeat and humiliation was forced to acknowledge that the internal conflict was a dynamic just as powerful in producing opposition. Resistance was thus a political response to political provocation, as well as a patriotic response to a national crisis. The result was an explicit identification of the Resistance with a left-wing, republican tradition, even among individuals and groups who had no particular liking for that tradition.

Thirdly, in the absence of Germans in the southern zone it was clear by 1942 that some of the major advances in Resistance had been made when *other* enemies had been openly identified. There were several of these, depending on the nature of the groups involved. For Communists and Socialists there had always been and continued to be the capitalist class; more specifically there were the 'two hundred families' who had been held responsible by Popular Front propaganda for carrying France towards Fascism and capitalist dictatorship. For trade-unionists there was an old enemy in yellow unions, instigated by the employers and now, with the *Charte du travail*, corporatist unions organized by the state; for old-style republicans of the Dreyfusard stamp there were the evils of censorship, injustice, clericalism, and anti-Semitism, all of which could be identified in the ideology of the National Revolution. For Resisters of any political stance there were the collaborators in their own town or region. For demonstrators in the streets there was the police; and for hungry urban families and desperate housewives there was scarcity, together with its parasite, the luxury of the black market, both of which could be laid at the door of the authorities.

None of these, except for the collaborator, was a new enemy, so that a recognition of these as acceptable objects for Resistance hostility and action was a successful enlistment of past conflicts into the current battle. The values and principles of the past, recognized by only a small minority in 1940 were thus rediscovered by a far larger proportion of society by the middle of 1942.

Fourthly, in addition to the belief, which can easily be defended, that Resistance was a coalition of widely differing individuals and groups, there was also the recognition that Resistance had prospered among groups with a common interest or character. Political affinities, the group mentality of refugees and victims, the shared traditions of a particular region, professional loyalties, family ties, the proximities of work, were some of the elements making for collective motivation, and they were of vital importance in the growth and spread of Resistance. Their importance does not easily lead to a sociology of Resistance since in many cases the same types of group also produced a collective motivation for Pétainism and inertia. But the recognition that affinities of place, past, ideas, and experience were a partial explanation of Resistance groupings prompted the search in 1942 for other collective affinities which might be put to good use. Surprise disappointments and strange bedfellows within Resistance made firm prediction of group behaviour impossible, but a certain predictability *within* groups made recruitment and planning more than an arbitrary gamble.

Finally, there was the significant element in the development of Resistance which was more to do with method than motivation. Propaganda through a clandestine Press, it was quickly discovered, was communication in two senses—communication between writers and readers, and communication between those who distributed and collected the actual papers. Running so many clandestine papers was therefore not just the self-indulgence of the French in their love of ideas and respect for the articulate, but also a familiar way of holding movements together and recruiting new members. Not all Resistance groupings started with a publication. The networks of espionage, escape, and sabotage, avoided publicity in order to keep their organizations as tight as possible, but the vast majority of Resisters found their way into the movements, whose populism was regretted by some of the more élite or military-minded members, but whose initial cohesion and growth were largely dependent on the two kinds of communication assured by their papers.

These major features in the growth of Resistance showed a wealth of different objectives, but it was usual in common parlance not to talk about the plurality and profusion, but to insist on one motivation, patriotism, and one objective, the liberation of France. These, of course, were the common elements which made for one unified struggle, but in the process of organization as in the first stages of Resistance the diversity was of the utmost importance. There was no single operation for which only a few selected people were carefully conscripted. The operation was constantly changing and enlarging owing to the different contributions of the volunteers, its structures and methods constantly adapted to the skills and ideas of those whose anger and defiance at different moments of time and in different ways and places had brought them to the point of Resistance. A patriot working for the liberation of France could have started Resistance for one or more reasons: because he or she had rejected the Armistice in June 1940; had refused to abandon the syndicalist movement; had continued to be involved in communist activities; had been determined to reconstitute the Socialist Party; had reacted against victimization as Freemason, Jew, Communist, republican, anti-clerical, or Gaullist; had continued to stand against the Nazi ideology; had demonstrated in the streets; had protested at the *mairie* for more food; had refused to be conscripted for labour in Germany; had come to reject the growing collaboration of Vichy; had realized that ideas apparently close to the National Revolution led in the opposite direction; or had grown critical of the developments in the Légion française des combattants, the Chantiers de la jeunesse, and many other institutions which Vichy had claimed represented the interests of the whole nation. Patriotism is a necessary explanation for many of these actions but it is not a sufficient one.

Most of these features of Resistance only became clear during 1942 when they were consciously embodied in the extended recruitment and organization of the various movements. The consolidation of Resistance during this period is the subject of numerous histories and memoirs and it is not the aim of this study to synthesize them. Some selective indication, however, must be given of how basic these features were and how they were of continuous importance not just at the outset but also in the period of accelerated growth and organization.

In the recruitment drive during 1942 instigated by all four major movements, Combat, Libération, Franc-Tireur, and Front National, the significance and potential of collective motivation was one feature which was highly developed. With the *Relève*, the campaign by syndicalists and Communists to reorganize the trade unions and form Comités populaires in defence of the workers assumed urgent dimensions, and produced new departures in collective action. The F.T.P.F. (Francs-Tireurs et partisans français), the activist movement organized by Communists with its monthly paper *France d'abord*, began to make substantial numbers of recruits, after a slow beginning in 1941, and the first units of the *maquis* were established in the last two or three months of 1942. These were composed of refugees or Jews sought by the authorities, deserters from Vichy youth camps, and workers escaping the *Relève*. In the Vaucluse Henri Frenay himself recognized that the collective avoidance of deportation was a significant new motivation towards Resistance, and the movement of Combat, no less than the Front National, began to encourage the formation of *maquis* units, and to provide them with false identity cards and ration books.[1]

In the Lozère, expectations by the Resistance movements even outran the realities of the collective protest against the *Relève*. It was expected by Combat, after the law of 4 September 1942, that rebellious workers would become instant Resisters, but there were some that sought escape by keeping themselves hidden in their own homes and others who tried living in the woods or on a farm, but found the *patois* of the peasants unintelligible and contracted dysentery from the change of diet. The result was an initial measure of disappointment for the Resistance movements, but also a spur to more planning and practical thinking.[2]

[1] Autrand, *Le Département de Vaucluse de la défaite à la libération*, pp. 84–6.
[2] Evidence from Henri Cordesse.

Before the deportation of Jews and labour, the activity of Alsace-Lorrainers as exiles in the southern zone had given some indication of the strength of collective motivation, though the full potential of this took some time to be realized. Systematic attempts to group all Alsace-Lorrainers had been made in Clermont-Ferrand, Saint-Étienne, and Lyon, partly on the initiative of Jean Nocher, the journalist on the Saint-Étienne paper *La Tribune* who wrote in the clandestine publication *Espoir*. It is estimated that some 1,500 refugees had been loosely grouped in these areas by 1942, but that organized activity in the southern zone was the province of much smaller units.[3] Franc-Tireur had recruited Alsace-Lorrainers in a systematic way, but there were also independent groups of refugees who attempted action on their own. One of these was created in 1942 at Agen in the Lot-et-Garonne, where Maurice Jacob, an administrator from the *préfecture* of the Haut-Rhin running the refugee services in Agen, joined a small group of local army officers who had constituted a movement called 'Victoire'. With him he brought most of his own refugee administration and established an organization strong enough to survive the occupation by the Germans in November 1942 and the dissolution of 'Victoire'.[4] In the Dordogne, one of the principal *départements* scheduled to receive exiles from the annexed provinces, a *maquis* group later called 'Bir-Hakeim' was formed by two exiled inspectors of police from Strasbourg, Charles Mary and Lucien Schneikert. Forced to leave Strasbourg in mid-1942 they arrived in the Dordogne and quickly brought together other exiles from Alsace and Lorraine who were living in the area of Bergerac.[5] In the Basses-Alpes at Manosque a small group of Resisters round Martin-Bret and Jean Vial joined up with Combat in June 1942 and began a more extensive recruitment for the A.S. (Armée secrète), the military side of Combat. It was quickly realized that exiles from Alsace-Lorraine were an important source of membership, and recruit-

[3] Bernard Metz, 'La Formation de la Brigade', in 'La Brigade Alsace-Lorraine', *L'Alsace française. Revue d'action nationale*, N.S. no. 1 (Oct. 1948), 7–15.

[4] Martin Rendier, *Quatre ans dans l'ombre* (André Bousquet, Condom, 1948), pp. 45–66.

[5] Rodolphe Kessler, 'Les "Terroristes"' (Strasbourg, 1948), pp. 33–4. The area of Bergerac, like the Cévennes, was another historical area of Protestant revolt.

ment was organized to maximize this potential.[6] Combat also took advantage of the existing groups of refugees in the Vaucluse, where a handful of Lorrainers had decided in the waiting-room at Avignon station on 14 November 1940 not to separate without creating groups of opposition. Among them was a Corporal Kessler who later by chance met Frenay on a train and informed him of the determination of the exiles in the area. They provided an organizational nexus throughout the *département*.[7]

Political affinity, no less than the experience of exile, had produced collective motivation from 1940 onwards. This continued to be important throughout 1942. For example, in July Jean-Pierre Lévy, one of the leaders of Franc-Tireur, assured the help of the socialist deputy in Grenoble Dr. Léon Martin in starting the movement in the Isère. Aimé Pupin became the local leader and the movement spread mainly through socialist contacts.[8] In the Allier the Socialists were collectively drawn to the movement Libération in the spring and summer of 1942 through the efforts of Pierre Kaan, a teacher sacked from the *lycée* at Montluçon for being a Jew.[9] When Jean-Pierre Bloch told de Gaulle in 1942 that Resisters in the Dordogne were still grouped together by 'political affinity'[10] he was speaking in terms of general political sympathies rather than specific party allegiance, and in these terms much of the recruitment into the various movements was political. Combat recruited more easily among left-wing Catholics, including Catholic trade-unionists, Libération and Franc-Tireur found it easier to gain the adherence of Socialists, radicals, Freemasons, members of the C.G.T., and individual Communists, while the Front National continued to be overtly communist in inspiration.

But no movement was politically exclusive, and the other side of collective motivation is the political heterogeneity of the Resistance. Henri Cordesse acknowledges the presence of right-wing individuals among the dominantly left-wing Resisters

[6] Vial, *Un de l'Armée secrète bas-alpine*, p. 27.
[7] Autrand, op. cit., pp. 74–6.
[8] Alban Vistel, MS. on origins of Resistance, p. 656.
[9] Rougeron, *La Résistance dans le département de l'Allier*, p. 12.
[10] See above, p. 97 n.38.

in the Lozère;[11] Raymond Chauliac, a dissident in the 1930s from the Socialist Party, along with Marcel Déat, whose position in 1940 he abruptly repudiated, recruited for Libération in Montpellier, and found old political ties no more than a marginal advantage;[12] Pascal Pavani, a militant Communist, became one of the local leaders of Combat at Sathonay-Calvaire in the Rhône in 1942, and remained in touch with the party, and Charles Tillon, the national organizer of the Francs-Tireurs et partisans français has said that the F.T.P.F. never had more than a minority of communist party members.[13] Madeleine Braun, who had worked with Spanish republican refugees and joined the party in 1942, became one of the directors of Front National with a fellow Communist Georges Marrane and stressed in an interview the political variety in both the F.N. and Resistance as a whole.[14] On the other hand, she also mentions the suspicion of the Socialist Daniel Mayer towards the F.N. which he saw as too closely linked with the Communist Party, a not uncommon attitude in the Resistance, particularly among those Socialists who had decided not to establish the Socialist Party as an independent movement of Resistance, but to join Libération.[15] Their insistence that Resistance should not be co-extensive with politics was repeated in several issues of *Le Populaire*, and yet *L'Humanité* was also calling for anyone to join the F.N. regardless of political background. Undoubtedly the origins of the F.N. made it more dependent on a single party in a way that none of the other movements was, but the recruitment of members by political affinity was never repudiated by any Resistance organization as long as it went hand in hand with the heterogeneous recruitment of individuals.

In many areas it was a question of stages, the first stage of recruitment depending to a considerable extent on political and social affinities, while once a movement was established its confidence to recruit more widely was increased. This was

[11] Evidence from Henri Cordesse.

[12] Evidence from Raymond Chauliac.

[13] Evidence from Charles Tillon. The figure he gave for 1944 was 25 per cent though he stated that it was higher in 1941–2. Better-known Communists than Pascal Pavani in Combat and Libération included Marcel Degliame in the former and Pierre Hervé and Lucie Aubrac in the latter.

[14] She was interviewed by Marianne Monestier for a book about women in the Resistance, *Elles étaient cent et mille* . . . (Fayard, 1972), pp. 1–30.

[15] See above, pp. 99–100.

the case at Tulle in the Corrèze where Martial Brigouleix recruited initially among socialist friends whereas by 1942 he was recruiting for Combat among all shades of political opinion in the area.[16] A typical example of the first stage is given by Alban Vistel for the town of Mâcon in the Saône-et-Loire. In the late summer of 1941 a signalman at Mâcon station, L. Gris, a militant trade-unionist, received a telephone summons from a barrister in the town, Me Denove. When he arrived at his office he found several men who were also members of the Socialist Party like himself, together with a member of the P.C.F. The barrister told him that a friend had come from Lyon to ask him to set up a local branch of Libération. The instructions were to recruit others in the jobs and professions in which each member was active. For L. Gris this meant recruiting among fellow railway-workers and trade-unionists. Within a short while he had created several such groups.[17]

No less important than collective motivation in 1942 was the aspect of Resistance that had grown steadily throughout 1941, the merging of opposition to the Germans with opposition to Vichy, and the identification of Resistance with a strong republican tradition. The necessity of this development was dramatically exposed within Combat in the spring of 1942. The movement had retained links with Vichy personnel, owing mainly to the contacts which Frenay had within the army but also to the reluctance of Frenay and others to repudiate Pétain, all the while they nurtured a dwindling hope that he was basically in favour of Resistance. The merger of Frenay's original movement with Liberté in November 1941 had extended the politics of the movement to the Catholic Left, and the incorporation of Renouvin's militant tactics against collaborators had set it firmly against the law and order of Vichy.[18] Yet the paper *Combat*, and Frenay himself, initially abstained from any political attack on Pétain or on the internal politics

[16] Chateau, 'Contribution à l'étude du maquis corrézien', p. 32. Even in the second stage the importance of the earlier political ties remained a feature of Combat in the Corrèze. The local leaders of the Armée secrète were all Socialists: Brigouleix at Tulle, Gontran Royer at Brive, and Chevalier and Lemoigne at Ussel. (Beau and Gaubusseau, *R.5.*, p. 43.)

[17] Alban Vistel, MS. on origins of Resistance, p. 603.

[18] See above, pp. 142–5.

of Vichy. Collaboration as a policy was roundly condemned but it was not until March 1942 that the first substantial shift towards politics was noticeable in the paper, when a paragraph on the *Charte du travail* denounced it as an authoritarian document placing economic power in the hands of 'the monopoly trusts and the anti-national mafia.'[19] The same issue pledged support for General de Gaulle as the 'symbol of resistance to the oppressor' but there was still no repudiation of Pétain, nor in the first issue of May which published de Gaulle's 'Declaration to the Resistance' where the notion of an internal revolution was nominally endorsed.[20]

It was in the next issue of May 1942 that the paper finally joined every other major clandestine publication by an attack on Pétain, not just for his external policy, but for his support of the internal politics of the regime. In an article couched as a 'Letter to Marshal Pétain', he was accused of capitulation, treason, collaboration, and cowardice, and held responsible 'for the suppression of our liberties, for parodies of justice, for a police state, for the odious anti-Semitic legislation, for the omnipotence of the monopoly trusts, for unemployment, and for the growing hunger of the people'.[21] After this attack the paper threw itself into the thick of internal politics, culminating in a programme for the Fourth Republic called 'Combat et Révolution' in September 1942.[22] Its articles became increasingly more socially aware and more left-wing politically, but without any hint of party. Clearly the movement was altering its tactics to reflect the needs of Resistance as well as the opinions of its members.

Since the war it has become fully apparent just what an internal struggle within Combat this change of tactics reflected. The memoirs of Frenay and Claude Bourdet, both designated as leaders of the movement in November 1941, and of René Cerf-Ferrière, nominated editor of the paper in 1942, all confirm that politics and personalities clashed within the leadership of the movement, and that the demands for a break with Pétain and the internal politics of Vichy long preceded the

[19] *Combat* (Mar. 1942).

[20] Ibid., no. 2 (May 1942). See above, p. 185 for de Gaulle's 'Declaration'.

[21] Ibid., no. 3 (May 1942).

[22] Ibid., no. 34 (Sept. 1942).

eventual statement of May 1942.[23] 'Frenay', wrote Cerf-Ferrière, 'lacked a political sense and the kind of flexibility necessary for leading civilians. . . . The military captain had known his men as soldiers, but he had still to discover his men as citizens.'[24] André Plaisantin, one of the leaders of Combat in Lyon and closely connected with all the left-wing Catholics in the town, shared this political mistrust and, like Cerf-Ferrière, voiced it in meetings with the directorate. Frenay, himself, knew their arguments and anxiety but maintained that to sever all links with Vichy would expose the movement to the full force of police repression and forfeit vital sources of information.

In January 1942 a courier was arrested carrying a list naming many of the leading Combat personnel, and within the month several of these had been found and imprisoned, including three of the major organizers of the movement, Maurice Chevance and Bertie Albrecht, who had been with Frenay since the beginning, and Jean-Charles Demachy, the first leader of the movement in the Lyon area, who had introduced Emmanuel Mounier to Frenay and had been influential in the reorientation of *Esprit*. Mounier was also imprisoned, and Frenay was faced not only with this loss of important leaders, but also with subsequent arrests which decimated the base of the movement in the area of Clermont-Ferrand. Bertie Albrecht, however, was shortly released by the Vichy Head of Police, Commandant Rollin, in exchange for a meeting with Frenay and a discussion of his activities. Frenay accepted, with the unanimous support of the leadership of Combat, and started a bizarre series of journeys to Vichy under safe conduct to meet first Rollin and later the Minister of the Interior, Pierre Pucheu. It was the meetings with Pucheu in February which threatened to split the movement at a level just beneath the directorate where political feelings were outraged by the thought that Frenay might make some sort of arrangement with Pucheu not to attack Pétain or Vichy's internal politics. This Frenay refused to do, and although the release of Mounier, Demachy, Chevance, and others was secured, he made no pact with

[23] Frenay, *La Nuit finira*, pp. 151–76; Claude Bourdet, *L'Aventure incertaine* (Stock, 1975), pp. 118–22; Cerf-Ferrière, *Chemin clandestin*, pp. 76–98.

[24] Cerf-Ferrière, op. cit., p. 64.

Pucheu but finally broke off relationships, first with Rollin and Pucheu, then with all his Vichy contacts within the echelons of the army, and finally, by the statement in *Combat*, with Pétain himself.

The 'Pucheu affair' caused Frenay an uneasy three months of relationships both inside Combat and between Combat and other Resistance movements, particularly Libération, whose militants in places as distant as Perpignan heard of the meetings and vigorously condemned both Frenay and Combat as a whole.[25] Throughout the affair Frenay had the agreement of his colleagues at the top of Combat, but the suspicion at lower levels was something he could ill afford. The complete restoration of trust was only achieved when the paper carried its full rejection of Vichy politics and a republican programme for the future. 'There was after all in our Resistance,' argued André Plaisantin in his meetings with Frenay, 'something more than the struggle against the enemy. In some way we were creating the future.'[26] Frenay had not started his Resistance through any sense of struggle against the internal politics of Vichy, but by the middle of 1942 the movement which he had largely envisaged and created had adopted that struggle as its own.

By holding Pétain responsible for such things as unemployment and hunger, Combat accepted the protests of the unemployed and the hungry as a legitimate part of Resistance activity. After six months of organization and expansion, and in the wake of the Pucheu affair, Combat had thus implicitly enlarged its concept of the enemy, something it had already begun when it sanctioned the attacks of Renouvin on shops, buildings, and individuals identified with collaboration. This feature of Resistance, involving action against several different enemies within the over-all struggle against Germany allowed the concept of Resistance to be realized at the most local of levels, in the place where people lived and worked. Demonstrations, in which people found themselves in conflict with the police, and protests against hunger where the enemy was the local authority or the black marketeers, were the most

[25] Personal evidence of Henri Noguères in Noguères *et al.*, *Histoire de la Résistance* ii. 551.

[26] Plaisantin, 'Sur les origines de Combat à Lyon', p. 7.

obvious expressions of this grass-roots opposition. They were, as we have seen, both encouraged and endorsed by all the Resistance movements.

There was also industrial action. Trade union activity throughout 1941 had succeeded in creating a climate of antagonism among workers towards the corporatist intention of the *Charte du travail*. Considering the absence of national federations to link the local efforts together, this was a considerable success, and in 1942 the demonstrations on 1 May were a public celebration of the achievement. By this point trade-unionists from both the C.G.T. and the C.F.T.C. had realized that some form of co-operation was vital, and *Libération*, in its issue of 18 May, announced the creation of the Mouvement ouvrier français (M.O.F.) which brought members of the two confederations together.[27] Its propaganda value was important whatever its organizational weakness, but the potential strength of trade-unionism remained very much at the local level, where it was found that clandestine activity could be cloaked in the legitimacy of the Vichy unions. Known militants surprised the Vichy authorities by registering within the law of the *Charte du travail*, thus enabling them to hold meetings and strengthen their contacts.[28]

Holding an effective strike was the real test of this strength, since, with strikes illegal, mounting unemployment, and only a small percentage of pre-war trade-unionists re-involved in union activity, the passive hostility to Vichy's labour policy was not a sufficient basis on which to mount industrial action. The successful miners' strike at Montceau-les-Mines in January 1942 therefore stood out as a rare achievement in this period. The town was on the demarcation line in the Saône-et-Loire and the strike encountered the opposition of both German and Vichy authorities as well as the employers. For twelve

[27] Including Marcel Poimbœuf, Lucien Rose, Yvon Morandat, and Jean Brodier for the C.F.T.C. and Robert Lacoste, Fourcade, and Julien Forgues for the C.G.T.

[28] Evidence from Albert Solié. In October 1942 a pamphlet representing the metal workers of Limoges and district stated that the Comités populaires were a sort of clandestine syndicalist movement, but urged workers not to desert the old unions even when they were run, as in Limoges, by administrators sympathetic to Vichy. 'For, comrades, despite the repugance you feel towards these traitors it's no good leaving the very house that you want to clean up.' (*Le Métallo du Centre-Ouest* (Organe des comités populaires de la métallurgie), no. 2, Oct. 1942.)

days the strike held up production not just in the mines but among metal workers and building workers who came out in support, and the result was an increase in rations, new pairs of boots, a promise from the Vichy Government to investigate the wage level, and the release of miners arrested in the first two days of the strike. The clandestine paper of the miners in the southern zone, *La Voix des mineurs*, was triumphant. The edition for the Gard in March gave full coverage to the achievements of the strike with no mention of its relationship to either the war or the Germans. It was sufficient that industrial action had been successful in a situation which needed no elaboration. There were, however, details of abuse and oppression in one of the local mines in the Gard and a report of the death of a trade union militant in one of the French concentration camps. The paper left no doubt as to who the immediate, accessible enemies were.[29] News of successful strikes by metal-workers at La Ciotat, on the coast east of Marseille, and by miners at Perronière in the Loire was carried in *La Vie ouvrière* in June 1942,[30] and in the same month the metal workers in Toulouse provided comprehensive guidance to militants by advocating force in the pursuit of their claims.[31]

It was not until the *Relève* that industrial action could be called more than spasmodic, and then the substantial difference between passive and active opposition to Vichy was vigorously stressed by the labour leaders. In *Revanche*, a paper produced in Toulouse by young workers, the front page carried a warning against armchair Resisters: 'There are some for whom resisting means simply reading a clandestine paper or turning the knob of the radio. They are cowards, *néo-attentistes*.' What was needed, continued the paper, was sabotage and armed Resistance. Encouraging the local Francs-Tireurs, it concluded, 'Young Frenchmen of the unoccupied zone, we too have our Boches and our traitors to destroy.'[32] The organ of the F.T.P.F., *France d'abord*, had popularized the slogan 'A chacun son boche' which applied most obviously to the occupied zone, but also to the factories which were supplying the Germans in the

[29] *La Voix des mineurs* (Organe régional de défense des revendications des mineurs et similaires du Gard) [Mar. 1942].

[30] *La Vie ouvrière*, no. 50 (10 June 1942).

[31] *Le Métallo* (Journal composé par les métallos toulousains), June 1942.

[32] *Revanche* (Organe du front patriotique des jeunes Français), no. 5 (Sept. 1942).

south, and during the autumn of 1942 the emphasis in industrial action moved from strikes for better pay and conditions, to sabotage and force. At the same time the Resistance movements as a whole recognized industrial action as legitimate Resistance, where before it had been encouraged only by the more left-wing Press. The *Relève*, to this extent, depoliticized the strike, the go-slow, sabotage, and any form of workers' obstruction, a fact made explicit in the notion of 'National Strikes' endorsed in a tract of mid-October signed by Libération, Combat, Franc-Tireur, Front National, the P.C.F., and the Mouvement ouvrier français. Shortly before, a tract stating 'Not a single worker for Germany' had been issued in Lyon carrying for the first time the combined names of all the Resistance movements, together with the P.C.F. It was a significant feature of Resistance in the southern zone that it should first proclaim its unity in these two tracts to support action which was anti-German, anti-Vichy, and anti-capitalist at the same time.

The acceptance of several enemies was part of the gathering strength of Resistance, and was built into its organization through the allocation to Resisters of separate functions. Of all developments this revealed most clearly the range of motivation, ability, and personality which people brought into the Resistance and which the Resistance was prepared to recognize. By the end of 1942 the special functions nurtured by the Resistance included information and intelligence, production of newspapers, the embryo formation of military units, activism by *groupes francs*, industrial action, welfare services, recruitment in public administration, the manning of escape routes, production of false papers and ration cards, the hiding of refugees, Jews, and Resisters on the run, and the strategic control of the movements themselves, involving negotiations between movements within both zones and between Resistance in France and in London. No less important than separate functions was the recognition of separate localities, not just regions, *départements*, towns and rural areas, but also universities, factories, railways, *préfectures*, and even police stations. These multiple divisions should not, in 1942, be seen as a sign of a powerful mass organization. It was still only a minority phenomenon, finance was only just beginning to arrive from London, and while Germans were still absent from the southern zone, the objectives of some sectors of the Resistance were often imprecise or merely theoretical. There was also duplication between the movements at local level and rivalries at the top, and the missions of Jean Moulin, empowered by de Gaulle both to allocate resources and to try and unite the various movements, served to highlight both the strengths and weaknesses of a highly diversified Resistance.

Nevertheless, the separation of tasks made it possible for Resisters to carry through their own original impulse and initiative and to recruit others whose skills were well-suited for specific roles in the developing movements. Combat was the most rationalized in this sense and the range of its services anticipated by Frenay's early plans in 1940 gave it the potential of being a large organization well before numbers guaranteed the reality. The character and staffing of these services have been thoroughly detailed by Marie Granet and Henri Michel in their excellent study of the movement and there is little to be gained here by repeating the material.[33] What can be underlined is that the separation of tasks within Combat was symptomatic of Resistance as a whole, and that this separation involved an increased recognition of skills and professions in their own right. In particular the professionalism within the clandestine Press was overtly acknowledged. In April 1942 Jean Moulin set up a Bureau d'information et de presse under the direction of Georges Bidault, ex-editor of *L'Aube*, which set out to link the clandestine Press of both zones. On the directing committee professional journalists from the southern zone were in the majority, including Pierre Corval and Yves Farge from *Le Progrès de Lyon*, Rémy Roure from *Le Temps*, and Louis Terrenoire from *Temps nouveau*. The Bureau later began to issue daily bulletins from which the rest of the clandestine Press gathered much of its news. In organizational terms it was a recognition of the vital significance of journalism and communication in the growth of the Resistance and a rationalization of the underground Press as a sector of activity on its own, manned by professionals.[34]

[33] Granet and Michel, *Combat*, pp. 127–202.

[34] See Claude Bellanger, *Presse clandestine 1940–44* (Colin, 1961), pp. 112–14, and Claude Bellanger *et al.*, *Histoire générale de la presse française*, vol. iv: *De 1940 à 1958* (P.U.F., 1975), p. 141. Shortly after Moulin's initiative with the Press he began grouping together a number of political thinkers within the Resistance

Other sectors harnessed skills and interests in the same way. Industrial activists were given an outlet in every movement: Marcel Degliame, once a permanent official of the communist trade unions, was recruited by Claude Bourdet in 1941 into the service of Combat where he organized the movement's 'Action ouvrière'. Yvon Morandat, from the C.F.T.C., spread Libération into the factories, and Yves Farge did the same for Franc-Tireur and Front National. Workers organized groups for all the major movements, as well as for the Comités populaires, for the clandestine unions, and for the Communist Party. Civil servants and other public employees were grouped in a special sector known as N.A.P. (Noyautage des administrations publiques), first suggested for Combat by André Plaisantin in Lyon and immediately taken up by Claude Bourdet, but not confined to that movement alone. In the clandestine Press the extension of Resistance into the town halls and *préfectures* was vigorously encouraged, especially if it meant making contacts within the local police. *Le Métallo* in Toulouse, for example, told its readers not to presume that all police were sympathetic to collaboration: on the contrary, it argued, many were anti-German and their solidarity could be gained by careful recruitment.[35]

Finally, the movements developed their military and intelligence sectors, their *groupes francs*, and their social and welfare services for Resisters and their families, all giving expression to different abilities and motivations. The activism of *groupes francs* against local collaborators was identified with Jacques Renouvin within Combat and with the F.T.P.F. within the Front National, both assuring similar groups of students and young workers an opportunity to experience the action they felt was lacking in the reading and distribution of newspapers.[36] The activist groups valued a temperament rather different

with a view to discussing the nature of France after the war. In June 1942 the group gained the title of Comité général d'études (C.G.E.); initially included were François de Menthon, Robert Lacoste, Paul Bastid, Alexandre Parodi, P.-H. Teitgen, and René Courtin. A detailed analysis of this organization together with an excellent introduction to the ideas within Resistance movements which provided a basis for the discussions in the C.G.E. can be found in Diane de Bellescize, 'Le Comité général d'études de la Résistance' (Thèse pour le Doctorat de Droit, Paris, 1974).

[35] *Le Métallo* (June 1942).

[36] Jean Pronteau was a member of Renouvin's *groupes francs* and was described by René Cerf-Ferrière as aged 21, a Marxist but not a member of the P.C.F.,

from that favoured by the intelligence sectors known as S.R. (Service de renseignements), though as the objects of immediate action became more military and strategic a strong liaison was necessary between the two. Neither found a full identity until the Germans arrived in the south, though intelligence services were widely dispersed throughout the southern zone well before then, serving escape routes as well as providing information for the British and French in London. Why some individuals involved in intelligence found themselves in networks and others in movements is not clear, though in many cases it was due to accidents of contact and recruitment.[37] In 1940 powerful personalities like Louis de la Bardonnie in the Dordogne, wine-grower and farmer, and André Boyer in Marseille, socialist lawyer with an outstanding war record, might well have found themselves at the start of movements rather than the networks C.N.D.-Castille and Brutus. It is important to stress that those whose aptitude was for collecting information or whose situation allowed them to belong to an escape network did not have to wait for one special organization to make its appearance in their locality. By the end of 1942 there were several.[38]

---

and above all an activist. He admitted that he had little interest in what was written in *Combat*. For him, as for hundreds of young members of Combat, 'the real passion was action against collaborators, then against the Germans. Under Renouvin's orders . . . he began by throwing stones through the windows of bookshops which sold collaborationist books'. (Cerf-Ferrière, p. 78.)

[37] e.g. two of the founder members of 'Azur-Transports' mentioned above, Robert Lynen and Pierre Henneguier (see pp. 66, 70), went into different organizations in autumn 1942. Lynen was recruited into the network Alliance and Henneguier into Libération. (Henneguier, *Le Soufflet de forge*, pp. 59–61.)

[38] This study has made no attempt to deal with the *réseaux* in France. The pseudonyms, coded messages, interzonal activity, and relationships with either France Libre in London or the British S.O.E. make them an especially difficult subject for the historian. There are some good memoirs, relating their activities, notably Rémy, *Mémoires d'un agent secret de la France libre*, vols. i–iii (France-Empire, 1959–61); Colonel Passy, *Mémoires*, vols. i–iii (Solar et Plon, 1947–51); and Fourcade, *L'Arche de Noé*; and there is the excellent inside history of S.O.E. by M. R. D. Foot *S.O.E. in France* (H.M.S.O., London, 1966). But when it comes to assessing the motivation of their members or attempting any political or sociological analysis the material is particularly intractable. Fourcade has a subsection called 'Motivation' in an essay on the *réseaux* in *Vie et mort des Français 1939–45* (Hachette, 1971), but it only serves to show that all the work is still to be done in that area. Henri Michel correctly observed just how daunting this would be in his *Bibliographie critique de la Résistance* (Institut Pédagogique National, 1964), pp. 116–21.

By organizing so many different sectors and by acknowledging such a range of different kinds of activity, the Resistance became an alternative way of life in Vichy France and not just a small pressure group or an élite military corps. In fact the argument of this study is that the Resistance could never have been a homogeneous, tightly knit group, since the very phenomenon known as The Resistance was developed between 1940 and 1942 by a plurality of groups in a plurality of ways. This argument repudiates the claim of several Resisters that the Resistance could have been carefully recruited from the beginning on the two criteria of efficiency and patriotism, without any concern for politics or social issues.[39] The mistake they make is in believing that there was either a group or a movement in 1940 or 1941 which could have established such criteria and could have made them exclusive. Resistance did not grow in such a way; there was no single centre from which concentric circles of Resistance radiated until they covered the whole country. People who resisted were not merely those who were encouraged to do so by centralized movements, but also those who reacted spontaneously, and often on their own, to a whole variety of events and provocations, some national and some local. Their defiant reaction was at the start of Resistance and they carried into their actions the diffuse motivations which had led them to reject the *status quo.* There was no ideal type of Resistance to which all others aspired.

There could have been an attempt in 1942 to reduce the variety and make one type of Resistance the norm, and there were individuals who would have preferred it that way. But no attempt was made, and the richness in the origins of Resistance was perpetuated in its organization. The diversity caused incredulity among the leaders of France Libre in London, where it was often seen as the perversity of the mainland French in following habitual lines of independent action. It also presented a challenge to those seeking a united military effort in the two years after the total Occupation. But the diversity could not easily have been otherwise. The problem facing the French after 1940 was to drive out the Occupiers, but it was also to break out of the closed, shuttered, and servile world in

[39] See Groussard, *Service secret*, p. 332, and Colonel du Jonchay, *La Résistance et les communistes* (Éditions France-Empire, 1968), *passim*.

which the Germans and the Vichy regime attempted to keep them, and to re-establish a sense of choice and self-direction. Resistance was reassertion and rediscovery as well as a new uncharted form of warfare and revolution, and in that recovery there was bound to be diversity. With so much lost, destroyed, and threatened there was much to recover, not least the collective freedom of the country and not least the individual freedom to be oneself.

XI. Profiles

AMONG those in the southern zone who began to undermine the *status quo* between 1940 and 1942, certain self-defined groupings have been stressed in this study: left-wing Catholics who had been opposed to the ideology of Nazism in the 1930s and were critical of the orthodox conservatism of the Church hierarchy; Communists who took up a position of outright political hostility towards Vichy; Socialists who kept the party alive after its split on 10 July 1940; army officers who refused the Armistice; nationalists whose militant anti-Germanism resisted the pull of Pétain; trade-unionists who defended union rights; Jews and refugees from Alsace-Lorraine who reacted against victimization; exiles from Paris and the occupied zone who formed a nucleus of dissidence in the large towns of the south; Protestants in historically rebellious areas; journalists, intellectuals, and academics who upheld free expression; urban workers and housewives who refused to accept hunger and deprivation, and young workers who resisted the compulsory recruitment of labour.

The polarity between these Resistance groups and those which actively served the interests of Pétain and Vichy gives the period its main political and social dynamic, though any political or sociological theory of Resistance based on this polarity remains a blunt instrument owing to the minority status of all Resisters, even within the most 'subversive' sections of society. Resisters themselves in their oral evidence are usually the first to stress this, arguing strongly against any attempts to construct a model of 'The Resister', or to define certain categories in society as those which 'produced Resistance'. Most of them acknowledge the left-wing tendencies of Resistance and its dominantly urban origins; most recognize the importance of exiled and refugee groups; and most emphasize the significance of pre-war hostility to Nazism and Fascism. But beyond such basic generalizations the Resisters produce profiles of themselves which, when collated, justify those who claim that Resistance in Vichy France had a richly varied background.

Eighteen such profiles are presented here, abridged from interviews which are too long to reproduce in full. The aim of the interviews was not so much to prompt colourful stories about Resistance activities as to arrive at a credible picture of individual Resisters in 1940–2 in terms of their pre-war attitudes and their reaction to events leading up to and following the defeat of France. The interviews, of which these are a sample, were conducted on the date and at the place shown, but they are grouped according to the area of the individual's activity within the southern zone between 1940 and 1942. When they were all completed, an attempt was made to subject them to statistical analysis, but without success. Their interest remained essentially individual though they helped to stimulate and guide many of the hypotheses on which this study is based. With all their obvious weaknesses as documentation, they provided a good deal of local information and suggested many paths to follow. It is characteristic of the Resistance in which they all converged, that these paths should take us back into French history and society in so many different directions.

M. Louis de la Bardonnie (20 Sept. 1972, Saint-Antoine-de-Breuilh, Dordogne)

I was 38 in 1940 and the father of eight children. A ninth was born in 1942. I was a property-owner and farmer at Saint-Antoine-de-Breuilh in the Dordogne where my family had been for six hundred years. I had nothing to do with politics, because anyone who is in politics gets himself dirty. I wanted to stay clean. I was a man of the Right, a man of order, and for this reason opposed the Popular Front because it was revolutionary. My education had been in the humanities up to the *Baccalauréat*, followed by two years at an agricultural college and my military service. I then returned to manage the family estate. For me 'patrie' and 'famille' were the cardinal values. In the locality I was respected by those who were worthy people. I couldn't care less what the rest thought of me. A practising Catholic myself, I was nevertheless in close touch with the Protestantism of this area of the Dordogne since my mother's family were long-standing Protestants. I never paid any attention to the political or religious bias of my friends and acquaintances. During the Resistance I saved many Jews, not because they were Jews but because they were persecuted.

I foresaw the danger of Hitler and condemned the Munich agreements, opposing the attitude of the political Right. I believed that once you began to give way you were finished. In 1939 I wanted to join up but was refused because of the pension which would have had to be paid to my widow and eight children if I had been killed. The defeat was due to several reasons: not enough notice had been taken of the French intelligence service which knew what the Germans were doing; the Maginot Line was ineffective; the military leaders and French equipment were not of the same quality as in Germany. There was also a low state of morale in the country. The schoolteachers before 1914 had inculcated a strong sense of patriotism and civic duty. They died in the trenches. The new generation of teachers was more political and no longer valued morality and patriotism.

In 1940 I stopped subscribing to *L'Action française* when I read the statement of Maurras that Pétain should be followed even if he was wrong. This was totally unacceptable. I entered Resistance from the moment I heard de Gaulle's first broadcast. I did not hear the start of the broadcast because I was too upset about the defeat to hear it properly, but when I realized what de Gaulle was saying I called out 'We've won the war'. I had never heard of de Gaulle until that moment, but immediately contacted seven good friends, all local land-owners of varying means, and we met on the day the Armistice was declared. We had to do something, but what? We started with trivial actions like turning round signposts on the other side of the demarcation line which was only eight kilometres away. The members of our group were mostly friends from childhood, all orientated towards the political Right.

We then began to collect details about the Germans in the occupied zone, and through a friend who was a chief pilot in Bordeaux harbour we gained information on all the ships going in and out of Bordeaux. On 14 July 1940 we took the first batch of information to Switzerland and delivered it at the British Embassy. I myself went with the second batch on 8 August, and we made further journeys in September and October. There was no reply, and yet despite the lack of results our group grew from seven to thirty-two. Finally, we decided to send a 71-year-old priest, abbé Dartein, through Spain to England. With him we sent a number of photographs of German and Italian ships and submarines in Bordeaux. Our earlier information had reached the English and French in London but they had believed it was too good to be true. It seemed too important to be genuine. The photographs convinced them and contact was made. France Libre sent us an envoy in the person of Rémy, and our network became known as C.N.D.—Confrérie Notre Dame.

Towards Vichy I never hid my views. I always rejected it and never believed Pétain was playing a double game. I didn't care what people thought of me. There were all types of people in the network by the end, though at the beginning it was the humble people who were most easily recruited. As Jaurès said, and Socialists do say something true occasionally, 'The fatherland is the only wealth of the poor'. No cottage door was ever closed to me in the Resistance.

In 1940 Resistance was the action of a very small minority but it became a mass movement overnight after the invasion of Russia in June 1941 when Communists suddenly found themselves automatically in the Resistance. There had been some magnificent exceptions before then, but very few, and personally I had not known any. There were a few Socialists at the beginning but no Radicals. The definition of a Radical is 'Red outside, white inside, and always on the side where the bread is buttered'. Most of the political Right supported Vichy as did over 80 per cent of the clergy, though I myself met a mixed reaction among local priests. At Sainte-Foy-la-Grande the priest had put a portrait of Pétain, 8 metres square, behind the altar and declared that Pétain was greater than Joan of Arc, for whereas she had saved France once, Pétain had saved France twice. On the other hand, another priest had willingly lent me his cassock for clandestine purposes. There were several Jesuits in the early Resistance. In November 1940 I met an elderly Jesuit in Bordeaux who confided to me that Hitler would lose the war. Jesuits are always well informed.

The clandestine Press was vitally important but not until the end of 1941. It was important because not everyone possessed a wireless. Personally I must have distributed thousands of copies of several different papers.

I do not believe that cold or hunger played any part in promoting Resistance in 1941 or 1942, though greater suffering of people in the occupied zone made recruitment marginally easier there. The difference, however, was not great. I had no contacts in England, no particular hatred of the Germans, but a real hatred of Nazism and racism. I had read *L'Action française* regularly, but also *Le Figaro* and *Le Temps*. Although I was more of a monarchist than a republican, I was not a fanatic. I merely favoured a regime of order and authority.

During 1940–2 the aim of our network was to do as much harm as possible to Germany, and to Vichy, which was the same thing. In 1941 I was arrested by Vichy after being denounced by a Frenchman in another network. I was imprisoned for four months, but they could find nothing substantive against me. Subsequently this denunciation and arrest became the rule: the vast majority of those arrested in our network were denounced by fellow Frenchmen and arrested by Vichy. The so-called *double-jeu* of Vichy was a lie.

M. le curé Alvitre (21 Sept. 1972, Brive, Corrèze)

I have always been known as a red priest. Before World War I I was a militant of Marc Sangnier's Sillon and took part in the fights against the Camelots du Roi who tried to break up our meetings. I enjoyed a good fight. During World War I I was decorated with the Croix de Guerre. In 1922 I became a priest at Tulle. I was always more of a soldier than a priest. In 1940 I had a parish in the suburbs of Brive in a communist area. I was 51 and still a fighter. There was a tendency towards Resistance in the area even before Hitler's invasion of Russia, but there were no Communists in the Resistance before the invasion.

I heard de Gaulle's first broadcast and went straight to Edmond Michelet in Brive and said 'I am a Gaullist'. 'What's that?' he said. I never accepted Vichy as a legitimate government. My superiors in the Church didn't approve of me at all. The Sillon had been suspect and they were always on the side of order and legitimate government. There were very few priests of my age in the early Resistance though some of the young ones were involved, like abbé Laire in Brive. I feel responsible for his death since I encouraged him in his resistance.

He hid a wireless transmitter in the belfry of his church. He was arrested and shot.

I knew Michelet extremely well. He was originally in the Action Française. I had given him a copy of *Le Petit démocrate*, Bidault's paper, which he called a filthy rag, but he read it and became interested in Christian Democracy. He left Action Française and became a Christian Democrat.

Jacques Renouvin came to Brive to blow up the house of a collaborator. He stayed with me and borrowed my bicycle and cassock. It came down to his knees. One bomb exploded. They searched everywhere for him in the hotels, but all the time we were in a religious procession. Another bomb went off. I started to laugh, and a woman behind said, 'M. le curé, you never take anything seriously'.

I sheltered many people, Jews, Resisters, anyone who was being hunted. I helped the network Alliance and was involved in Combat. I was a Resister because I was a soldier and never accepted Vichy. People became patriotic when they were deprived of freedom. Communism and Nazism had both been condemned by the Pope and I accepted neither. In the 1930s I supported the Republicans in the Spanish Civil War. I was in favour of the Popular Front. I was a man of the Left and as a member of the Sillon I was in favour of social reforms. I believe in heredity. My mother's side was religious and my father's revolutionary. I inherited both but felt closer to my father.

I had nothing against Pétain. He had decorated me in World War I. I never believed he was a collaborator. He was a victim of those round him, particularly the Action Française and Pierre Laval.

In Brive there was a radical administration. They treated Michelet with scorn. They were hostile to all practising Catholics. Very few people in Brive praised Michelet's actions when he distributed his first tracts, certainly not the Communists or the Radicals.

M. Roger Pestourie (24 June 1969, Lyon)

In 1940 I was a bachelor aged 20 with a peasant background on both sides of the family. My father had died when he was 32 as a result of his injuries in the First World War. My brother was mobilized in 1939 and captured and made a prisoner of war in 1940. As a result I had to leave the job I had in a transport firm in Brive and return to the family farm of seventeen hectares in the Lot. I had been a member of the Young Communists since 1937 and a member of the party since 1938.

When war had been declared I felt the same kind of shock as the rest of my generation. I was convinced that war was inevitable after the refusal of Britain and France to form an anti-Fascist pact with Russia. During the *drôle de guerre* I saw the bourgeoisie use the pretext of the Nazi–Soviet pact to revenge themselves on the working class by turning the French people against the P.C.F.

I was stupefied by the signing of the Armistice, even though my party had led me to expect it. I felt a deep anger and resentment against those who had produced the disaster and the humiliation. I would quite happily have used violence at once against the traitors.

By and large the great majority of the communist militants in Brive remained faithful to the party. I myself had confidence in the U.S.S.R. and this allowed me to understand the pact. But we had to think things out for ourselves as the liaisons with the party were broken and we had to take the initiative at the grass roots. The pact had traumatized public opinion and the party was even more isolated than it had been at the time of Munich. Our first reaction was one of self-defence against all this suspicion and hostility. There were several different ideas about the situation within the party and many comrades were at first influenced by the public hostility. They were honest party members who just didn't understand. Several of them had been soldiers in the 1914–18 War and were affected by the government propaganda of 1939–40 which declared that this was another patriotic war. But it wasn't, and they could soon see that. It was an imperialist war in 1939 and *not* a war against Fascism. You could see that by the way in which the working class were opposed by a hostile bourgeois government. And then comrades came back from the front and told us that the whole war was a bluff. No one was fighting against Hitler; there was no intention at all to wage war against him.

So from the start our Resistance was a class struggle, a struggle against Fascism which we had started before the war. Once we were invaded we added propaganda for the liberation of the country to the class war.

You mustn't forget that we were very dispersed in 1939–40, not just because of persecution but also because of mobilization and all the prisoners of war. So we had to start our activity by making lists. Our job was to find out who was still there and to contact them. We contacted the wives when the husbands were missing. We had to show we still existed. This was Resistance because it was illegal. Only then did we go on to reform the party in groups of three. I remember investigating the *lycée* at Cahors and schools in Brive during 1941–2 still looking for Communists but also good republicans who were not necessarily members of the party. Bit by bit we built up an underground organization.

At that time we didn't hear of any other movements, though we knew of de Gaulle's broadcast. Gaullism spread much faster than we did. It had the benefit of the radio, and there were many popular ways of showing you were a Gaullist. I remember people coming out of mass in our village in the Lot and just saying 'Vive de Gaulle' to each other.

Pétain's influence did enormous damage to Resistance. His hold over the families of prisoners of war was very strong. The trouble was that people's bitterness about the defeat didn't make them want to do something active to change the situation but made them even more submissive to Pétain. They also thought he was playing a double game and was getting ready to defeat the Germans. The officers in the Armistice Army believed that, and in Brive they thought he would call for armed Resistance when the Germans invaded the southern zone. They were bitterly disillusioned.

M. Alban Vistel (10 Aug. 1969, Lyon)

I was 35 in 1940 and was living just outside Lyon. I had never been a member of a political party, yet had formed strong political convictions. For five years in the early 1930s I had lived in South America where I was made acutely aware of social problems and human misery. In a small way I had been involved in political activities there: it was where I began my career as a conspirator. I felt I was being prepared for something but didn't know what. In 1935 I returned to France and was shocked by the public's indifference to the Nazi danger. I believed that another war was imminent—I was absolutely convinced of that after reading *Mein Kampf* and *Hitler speaks*. When the war in Spain started I was emotionally involved on the republican side due to the Spanish-American origins of my wife as well as my anti-Nazi ideas. I would have gone to fight as a volunteer but my wife was pregnant. The Czech crisis confirmed my belief that World War II was near.

I was in favour of the Popular Front and marched on its behalf, singing The Internationale. I was an engineer in a small factory, where I was the only member of the C.G.T. My position made me a mediator between the employers and the unions. I never identified with the employers, but because I was seen as a member of the ruling class my left-wing ideas were constantly under pressure.

In educational terms I had a legal and scientific university training, but my vocation was for the humanities. I had undergone a solid religious education, but at the time had moved away from religion, though I was very interested in the *personnaliste* ideas of left-wing Catholics. My passion was 'revolution' —I wanted to change the world, transform society, and revolutionize man. Everything else was secondary, and I valued literature only if it shed light on man's condition.

My South American experience had strongly marked me. I had seen the realities of colonization and the imperialism of the dollar. I had been particularly horrified by the American humiliation of the Cubans: Havana was an American brothel. I was determined to fight against these social inequalities. Then on my return to France I encountered unemployment and economic crisis and was convinced that capitalism was incapable of resolving the current economic problems.

The failure of the Popular Front I believed was due to the hostility of the capitalist classes who were attracted by the Fascist regimes where order had been defended against the threat of social revolution. The Popular Front Government was too weak and Blum did not have the personality to deal with the situation, though he could have stopped Nazism by a firm stand.

When war arrived, the war I had predicted, I declared it to be a just war against an inhuman enemy. Nazism was the opposition of everything I stood for. As a *personnaliste* I could not have done anything else but oppose the Nazi values. I was mobilized in the reserve army and given the command of a fortress in the Alps near Grenoble. I saw no action. From my military service in Morocco I had retained a sympathy for the self-respect and fraternity which the army induced, but I was far from being a militarist.

The French were used to the idea of victory since World War I, so that defeat was a thunderbolt. It was utterly unbelievable to see the Germans thirty kilometres from Grenoble. After panic on the roads and the ridiculous exodus of people, some of whom fled merely from the Jura to Grenoble, the sigh of relief when it was all over was enormous. It was easy for the vast majority of the French to accept Pétain as a saviour. I saw both sides of Pétain—the image of the famous soldier and yet also an old hypocrite. For a while I experienced a certain doubt since it was possible to believe that Pétain could get the best out of the defeat, but my hesitation did not last long. I became determined to do something constructive. I began to collect round me young workers from my factory and in November 1940 I held my first secret meeting in a disused sports stadium with about fifteen young people. I read some of Churchill's and de Gaulle's speeches, talked of the heritage of France, my belief that the scandalous Nazi–Soviet pact could not last, my conviction that America would enter the war, and the need to show that France was capable of independence from the Germans.

My main quarrel with Vichy was its suppression of the Republic and democracy. I was no great admirer of the Third Republic, but I was prepared to fight to defend democracy against totalitarianism. Resistance was individual and spontaneous at this time and the main problem for me was to keep hold of my circle of young workers by holding regular meetings, typing out tracts, and writing slogans on walls. I had meagre means at my disposal but I pretended to have a contact with London. It was essential to say this otherwise I would have lost my support. For a year I searched for something concrete in the way of contacts.

In November 1941 I decided to cycle from my home outside Lyon to see Emmanuel Mounier who was trying to keep *Esprit* alive in the face of censorship. Mounier was very friendly and after discovering my ideas suggested I should join Libération through André Philip. I fixed a meeting with Philip, who was my old professor at the Faculté de Droit, and talked with him enthusiastically more about plans for France after the war than about action against the Nazis. From that point I received packets of clandestine newspapers and I began to reconstruct my following into organized groups of six. At the time I did not know Emmanuel d'Astier.

Within Libération there were a good number of Jews and intellectuals while among the *gens de base* there were trade-unionists and workers who had left the Communist Party after the Nazi–Soviet pact. One of the most important sources of support was the C.F.T.C., and the left-wing Catholics who had belonged to such movements as the Jeune République and the Parti Démocrate Populaire (P.D.P.) before the war. Resistance as I knew it was essentially an anti-Fascist activity by left-wing people, even anarchists in the best sense of the word.

Within the Resistance, prejudices tended to disappear since people were united by something essential—the defence of liberty, justice, dignity, and the fatherland. For myself Resistance was a direct continuation of my pre-war ideas. I had always dreamed of revolution, the remaking of the economic and political structure, and the movement towards a peaceful world of people united in a common cause. Resistance was a sense of Utopia, and it is always necessary to envisage Utopia, even though serious-minded people at the time saw this Resistance as mad and ridiculous.

M. André Plaisantin (30 Aug. 1969, Lyon)

I was aged 34 in 1940 and was the father of four children. I was a building engineer in Lyon and before the war had been a member of the Christian Democratic movement Jeune République. Marc Sangnier had been a strong influence on me, and my outlook on life was religious and social rather than political. My friends were mostly Christian Democrats and I was close to the group which published *L'Aube*, the Christian Democratic newspaper of the 1930s. In common with this group I was appalled by the Munich agreements of 1938, and although a small minority of Jeune République placed the maintenance of peace above all else, the majority condemned Munich. I myself was basically a pacifist but had rallied to the majority view in the face of events.

As a father of four I was not mobilized for the war, but my building business had to be closed owing to mobilization and I worked in my brother's carpentry business.

I condemned the Armistice outright and rejected Pétain because he had signed it and because he had not put an end to the Munich policy. I found it inadmissible that France should negotiate with the Germans. I was also completely against the internal policy of Vichy which I dismissed as an antiquated programme. I rejected its corporatism and was in no way seduced by the Catholic support for Pétain. Although I was by nature a pacifist I was determined to fight to avoid Nazi domination and accepted all means of Resistance including the notion of armed rebellion.

It was I who contacted others to share my individual defiance, and my Resistance took shape through numerous discussions, particularly with friends who belonged to the Amis de Temps présent, reassembled round Stanislas Fumet and the sequel to the paper, *Temps nouveau*. I was soon in contact with Jean Demachy and Henri Frenay. My Resistance was essentially an anti-Nazi struggle, seen as one of European dimensions. I condemned France for having continued a legal government under the Occupation.

Almost all my first contacts were within the Christian syndicalist movement, whose local centre in the rue Saint-Polycarpe in Lyon was a centre for recruitment and discussion. Exiles and refugees, particularly from Alsace, were important in the early stages. There was a common bond in the beginning within Christian Democracy, but this was soon replaced by a wider bond of free-thinkers, Catholics, Socialists, and Communists united behind a Resistance Charter for liberated France.

Most jobs were represented in the early Resistance of Combat though the majority were wage-earners. The leaders were at first linked by a common heritage of left-wing Christianity in Jeune République or the Parti Démocrate Populaire, but their ranks were soon enlarged by others who shared a common liberalism. The word 'Resistance' was used from the start, though there was an equivocal attitude towards Vichy. Frenay hoped that Vichy would protect Combat, a tactical position I rejected. A meeting with Frenay was held at my house in Lyon at which I expressed my disapproval after Frenay had explained why he had met the Minister of the Interior. On the whole Frenay's view, shared by Demachy, was a class position. The bourgeoisie did not like the idea of civil violence and preferred to keep the possibility of rebellious action at arm's length. The working class, on the other hand, were used to fighting for their rights and were more imbued with a revolutionary spirit. They wanted action and were prepared for violent conflict.

Within Combat I worked out a scheme for mobilizing groups within the administration, in order to gain the support of experts. It was taken up by Claude Bourdet and became N.A.P. (Noyautage des administrations publiques). The most difficult organization to penetrate was the police, but it was easier among officials in the *mairies* administering food and supplies. My relationship with Communists was excellent.

M. Pavoux (2 June 1969, Lyon)

In 1940 I was a railway-worker at Oullins near Lyon, was married with one child, and was aged 34. I was a member of the organization Amis de l'U.R.S.S. and in 1937 had paid a visit to Russia. The organization had as its aim to stimulate interest in Soviet Russia, and most of its members did not belong to the Communist Party. Neither did I before 1939.

When war was declared I thought at first that it was a just war, but when I saw that the first act of Daladier was to dissolve the Communist Party, I saw that it was not really a war against Hitler. Instead, militant Communists were being arrested and liberties imperilled. I had taken part in the strikes at Oullins in 1938 and had seen soldiers sent to occupy the factory, so I knew this was another action against the working class. My wife and I immediately decided to join the party and we started producing tracts to keep the party together at Oullins.

Our first task was to inform people. We explained why the government had dissolved the party of the Left, and that the government was waging war not against Hitler but against the Communist Party and the communist trade unions. We tried to explain the Nazi–Soviet pact, saying that it was an attempt to create peace. It was a big question and a great problem for us. Several militants didn't understand. I myself had confidence in the Soviet Union and couldn't believe that it would let us down. There were very few defections from the Amis de l'U.R.S.S.

There were three thousand railway-workers at Oullins, and our task was to inform them of the facts and to regroup the party in groups of three. Admittedly we made mistakes early on. We were not cautious enough and several comrades were arrested. But we were then more careful. It was just lack of clandestine experience.

As a railway-worker I was not mobilized to fight, but employed in the pioneer corps attached to the Alpine Army. At the Armistice we were not sent home but transferred to the fortress of Fort Barreau in the Isère where we were kept as 'undesirables'. That showed that Vichy and the Germans were hand in hand. There were about 720 of us, all skilled workers, and yet at that time France desperately needed labour. Comrades wrote to us and said they were working twelve hours a day, and yet there we were with nothing to do. After four months I was transferred to Lyon to face trial for reconstituting an illegal party. A young comrade had been arrested and he had talked, giving a lot of names. Luckily we had a secret organization inside Fort Barreau, which even produced its own newspapers, and it found out everything the young comrade had said. So when it came to the trial I knew exactly what to say and what not to say, and was acquitted.

I returned to Oullins but shortly afterwards was dismissed, with no reasons given. I found a job in a small workshop and from there became one of those principally responsible for the party at Oullins. I also took part in syndicalist propaganda for the Metalworkers' Union. Our struggle was still mainly to re-establish the party. Pétain had a certain prestige and many veterans let themselves be taken in by the Légion. In my own family, those who had fought in World War I believed it was really something. But that didn't last long. Also for a while some unionists were taken in by the labour plans of Vichy but, as the arrests of militants continued, they saw through the

Charte du travail. The same was true in 1942 of the *Relève*. To begin with it looked good to some workers, but they soon changed.

The invasion of Russia in 1941 didn't change our activity, but it accentuated it. People could now see clearly what Hitler's intentions were. What was difficult to understand was how Russia was so easily invaded. That needed explanation, because we all thought Russia was stronger than Germany.

Explaining and informing: that's what the early period was all about. I emphasize it not just because I work in a bookshop now but because people think Resistance was all machine-guns. But the armed struggle grew out of the ideological struggle. We had to explain why? and how? all the time. Most of our explanations came from Paris and I saw nothing of any clandestine Press outside communist and trade union publications. I was amazed there were so many others at the Liberation.

Before 1942 Resistance was only a minority movement. The real break through came when the southern zone was occupied. This made it much easier.

M. Ferdinand Paloc (10 Sept. 1970, Montpellier)

In 1940 I was 44, the father of two children, and general editorial secretary in the local paper *L'Éclair* in Montpellier. I was not a member of any political party but had been secretary to a deputy in the departmental assembly who was a Républicain indépendant, in other words moderately right-wing. *L'Éclair* was also right-wing and monarchist in its attitudes. I was critical of the Third Republic which did not do enough to safeguard the country against the danger from Hitler's Germany. I was opposed to the Popular Front because it was extremist and could only weaken the potential of national resistance to any attack from outside. At the time of Munich I tried for some time to believe that there was good faith on the German side but my naïvety didn't last long. I saw that Hitler only took advantage of any concessions. As for the Nazi–Soviet pact, I was deeply indignant that Russia after all its statements in the previous years could ally with Nazi Germany and stab France and Britain in the back. *L'Éclair* published a column by the historian Pierre Gaxotte condemning the Soviet Union. There was no justification whatsoever for the pact.

I was not mobilized for the war because I had been badly

wounded in the 1914–18 War in which I had fought as a volunteer. The two wars had nothing in common. In 1939–40 there was no energy, no foresight, and no preparation.

I held many things responsible for the defeat, particularly negligence, lack of preparation, and a terrible failure to get all the arms and munitions out of the arsenals and depots into the hands of the soldier on the front. When the Germans occupied France they found enormous unused stores of weapons.

Like most Frenchmen I believed Pétain could rally the country and could save what was left. He was the victor of Verdun and didn't like the Germans. He could have played a role in crystallizing Resistance, but he was too old and was surrounded by ambitious men like Pierre Laval. Within two months I was disillusioned with Pétain, well before his meeting with Hitler at Montoire.

It was in October 1940 that I received Jacques Renouvin, an old member of the Camelots du Roi and Professor of Law in Paris. He was sent to me by Moulin de Labarthète, who was a personal assistant to Pétain. I was at the time local president of the Association of War Veterans and therefore had certain contacts with the Vichy ministries. Despite my veteran loyalties I was a member of Pétain's Légion française des combattants for only eight days, not long enough to receive a membership card. I realized at once that it was designed for political ends.

Before Renouvin came I had assisted eight Belgian officers to escape. They were refugees along with many other Belgian government and military figures in Montpellier, and they escaped from Sète to Britain via Spain and Portugal. That was on 26 September 1940. When Renouvin arrived he began to group together the elements of spontaneous Resistance in Montpellier and formed an embryo core of Resistance which later became part of Combat. My job in 1940–2 was to pass on information from *L'Éclair*, particularly the oral instructions from Vichy and the Germans which were not written down.

The reasons for my Resistance, which led eventually to my deportation to Germany, were simple. As a veteran of World War I, I could not accept occupation by the traditional enemy whom we had beaten in 1918. Nor could I accept the nature of the Hitlerian regime. We had to fight on; I could not agree with the policy of 'wait and see'.

One or two colleagues on *L'Éclair* supported me, but the director of the paper was a strong Vichy supporter and I kept my opinions quiet. When Pétain visited Montpellier I refused to join in the procession. The town became a centre for active Resistance, not just verbal Resistance. There were bomb attacks, sabotage, and regular escapes from the coast. All sorts of people were involved, though the active Resistance was mostly undertaken by ordinary people for whom Resistance was a movement of social progress. Politics throughout was subordinated to the unity of Resistance. The clandestine Press was very important and we distributed *Petites Ailes* and *Vérités* from the beginning. My two children acted as distributors, since children were less suspected.

There were, unfortunately, many denunciations by Frenchmen. Without French traitors the Gestapo would have achieved only a tenth of their arrests.

Living conditions were very hard, particularly in the winter of 1942–3. Some villages helped us and provided food, but the myth of Pétain was deeply rooted in the countryside and some villages were entirely loyal to Vichy. Pétain himself could not have known when he came to power just how many demands would be imposed on him. Laval was mainly responsible, but Pétain had several moments when he should have protested or resigned, like the time of the hostage-shooting at Châteaubriant, or the deportations. But it is still too soon to pass judgement on him. Charles Maurras, whom I knew personally through *L'Éclair*, was a bitter disappointment. I had a fervent admiration for his logic and his doctrine but I was totally disillusioned, as with Brasillach, whom I also admired. All the members of Action Française should have followed Jacques Renouvin. He didn't hesitate, but resisted at once.

M. Albin Tixador (17 Sept. 1970, Montpellier)

I had been a militant Socialist and member of the Socialist Party since about 1925. I was 43 in 1940, married with no children of my own, but we had adopted my wife's nephew. I was a humanitarian Socialist, an admirer of Jean Jaurès, and a good friend of Léon Blum. I fought the whole of the First World War and in May 1918 lost my left leg in action. My job in Montpellier in 1940 was as a civil servant under the Ministère des Anciens Combattants, involved with the creation and running of a retirement home for war veterans.

In the 1930s I had been completely on the side of the Spanish Republicans, and thought that our own Popular Front Government should have intervened to help them: it might have done so if the English had been in favour. As it was, I was closely involved with the Spanish refugees when they arrived in Montpellier. I was opposed to the Munich agreements, which I saw as a trap.

The defeat of France in 1940 I felt was due mainly to the subversive activity of the Fifth Column and the failures of the General Staff. There was no lack of material: it was stacked up everywhere. It wasn't the fault of the Third Republic. One of the first victims of the Fifth Column after the defeat was one of the leaders of our party, Marx Dormoy, assassinated by them.

Among the political parties there was a period of dislocation after the defeat and I don't really blame the Socialists who voted in favour of Pétain on 10 July. They lacked a clear sense of direction and firm leadership. After all, Paul Faure was in favour of Vichy and he had been General Secretary of the party in the 1930s. The myth of Pétain and his great reputation as victor of Verdun took most people in, especially veterans and army officers. His Légion seemed a good thing because it united all the veterans' movements. I myself didn't join. I waited to see what it was intended for. So, too, did my own veteran association, the Association générale des mutilés de guerre. I stayed at my job, and pressure was put on me to join, but I never gave in.

I was immediately against the Armistice. I had heard de Gaulle's appeal from London and tried to create a small group in Montpellier to do something. We didn't know what. It wasn't easy to find others. Most of them produced some sort of excuse and said, 'We'll be with you when it comes to it, but . . .' Our first meeting—about fifteen of us—was at a photographer's house. His name was Gounel. Later we met at Paloc's. That was in November 1940. Contact was made with Jacques Renouvin in the same month. He was an old Action Française member and Paloc was a monarchist. You can see therefore that there were no politics in early Resistance. Paloc and I were both wounded veterans and we knew each other well, despite our political differences. Renouvin brought enormous enthusiasm to Resistance.

We recruited mainly among workers and intellectuals. There were plenty of young recruits but we had to restrain them. They were not very cautious. I myself helped organize one of the *groupes francs*, though naturally I couldn't take part in their action. I worked with Chauliac who had been on the municipal council. The ex-mayor was also in the early groups. There were several fights at the University, in the Faculté de Droit, between students who were for Pétain and those who were against. On 14 July 1942 there was an enormous demonstration in the town: it showed that the vast majority of the population was in favour of Resistance.

As for party politics, there weren't any. I was contacted by Daniel Mayer and Froment and I made regular journeys to Toulouse to attend meetings to set up the Comité d'action socialiste (C.A.S.), but it was set up as a Resistance operation not for party-political ends. Of course we were political in the sense of being anti-Vichy, but that was the politics of Resistance. In Toulouse we met mainly at the Café de la Poste.

M. Jean Baumel (15 Sept. 1970, Montpellier)

I gained my doctorate in History at the Sorbonne and in 1940 I was General Secretary to the municipal administration of Montpellier, a job which I held throughout the Occupation until my arrest in mid-1943. I was 33 years old, married, and father of three children. During the 1930s I was a member of the Radical Party with sympathy for the Independents. I was not a supporter of the Popular Front which I believed was only causing social unrest. The Munich agreements seemed to me to offer a possibility of peace and I was not opposed to them.

At the declaration of war I was mobilized as a captain, and was made aide-de-camp to General Charles Hanote in Algiers. He had the temperament of Resistance even before the defeat and I think my own Resistance owes much to having been his aide-de-camp. The defeat was due to failures by the Third Republic governments and the military leaders. The *drôle de guerre* had allowed soldiers to develop a mentality which was far from warlike and consequently the army was quite unprepared. I didn't believe in the Fifth Column, and the Communists were not opposed to a French victory. They were merely passive at the time.

I accepted the Armistice although I was no partisan of Vichy, and I returned to my job in Montpellier. One of my friends there was Vincent Badie, the radical-socialist deputy for the town, who had voted against Pétain on 10 July. We talked a lot about what could be done and held meetings of friends at the end of 1940. A group of professors at the University criticized the Armistice and there was a demonstration against them by nationalist students in favour of Vichy. They only represented a minority of the student body.

I was very hostile to the National Revolution but at the start I accepted Pétain as a Resister. I was disillusioned by Montoire. I blame Laval for this. He wanted a German victory.

We made very little progress before 1942 although we distributed tracts on an individual basis. We had no organization. It was easy in the southern zone to remain inactive because there were no Germans, but the lack of food and conditions of life gradually changed public opinion. It was difficult to find enough food in an area almost wholly devoted to vines, and hunger undoubtedly provoked acts of Resistance. At the beginning, Resistance in Montpellier was uniquely composed of intellectuals because they were more in touch with events. The majority of the public in Montpellier were anti-German but had confidence in Pétain. I myself never swore an oath of allegiance to Pétain even though I was involved in the formalities of his visit to the town. I was not reproached for this by my friends because they knew my Resistance attitudes. My active Resistance did not begin until after the invasion of the southern zone when I became an active member of Combat until I was arrested and deported to several camps, including Auschwitz. I had no particular love of adventure. Resistance for me was something that I just had to do. In the early stages I particularly valued the Resistance Press and in 1942 we distributed *Combat* and *Cahiers du témoignage chrétien*. The radio was also important and many people who were not Resisters were nevertheless made sympathetic by listening to the BBC. From the Swiss radio we received objective information about events in the war.

M. Raymond Chauliac (20 Sept. 1970, Montpellier)

I was 36 in 1940 and was an engineer in Montpellier. I was a Catholic and was married with three children. I was on the municipal council and was well known in the town. I was a dissident from the Socialist Party along with Marcel Déat, and had been in favour of the Munich agreements of 1938 and against the war. I suppose I was a pacifist, more or less.

During the war I was attached to aircraft control in the air force, but mainly dealing with civil aviation. In June 1940 I tried to cross to Algiers from Bordeaux but was overtaken by the Armistice. I returned to Montpellier, where, to begin with, I was fairly undecided what to do. Mers-el-Kébir was a severe blow. But I rejected the defeatism of Déat and also that of the Communists. I had read *Mein Kampf* and was strongly opposed to Nazism.

In Montpellier I resigned as a municipal councillor before the Vichy suppression of local government. I was hostile to Pétain and never thought he was playing a double game. Before the war I was an official of the Fédération des officiers de réserve républicains, which was left-wing, and on the whole most of us refused to join Pétain's Légion.

My Resistance was a progressive activity, starting from talking to friends whose attitudes I was confident about. I knew the professors in the University who were hostile to the Armistice and collaboration, and I became involved with Renouvin's activities and with Combat. I recruited mainly among my friends, though by 1943 there were a lot of Jews under my command in the Armée secrète (A.S.). Resistance was not a movement of the people until August 1944.

The clandestine Press was very important, so too was the fact that there were all types of people in the Resistance. There was a great fraternity of different jobs and different political backgrounds.

The Armistice Army missed a great chance in November 1942. It refused to give the arms it had camouflaged to the Resistance, but either threw them into rivers and ponds or surrendered them. Nevertheless, we had organized the first armed *maquis* in the area before the end of 1942, in fact before the total occupation of the southern zone.

M. Albert Solié (9 Sept. 1970, Montpellier)

I was 34 in 1940, married without children. I was a fitter at the Fouga works in Béziers and was secretary of the Metalworkers' Union in Béziers. My militant union activity in the C.G.T. took shape during the period of the Popular Front when I organized the strikes at the Fouga works in 1936. I was not a Communist at that time.

When war was declared I was mobilized to the front near the Maginot Line where I experienced the absurdity of the *drôle de guerre*. Everyone there felt that it was not an ordinary war. It was a caricature. As a skilled worker I should really not have been mobilized, and my unit administrator finally told me to return to Béziers in early May 1940. I left on 9 May and reached Béziers, not knowing anything of the German attack. I was given a special job, then this was revoked, so really I was hanging around during the whole invasion and defeat. I was finally demobilized officially on 28 July.

A few days later I was contacted by a railway-worker who was a militant Communist and who suggested I should reconstruct my union as a member of the Communist Party. I agreed, and although there were no party cards at that time I became a Communist. To restart the Metalworkers' Union at Fouga it was necessary to have one eye on legality, since union activity was controlled by Vichy. I began to republish clandestine issues of *Le Métallo* from the Fouga works and reconstituted the union. I was nominated as its secretary. We were a very small group, only 24 out of 2,200 workers at Fouga, and all our meetings were watched by the police. I was arrested briefly in December 1940, but released when it was shown that my activity on the surface was legal.

In *Le Métallo* we set out our wage claims and other demands and condemned the high cost of living and Vichy's restrictions on the freedom of the unions. This was the only content of the paper at the beginning, purely economic and union claims. Later the union had a role in creating the Front National in Béziers. Early on, about ten of us, including my union colleague Montagné who was a Socialist, met at the home of Me Pierre Malafosse, a barrister who had defended workers against the management of Fouga during the 1930s. As members of the

Communist Party we were one of the very few forces making for Resistance at the time in Béziers.

It was extremely difficult to persuade fellow comrades to resist and we were a small minority within the party. Vichy had instilled a climate of fear and anxiety and even good Communists turned their heads away from any action. The Nazi–Soviet pact had left the position of the party very unclear, and it wasn't until later that things began to change. But for us at the grass roots, without any instructions from the top, the basic activity of making economic demands and regrouping the union was the way to start Resistance. As Lenin said, you have to work within people's capacity for action, so that we could not move very fast.

I was arrested again in April 1942 and defended by Me Malafosse. After a month I was acquitted because no proof of my clandestine activity could be found. I was helped all the time by having my name openly on the form by which Vichy had authorized meetings of our local union in the period before the *Charte du travail*.

Frédéric Montagné (16 Sept. 1970, Béziers, Hérault)

I was a metalworker in Béziers in 1940 and was 30 years old. I had been a member of the Socialist Party since 1932, and was still a member in 1940. The party had survived several splits, particularly those caused by Pivert and Zyromski, but in 1940 after the defeat it had no policy and no position. I was a militant in the local Building-Workers' Union and we'd always had close liaisons with the Communists. I knew a lot of comrades from the Fouga works where I used to work.

When I returned from the war some fellow workers who were Communists said we should restart the union on a legal basis. I said No. I was not in agreement with them. But then Albert Solié who had only just become a Communist said that it was a question of making the unions legal and illegal at the same time. What he was proposing was a parallel activity. I agreed to do this. He restarted the Metalworkers' Union and I did the same for the Building-Workers' Union. I also started, like Solié, to work as a Communist.

When the *Charte du travail* was passed there were meetings in Béziers between employers and workers. They wanted to start a mixed union. The workers who went to the meetings had no union experience. We went along to one and when they saw us they shouted 'Don't let the Communists speak'. But I was known as a Socialist and I was allowed to speak and I said that the interests of employers and workers were not the same. Then my own employer said to me, 'If you go on like that we'll have you thrown out'. At that, one of our comrades crossed the floor and shouted 'Salaud'.

Albert Solié had the confidence of the Fouga workers, but the public authorities—the prefect, the police, and the Labour Inspector—didn't want him to be secretary of his union. They kept arresting him. A bourgeois barrister Pierre Malafosse defended him. He didn't know what we were doing illegally, but he stood out against the rest of the authorities.

The Socialist Party made no attempt to contact me. It didn't operate as a party in the Resistance, though I worked with several old Socialists later on. What we did at the beginning in 1940–1 was to place our action firmly on a union basis, reviving all the workers' claims and pressing for the release of our comrades who had been imprisoned. This was Resistance because the Germans and Vichy were the same.

M. Pierre Malafosse (20 Sept. 1970, Cap d'Agde, Hérault)

When war broke out I was an artillery officer in the reserve. I volunteered shortly afterwards to go on the Norwegian campaign, and on the way back in April 1940 I passed through England. From that point I knew the determination of the English.

I was 27 at the time, had received my doctorate in law at Montpellier, and was a barrister at Béziers. I had no party politics, but I had rejected the Munich agreements of 1938 because I knew what Hitler's game was. Those responsible for the French defeat were firstly the General Staff, secondly the French people, and thirdly Daladier, who admitted that he couldn't get rid of incompetent generals. As a barrister I was asked to talk to the troops I was with about the German danger. They didn't know what it was. The average Frenchman thought the French army was the strongest in the world. Once it was defeated he thought nothing else could possibly resist. I myself was totally opposed to Pétain's Armistice decision since he knew the power of England and the U.S.A.

When I arrived back in France in mid-May 1940, I was sent to Chantilly but the Germans were already on their way. I was then sent to Briançon to fight against the Italians. When the Armistice was declared, I was told to surrender our arms to the Italians. I refused to do so.

I returned to the bar at Béziers but still had the spirit of adventure. I had volunteered for Norway and I had volunteered for the anti-tank units. My anti-Vichy ideas were soon well known in Béziers. I made no secret of them in the corridors of the law courts. In 1940 I had no colleagues who shared my opinion and by 1942 there were still very few. They were almost all Pétainist.

In October 1940 I had my first conversation with another barrister, André Boyer in Marseille. By the spring of 1941 we were in contact with London, and I was part of the network Brutus, seeking out military information. It was difficult in the southern zone because there were no Germans. I also distributed propaganda from Combat and defended Communists in Béziers. I defended Solié because I had known him before the war. But I had been very critical of the Nazi–Soviet pact, and before the invasion of Russia the Communist Party in the area did nothing, *qua* party. But individuals did do something as individual Communists.

I myself was of independent means and had plenty of money. This was an important facility in my Resistance activity. I became a Resister, I suppose, because I was against Hitler, but chance had a lot to do with it. I was also a patriot, and more and more of a democrat. We recruited mainly among workers.

M. Joseph Pastor (13 Sept. 1971, Marseille)

I was 47 in 1940 and was by training an engineer, though because of my Communist ideas I did not want to be caught in a factory between employers and workers, so I became self-employed. I lived in Marseille, and was married with two children. Since 1930 I had been a member of the Communist Party, though in the 1930s I was already critical of the party for failing to become genuinely revolutionary. All it could do was to follow Stalin's wishes. The Nazi–Soviet pact was part of Stalin's determination to look after Russian interests at all costs, but although I rejected the pact I stayed in the party. I always thought France would lose the war because it was deceived about the power and organization of Hitler's Germany.

I was mobilized at the start of the war but only to be imprisoned as a 'notorious Communist and propagandist who must be locked up'. I remained in prison for ten days but was freed due to pressure from the Ligue des droits de l'homme.[1] I was then placed under house arrest at Tournon and Privas until the end of January 1940 when I was finally allowed home to Marseille. They came to arrest me again once Vichy was in power but I had left the notice saying 'Mobilized' on the front of my shop and they went away. Owing to this notice I remained free until September 1940.

When I returned to Marseille at the end of January I tried to contact the party but found no trace of it. It had disappeared entirely after being dissolved, but not before condemning me for my attitude to the Nazi–Soviet pact. I started, therefore, to reconstruct the party in the south of Marseille among my old comrades. Some, who rejected me, had little concern to restart the party and made no attempt to stay hidden. As a result many were arrested.

By August 1940 I had reconstituted the party in my area, and in that month the party sent an official from Montpellier to contact me. I duly passed on all my information and gave him the names of my comrades. A month later I was arrested, when a neighbour told the police that I was living behind the 'mobilized' sign, and shortly after almost all of my group were rounded up and arrested. A police spy, Nau, had penetrated the very heart of the organization pretending to be an official from Saint-Loup, and had used my documents to destroy the party. When I heard this I escaped from my concentration camp knowing that I would be held more firmly as a result of his discoveries. As soon as I was free, the Vichy police circulated a rumour that it was I who had betrayed all my comrades. The party in Marseille believed the stories. They were still

[1] Founded in 1898 at the height of the Dreyfus Affair to defend human liberties threatened by arbitrary decisions of political and judicial authority, the Ligue des droits de l'homme had almost 200,000 members in 1933. Later in the 1930s there were a number of splits within the movement as the Radicals lost control to the Socialists.

opposed to me because of my attitude to the Nazi–Soviet pact. They at once said I was a Vichy agent and in the pay of the police.

I came back clandestinely to Marseille and began again to construct a group, this time only among comrades who shared my views. We were about 30 and we brought out about five or six numbers of *Rouge-Midi* in 1941, calling for sabotage of material going to Germany and a front against the Occupiers. The party also had its publications, including *Rouge-Midi*, and in their editions they totally rejected mine and condemned my proposals for an anti-German front. During this time I can certify that the party did nothing in the way of Resistance.

My activity expanded when I was contacted by Chevance, the friend of Henri Frenay, through a local doctor who knew me, Dr. Recordier. I agreed to constitute Resistance groups of three among my comrades and among fellow engineers in Marseille.

Between 1940 and 1942 there was virtually no Resistance in Marseille except for a few individuals and small groups. Among the workers this was due to the rivalry between Communists and Socialists and the fact that there were very few militants among them. A militant is someone who is born that way. One is a fighter by nature. For that reason there was no merit in being a Resister. One was there by nature. People rarely became Resisters by conscious deliberation. There were many jobs and professions represented in the Resistance, simply because it was a question of character, not politics.

On the whole Resistance was a young man's activity. I was the oldest among my comrades. There were no veterans of World War I among us except myself. I had escaped three times from the Germans in 1914. My wife was not a natural Resister. She shared my ideas but the life didn't come easily to her. She was arrested twice. I myself avoided capture but was under sentence of death by Vichy proclamation, while the Communist Party continued to call for my death, calling me a police agent. They also rejected my comrade Mecker, who started the *groupes francs* in Marseille. He too had disowned the Nazi–Soviet pact, as had most of those we recruited for Combat. Some re-entered the party in the last years of the war. Eventually I was responsible for bringing the party in

Marseille into contact with the three movements of Resistance—Combat, Libération, and Franc-Tireur—in a meeting in my clandestine hiding-place. This was done without telling the party that I was behind the meeting. But I was there—listening from the kitchen.

I don't think that cold and hunger were very important in stimulating Resistance. There were demonstrations for more food in Marseille but these were not held for Resistance purposes. Resistance was an armed struggle and the sabotage of everything that served the German army. It never became a mass movement. Most people were against it until it was obvious that Hitler was going to lose.

Mlle Madeleine Baudoin (6 Sept. 1971, Marseille)

In 1940 I had just finished my first year in the Faculté des Lettres at Aix-en-Provence and was 19 years old. I came from a family whose politics were in the Centre, but from the time of the Popular Front in 1936 I myself had been passionately left-wing although I had not joined any party. I felt angry about the Munich agreements because France had repudiated its pact with Czechoslovakia. I had also supported those who called for intervention in Spain against Franco. The declaration of war seemed logical to me. But no one wanted to go to war. The people of France were more afraid of Bolshevism than Fascism. So too was the government.

The Nazi–Soviet pact deeply shocked me. I found it inexcusable. It was more than a non-aggression pact: the Germans and Russians made several agreements to aid each other with petrol and raw materials. The pact caused all the ambiguities in the French Communist Party before June 1941.

The Armistice was inevitable. The whole public wanted it. I was against Pétain from the start because he was defeatist. But the people of France were to blame. They wanted him. They followed him blindly. At the time it was said, 'Pétain is France: France is Pétain'. It was absolutely true. I approved of the English attack on the French fleet at Mers-el-Kébir. I understood why the English had done it. The French fleet ought to have gone over to the English side in defiance of the Armistice.

We talked about all these events in the Faculté. Most

students were very shocked by the events and when the Dean made an obsequious speech in homage to Pétain there were a lot of shouts from the audience.

No one heard de Gaulle's appeal of 18 June: it was far too badly jammed. People in Marseille were fairly content with the situation because there was no Occupation. They talked about nothing else but rationing. The more the Germans took the more they thanked Pétain for saving what was left. However bad the food situation was they believed it would have been worse without Pétain. Their attitude was 'Pétain saves every day'. The word 'resist' was used right from the beginning. But it meant resisting the system of rationing, getting round it, finding a bit more food somehow from somewhere.

The Communists in the Faculté were completely blocked by the Nazi–Soviet pact. It's true they were hostile to Vichy and Pétain but they had nothing to say about the Germans. They were against the valet but not against his master.

To stand out against all this and to resist by wanting to go on fighting against the Germans was like being in a foreign country. No one agreed with you and they happily denounced you. They were obsessed by day-to-day problems of food and any goods in short supply. If hunger could have caused Resistance, everyone in the south would have been Resisters. There was hunger everywhere, but very, very few Resisters. In Marseille the hunger was even worse than most places, but did it produce more Resisters? No.

What was done before 1942? Very little. A few students circulated tracts, and demonstrated against the raising of the colours on the festival days authorized by Vichy. But there was no really active Resistance until after 1942. I don't believe that there was anything called 'Resistance ideas' or 'Resistance opinion.' You either *did* something or you were one of the mass who wouldn't do anything. France was Pétainist and *attentiste* to the end. If you wanted to do anything you had to mistrust everyone.

The Légion was very popular and when Pétain visited Marseille the enthusiasm was enormous. People at first believed that the Germans were protecting them against the Bolsheviks. And there was a lot of Anglophobia. Members of the Légion made continuous speeches against Russia and against England.

Everyone found ways of getting bread, more vegetables, more food. But they didn't resist the Germans. There were a few individuals in Marseille before 1942: a few small groups of Resisters. That's all. Combat was the first to be established, but it was mostly a question of discussion and writing tracts. Very few of those who wrote or read tracts went into active, armed Resistance after 1942. Even after 1942 there was no patriotic upsurge; that's a myth. There was no national insurrection; that's another myth, created by the Gaullists and the Communists for different reasons. Real Resistance was anti-Fascist; a small minority, fighting international Fascism. It was 'gauchiste' before the word was known: independent action without orders from the top and without a hard political line. This was the character of the *groupes francs* in the area after 1942 in which I was involved. I myself was no patriot, though I was prepared to fight to defend the Canebière.[2] But I would have fought in the same way in Spain or anywhere else against Fascism. It was an international fight.

M. Henri Cordesse (23 Sept. 1970, Montpellier)

My father was killed at the front in 1917 when I was 7. In 1940 I was a teacher in the small town of Marvejols in the Lozère. I was a militant trade-unionist in the Schoolteachers' Union, and although I was not a member of a political party I was close to the Communists and was often taken for one.

During the Spanish Civil War I organized the reception of Spanish republican refugees, and I constantly opposed the policy of non-intervention pursued by Léon Blum. I was also anti-Munich, but in a general assembly of the Schoolteachers' Union of the Lozère I was one of only about 50 out of 400 who voted against Munich. Forty out of those 50 were probably Communists.

I discussed the Nazi–Soviet pact at length with communist friends who said it must be a case of high diplomacy since Communism was the main enemy of Fascism and there could be no fundamental agreement between them. There was very little documentation on the pact. People were in the dark about it.

In 1939 I was mobilized as a reserve officer and sent to the

[2] The central boulevard of Marseille.

Alpine front south of Mont Blanc. The *drôle de guerre* was largely responsible for the disorientation of French people both at the time and during the defeat.

As teachers we did not like to blame the ordinary officers for the defeat since so many of us were officers from the reserve. But the higher echelons of the army were to blame for their Fascist sympathies of the 1930s. Pétain played a considerable right-wing political role in the 1930s. But I didn't really believe in the Fifth Column. That was an explanation used to cover more complex causes.

I myself had read *Mein Kampf* in translation and had discussed it with a colleague who had read it in German. I was passionately convinced that Nazism was evil.

After the defeat there were several months of lassitude in the area. I returned to my job like everyone else. But by early 1942 positions had been taken up and most people who became active Resisters had made their choice by then. I reckon 80 per cent of the *département* were *attentistes*. The Lozère is rural, mountainous, and sparsely populated and the *chef-lieu*, Mende, is a small town where employment was split between working for the *préfecture* and those working for the episcopacy. There was no industry and no university. Peasants were cautious and never did anything *en masse*. Catholicism in the area was very reactionary and pro-Pétain.

Most veterans joined Pétain's Légion, but it soon became clear that it was an organ of Vichy propaganda. Nascent Resistance took issue with the Légion very early on. Two of the first local Resisters, Peytavin and Bourrillon, were both veterans of the last days of World War I, but neither joined the Légion.

Resistance in Marvejols grew initially quite independent of both de Gaulle and the internal movements like Combat, though once Combat penetrated the region through Bourrillon most Resisters, including several Communists and myself, joined it. Before that, Resistance was a gradual but firm orientation in people's attitudes towards the events of 1940–1. For example, there were several Freemasons among my colleagues who reacted to victimization by Vichy. By 1942 most people knew where everyone stood. Undoubtedly Resistance in this area was heavily biased to the political Left, especially in the Cévennes where peasants were both Protestant and socialist. They provided a safe asylum for people like Grumbach, a socialist deputy and a Jew, who arrived as a refugee from Alsace in 1940. But there were also some right-wing Resisters, though not very many.

Among the first Resisters in the area, Bourrillon was a barrister in Mende, a notable of the town who had been in favour of republican Spain and had welcomed the Spanish refugees. He was dismissed as a municipal councillor by Vichy, and it was through him that Combat established itself in the Lozère. There was also Gilbert de Chambrun, whose father was the Marquis and had voted against Pétain in the Senate. Gilbert and his wife Noëlle became great organizers in the region. He and I met Peytavin and Bourrillon at Mende to set up Combat in the *département*.

Hunger played very little part in promoting Resistance, since the Lozère, as a rural area, did fairly well. Nor do I think the clandestine Press was particularly important: attitudes had hardened before the arrival of the first Resistance papers. As for my own professional sphere, I don't think Vichy's attack on secularism in the schools was very important: it was only a secondary matter.

I think it was important that I was a married man with a family. I felt more responsible for the future of France and a greater need to keep it free from Nazism. This was true of many parents, and in the early Resistance there were a large number of family men.

As for my trade union, I had felt estranged from it ever since the vote over Munich and had little to do with it. I talked at one point to a teacher from Lyon who had set up a legal Vichy union and to my surprise very few of my colleagues repudiated it.

M. Jean Vittoz (19 May 1969, Annemasse, Haute-Savoie)

I was a bachelor aged 32 in 1940 and I was working as a chemist in Annemasse. In 1925 I had joined the Communist Party, influenced by my father who had been a militant Socialist and who had brought me up in the tradition of those soldiers of World War I who rejected the war in favour of social revolution.

In 1939 the refusal of England and France to form an anti-Fascist front with Russia led Russia momentarily to nurture the illusion of a pact with Hitler. When war broke out I was mobilized in the Alpine Army, but my unit commander refused to victimize the Communists under his command, despite orders to 'unmask' them.

My own Resistance was a self-defensive reflex against the persecution of Communists and the anti-Russian propaganda of 1939–40. I also responded to the appeal launched by Maurice Thorez and Jacques Duclos in July 1940, shortly after the similar appeal of de Gaulle from London. My first act of Resistance was the distribution of this appeal from our leaders. I acted because I was a Communist and as a Communist I believed the party was right. I was obviously anti-German, because it was the Germans who were occupying the country.

Since I had only arrived in Annemasse in 1937 I wasn't well known there. This helped me a lot.

There were very few Communists in the Haute-Savoie: a few railway-workers in Annemasse, a few customs workers on the border, and a few fishermen on the lake at Annecy who had been militant Socialists but had become Communists in 1920. It was difficult to persuade my communist comrades to resist: some were confused by the events and found it particularly difficult to believe Pétain was a collaborator. Since my father had been a vigorous anti-militarist and I had been brought up to know all about Pétain's savage repression of the mutineers in World War I, I was able to argue with them and convince them.

My first job was to reconstitute the party in the area in groups of three. There had been so many arrests, and the wives of the Communists didn't want their husbands to get involved again. At the start in Annemasse we had no more than about fifteen groups of three. I got married in 1941 and my wife shared all my opinions and helped in all my activities.

I was also involved in air-raid duties so whenever there was a raid I was able to circulate freely. For this I had been given an *Ausweis* so I was able to cross the frontier in Annemasse without difficulty. As a chemist I was also well placed to supply the chemicals necessary for explosives later on.

I was one of the creators of the first groups of the F.T.P. in the area. They were mostly formed of young men who refused the labour conscription which began in June 1942. In late 1942 they started forming camps in the mountains and we had to feed them. In all this activity I was in weekly contact with party leaders in Lyon.

The area of Haute-Savoie was particularly open to Resistance since it was passionately anti-Italian. Mussolini's claims on Savoy made the people extremely patriotic in reaction. For example, we received a lot of help from patriotic village priests.

M. Romain Baz (10 May 1969, Annemasse, Haute-Savoie)

I was recently married in 1940 and was aged 30, with a job as a teacher at Gaillard in Annemasse. I was a militant trade-unionist and had been a member of the Socialist Party until 1938. I left because I thought Léon Blum was selling out to the bourgeoisie. I was then politically unattached for a while. I had opposed the Munich agreements because they were obviously in the interests of the bourgeoisie, who were preparing for the defeat of France. When it happened in 1940, it was no surprise to me. It had been carefully prepared for years. The ruling classes had betrayed the country.

When the defeat at the front was known, I asked for arms to be distributed to the citizens of Annemasse. My demand was dismissed out of hand by the police. As soon as the Vichy Government was in power, I was removed from my job in Annemasse because I was a 'danger to the youth of the town', and I was sent to a reactionary rural commune at Boëge,[3] under strict observance. But the result was the opposite of the one intended. I didn't change, the rural commune did, and it became almost totally a Resistance area.

At the start there was complete resignation among the people. Very few wanted to continue the fight. My wife was a typist and we typed and distributed our own tracts in 1940 telling people to be patriots and not to accept the defeat. I was against the Armistice and Pétain from the start. I suppose my reasons were both patriotic and political. I was utterly scornful of the claim by Pétain that the Armistice had been an honourable event: it was a real swindle. But 90 per cent of the veterans joined Pétain's Légion, and although I argued with many of them, they usually answered by saying that Pétain knew best how to get the better of the Germans.

[3] Fifteen kilometres due east of Annemasse.

The first group we created in the Boëge valley was in the shape of a sports association. It was above suspicion because it had a priest attached to it. The young members distributed tracts and organized listenings to the BBC. The tracts came first from Combat, then from the Communist Party and other Resistance movements. We distributed everything. Recruitment was steady but quickest among young people.

In the middle of June 1942 a local meeting was called by the collaborators in the Légion, the Service d'ordre légionnaire (S.O.L.). At the time, one of the local regiments, the 27ᵉ Chasseurs from Annecy, was on manœuvres in the area, so we asked their band to attend the meeting. When the leader of the S.O.L. started to speak, he was drowned by catcalls and shouts of 'Traitor', and then the band struck up 'Vous n'aurez pas l'Alsace et la Lorraine'. It was a total defeat for the S.O.L., and I'd say that by mid-1942 the Resistance was a popular position, even if not always an active one. People had gradually realized that the promises of 1940 had not been fulfilled. For example, the prisoners of war had not come home. They also realized just how much France was being exploited by the Germans, even if there was very little real hunger in the countryside. Nothing to compare with Nice or Marseille, where people really starved.

I was arrested in the evening of 14 July 1942, while distributing tracts in Annemasse, calling on young workers not to fall for the *Relève* and not to go to Germany. I was sentenced to eighteen months' imprisonment for 'action harmful to the government and the nation' and was imprisoned first at Annecy, then at Chambéry, then, after fourteen months, in a camp from which I escaped and returned to the Boëge valley. At Chambéry I met a lot of communist prisoners, some of whom were under sentence of death. I then joined the party myself.

In our valley there wasn't much difference between those who joined Combat, Libération, or the Front National. Party politics didn't enter into it. There was a saying at the time that if you have to make a pact with the devil to drive out the Germans, you choose the devil every time. We used to call ourselves 'Les Rouges et les Noirs', because we combined extreme left-wingers with right-wing clericals.

* * * *

There is one point to add by way of a postscript to this oral evidence. Most of the Resisters interviewed, including those presented here, had some difficulty in reconstructing the period before the total occupation of France in November 1942. The conflicts after 1942 leading to the Liberation were considerably more vivid, and in most cases had provided the individuals with their dominant memory and understanding of Resistance, for which the period 1940–2 often seemed no more than a mild preparation. Many would insist that the roots and origins traced in this study lost much of their significance in the stark confrontations of 1944 when areas barely affected by the Occupation for four years experienced the brutal reality of German repression and reprisals carried out with the collaboration of the French *milice*. A woman at Tulle in the Corrèze who wanted to remain anonymous, gave an interview of one minute only. 'I was a Resister in 1941 but only have one thing to say. I came home from shopping on 9 June 1944 to find my husband and my son hanging from the balcony of our house. They were just two of a hundred men seized at random and killed in cold blood by the German S.S. The children and the wives were forced to watch while they strung them up to the lamp-posts and balconies outside their own homes. What else is there for me to say?' On the following day occurred the horrific massacre of the inhabitants of Oradour-sur-Glane, shot and burnt alive in the church and barns of the village, and there were few areas which did not experience some incident of savage retaliation as the Germans were driven into retreat.[4]

The period of 1940–2 in the southern zone lacks this degree of violence and tragedy, though the deportation of foreign

[4] Accounts of the hangings at Tulle perpetrated by the S.S. division 'Das Reich' can be found in A. Soulier, *Le Drame de Tulle, 9 Juin 1944* (Tulle, 1946); abbé Jean Espinasse, *Témoignage sur la journée du 9 Juin 1944* (Tulle, 1953); and Rémy, *Les Balcons de Tulle* (Librairie Académique, Perrin, 1962). On the massacre at Oradour, for which the same S.S. division was responsible, there is the account, carefully pieced together from eye-witness evidence, by G. Pauchou and P. Masfrand, *Oradour-sur-Glane* (Charles-Lavauzelle, 1945). For other areas, in addition to memoirs and local accounts, there are the statistics of death and deportation at the hands of the Germans compiled by the official representatives of the Comité d'Histoire de la Deuxième Guerre Mondiale in each *département*. Some of these are already published by the Comité and others exist in manuscript or on index cards.

Jews in the summer of 1942 had established something of the inhumanity inseparable from the German Occupation. But what the emphasis on the later phase of Resistance tends to produce is a constant re-evaluation of its military importance in the context of the Allied victory over Germany. Arguments and counter-arguments proliferate in this area. By contrast, a study of the earlier period produces an emphasis on the ideological conflict which belongs to the internal history of modern France as much as to the history of German-occupied Europe. As a result of this ideological conflict the armed Resistance of 1943–4 could safely assume that its actions were firmly grounded in both patriotism and the traditions of revolutionary France. The ideas and motivations of 1940–2 had created the basis for a complex but powerful resurgence of moral and political certainty which gave the French Resistance its own justification whatever the ultimate calculations of its strategic and military value.

Bibliography

The place of publication of all works in sections 1, 2, 5, and 7 is Paris unless otherwise stated.

1. BIBLIOGRAPHIES

Catalogue des périodiques clandestins diffusés en France de 1939 à 1945, Bibliothèque Nationale, 1954.

MICHEL, HENRI, *Bibliographie critique de la Résistance*, Institut Pédagogique National, 1964.

Revue d'histoire de la Deuxième Guerre Mondiale, P.U.F. Each issue keeps the bibliography up to date.

2. PUBLISHED DOCUMENTS

Centre de documentation juive contemporaine, *Les Juifs sous l'occupation. Recueil de textes français et allemands 1940–44*, Éditions du Centre, 1945.

MICHEL, HENRI, and MIRKINE-GUETZÉVITCH, BORIS, *Les Idées politiques et sociales de la Résistance*, P.U.F., 1954.

PÉTAIN, PHILIPPE, *Les Paroles et les écrits du Maréchal Pétain*, Édité par la Légion française, n.d.

Principes de la rénovation nationale, Société d'Éditions Économiques et Sociales, 1941.

RIBET, MAURICE, *Le Procès de Riom*, Flammarion, 1945.

3. UNPUBLISHED MATERIAL, THESES, AND DISSERTATIONS

BARDONNIE, LOUIS DE LA, 'Historique de la création du réseau Confrérie Notre Dame–Castille'.

BELLESCIZE, DIANE DE, 'Le Comité général d'études de la Résistance', Thèse pour le Doctorat de Droit, Paris, 1974.

BOULADOU, G., 'Contribution à l'étude de l'histoire de la Résistance dans le département de l'Hérault', Thèse 3e cycle, Montpellier, 1965.

CHATEAU, MARTINE, 'Contribution à l'étude du maquis corrézien', Mémoire de Maîtrise, Poitiers, 1969.

ESCHALIER, JACQUES, 'Le Journal *Libération* (zone sud) 1941–4', Diplôme d'Études Supérieures d'Histoire Contemporaine, Paris, 1962.

FIAT, R., 'L'Insurgé. Un Mouvement de Résistance. Un Journal', Diplôme d'Études Supérieures d'Histoire, Lyon, 1961.

JOSSE, DANIELLE, 'Brive-la-Gaillarde 1940–42', Mémoire de Maîtrise, Académie de Poitiers, 1971.

KESSLER, R., 'Les "Terroristes" ', Strasbourg, 1948.

LARIVIÈRE, RENÉ, Private Files on the Dordogne 1940–42.

MOUTERDE, P., 'La Résistance chrétienne dans la région lyonnaise', Diplôme d'Études Supérieures, Faculté des Lettres, Lyon, 1946.

PLAISANTIN, ANDRÉ, 'Sur les origines de Combat à Lyon', May 1949.

— — 'Historique du mouvement Combat dans la région lyonnaise R.I'.

VEILLON, DOMINIQUE, 'Le Mouvement Franc-Tireur', Thèse 3e cycle, Paris, 1975.

VIROULAUD, ANNIE, 'Contribution à l'étude des maquis A.S. du Secteur-Centre de la Dordogne', Mémoire de Maîtrise, Poitiers, 1969.

VISTEL, ALBAN, MS. on the origins of Resistance in ten *départements* of the south-east (see book title under sect. 7).

4. CLANDESTINE PRESS

L'Avant-Garde
Bibendum
Bulletin d'information et de propagande
Ça ira
Cahiers du bolchevisme
Cahiers du témoignage chrétien
Combat
Le Coq enchaîné
Le Cri du Gard
Le Cri du peuple (*Loire*)
L'Émancipateur du Cher
Espoir
L'Étincelle
L'Étincelle des Basses-Pyrénées et Landes
Femmes de Provence
Le Franc-Tireur
L'Humanité
L'Humanité (région marseillaise)
L'Humanité (zone sud)
L'Humanité de l'Allier
L'Humanité de la femme
L'Humanité des paysans
L'Humanité du soldat

Informations sur les atrocités nazies
L'Insurgé
J'arrive
Jeunes de France
Journal d'usine de Libérer et fédérer
Lettres à François
Libération (sud)
Libérer et fédérer
Liberté
Libre France
La Lutte des classes
Le Métallo (Toulouse)
Le Métallo du Centre-Ouest
Le Midi ouvrier
Notre bulletin
Notre voix
Le Père Duchesne
Les Petites Ailes
Pointe rouge
Le Populaire
93
Revanche
Rouge-Midi (édition de Marseille)
Rouge-Midi (région vauclusienne)
La Terre
Tour d'horizon
Le Travailleur alpin
Le Travailleur alpin des Deux Savoies
Le Travailleur de la Corrèze
Le Travailleur de la Creuse
Le Travailleur de la Dordogne
Le Travailleur du Languedoc
Le Travailleur limousin
Le Travailleur sétois
La Tribune des cheminots
La Tribune des mineurs (Gard)
La Tribune des mineurs (Loire)
Vérités
La Vie du parti
La Vie ouvrière
La Vie ouvrière (Puy-de-Dôme)
La Voix des femmes de Saône-et-Loire
La Voix des vignerons beaujolais

La Voix du Midi
La Voix du peuple (Puy-de-Dôme)

Other periodicals

Confluences
Esprit
Poésie 40
Poésie 41
Positions

5. MEMOIRS, DIARIES, BIOGRAPHIES, AND PUBLISHED INTERVIEWS

D'ASTIER, EMMANUEL, *Sept fois sept jours*, Éditions 10/18, 1961.
AUBRAC, LUCIE, *La Résistance, naissance et organisation*, Robert Lang, 1945.
BEAUFRE, ANDRÉ, *Le Drame de 1940*, Plon, 1965.
BÉNOUVILLE, GUILLAIN DE, *Le Sacrifice du matin*, Laffont, 1946.
BERGERET, H. G., *Messages personnels*, Éditions Bière, Bordeaux, 1945.
BIDAULT, GEORGES, *D'une Résistance à l'autre*, Les Presses du Siècle, 1965.
BLOCH, J.-PIERRE, *Mes jours heureux*, Bateau Ivre, 1946.
L'Œuvre de Léon Blum 1940–45, Albin Michel, 1955.
BONTE, FLORIMOND, *Le Chemin de l'honneur*, Éditions Hier et Aujourd'hui, 1949.
BOURDET, CLAUDE, *L'Aventure incertaine*, Stock, 1975.
CALAS, RAOUL, '1938–41. Une Période sombre', *Notre musée*, no. 32 (Feb. 1969).
CASSOU, JEAN, *La Mémoire courte*, Éditions de Minuit, 1953.
CAZARD, GEORGES, assisted by METGES, MARCEL, *Capitaine Philippe. 1909–44 (J.-J. Chapou)*, Imprimerie A. Coueslant, Cahors, 1950.
CERF-FERRIÈRE, RENÉ, *Chemin clandestin 1940–43*, Julliard, 1968.
CHOISEUL-PRASLIN, *Cinq années de Résistance*, Éditions F–X, Strasbourg–Paris, 1949.
CLAVIER, N., 'Franc-Tireur. Tel que je l'ai vu naître', *Bulletin des AMUR*, no. 6 (June 1947).
CORDESSE, HENRI, *Histoire de la Résistance en Lozère*, Cordesse, n.p., 1974.
CROUZET, PAUL, '*Et c'est le même ciel bleu . . .' Journal d'un maire de village 1939–40*, Didier, 1950.
DÉCHELETTE, VICTOR, *Le Curé de Mailly*, Imprimeries Réunies de Roanne, 1956.

DOMENACH, JEAN-MARIE, *Celui qui croyait au ciel. Gilbert Dru*, Elf, 1947.

DUHAMEL, JEAN, *Le Journal d'un Français moyen 1940–44*, Imprimerie de la Vallée d'Eure, Pacy-sur-Eure, 1953.

FARGE, YVES, *Rebelles, soldats et citoyens*, Grasset, 1946.

FAURE, PÉTRUS, *Un Témoin raconte . . .* , Imprimerie Dumas, Saint-Étienne, 1962.

FERRY, GILLES, *Une Expérience de formation de chefs*, Seuil, 1945.

FLAVIAN, C. L., *Ils furent des hommes*, Nouvelles Éditions Latines, 1948.

FOURCADE, MARIE-MADELEINE, *L'Arche de Noé*, Fayard, 1968.

FRENAY, HENRI, *La Nuit finira*, Laffont, 1973.

GAULLE, CHARLES DE, *Mémoires de guerre. L'Appel 1940–42*, Plon, 1954.

GOSSE, LUCIENNE, *Chronique d'une vie française: René Gosse 1883–1943*, Plon, 1962.

GROUSSARD, GEORGES, *Service secret 1940–45*, La Table Ronde, 1964.

GUITTON, JEAN, *Le Cardinal Saliège*, Grasset, 1957.

HASQUENOPH, MARCEL, *Ces prêtres qui ont su mourir*, Apostolat des Éditions, 1971.

HENNEGUIER, PIERRE, *Le Soufflet de forge*, Éditions de la Pensée Moderne, 1960.

JOANNES, VICTOR, 'Souvenirs de l'année 40', *Notre musée*, no. 29 (Nov. 1968).

LABARTHÈTE, H. DU MOULIN DE, *Le Temps des illusions*, Bourquin, Geneva, 1946.

Pierre Lamy. Un Héros de la Résistance savoyarde, Éditions Port-Royal, 1948.

LOUSTAUNAU-LACAU, G., *Mémoires d'un Français rebelle 1914–48*, Laffont, 1948.

LYTTON, NEVILLE, *Life in Unoccupied France*, Macmillan, 1943.

MARTIN DU GARD, M., *La Chronique de Vichy 1940–44*, Flammarion, 1948.

'Le Père Maydieu', supplément à *La Vie intellectuelle* (Aug.–Sept. 1956), Éditions du Cerf.

MEIFREDY, FRANÇOISE, *Missions sans frontières*, France-Empire, 1966.

MICHEL, HENRI, *Jean Moulin. L'Unificateur*, Hachette, 1964.

MICHELET, EDMOND, *La Querelle de la fidélité. Peut-on être gaulliste aujourd'hui?* Fayard, 1971.

MONTARON, ANDRÉ, *Le Maquis de Corlay*, Imprimeries Jobard, Dijon, 1950.

MOULIN, LAURE, *Jean Moulin*, Presses de la Cité, 1969.

Mounier et sa génération. Lettres, carnets et inédits, Seuil, 1956.

Nouveau, L. H., *Des Capitaines par milliers*, Calmann-Lévy, 1958.

Ophuls, Marcel, 'Le Chagrin et la pitié', *L'Avant-Scène*, nos. 127–8 (July–Sept. 1972).

Pestourie, Roger, *La Résistance, c'était cela aussi*, Éditions Sociales, 1969.

Peytavin, le Lieutenant-Colonel, *De la 'Résistance' au combat*, Chaptal, Mende, 1945.

Picard, Henri, *Ceux de la Résistance*, Éditions Chassaing, Nevers, 1947.

Ploton, Romain, *Quatre années de Résistance à Albertville*, Ploton, Albertville, 1946.

Pons, Commandant, *De la Résistance à la libération* (*Défense du Vercors Sud*), Passas et Deloche, Valence, 1962.

Pougatch, I., *Charry. Vie d'une communauté de jeunesse*, Chant Nouveau, 1946.

Quelques actions des protestants de France en faveur des Juifs persécutés sous l'occupation allemande 1940–44, CIMADE, n.d.

Ramonatxo, H., *Ils ont franchi les Pyrénées*, Éditions de la Plume d'Or, 1954.

Rémy *Mémoires d'un agent secret de la France Libre 1940–42*, Aux Trois Couleurs, 1946.

—— *Mémoires d'un agent secret de la France Libre*, vols. i–iii, France-Empire, 1959–61.

Rendier, Martin, *Quatre ans dans l'ombre*, André Bousquet, Condom, 1948.

Rocal, Georges, and Bouillon, Léon, *Jean Sigala (1884–1954)*, Éditions Coquemard, Angoulême, 1954.

Roure, André, *Valeur de la vie humaine*, Oeuvre posthume, Sfelt, 1946.

Rude, F., Vistel, Alban, and Lacour, R., *Trois témoignages sur la 2e Guerre Mondiale*, Imprimerie Nouvelle Lyonnaise, Lyon, 1966.

Un Évêque français sous l'occupation. Extraits des messages de S. Ex. Mgr. Saliège, Éditions Ouvrières, 1945.

Seghers, Pierre, *La Résistance et ses poètes*, Éditions Seghers, 1974.

Segonzac, Dunoyer de, *Réflexions pour de jeunes chefs*, Éditions de l'École Nationale des Cadres, Uriage, n.d.

Stéphane, Roger, *Chaque homme est lié au monde. Carnets 1939–44*, Sagittaire, 1946.

Truffy, Jean, *Les Mémoires du curé du maquis*, Imprimerie Abry, Annecy, 1950.

Vial, Jean, *Un de l'Armée secrète bas-alpine*, Imprimerie Villard, Marseille, 1947.

VIRET, PAUL, *L'Affaire François de Menthon*, Gardet et Garin, Annecy, n.d.

VISTEL, ALBAN, *Héritage spirituel de la Résistance*, Lug, Lyon, 1955.

6. AUTHOR'S INTERVIEWS

All the following gave formal interviews, replying to questions asked by the author, and almost all these interviews are recorded on tape. Other oral evidence from a much larger number of Resisters was gathered more informally, for example at meetings and social reunions of various Resistance associations. The names of those who contributed in this way are not given.

MM.	ALVITRE, CURÉ	Brive-la-Gaillarde, Corrèze
	BARDONNIE, LOUIS DE LA	Saint-Antoine-de-Breuilh, Dordogne
Mlle.	BAUDOIN, MADELEINE	Marseille
MM.	BAUMEL, JEAN	Montpellier
	BAZ, ROMAIN	Annemasse, Haute-Savoie
	CALAS, RAOUL	Paris
	CANET, HENRI	Marseille
	CARRIER, RENÉ	Lyon
	CHAULIAC, RAYMOND	Montpellier
	CHAUSSADE, PIERRE	Paris
	CHAVANET	Lyon
	CORDESSE, HENRI	Montpellier
	DEFFAUGT, Jean	Annemasse, Haute-Savoie
	DOUMENC, GEORGES	Montpellier
	DUPIC, LOUIS	Lyon
	DUTARTRE, MARCEL	Lyon
	FOURNIER, GUSTAVE	Montpellier
	GAZAGNAIRE, LOUIS	Marseille
	GIGNOT	Reignier, Haute-Savoie
	GIMPEL, JEAN	London
	HERVET, ROBERT	Paris
	JOANNES, VICTOR	Paris
	JUGIE, RENÉ	Brive-la-Gaillarde, Corrèze
Mme.	LAMBOLEZ-WEINSTEIN, SUZANNE	Paris
MM.	MALAFOSSE, PIERRE	Cap d'Agde, Hérault
	MICHAUT, VICTOR	Paris
	MONTAGNÉ, FRÉDÉRIC	Béziers, Hérault
	PALOC, FERDINAND	Montpellier
	PASTOR, JOSEPH	Marseille
	PAVOUX	Lyon

Pestourie, Roger	Lyon
Petit, Edmond	Marseille
Plaisantin, André	Lyon
Simon, Louis,	Annemasse, Haute-Savoie
Solié, Albert	Montpellier
Tillon, Charles	Aix-en-Provence, Bouches-du-Rhône
Tixador, Albin	Montpellier
Vistel, Alban	Lyon
Vittoz, Jean	Annemasse, Haute-Savoie

7. HISTORIES AND SPECIAL STUDIES

Those titles marked by an asterisk are recommended for general reading and are currently easily available.

Activité des organisations juives en France sous l'occupation, Éditions du Centre, 1947.

Adam, Gérard, *La C.F.T.C. 1940–58*, Colin, 1964.

Amoretti, H., *Lyon Capitale 1940–44*, France-Empire, 1964.

*Amouroux, H., *La Vie des Français sous l'occupation*, Fayard, 1961.

Angeli, Claude, and Gillet, Paul, *Debout, partisans*, Fayard, 1969.

Argenson, Marquis d', *Pétain et le pétinisme*, Éditions Créator, 1953.

*Aron, Robert, *Histoire de Vichy*, Fayard, 1954.

Autrand, Aimé, *Le Département de Vaucluse de la défaite à la libération. Mai 1940–25 août 1944*, Aubanel, Avignon, 1965.

Baudoin, Madeleine, *Histoire des groupes francs (M.U.R.) des Bouches-du-Rhône de septembre 1943 à la libération*, P.U.F., 1962.

*Bayac, Jacques Delperrié de, *Le Royaume du maréchal*, Laffont, 1975.

Beau, Georges, and Gaubusseau, Léopold, *R.5. Les S.S. en Limousin, Périgord, Quercy*, Presses de la Cité, 1969.

Bédarida, F. and R., 'Une Résistance spirituelle: Aux origines du Témoignage chrétien 1941–2', *Revue d'histoire de la Deuxième Guerre Mondiale*, no. 61 (Jan. 1966).

*Bellanger, Claude, *Presse clandestine 1940–44*, Colin, 1961.

— — *et al.*, *Histoire générale de la presse française*, vol. iv: *De 1940 à 1958*, P.U.F., 1975.

Besson, André, *Une Poignée de braves*, Nouvelles Éditions Jurassiennes, Poligny, 1965.

Bonte, Florimond, *Les Antifascistes allemands dans la Résistance française*, Éditions Sociales, 1969.

Cépède, Michel, *Agriculture et alimentation en France durant la 2e Guerre Mondiale*, Éditions Génin, 1961.

*Cotta, M., *La Collaboration*, Colin, 1964.

Demontès, A., *L'Ardèche martyre. Histoire de l'Ardèche 1939–45*, Imprimerie Mazel, Largentière, 1946.

Diamant, David, *Héros juifs de la Résistance française*, Éditions Renouveau, 1962.

— — *Les Juifs dans la Résistance française 1940–44*, Roger Maria, 1971.

*Duquesne, Jacques, *Les Catholiques français sous l'occupation*, Grasset, 1966.

Faucher, J.-A., and Ricker, A., *Histoire de la franc-maçonnerie en France*, Nouvelles Éditions Latines, 1967.

Faure, Pétrus, *Histoire du mouvement ouvrier dans le département de la Loire*, Imprimerie Dumas, Saint-Étienne, 1956.

Le Gouvernement de Vichy 1940–42, Fondation Nationale des Sciences Politiques, Colin, 1972.

*Granet, Marie, and Michel, Henri, *Combat*, P.U.F., 1957.

Grenier, Fernand, *Ceux de Châteaubriant*, Éditions Sociales, 1961.

*Jäckel, E., *La France dans l'Europe de Hitler*, Fayard, 1968.

Josse, R., 'L'École des Cadres d'Uriage', *Revue d'histoire de la Deuxième Guerre Mondiale*, no. 61 (1966).

Kedward, H. R., 'Behind the polemics. French Communists and Resistance 1939–41,' in *S. F. Hawes and R. T. White (eds.), *Resistance in Europe 1939–45*, Allen Lane, London, 1975.

Knout, David, *Contribution à l'histoire de la Résistance juive en France 1940–44*, Éditions du Centre, 1947.

Latour, Anny, *La Résistance juive en France 1940–44*, Stock, 1970.

Lecœur, Auguste, *Le Parti Communiste Français et la Résistance 1939–41*, Plon, 1968.

Loubet del Bayle, Jean-Louis, *Les Non-Conformistes des années 30*, Seuil, 1969.

Lubetzki, J., *La Condition des Juifs en France sous l'occupation allemande 1940–44*, Éditions du Centre, 1945.

Mayer, Daniel, *Les Socialistes dans la Résistance*, P.U.F., 1968.

*Michel, Henri, *Les Courants de pensée de la Résistance*, P.U.F., 1962.

— — *Vichy, année 40*, Laffont, 1966.

*Milward A. S., *The New Order and the French Economy* Clarendon Press, Oxford, 1970.

Mollard, André, *La Résistance en Savoie 1940–44*, Mollard, Chambéry, 1972.

Morquin, G., *La Dordogne sous l'occupation allemande 1940–44*, Imprimerie Joucla, Périgueux, n.d.

Monestier, Marianne, *Elles étaient cent et mille . . . femmes dans la Résistance*, Fayard, 1972.

NÉGIS, ANDRÉ, *Marseille sous l'occupation*, Éditions du Capricorne, Paris–Marseille, 1947.

*NOGUÈRES, HENRI, assisted by DEGLIAME-FOUCHÉ, M., and VIGIER, J.-L., *Histoire de la Résistance en France de 1940 à 1945*, vols. i and ii, Laffont, 1967–9.

ODIN, JEAN, *Les Quatre-Vingts*, Éditions Tallendier, 1946.

OLLIER, NICOLE, *L'Exode sur les routes de l'an 40*, Laffont, 1970.

PALMER, M. B., 'L'Office français d'information (1940–44)', *Revue d'histoire de la Deuxième Guerre Mondiale*, no. 101 (1976).

PARROT, LOUIS, *L'Intelligence en guerre*, La Jeune Parque, 1945.

**Le Parti Communiste Français dans la Résistance*, Éditions Sociales, 1967.

*PAXTON, R., *Vichy France: Old Guard and New Order, 1940–44*, Barrie and Jenkins, London, 1972.

POLONSKI, JACQUES, *La Presse, la propagande et l'opinion publique sous l'occupation*, Éditions du Centre, 1946.

RAYMOND-LAURENT, *Le Parti Démocrate Populaire 1924–44*, Imprimerie Commerciale, Le Mans, 1965.

'Le Réseau F2', *Revue historique de l'armée* (Dec. 1952).

ROSSI, A., *Les Communistes français pendant la drôle de guerre*, Îles d'Or, 1951.

ROSSI-LANDI, GUY, *La Drôle de guerre*, Colin, 1971.

ROUGERON, G., *Le Mouvement socialiste en Bourbonnais 1875–1944*, Éditions du Beffroi, Vichy, 1946.

— — *La Résistance dans le département de l'Allier 1940–44*, Typocentre, Montluçon, 1964.

— — *Le Département de l'Allier sous l'État français 1940–44*, Typocentre, Montluçon, 1969.

SEREAU, RAYMOND, *L'Armée de l'armistice*, Nouvelles Éditions Latines, 1961.

*TILLON, CHARLES, *Les F.T.P.*, Julliard, 1962.

VERDIER, ROBERT, *La Vie clandestine du Parti Socialiste*, Éditions de la Liberté, 1944.

VIDALENC, JEAN, *L'Exode de mai–juin 1940*, P.U.F., 1957.

Vie et mort des Français 1939–45, Hachette, 1971.

*VISTEL, ALBAN *La Nuit sans ombre. Histoire des Mouvements unis de Résistance, leur rôle dans la libération du Sud-Est*, Fayard, 1970.

*WARNER, GEOFFREY, *Pierre Laval and the Eclipse of France*, Eyre & Spottiswoode, London, 1968.

WILLARD, GERMAINE, 'La Drôle de guerre', *Cahiers du communisme* (Dec. 1959).

— — 'La Résistance française et la Seconde Guerre Mondiale', *Cahiers du communisme* (July–Aug. 1965).

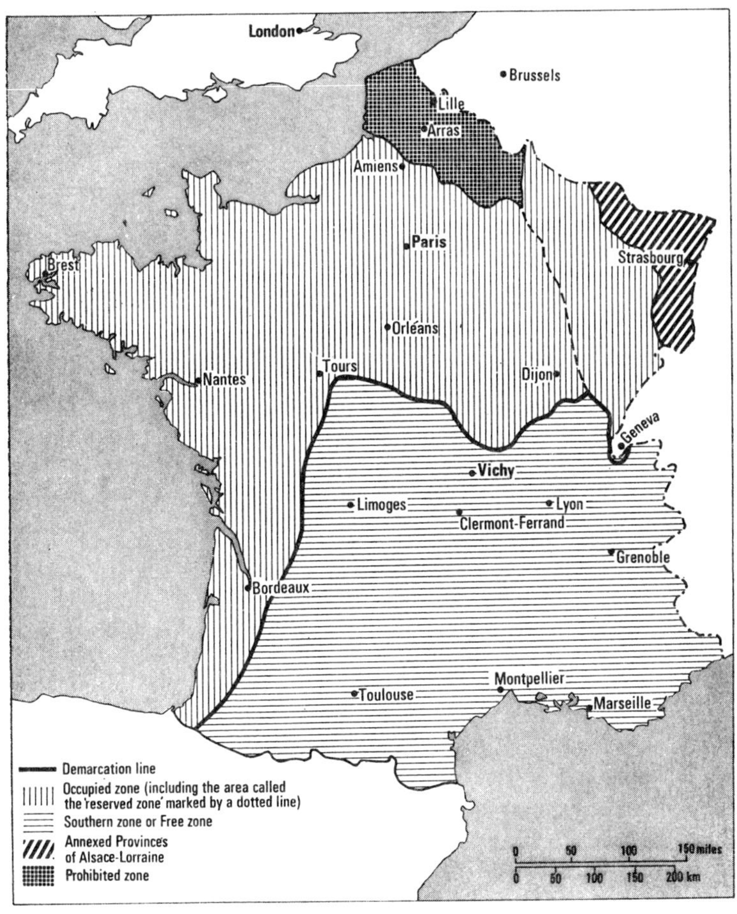

MAP 1. France 1940-42

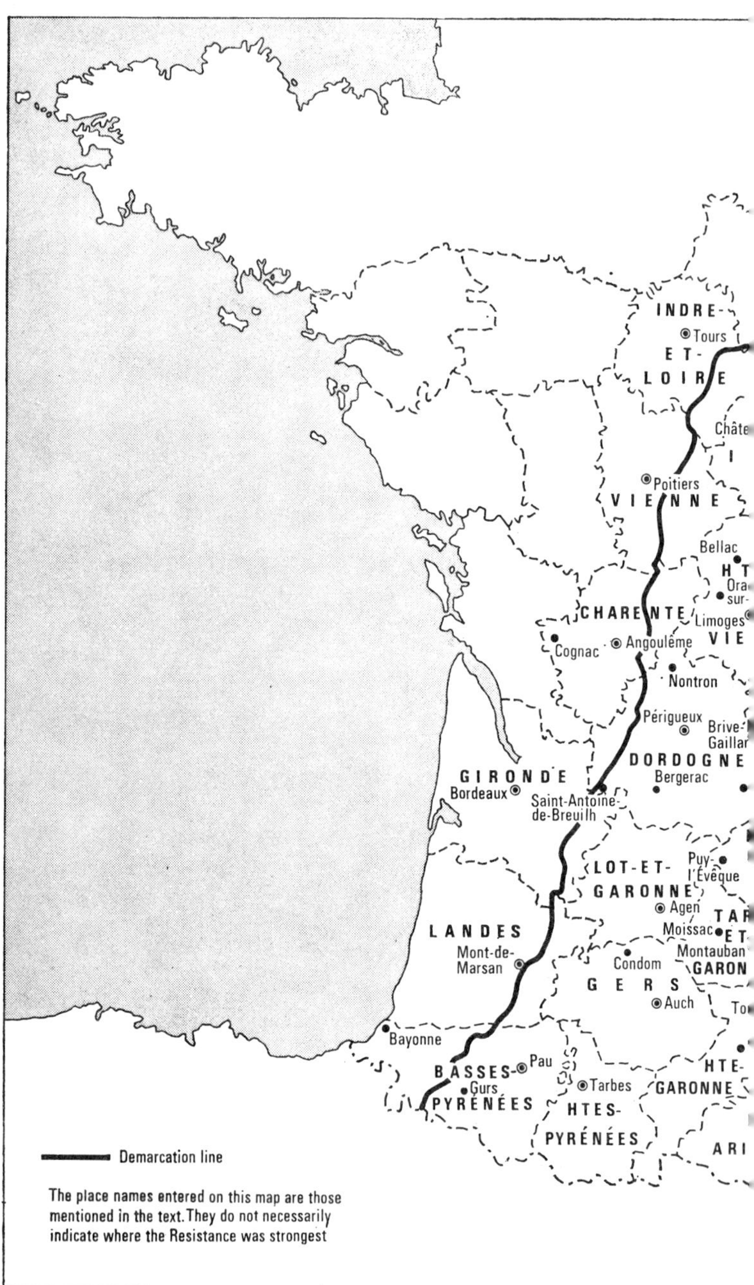

MAP 2. Southern Zone 1940-42

Paris
GERMANY
SWITZERLAND
ITALY
CHER
Vierzon
Bourges
NIÈVRE
Nevers
Le Creusot
Chalon-sur-Saône
Poligny
Lons-le-Saunier
JURA
Montceau-les-Mines
Saint-Amand
Moulins
SAÔNE-ET-LOIRE
ALLIER
Montluçon
Gex
Bourg-en-Bresse
Mâcon
Annemasse
Geneva
Bonneville
AIN
Nantua
Vichy
Roanne
RHÔNE
Trévoux
Villefranche
Annecy
HTE-SAVOIE
Thônes
Aubusson
PUY-DE-DÔME
Riom
Clermont-Ferrand
Gergovie
Issoire
LOIRE
Lyon
Oullins
Montbrison
La-Tour-du-Pin
Vienne
Albertville
Chambéry
SAVOIE
Saint-Étienne
ISÈRE
Grenoble
Uriage
CANTAL
Aurillac
HTE-LOIRE
Le Puy
Yssingeaux
Chambon-sur-Lignon
Tournon
Valence
Briançon
HTES-ALPES
Gap
Privas
ARDÈCHE
Largentière
Crest
DRÔME
Montélimar
Nyons
Marvejols
Mende
LOZÈRE
Florac
Rodez
AVEYRON
Millau
Villeneuve-lès-Avignon
Carpentras
VAUCLUSE
BASSES-ALPES
Digne
ALPES-MMES.
Alès
Uzès
GARD
Avignon
Apt
Manosque
Castellane
Albi
Nîmes
Arles
BOUCHES-DU-RHÔNE
Aix-en-Provence
Nice
Antibes
Cannes
Lodève
HÉRAULT
Bédarieux
Castres
Frontignan
Montpellier
Sète
Béziers
Draguignan
Sainte-Maxime
VAR
Marseille
Saint-Tropez
Toulon
Hyères
Narbonne
Carcassonne
AUDE
Perpignan
Collioure
Argelès
Port-Vendres
0
50
100
150 miles
0
50
100
150
200 km

Index

1) What he is doing

2) How he does it

3) Why/where is it effective

4) Compare to other book — synthesize w/ other book